Oh Lordy!

A Story of One Family's Trials During the Struggle for Southern Independence As Told Through the Letters of Private Young H. E. Hitch, Company I, 16th South Carolina Volunteer Infantry

BY

Michael G. Hitch & Elinor H. Mowbray

Elinor H Mowbray

Oh Lordy!
A Story of One Family's Trials During the Struggle for Southern Independence As Told Through the Letters of Private Young H. E. Hitch of the 16th South Carolina Infantry

v2.0

Cover Art: With the backdrop of the original 16th South Carolina Volunteer Infantry battle flag, we see (clockwise from top left) a period photograph of Young H. E. Hitch (likely from January 1863), a battlefield doodling done by Hitch presumably of his wife Mary Ann Hitch on Jun 8 1863, a letter addressed to Young Hitch from his son John Joseph Hitch dated Jan 25 1863, a clipping from the envelope of one of Y.H.E. Hitch's letters stating "A Soldiers Letter, Co. / I / 16th regt S.C.V." and, finally, the index card introduction to Young Hitch's service files at the National Archives in Washington, DC.

Webpage: *www.mikehitch.com* E-mail: mikehitch@mikehitch.com

Outskirts Press, Inc.
http://www.outskirtspress.com

ISBN: 978-1-4787-6247-8

Library of Congress Control Number: 2015912966

PRINTED IN THE UNITED STATES OF AMERICA

DEDICATION

Dedicated to my mother, Azilee Hitch Holland Mowbray, who gave me the house in which Young Hitch's letters were found.

- *Elinor Mowbray*

Dedicated to my wife, Jonna Hitch, for her understanding of the long hours needed to put together this work and my son, Michael Carroll Hitch (1992-1993), who passed way too young.

- *Mike Hitch*

TABLE OF CONTENTS

TABLE OF FIGURES

Figure 21	Major General William Henry Talbot Walker (1816-1864), commander of Walker's Division for which the 16th South Carolina served in the Atlanta Campaign. Gen. Walker was killed in Atlanta on Jul 22 1864.
Figure 22	Brig. General States Rights Gist, the commander of Gist's Brigade of which Young Hitch and the 16th South Carolina were a part during the Atlanta Campaign. He was killed at the Battle of Franklin (Tennessee) on Nov 30 1864.
Figure 23	CSA War Bond Receipt for $100 paid by Y.H.E. Hitch on Mar 29 1864
Figure 24	An envelope in the Mowbray collection addressed to "Y.H.e. Hitch" in Dalton, Georgia franked with a postally-used CSA ten cent stamp. Note that it includes his unit named as "Gists Brigade 16 reg. Com I. So C. V." The handwriting on this envelope for the address portion is that of Aunt Sally Hitch whom Young states on April 21st sent him a letter on April 16, 1864 (the actual letter is missing, however). It is notable that this envelope was folded inside out to be reused at a later date given the scarcity of paper.
Figure 25	Civil War Enfield rifle-musket much like Young Hitch took to war with him.
Figure 26	Atlanta Campaign map for the Dalton to Kennesaw portion that occurred from May to July 1864.
Figure 27	The Battle of Rocky Face Ridge, May 7-12 1864. Also note the area called Spring Place where Young said he had tramped in the days before May 7th and where Company I of the 16th South Carolina conducted picket duty.
Figure 28	Battles of Rocky Face Ridge and Dug Gap, near Dalton, GA. Note the position of Gist's brigade (including the 16th South Carolina and Young Hitch) occupying the center of Walker's Division. They are situated atop Hamilton Mountain and out of the main lines of battle.
Figure 29	The action that occurred on the retreat from Resaca. Lay's Ferry provided some minor skirmish action for Walker's Division on May 15 followed by more meaningful heavy skirmishing, especially with the 66th Illinois at Rome Crossroads near Calhoun on May 16 1864.
Figure 30	The route of Johnston's retiring army from Resaca back towards Cassville on May 17-19, 1864.
Figure 31	Cassville area operations on the evening of May 19 1864. Note, Hardee's corps (with the 16th South Carolina) dug in around the Cassville railroad depot.
Figure 32	Detail of the Cassville and Cartersville area in May 19-27, 1864. Note Hardee's Corps position within which Young Hitch was participating. After retiring back from Cassville, Hardee's Corps set up near where the Battles of New Hope Church and Pickett's Mill took place on May 25 and 27, respectively.
Figure 33	The Lost Mountain and Brushy Mountain Lines of defense set up by the Army of Tennessee in the time from June 4-18, 1864. Our Young Hitch was entrenched for most of this period with Walker's division on the Brushy Mountain Line between Cleburne and French's divisions where they engaged the enemy on June 18th during the Latimer's Farm affair.
Figure 34	Page 1 of the original letter from William Scruggs to Mary Hitch informing her of the death of her husband, Y.H.E. Hitch (1825-1864).
Figure 35	Retrenchment of the Confederate army in the vicinity of Kennesaw Mountain after June 18th and the action of the Battle of Kolb's Farm on June 22nd. The location of Gist's brigade is shown at a position near Hardage's sawmill. As depicted, this is very near the exact spot where Young Hitch was killed while on picket duty on Jun 19 1864 (denoted by the green star).

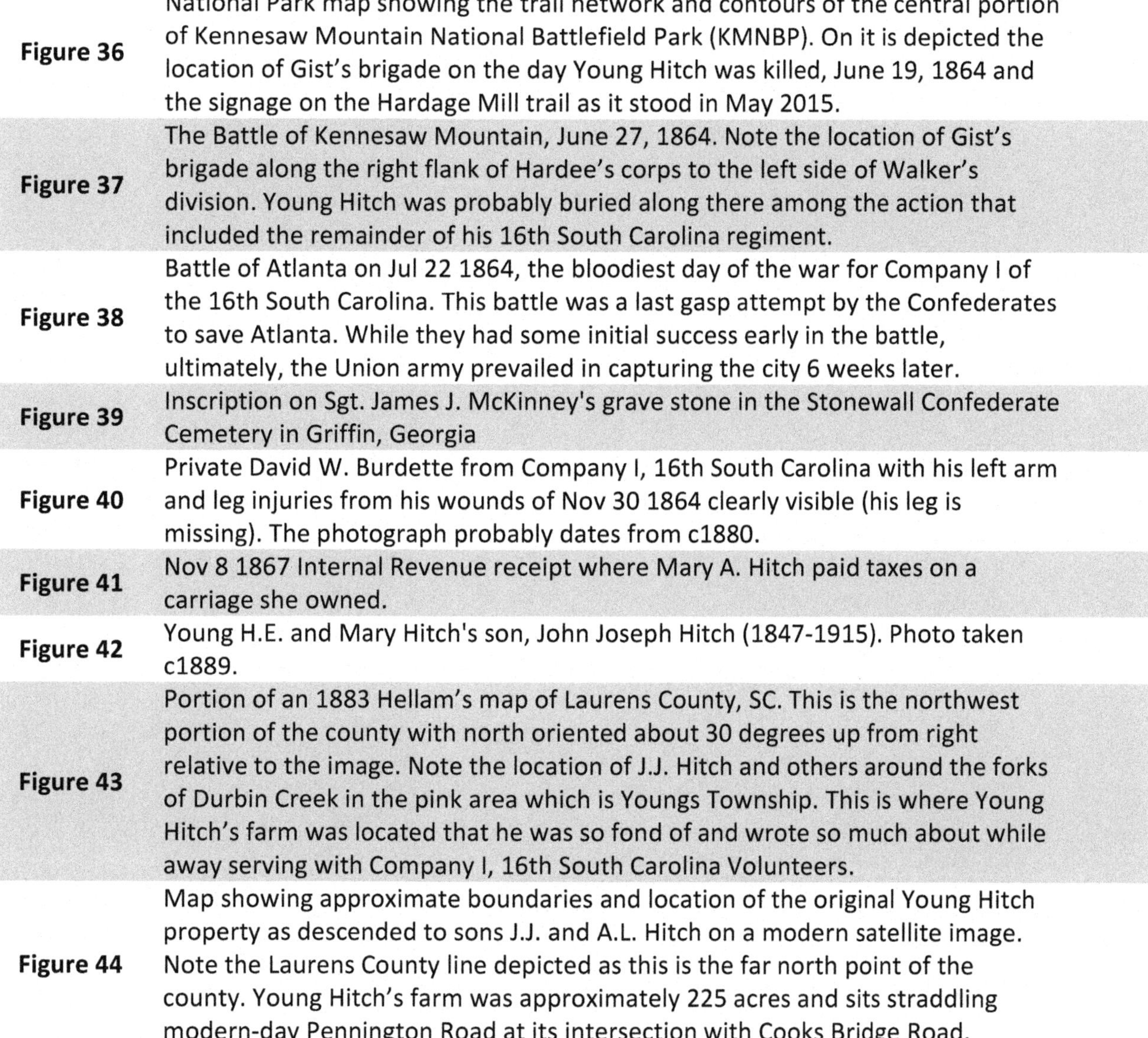

Mowbray Collection Transcriptions in the Appendix

LETTERS (UNTIL AUGUST 1862) DATING FROM BEFORE THE WAR TO YOUNG HITCH'S TIME IN COMPANY C, 9TH SOUTH CAROLINA RESERVES	
Item I	"Scribbling" Notes of Young Henry Elkanah Hitch dating from 1846 and from several pages that were folded inside an 1806 school notebook of his father, Joseph N. Hitch
Item II	The "Grand Rascal" Letter, James B.F. Bruce to Y.H.E. Hitch dated September 30, 1851, Laurens District, South Carolina
Item III	Young Hitch's List of Members of Number 1, 2nd Battalion 41st Regiment of the Beat Company, January 14, 1854
Item IV	Letter from "Nan" to Y.E. and Mary Ann Hitch dated June 20, 1854 from Marshall County, Mississippi
Item V	Letter from William P. Edwards to Y.H.E. and Mary E. Hitch dated February 2, 1855 from Lauderdale County, Alabama
Item VI	Letter from William Scruggs to Y.H.E. and Mary Hitch dated August 16, 1855
Item VII	Letter from "Aunt Sally" (Sarah) Hitch to Y.H.E. and Mary Hitch dated April 25, 1856.
Item VIII	Letter from Elijah and Emily Scruggs to Y.H. and Mary Hitch dated May 16, 1856 from Marshall County, Alabama
Item IX	Letter from Sarah Hitch to Y.H.E. and Mary Hitch dated September 26, 1856
Item X	Letter from Sarah Hitch to Y.H.E. Hitch dated March 20, 1857
Item XI	Y.H.E. Hitch Diary from Jan to Aug 1858
Item XII	Letter from Caroline L. Brown and Emily (Brown) to Y.H.E. Hitch dated May 30, 1858 from Marshall County, Alabama
Item XIII	Letter from J.C. Brown to Y.H. Hitch dated August 7, 1859 from Marshall County, Alabama
Item XIV	Letter from ____ Hughes to John J. Hitch dated April and May 1860
Item XV	Letter from John C. Brown to Y.H.E. Hitch dated July 3, 1860 from Marshall County, Alabama
Item XVI	Letter from Sarah Hitch to Y.H.E. and Mary Hitch dated July 25, 1860
Item XVII	Letter from William P. Edwards to Y.H.E. and Mary Ann Hitch dated March 11 1861 from Marshall County, Alabama
Item XVIII	Letter from G. Lafayette Brown to Young Hitch dated June 25, 1861 from Moulton, Alabama
Item XIX	Two Letters from W.P. Edwards to Y.H.E. and Mary Hitch dated September 11, 1861 from Lauderdale County, Alabama with codicil from J.P. Garrett
Item XX	Letter from S.R. Thackston to Young Hitch dated October 7, 1861 from "Army of the Potomac", Fairfax County, Virginia
Item XXI	Receipt from E. Watson to Y.H.E. Hitch for Confederate States War Tax dated July 12, 1862
Item XXII	Note from Capt. S.D. Thackston to Y.H.E. Hitch to be Captain of a patrol dated August 16, 1862 at a Camp near Charleston, South Carolina
LETTERS (UNTIL MARCH 1863) DATING FROM YOUNG HITCH'S TIME IN COMPANY C, 9TH SOUTH CAROLINA RESERVES	
Item XXIII	Letter from Y.H.E. Hitch to Mary A. Hitch dated December 8, 1862

Item LI	Letter from Y.H.E. Hitch to Mary A. Hitch dated May 1, 1863
Item LII	Letter from Y.H.E. Hitch to Mary Hitch dated May 3-4, 1863 from Colleton District, South Carolina
Item LIII	Letter from Y.H.E. Hitch to Mary Hitch dated May 6, 1863 from Camp Roberts, South Carolina
Item LIV	Letter from Y.H.E. Hitch to Mary Hitch dated May 9, 1863 from West Point, Alabama
Item LV	Letter from Y.H.E. Hitch to Mary A. Hitch dated May 14, 1863 from McDowell's Landing, Alabama
Item LVI	Letter from Y.H.E. Hitch to Mary A. Hitch dated May 15, 1863 from Lauderdale County, Mississippi
Item LVII	Letter from Y.H.E. Hitch to sons Joseph and Lucian Hitch dated May 15, 1863 from "Hospital Ward 5", Meridian, Mississippi
Item LVIII	Letter from Y.H.E. Hitch to Mary A. Hitch dated May 16, 1863 from Meridian, Lauderdale County, Mississippi
Item LIX	Letter from Y.H.E. Hitch to Mary A. Hitch dated May 21, 1863 from Lauderdale County, Mississippi
Item LX	Letter from Y.H.E. Hitch to Mary A. Hitch dated May 24-25, 1863 from Meridian, Lauderdale County, Mississippi
Item LXI	Letter from Y.H.E. Hitch to Mary A. Hitch dated June 2-3, 1863 from Meridian, Lauderdale County, Mississippi
Item LXII	Letter from Y.H.E. Hitch to son Joseph Hitch dated June 4, 1863 from Hospital Ward 5, Meridian, Lauderdale County, Mississippi
Item LXIII	Letter from Y.H.E. Hitch to son Lucian Hitch dated June 5, 1863 from Hospital Ward 5, Meridian, Lauderdale County, Mississippi
Item LXIV	Letter from Y.H.E. Hitch to Mary A. Hitch and sons J.J. and A.L. Hitch dated June 8, 1863 from Jackson, Mississippi
Item LXV	Letter from Y.H.E. Hitch to Mary A. Hitch dated June 12, 1863 from Yazoo City, Mississippi
Item LXVI	Letter from Y.H.E. Hitch to Mary A. Hitch dated June 15, 1863 from Camp Woods, Mississippi
Item LXVII	Letter from Y.H.E. Hitch to Mary A. Hitch dated June 16, 1863 from Madison County, Mississippi
Item LXVIII	Letter from Y.H.E. Hitch to Mary A. Hitch and sons J.J. and A.L. Hitch dated June 22, 1863 from Madison County, Mississippi
Item LXIX	Letter from Y.H.E. Hitch to Mary A. Hitch dated August 11, 1863 from Scott County, Mississippi
Item LXX	Letter from Y.H.E. Hitch to A. Lucian Hitch dated August 20, 1863 from near Morton Station, Scott County, Mississippi
Item LXXI	Letter from Y.H.E. Hitch to Mary A. Hitch dated August 21, 1863 from Morton Station, Mississippi
Item LXXII	Letter from Y.H.E. Hitch to Mary A. Hitch dated September 7, 1863 from "Three miles west of Rome," Floyd County, Georgia
Item LXXIII	Letter from Y.H.E. Hitch to Mary A. Hitch dated September 18, 1863 from Kingston, Georgia
Item LXXIV	Letter from Y.H.E. Hitch to Mary A. Hitch dated November 6, 1863 from "near Chattanooga, Tennessee

Item LXXV	Letter from Y.H.E. Hitch to Mary Hitch dated November 15, 1863 from near Chattanooga, Tennessee
Item LXXVI	Letter from Y.H.E Hitch to Mary A. Hitch dated December 19, 1863
Item LXXVII	"Anniversary Letter" from Y.H.E. Hitch to Mary Hitch dated January 19, 1864 from camp near Dalton, Georgia
Item LXXVIII	Letter from Y.H.E. Hitch to Mary A. Hitch dated January 25, 1864 from camp near Dalton, Georgia
Item LXXIX	Letter from Sarah Hitch to Y.H.E. Hitch dated January 31, 1864 from Laurens District, South Carolina
Item LXXX	Letter from Y.H.E. Hitch to Mary Hitch dated February 2, 1864 from camp near Dalton, Georgia
Item LXXXI	Letter from Y.H.E. Hitch to son A.L. Hitch, undated but probably early February 1864
Item LXXXII	Letter from Y.H.E. Hitch to J.J. Hitch dated February 8, 1864 from camp near Dalton, Georgia
Item LXXXIII	Letter from Y.H.E. Hitch to Mary A. Hitch dated February 28, 1864 from camp near Dalton, Georgia
Item LXXXIV	Letter from Y.H.E. Hitch to Mary A. Hitch dated March 6, 1864 from camp near Dalton, Georgia
Item LXXXV	Letter from Y.H.E. Hitch to J.J. Hitch dated March 7, 1864 from camp near Dalton, Georgia
Item LXXXVI	Letter from Y.H.E. Hitch to Mary A. Hitch dated March 13, 1864 from camp near Dalton, Georgia
Item LXXXVII	Letter from Y.H.E. Hitch to J.J. Hitch dated March 20, 1864 from camp near Dalton, Georgia
Item LXXXVIII	Letter from Young H.E. Hitch to Mary A. Hitch dated March 24, 1864 from camp near Dalton, Georgia
Item LXXXIX	Letter from Young H.E. Hitch to Mary A. Hitch dated March 27, 1864 from camp near Dalton, Georgia
Item XC	Letter from Y.H.E. Hitch to Mary A. Hitch dated April 21, 1864 from camp near Dalton, Georgia
Item XCI	Letter from Y.H.E. Hitch to sons J.J. and A.L. Hitch dated April 21, 1864 from camp near Dalton, Georgia
Item XCII	Letter from Y.H.E. Hitch to Ellen (?) dated April 21, 1864 from camp near Dalton, Georgia
Item XCIII	Letter from Y.H.E. Hitch to sons J.J. and Lucian Hitch, undated (probably Spring 1864 sent with a letter to Mary Hitch)
Item XCIV	Letter from Y.H.E. Hitch to Mary A. Hitch dated April 25, 1864 from camp near Dalton, Georgia
Item XCV	Letter from Young H.E. Hitch to Mary A. Hitch dated May 1, 1864 from camp near Dalton, Georgia
Item XCVI	Letter from J.J. Hitch to father Young H.E. Hitch dated May 1, 1864 from Laurens District, South Carolina
Item XCVII	Letter from Young H.E. Hitch to sons J.J. and Lucian Hitch dated May 7, 1864 from camp near Dalton, Georgia
Item XCVIII	Letter from Y.H.E. Hitch to Mary A. Hitch, undated but probably early May 1864
Item XCIX	Letter from Sarah Hitch to Y.H.E. Hitch dated May 9, 1864 from Laurens District South Carolina

PREFACE

The story behind how this book came to be begins back in the early 1990s when one of the authors, Mike Hitch, began a quest to search for his family roots. It had been an interest since he was a child and that interest came to the fore after losing his son, Michael Carroll Hitch to SIDS in 1993. Call it a compulsion, call it therapy, but what resulted was a huge undertaking to find out as much about the Hitch family in the United States as possible – its beginnings, how the family evolved through the years and, even where it stands today.

By the autumn of 1994, he had collected enough information from various libraries and other historical repositories that he decided to publish a newsletter dedicated to the Hitch surname. At the time, he used phonebooks and was able to identify about 600 Hitch families in the U.S. and sent an inaugural issue of the newsletter to all of them! But, in the letter, he stated that he would be happy to continue to send the newsletters free of charge but only to those families that might be interested. From that inquiry, he received about 125 positive responses and the newsletter was kept alive through 16 quarterly publications that finally ended in the summer of 1999.

The response to the newsletters was tremendous. People began sending information on their various branches and connections to the Hitches here in this country. He dutifully reviewed, noted and saved everything that was sent. Examples of the material received ranged from old photos, letters, family trees, and very precious original documentation. One gentleman, Don Hitch of Pendleton County, Kentucky, in the mid-1990s, sent a box of old papers randomly stacked together and dating from 1807 of his branch of the family that had migrated there from Maryland at that time. Those papers were carefully recorded and scanned into digital format. They were then placed in separate acid-free archival plastic sleeves and put into a notebook for safe keeping before being sent back to Don Hitch in Kentucky. Caches of items like this are getting harder to find and contain valuable clues to the history of our families and even our nation. Also received was a file of information on the subject of this book, Young H.E. Hitch from a Mr. Michael Givens of South Carolina – we will cover much more on Private Young Hitch later in this book.

Using the information received from many dozens of Hitch folks as a foundation, Mr. Hitch then began conducting many years of primary research at various historical repositories throughout the country. He spent many man YEARS of time at the National Archives in Washington, DC, the Hall of Records in Annapolis, Maryland and many, many county courthouses in many different states from Maryland to Virginia, Delaware, Mississippi, Ohio, Pennsylvania, even Massachusetts and beyond. All of the information sent by the Newsletter patrons and all of the information collected in those research travels was donated to the Edward H. Nabb Center for Delmarva History and Culture at Salisbury University (Salisbury, Maryland) in early 2014 for safe keeping and for use by future researchers.

As Mr. Hitch found new information, it was added in a systematic way into organized files and family history software package. He also made sure to provide copious and accurately documented source citations to help create a true account of the various Hitch families through the years. Today, that software contains over 25,000 people and is probably the most comprehensive and documented treatise of the Hitch family is this country. There are 15 separate Hitch lines that came to this country as early as the 1680s (maybe earlier) and some into the 19th century. The primary line is Adam Hitch (1658-1731) of Maryland who settles around modern day Salisbury, Maryland in about 1685 at the age of 27 (the line from which Young Hitch descends). All 15 lines are chronicled on his web page at www.mikehitch.com which was established in 1998 and is still active today (2016).

After about 12 or 13 years of the initial "hunting and gathering" of the data, Mr. Hitch began to contemplate publishing a book about all his research. With so much information, the initial scope was limited to one family line and the book, Adam Hitch (1658-1731) of Old Somerset in ye Province of Maryland, His Descendants was completed and published in the fall of 2007. The magnitude of the effort to get it into print was immense and resulted in a book with over 700 pages and to permit fitting everything into one volume, the font type had to be reduced to 7-point on large format 8½" x 11" paper! Nevertheless, the book was an immediate success and won the Washburn Prize for Delmarva History & Culture at Salisbury University in early 2008.

However, the intent here is not to boast about that book but rather, to complete the story of how we get to the writing of THIS BOOK! You see, one of those Adam Hitch books over the years found its way to a Mr. Gordon Garrett in Fountain Inn in Greenville County, South Carolina. Serendipitously, Ms. Elinor Mowbray, a retired paralegal living in that same vicinity, was rummaging through her attic one day and came across a large cache of old books, paraphernalia and letters of her direct line ancestors in the Hitch family. The majority of the find was correspondence between Young Henry Elkanah Hitch and his wife Mary Ann (Edwards) Hitch and young children John Joseph and Augustus Lucian Hitch during the Civil War when Young was a Private, first in the 9th South Carolina Reserves and then, in Company I of the 16th South Carolina Volunteer Infantry.

In finding this cache of priceless memorabilia, Ms. Mowbray began investigating more into her family and determined Young H.E. Hitch was her great great grandfather with his son, Lucian, as her great grandfather. In her quest, she happened to talk to Mr. Garrett and he referred her to the book on Adam Hitch who just so happens to be Young H.E. Hitch's 3x great grandfather! The book offers a good assessment of the line of Hitches that had moved to South Carolina (even though Young's second name was listed incorrectly) thanks to the people who had responded to that Hitch newsletter years earlier[1]. So, Ms. Mowbray, upon reviewing the book, contacted Mr. Hitch about the fabulous find she had discovered and he was very grateful she did!

New cousins introduced, they began to communicate about the contents of the discovered documents and interest levels piqued at a very high level in both of them. These types of finds are becoming ever more scarce and, for this documentation to have survived through so many years is simply incredible. Ms. Mowbray drove from South Carolina to Mr. Hitch's house in Maryland in the autumn of 2014 and they spent all day digitally scanning the letters one-by-one into a computer at the Edward H. Nabb Center at Salisbury University. A common conclusion was then realized – the contents of this cache of information has to be told to a larger audience and it would best be told in the form of a book! They immediately agreed to collaborate and so here we are! What has resulted is a book that not only covers

[1]Including Michael Givens (who is another descendant of Y.H.E. Hitch and originally provided a photograph of Y.H.E. Hitch along with a treasure of other things), Michelle (Manley) Wells, Jim Boling, Marge Motes and others.

the exploits of Private Young H.E. Hitch through his life as a private citizen and soldier, but also a treatise of his compatriots in Company I of the 16th South Carolina Volunteer Infantry. This includes service records for most of the men in the unit and even some genealogical research regarding their friends and families near to them. We find it a fascinating, historically accurate tale that we hope you enjoy reading as much as we enjoyed writing it.

The Appendix presents most of the items from the Mowbray collection in transcribed form and uncorrected for grammar or spelling from the way they were originally composed. The collection is presented in a chronological manner to aid the reader and to offer this important information in one central place for the user to review. The final home for the original material in the collection is the Edward H. Nabb Center at Salisbury University in Salisbury, Maryland.

CHAPTER 1
Hitch Family to South Carolina

This story begins in Maryland in the mid-1700s. Louther Hitch was born to John and Isabell Hitch on Nov 5 1750 in Somerset County, Maryland in an area that is now Wicomico County about 3-4 miles west and slightly north of the city of Salisbury. Louther eventually moved with his family to the Laurens area of South Carolina about the year 1801 and established roots that became the basis of many families from that area who would later serve in the Civil War.

Louther's father, John Hitch, was born in about 1723 to William and Rachel (Humphreys) Hitch and this William was the first son of Adam Hitch (1658-1731), the original patriarch of the Hitch line in Maryland. Adam Hitch appears in the Salisbury, Maryland area in the mid-to-late 1680s as a wealthy land owner of the time. By the time of his death in 1731, Adam had amassed a large estate of over 2000 acres of land, a mill, at least 10 slaves and an established influential reputation in his community.

His son, William Hitch, preceded him in death by about one year but Adam assured in his will that the children of William Hitch received their share of his estate. Also, prior to the death of each of them, Adam Hitch began to prepare his estate for his children when he allocated "deeds of estate" of some of his land and chattel in 1728. For William Hitch, we find this entry in the old records:

> William Hitch is assigned 405 acres of land from part of tract named High Suffolk – *"Beginning at southwest end of a line of marked trees dividing it from a part of the said tract called High Suffolk given to my son Solomon Hitch on the west side of a glade that comes by where Jno. Price now lives thence by a line of marked trees S46E 180 poles partly dividing it from the land I have given to my son Saml Hitch thence by a line of marked trees NE 200 poles dividing it from a part of said land given to Jno. Hitch thence by a line of marked trees NE by N 168 poles to the easternmost bounds of ye said tract called High Suffolk from thence bounded by ye outside line of ye said tract to ye eastern side of ye land I gave to my son Solomon from thence SW by a line of marked trees dividing it from my son Solomon's land 375 poles to ye first beginning."*[2]

William Hitch died less than two years later and we find his will probated on Apr 10 1730 as; ·*I give my real estate to sons William, Thomas, John, and Nehemiah, the eldest to have first choice. ·To my son Ezekiel I give £10 to be paid to him when he reaches the age of eighteen. ·All sons to be free at age 18. ·Wife to be executrix. ·To my daughter Rachel a bed and other household goods. ·My father, Thomas Humphries, and my brother Solomon Heatch to be trustees. Testators John Heatch, Samuel Heatch, and Cornelius Linch.*[3] Here, we see listed John Hitch, the eventual father of Louther Hitch, getting a share of the real estate in Maryland, no doubt part of the 405 acres given to William Hitch in 1728. Note that all the sons were under age 18 at the time of the will in 1730 but were to be freed of their apprenticeships

---

[2] Adam Hitch Deed of Gift to William Hitch from the Somerset County, MD Land Records for May 6 1728; Liber SH, Folios 23-26, Maryland Hall of Records, Annapolis, MD.

[3] Somerset County, MD Wills-Liber EB9, Folio 131, also Somerset original Wills file, all in the Maryland Hall of Records.

at that age. We can establish a very close approximation of John Hitch's birth year to 1723 as he turned age 15 in 1738[4]. It is interesting to note that John Hitch, father of Louther, was referred to by his contemporaries as "John Hitch Jr." though he was not son of John Hitch (who became known as John Hitch Sr.). This is a confounding issue sometimes for modern genealogists as it is a different convention from modern day where one could assume a "junior" to be a son of a "senior." In the 1700s, a "junior" simply could mean that, for instance, the John Hitch Junior was just a younger John Hitch than another of the same name, regardless of how they were related. One case of such confusion occurs when there were three contemporary William Hitches; a William Hitch Sr., William Hitch Jr. and William Hitch, the younger! Here, William Hitch Jr. was son of Solomon Hitch and William Hitch the younger was son of William Hitch Sr. – this makes for some interesting research problems that must be carefully discerned.

Back to our John Hitch "Jr.", son of William Hitch and father of Louther Hitch. John was born in 1723 and died certainly after Jul 30 1767 when he wrote his will but probably closer to the time it was probated on Aug 10 1769. In his early years, John led a rather unremarkable life as we only find him appearing each year in the tax records as head of household. He probably married sometime around 1743 and began a family. We do not find out John's wife's names until we see, in his will, where "Isable Hitch made oath." Then, when his estate was inventoried in 1769/70 and valued at £55.0.4, we find as administrator and executrix, "Isabel Hitch". We can determine Isabell's maiden name from the will of James Nicholson written on Feb 19 1749 and probated Mar 22 1749, where he lists daughter "Isable Hitch" along with his wife Mary Nicholson and sons Joshua Nicholson, Charles Nicholson, James Nicholson, John Nicholson, Joseph Nicholson and other daughters Mary Nicholson, Rachel Nicholson and Phillis Nicholson[5].

In 1748/49, John Hitch Jr. is indicated under a list of soulgers (sic, soldiers) commanded by Captain Nath'll Waller[6] establishing him as the first of his line to be in a formal military position for his country. On Mar 27 1754, William Hitch, with Nehemiah and John Hitch, sold land to our John Hitch. The record states, "this was land conveyed as 1,450 acres called "High Suffolk" to Adam Hitch who, on May 6 1728, conveyed 400 acres of this to his son William Hitch who divided it equally among his four (4) sons, William, Thomas, Nehemiah and John through his will. Thomas died before reaching age 21 so his portion conveyed to William, the eldest son. For £75, John Hitch bought the part assigned to Nehemiah Hitch."[7]

Furthermore, on Feb 21 1757, John and William Hitch bought 100 acres of land in "High Suffolk" for £60 from Solomon Hitch. This is described in the records as "part of 405 acres Adam Hitch gave to son William in 1728." It also references the 100 acres John Hitch Sr. purchased Mar 27 1754 that was originally Nehemiah Hitch's share. So, with this, brothers William and our John Hitch then own all 405

---

[4] Tax lists for Somerset County, MD for the years 1722-1756 survive nearly fully intact and list heads of household and males of age 15 and older. John Hitch first appears in these records in 1738 suggesting he turned age 15 around that time.

[5] Somerset County, MD Wills; Liber EB9, Folio 280.

[6] Somerset County Militia, Box 1, Folder 22; Colonial Wars; Maryland Hall of Records, Annapolis, MD.

[7] Somerset County, MD Land Records; Liber B, Folio 26.

acres of the original bequest of their father William Hitch and, they are selling 100 acres of it to John Hitch Sr.[8]

So, here we see in the records, a verification that John Hitch originally received one-fourth (approximately 100 acres) of land from his father in 1730 and, in 1754, purchased another 100 acres from his brother Nehemiah Hitch, increasing his total holdings to 200 acres and, he sold a portion of the whole to John Hitch Sr. in 1757.

Finally, to establish John and Isabell (Nicholson) Hitch as the parents of Louther Hitch who moved to South Carolina, requires one more fragment of information that eluded this researcher for many years. In fact, most established loose genealogies of the Hitch family have surmised Louther Hitch to be a son of Ezekiel Hitch[9], who happens to be a brother of our John Hitch Jr. All the existing records pointed circumstantially to Louther Hitch belonging to this particular lineage BUT there was no definitive proof to be found. That is, until this researcher stumbled across an inventory for the estate of an "Isabella Waller" from Aug 29 1791 with Curtis Hitch, as administrator. From the estate, payments were made to John Pope Mitchell, Isaac Holland for coffin, William Handy and John Scroggin appraisers, "money due to the orphans of Elijah Vincent, for the money made use of by the deceased received by her as their guardian and retained by this accountant." But, most importantly for this discussion, distributions were made to her seven children as "this accountant Curtis", Louther and Elijah Hitch, Annis Vincent's heirs, Phillis Short, Letty Nicholson's representatives and Lilah Culver[10]. This was final proof showing definitively that Louther Hitch was son of John and Isabell (Nicholson) Hitch that even offers a listing of his siblings.

With the groundwork successfully laid, Louther Hitch now becomes the focus of our discussion. Louther, who was affectionately called "Loudy" and "Ludy" (hence, the pronunciation was probably like LOODY) throughout the years, becomes the foundation by which many accepted memberships into the Daughters of the American Revolution (DAR) for his service as a Private with the Maryland Militia, Blackwater Regiment in 1780. The DAR files state Louther's birth in 1743, however, birth records from the family bible in South Carolina indicate that he died on Aug 19 1838 at age 87 years, 9 months, 14 days placing his birth at Nov 5 1750, which is probably much closer to being correct than 1743.

The first time Louther Hitch appears in the historical record is having an account in John Nelms' store in Salisbury, Maryland for the years 1775 and 1777. Only a couple of ledgers survive of this ancient establishment but Louther shows as, in 1775, owing a balance with interest from Ledger H of £1/8/1. He bought 9 yards of duck and 1 lb. of brimstone for a total of £2/11/7. His brother, Elijah Hitch, delivered a bushel of peas for credit to his account in 1776. He paid the balance in cash in 1777.

To give some more perspective on Louther Hitch while he was a younger man and still in Maryland, we see that, on Nov 6 1779, he bought land on the north side of the Wicomico River called "Ellis's Addition"

---

[8] Somerset County, Maryland Land Records, Liber B, Folio 153.

[9] The records in the Daughters of the American Revolution (DAR) Library in Washington, DC incorrectly claim Ezekiel Hitch as father of Louther as well.

[10] Somerset County, MD Administrative Accounts; Liber EB16, Folios 476-477.

from Joseph Ellis, 23¼ acres, for £20[11]. As indicated in the Maryland Tax Assessment of 1783, Louther Hitch has a modest estate in Rewastico Hundred of Somerset County including land "Gravelly Hill" (50 acres) and "Ellis's Addition" (20½ acres) plus two horses and five cattle. This same record shows the household consisting of four white males and two females. On Apr 22 1784, Louther acquired from his uncle Ezekiel Hitch 50 acres of land called "Gravelly Hill" for £80[12]. On May 16 1789, Louther Hitch acquires more property when he purchased from Stephen Ellis of Sussex County, Delaware the tracts "Ellis's Chance" and "Ellis's Addition," a total of 56¾ acres, for £52.9.10½ "current money of Maryland"[13].

Louther Hitch had first married Mary Nicholson on Jun 30 1771 who may have been a first or second cousin through his mother Isabell (Nicholson) Hitch's line. Mary was born in Nov 1750 and died November 28, 1779. There are only two known children from this bond, brothers John and Joshua Hitch. John was born Feb 4 1773 and Joshua on Jun 1 1779, both in Somerset County, Maryland. John was just a small child six years of age and Joshua, an infant, when their mother died in late 1779.

On Apr 13 1790, Loudy Hitch, along with Joseph Humphris (sic, Humphreys), made surety when Curtis Hitch (Louther Hitch's brother) was appointed guardian to Eli Vincent[14] who was over age 14[15]. In the Nov 1791 court session, there was a case Joseph Scroggin versus Elias Hitch, Loudy Hitch, and Elijah Moor (sic, Moore). The Hitch-Moore side confessed judgment to Scroggin for £0.7.6 debt and 3 shillings, 10 pence cost[16]. On Nov 3 1792, Louther Hitch sold to Stephen Ellis of Sussex County, Delaware the same land he bought of Ellis on May 16 1789[17]. On the same date, this Stephen Ellis sold to Louther Hitch part of tracts "Ellis's Chance" and "Ellis's Addition" laid out for 61¼ acres[18].

After the death of his first wife, Mary, Louther raised his young sons on his own until he remarried in 1792 to Elizabeth Douglas. She was born on Apr 27 1769 and was only four years older than her stepson John Hitch and 10 years older than John's brother, Joshua Hitch. With Louther beginning a new family with his new wife, it can easily be surmised that the two sons of the previous marriage, who were ages 19 and 13, might have been alienated by the new step mother. This is sometimes cited by genealogies as the reason they go to South Carolina in the late 1790s. Whether that actually happened is not known but we do know that sometime over the next 6 years, John and Joshua Hitch departed Maryland for South Carolina on their own.

John and Joshua Hitch do not show up in the Maryland records on their own. The first record this researcher finds of them is in a document entitled "J. Hitch - Journal - March 26th 1799 to Maryland, (eastern shore) and back to So Carolina Laurens County, 96 District." This record is in the Manuscripts Division of the South Caroliniana Library at the University of South Carolina and is attributed there as being the journal of Joshua Hitch. However, in reviewing the contents of the document, it is instead found to be the journal of Joshua's brother John Hitch (the journal refers to "brother Joshua" at one

---

[11] Somerset County, MD Land Records; Liber G, Folio 201.
[12] Ibid; Liber G, Folio 483.
[13] Ibid; Liber H, Folio 477.
[14] Eli Vincent was Louther Hitch's nephew, son of Elijah Vincent and Louther's sister, Annis Hitch.
[15] Somerset Orphan's Court Proceedings 1777-1792, Folio 94
[16] Somerset County Judicials, Liber 1791/94, Folio 11
[17] Somerset County, MD Land Records; Liber I Part II, Folio 433.
[18] Ibid; Folio 474.

point in the writings). From this record, it can probably be estimated that John and Joshua headed to South Carolina to live in about the year 1798.

Louther remains in Somerset County for the years 1793-1796, when he is shown as Lowther Hitch in Broad Creek Hundred and assessed for 127 acres of land, £90; and other property, £30. Total assessment was £120, £120, £120 and £120 for years 1793, 1794, 1795, and 1796 respectively. On September 23, 1797, Louther Hitch and wife Betsy sold land called "Gravelly Hill", "Ellis's Chance", and "Ellis's Addition", a total of 58¾ acres, for £56 to his brother Curtis Hitch[19].

In 1798, Ezekiel Hitch was listed as the occupant of property in Broad Creek Hundred owned by Louther Hitch "situated about 2¼ mi. from Spring Hill Chappel" and consisting of "one old dwelling house, framed, one story, 20'x16' under repair; one cook house of round poles, 14'x12', the roof rotten; one blacksmith shop, 12'x14' of slabs; 73 acres of land. Total was assessed at $25 for the buildings and $80 for the land. Loudy Hitch is shown as occupant of a house owned by Isaac Handy's heirs in Rewastico Hundred "near Salisbury" in a "very old dwelling house framed 20'x16', cookhouse (of) slabs 12'x14'.[20]" Lowday Hitch then shows in the records for the years 1798-1803 in Broad Creek Hundred of Somerset County where he was assessed for 73 acres of land at £55 and other personal property at £30 for the years 1798-1801, and just £30 for personal property for 1802-1803[21].

Finally, Louther Hitch appears for the last time in Maryland records on Mar 11 1801 when he sold his land "Gravelly Hill" and "Ellis's Addition" to Ezekiel Hitch, 83¼ acres, for $275[22]. This appears to be the time Louther Hitch decides to join his sons John and Joshua Hitch in Laurens County, South Carolina who had relocated there sometime around 1798. We do not know for certain why the family moved but, it seems the ultimate reason Louther relocates his entire family to South Carolina is the promise of new and productive farmland. By 1800, the Eastern Shore of Maryland where Louther's ancestors had lived for over 100 years had become more crowded (for the time) and the farmlands depleted due to years of growing tobacco and other crops making it hard to make a productive living. The Laurens area of South Carolina was relatively new land and more sparsely settled at the time, a prime venue to offer a new start for the adventurous farm family.

By the time Louther leaves for South Carolina in 1801, he has, in his new family, five known children: Joseph N. Hitch (born 1794), Mary (born 1794), Letitia[23] (born c1795), Sarah (born 1796) and Louther D. Hitch (born 1798), with wife Elizabeth (Douglas) Hitch accompanying him. Joseph N. Hitch[24] will become

---

[19] Ibid; Liber L, Folio 87.

[20] Federal Direct Tax of 1798 for Somerset County, Maryland.

[21] Somerset County Commissioners of the Tax assessment for 1798-1803, microfilm at the Edward H. Nabb Center at Salisbury University.

[22] Somerset County, MD Land Records; Liber N, Folio 148

[23] Unproven linkage here. Circumstantial evidence may support that Letitia (?), who married James Duvall in South Carolina, is daughter of Louther Hitch but this researcher has not seen any definitive evidence proving it. Nevertheless, it is rather compelling, and is included here with the note that it MAY prove FALSE.

[24] Joseph N. Hitch: We know his middle initial is "N." from the records but we do not know what it represents. It MAY stand for "Nicholson", a name that runs through his paternal grandmother's line, Isabell (Nicholson) Hitch Waller. Isabell had a brother Joseph Nicholson who may be the origin of Joseph N. Hitch's name. No known proof exists, however.

the father to the subject of this book, Young H.E. Hitch, in 1825. This family, as well as John Hitch[25] from Louther's first marriage, resulted in descendants that populated areas in South Carolina, Georgia, Alabama and Arkansas in the years leading up to the Civil War and, will be covered in more detail later in this book. In the Mowbray collection, besides the letters of Y.H.E. Hitch and his wife and sons, there are also surviving letters of some of these other family members that will bring perspective to the story here. "Aunt Sally," Sarah Hitch (1796-1871), daughter of Louther Hitch, for instance, was quite the prolific writer to Young Hitch and his family, and shares much with respect to the Louther Hitch family lineage in the years 1850-1870.

In the Federal Census of 1810, "Lowther" Hitch is indicated in Laurens County in a household comprised of one male age 10-16, one male age 16-26, one male over age 45, one female age 10-16, one female age 16-26 and one female over age 45. Then, on Apr 14 1812, Louther Hitch deeded land to William Adair for $150, 50 acres, on Duncan's Creek including Browns Mill and Mill Shoals[26]. Witnesses were James Hanna, John Hitch, and J.A. Elmore, JQ. Dower renunciation was confirmed by his wife, Betty Hitch. In the census of 1820, "Luther" Hitch is indicated in Laurens County in a household comprised of one male age 16-26 (with none age 16-18), one male over age 45, one female age 16-26 and female over age 45 and, in the census of 1830, he is indicated in Laurens Township, Laurens County, in a household comprised of one male age 60-70, one female age 30-40, one female age 50-60 and one female age 60-70. In 1835, Louther and Elizabeth Hitch gave a 129 acre deed of gift to Sally Hitch[27].

Young Hitch's father, Joseph N. Hitch was a fraternal twin with Mary Hitch, both born Oct 10 1794 in the area that is modern-day Wicomico County, Maryland (was Somerset County till Wicomico was formed in 1867). Joseph was very well-educated as were most of the children of Louther Hitch. In the Mowbray collection, there is a very old cloth-bound book that was originally Joseph N. Hitch's entitled, *"A Book of Arithmetic for Mr. Joseph Hitch Under the Tuition of John S. Carwile, May 13th Day Anno Domini 1806."* The book is a beautiful collection of mathematical tables, conversions, charts and word problems. Joseph was 11 years old when this book was made and the math is very advanced for someone of his age where he would have been the equivalent of a 6th grader today. Interspersed among the pages are various notes that Hitch made during his studies, notes about his surroundings and the people he knew in the Laurens vicinity. For instance, here are a few interesting notes:

- Snow fell March 23rd 1806
- Snow fell November 23rd 1809
- Joseph Hitch his Book of Arithmetic, Matthew Cunningham his hand and pen (the writing of Cunningham)
- Sally Holcombe her name
- Matthew Cunningham was born December 17th Anno Domini 1792
- Joseph Hitch his name December 28th Day of the month in the Year of Our Lord 1813
- October 1st 1806 Acton School J. Hitch
- Nancy Hanna

[25] John Hitch's brother, Joshua, died in 1808 with no known descendants. He had married in Laurens County on Apr 19 1807 to Elizabeth Compton.
[26] Laurens County, SC Deeds and Wills, Deed Book J-261 (as reviewed in the DAR Library).
[27] Laurens County, SC Deed Books Index, Book N-110.

- Joseph Hitch his Cyphern book July 15th 1809
- Joseph Hitch was born October 10th Anno Domini 1794
- Amen for our potatoes; they lasted till the 26th of January 1812 Joseph Hitch his hand & pen
- Joseph N. Hitch Spring Hill July 30th Day A.D. 1814
- Joseph Hitch entered into Interest February 19th 1808 (calculations of interest)
- Married Friday May 13th in the year 1808 By the Reverend Joshua Palmer Mr. John Bishop to Miss Fereby Brown both of Laurens County
- Maryland Summerset County, Maryland state summerset county
- Entered into Exchange Thursday July 7th 1808 Mr. Joseph Hitch
- Entered into the Double Rule of three July 25th 1808 Joseph Hitch
- Entered into Permutation August 18th 1808 Joseph Hitch

The book shows a fascinating progression of Joseph Hitch's growth as a student in the years from 1806 to about 1814. The notes above also offer us some interesting mini-facts about some people in the area, a marriage, birthdates and even a mention of the place Joseph was born, "Maryland state summerset county." Joseph's penmanship and command of his studies was excellent and he received an education, much above the standard for the day.

Unfortunately, Joseph N. Hitch died young, on Oct 20 1827, just ten days after his 33rd birthday. His son, Young Henry Elkanah Hitch was just over two years old at the time. Young's mother, Rosanna Hitch remarried quickly, to Captain William Brown, in c1828 and he was raised by his mother and step-father, with many step-siblings, in Laurens County, South Carolina.

CHAPTER 2
Family and Close Acquaintances leading up to the Civil War

Young Henry Elkanah Hitch, by the time the Civil War broke out, was surrounded by many family, friends and other acquaintances as we will see from the correspondences and other notes he composed and received. After all, close to 60 years had passed from the time when the original Hitch patriarch, Louther Hitch, had moved to Laurens County, South Carolina. So the existing families, and those new to the area in the 1800 timeframe, had fully integrated and acclimated to one-another by the advent of the War. In the Louther Hitch line, young men that had reached maturity by 1860 were either his grandsons or great-grandsons and, as such, were the candidates to serve in the army. These men and their families are some of the ones that we find mentioned in the Young Hitch letter collection, from the Hitch side of the family.

We know that Young Hitch married Mary Ann Edwards in Jan 1847, she the daughter of John Edwards (1788-c1869[28]). The John Edwards family was large as he had two wives and many children through the years. His wives were Jane Bradley (1793-1838) and Rebecca Gilbert (1809-1880). With his first wife, Edwards had nine (9) known children; Jonas M., Lemuel, Ceborn, John Bradley, Nancy, William P., Patsy E., Mary Ann (Young's wife) and Jane Caroline (Jinsey C.) Edwards. Jane Edwards died c1838 and John remarried to Rebecca Gilbert and fathered six (6) more known children; Sarah E., Samantha, Milly Malinda, Little Berry, Willie and Euphrates Lafayette Edwards. Young Hitch was born at a time that corresponds roughly at the center point of when all these Edwards children were born, and he even married one of them, so it is no doubt that he was very well acquainted with the entire family during the years he was growing up.

There were other families and relatives in the vicinity of where he lived of whom Young Hitch would also have been very familiar and who appear in his correspondence before and during the War. These are the Bruces, Scruggs, Edwards, Vaughns, Garretts, Thackstons, Mocks and many others. We will hear much more of them as this story progresses.

Finally, in the broader sense, the War touched every American in some way or another. Within the microcosm of the Hitch family, there were families similar to Young's that stayed in Maryland and some that moved to other parts of the country like Delaware, Massachusetts, Kentucky, Ohio, Indiana, Mississippi, etc. These various cousins of Young Hitch faced many of the same experiences as Young and his direct colleagues did but serving and fighting for other distant units in both the Confederate States and United States forces. It was truly a nation-divided time and especially intriguing to know that all these people originated from a single family living on the Eastern Shore of Maryland in the late 17th and early 18th centuries.

---

[28] There is some uncertainty of the death date of John Edwards. We know he was living in late 1864 as he is mentioned in some of the Hitch letters. We also know that Mary (Edwards) Hitch signed a receipt that she had received her share of his estate in May 1871. For this, and the fact that he is not listed in the 1870 census, narrows the estimate of his death to the 1864-1870 timeframe and, probably closer to the 1870 side of that range.

The chart in **Figure 1** graphically illustrates Louther Hitch's descendants that we know served in the Civil War. All served for the Confederate cause and the ones who served were either grandsons or great grandsons of Louther. With his first wife Mary Nicholson, only Louther's son John Hitch had descendants who served (in fact, his other son Joshua, had no known descendants). Under John Hitch, we see the following who served, and their respective units and, all were great-grandsons to Louther Hitch:

JOHN HITCH line

NAME	HOW RELATED	RANK	UNIT
Benjamin Franklin Hitch	Great Grandson	QMSGT	39th Georgia Infantry
Robert Marcus Hitch	Great Grandson	MAJ	30th Georgia Infantry
Augustus Simpson Hutchinson	Great Grandson	LTCOL	19th Arkansas Infantry
Thaddeus McDuffie Templeton	Great Grandson	PVT	Hampton Legion (SC)
James Ludy Templeton	Great Grandson	PVT	3rd South Carolina Infantry
John Pulaski Templeton	Great Grandson	PVT	3rd South Carolina Infantry
Henry Tyler Templeton	Great Grandson	PVT	3rd South Carolina Infantry
John Wistar Simpson Stewart	Great Grandson	PVT	22nd South Carolina Infantry

The other members of the Louther Hitch line who served descend from him and his second wife, Betsy Douglas. The list of these soldiers are as follows, listed under their direct Louther Hitch descendant:

JOSEPH N. HITCH line

NAME	HOW RELATED	RANK	UNIT
Young Henry Elkanah Hitch	Grandson	PVT	16th South Carolina Infantry

MARY HITCH line (married Henry Pitts)

NAME	HOW RELATED	RANK	UNIT
Edwin Leroy Pitts	Grandson	PVT	4th South Carolina Battalion
James Young Pitts	Great Grandson	PVT	27th South Carolina Infantry
Young Joseph Harrington Pitts	Grandson	PVT	19th South Carolina Infantry
John Wesley Pitts	Grandson	PVT	3rd South Carolina Battalion

LETITIA HITCH line (married James Duvall)

NAME	HOW RELATED	RANK	UNIT
Lewis J. Duvall	Grandson	PVT	9th South Carolina Reserves
H. James Duvall	Great Grandson	PVT	3rd South Carolina Infantryantry
Chesley W. Duvall	Grandson	PVT	3rd South Carolina Infantry
Francis Marion Duvall[29]	Grandson	PVT	Holcombe Legion Cavalry (SC)

[29] Married Susan T.E. Hitch, daughter of Louther Douglas Hitch.

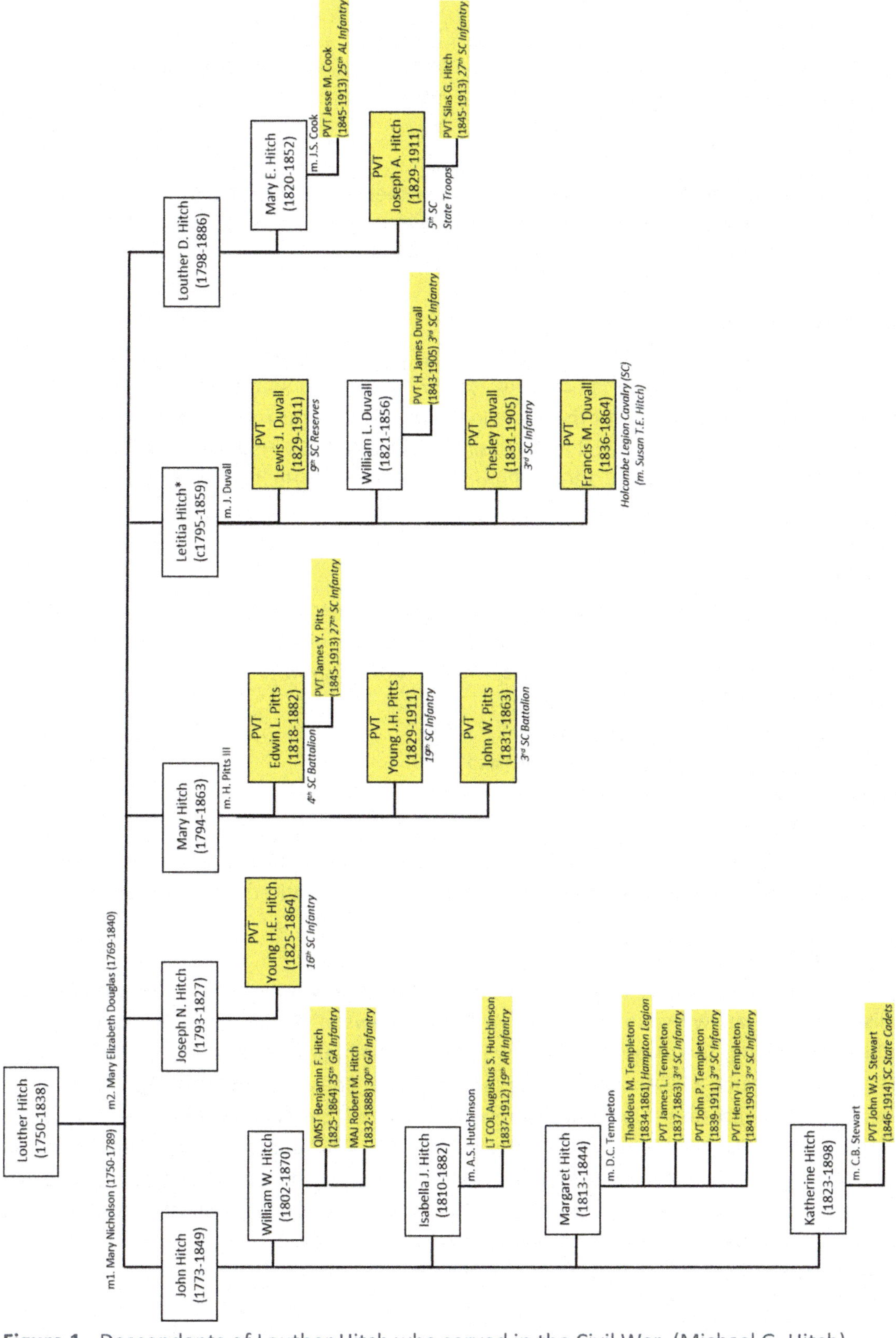

Figure 1 - Descendants of Louther Hitch who served in the Civil War. (Michael G. Hitch)

LOUTHER DOUGLAS HITCH line

NAME	HOW RELATED	RANK	UNIT
Jesse Madison Cook	Great Grandson	PVT	25th Alabama Infantry
Joseph Allen Hitch	Grandson	PVT	5th SC State Troops
Silas Green Hitch	Great Grandson	PVT	27th South Carolina Infantry

The following are brief military biographies of each of these men as obtained from the surviving Confederate military service records at the National Archives in Washington, DC. More information will be provided on some of these men in later sections of this book.

SGT Benjamin Franklin Hitch

Benjamin F. Hitch (1825-1864) was born in Laurens County, SC but moved to Georgia in the late 1850s. He enlisted as Quartermaster Sergeant in Company F/S, 35th Georgia Volunteer Infantry in Atlanta on Sep 17 1861 with Captain D.B. Henry "for the war." In the muster records for Sep 1862 through Oct 1864, he is listed as "present." He received a $50 bounty on Oct 31 1863. However, the muster records of Nov/Dec 1864 state he died on Nov 7 1864 in Petersburg, Virginia[30]. He died single and is buried in the Beaufort National Cemetery, Beaufort, SC.

MAJ Robert Marcus Hitch

Robert M. Hitch (1832-1888) was born in Laurens County, SC but moved to Georgia in the late 1850s. He was a Doctor and enlisted as a Captain in Company B, 30th Georgia Volunteer Infantry on Sep 25 1861. He received a promotion to Major in January 1863. Muster records show the following:

- May 1862: Absent, on furlough recruiting
- Jun/Jul 1862: Present at Camp Hardee
- Aug 1862: Absent, recruiting since Aug 8 1862
- Sep 1862: Absent, sick in Savannah
- Oct/Nov 1862: Present
- Jan 1863: As Senior Captain, he applied for and got a promotion to Major to fill a vacancy
- Aug 17 1863: He resigned his service and, on Oct 26 1863, he retired from service

LTC Augustus Simpson Hutchinson

Augustus S. Hutchinson (1837-1912) was born in Laurens County, SC but moved to Arkansas prior to the war. He enlisted as a Private with Company C, 19th Arkansas (Dawson's) Infantry on Oct 19 1861 with C.L. Dawson in Pike County, AR. The records show he was captured on Jan 11 1863 at the surrender of the "Arkansas Post" and became a POW where he was sent to Camp Chase on Jan 30 1863, then to St. Louis. He was described in the records while he was captive as 5'-10" tall, 25 years old, blue eyes, dark hair, and fair complexion. He was then sent to Ft. Delaware on Apr 10 1863 and on to City Point for exchange Apr 29 1863. He immediately rejoined the service on May 5 1863 at Camp 8 & 19 in Arkansas and was appointed Lieutenant Colonel by election on May 8 1863 delivered by General Johnston to take the rank on Aug 13 1863. The muster records then chronicle his service as follows:

- May/Aug 1863, Present; Oct to Dec 1863, absent on leave starting Dec 18 1863

---

[30] There is a discrepancy between this and the date shown on-line for his gravestone in the Beaufort National Cemetery, Beaufort, SC where it indicates his death date as Jan 8 1864.

- Jan/Feb 1864, absent, sick leave beginning Feb 5 1864; Mar/Apr 1864, present
- Jul/Aug 1864: Absent, wounded on Jul 22 1864, on sick furlough
- Jul 27 1864, Ocmulee Hospital, Macon, GA, indicates he received a gunshot wound in his left arm, the ball entered 3" or 4" above the joint and passed out the arm near the joint.

PVT Thaddeus McDuffie Templeton

Thaddeus M. Templeton (1834-1861) was born in Laurens County and brother to the other three Templetons in this list but the only one not to serve in the 3rd South Carolina Infantry. He enlisted as a Private in Company E, Hampton (South Carolina) Legion on Jun 19 1861 for 12 months at Columbia, SC. He shows as present through September 1861 on the muster rolls. However, the records state that he died while home on furlough on Oct 19 1861 of typhoid fever. He is buried in the Rocky Springs Presbyterian Church Cemetery, Laurens County, SC.

PVT James Ludy Templeton

James L. Templeton (1837-1863) was born in Laurens County and one of three Templeton brothers who became part of the 3rd South Carolina Infantry. He enlisted there as a Private on Apr 14 1861 for 12 months with Company A and mustered in at Columbia, SC on Jun 6 1861. On May 13 1862, after his initial 12 month hitch was over, he reenlisted for 2 years. Later that year, on Dec 13 1862, he was gravely wounded at the Battle of Fredericksburg and sent to the hospital in Charlottesville, VA. He never recovered from his wounds and died at the hospital on May 30 1863. He is buried in the Rocky Springs Presbyterian Church Cemetery, Laurens County, SC where the inscription on his tombstone states, "Mortally wounded at Fredericksburg, VA, on Dec 13 1862."

PVT John Pulaski Templeton

John P. Templeton (1839-1911) was born in Laurens County. He enlisted at Laurens Courthouse on Apr 14 1861 for 12 months with Company G, 3rd South Carolina Infantry and then re-enlisted on May 13 1862 for 2 years. The muster records show that he was sick in a hospital in Richmond, VA with typhoid fever and pneumonia on Jan 12 1862 and returned to duty Mar 24 1862. On Jun 29 1862, he was wounded casualty in a battle near Richmond. He was wounded again at the Battle of Chancellorsville on May 3 1863 and sent to the hospital and then furloughed home where he stayed until about January 1864. He reenlisted yet again on Mar 2 1864 for three years.

PVT Henry Tyler Templeton

Dr. Henry T. Templeton (1841-1903) was born in Laurens County and enlisted at Laurens Courthouse as a Private, Company A, 3rd South Carolina Infantry on Jul 1 1862 with Colonel Preston "for the war." Muster records show that he was present from September 1862 to February 1863, He was sick in Howard's Grove General Hospital, Richmond, VA on from Jun 6 1863 till he returned to duty on Sep 7 1863. He was captured by the enemy near Knoxville, TN on Dec 3 1863 and processed as a POW where he was sent to Camp Chase, OH on Dec 15 1863 and then to Rock Island, IL on Dec 31 1863. He was released from there on Jun 22 1865 after signing an Oath of Allegiance to the U.S. (where he is described as age 23, fresh complexion, dark hair, grey eyes and 5'-8" tall).

PVT John Wistar Simpson Stewart

John W. Stewart (1846-1914) was born in Laurens County and won a college scholarship to the Arsenal in Columbia, SC and reported there on Jan 1 1863. However, in a few months, the institution was closed for 17 years. He then enlisted as a Private with Lieutenant Patrick in Company B, Battalion State Cadets, South Carolina Local Defense Troops in Charleston, SC. He served on Post Duty on James Island near Charleston.

PVT Young Henry Elkanah Hitch

Young H.E. Hitch (1825-1864) was born in Laurens County and first enlisted as a Private with the 9th South Carolina Reserves at Laurens Courthouse by William Stewart for 90 days on Nov 17 1862 where he served until Feb 14 1863. He then reenlisted as a Private with Company I, 16th South Carolina Infantry Volunteers on Feb 13 1863 in Adams Run, SC with Captain McCullough "for the war." His muster records show him present (with only occasional sickness absences) from February 1863 through June 1864 when he was killed while on picket duty at Kennesaw Mountain (Georgia) on Jun 19 1864.

PVT Edwin Leroy Pitts

E. Leroy Pitts (1818-1882) was born in Laurens County. He served as a Private for Company D, 4th Battalion South Carolina Reserves where he enlisted on Jul 20 1864 at Laurens Courthouse under Lt. McGowan "for the war." On Jul 27 1864, the records indicate he was detailed by General Ordnance No. 30 but that was revoked by General Jones. He reported for duty on Aug 14 1864 and was listed as "present" in a muster for Nov/Dec 1864.

PVT James Young Pitts

James Y. Pitts (1845-1913) was from Laurens County and the son of E. Leroy Pitts. He enlisted as a Private in Company D, 1st Battalion (Gaillard's) South Carolina Infantry which later became the 27th South Carolina. He enlisted on Feb 28 1863 at Charleston, SC with Captain Hopkins "for the war" and was generally present on extant muster rolls from March to October 1863.

PVT Young Joseph Harrington Pitts

Young J.H. Pitts (1829-1911) was brother to E. Leroy Pitts and first enlisted as a Private with Company B, 9th South Carolina Reserves on Nov 17 1862 for 90 days, and serving until Feb 14 1863. He then enlisted as a Private with Company D, 19th South Carolina Infantry on Nov 3 1863 (another record shows the date as Oct 27 1863) in Columbia, SC by Captain Peterson "for the war." He was captured and taken prisoner on Nov 25 1863 during the action at Missionary Ridge and forwarded for processing to Louisville, KY and sent to Rock Island, IL where he was exchanged on Jan 17 1864.

PVT John Wesley Pitts

John W. Pitts (1831-c1863) was brother to E. Leroy and Young J.H. Pitts from Laurens County. He enlisted as a Private in Company C, 3rd (Laurens) Battalion South Carolina Infantry on Dec 2 1861 at Columbia, SC by Colonel John S. Preston for 12 months. He was sick for most of his tenure in the army at camp near Adams Run, SC and finally discharged by authority of the Army Medical Examiner's Board on Mar 18 1863.

PVT Lewis J. Duvall

Lewis J. Duvall (1818-1895) was born in Laurens County and enlisted as a Private on Nov 17 1863 for 90 days in Company D, 9th South Carolina Reserves at Clinton, SC. The only muster entry shows him as sick on furlough. No other service record is found for him.

PVT H. James Duvall

H. James Duvall (1843-1905) was from Laurens County and enlisted on Apr 25 1862 at Camp Brooks, SC with LTC George S. James for 12 months as a Private with Company C, 3rd (Laurens) Battalion South Carolina. Muster records show the following:

- Mar/Apr 1862: Present, recruit for the war, $50 bounty paid
- May/Dec 1862: Absent, sick at Winchester since Oct 12 1862
- Nov 1862 to Mar 1863: $94 bounty paid
- Jan/Feb 1863: Absent, sick since Nov 29 1862
- Jul/Aug 1863: Present
- Sep 22 1863: wounded at Chickamauga
- Nov/Dec 1863: Absent with leave since Sep 22 1863, wounded
- Dec 1863 to Apr 1864: Absent with leave since Sep 22 1863, wounded at Chickamauga
- May/Jun 1864: Returned to service
- Apr 27 1865: Present
- May 2 1865: Paroled

PVT Chesley W. Duvall

Chesley W. Duvall (1831-1905) enlisted as a Private with Company I, 3rd South Carolina Infantry on Jul 1 1862 in Clinton, SC with Colonel Preston "for the war." Other than being sick for about a 60-day period from June to August 1863 in Howard's Grove hospital in Richmond, he was present from September 1862 until he was paroled on May 2 1865.

PVT Francis Marion Duvall

F. Marion Duvall (1836-1864) enlisted on Jul 1 1862 with Company C, Holcombe Legion Cavalry, South Carolina Volunteers. Muster records detail how he was sick for most of his tenure in the army:

- Jan/Feb 1863: Present
- Mar/Apr 1863: Absent, sick in camp; May/Jun 1863: Absent, sick in hospital at Richmond, VA
- A note in the file indicates he was admitted to the General Hospital in Richmond on Jun 4 1863 with "int. fever" and discharged on Jun 19 1863
- Jul/Aug 1863: Absent, sick in hospital at Richmond, VA
- Another note in the file states he had "debilities" and admitted to the Hospital in Richmond on Jul 3 1863 and put in Jackson Hospital in Richmond on Aug 10 1863. He was returned to duty on Sep 7 1863.
- Sep/Oct 1863: Absent, sick, admitted to Hospital 9 in Richmond on Sep 21 1863 then, on furlough from Brigade hospital on Oct 17 for 30 days
- Nov/Dec 1863: Absent, sick, on furlough from Brigade hospital on Oct 17 for 30 days

- Apr 4 1864, F.M. Duvall appears on claims of deceased soldiers by widow "S.T.E. Duvall" (this is Susan Hitch Duvall) saying he died in Laurens District, SC; Apr 26 1864 it is noted that he died on Jan 11 1864 in Laurens District, SC.

PVT Jesse Madison Cook

Jesse M. Cook (1842-1914) was born in Laurens County but entered service in Alabama when he enlisted on Oct 11 1861 as a Private with Company E, 25th Alabama Infantry. Surviving muster records show that he was seriously wounded on Apr 6 1862 presumably at the Battle of Shiloh where the 25th Alabama was engaged. He served out through the rest of the war and was paroled with the rest of his unit on May 30 1865.

PVT Joseph Allen Hitch

Joseph A. Hitch (1823-1897) was born in Laurens County and served as a Private in Company D, 5th South Carolina State Troops where he enlisted for 6 months at Boyd's Old Field, SC by W.J.M. Jones for a term that lasted from Aug 1 to Nov 11 1863. He then reenlisted as a Private with Company B, 9th South Carolina Reserves for 90 days at Clinton, SC by W.J.M. Jones, for a term that lasted from Nov 17 1863 to Feb 14 1864.

PVT Silas Green Hitch

Silas G. Hitch (1845-1874) was the son of Joseph A. Hitch and served as a Private, Company D, 1st (Charleston) Battalion South Carolina Infantry/Sharp Shooters/Sumter Guards which later consolidated into Company D, 27th (Gaillard's) South Carolina Infantry. He enlisted just after his eighteenth birthday on Sep 26 1863 at Charleston, SC by Captain Hopkins "for the war." He served as present through the war except for a period in the summer of 1864 when he went absent near Richmond and received a 30 day furlough.

The preceding covers the Louther Hitch blood line relatives of Young Hitch who served in various capacities during the War Between the States. Besides these men, there were many other family in-laws and friends that we know served at the same time as, and sometimes directly with, Young Hitch in his travels during the War. We will cover many of them in the chapters ahead.

CHAPTER 3
Young Henry Elkanah Hitch and Life in the Years Prior to the War
1851-1860

The author first became acquainted with Young H.E. Hitch in 1994 when he was entrenched for many days in the microfilm room in the National Archives in Washington, DC, perusing Civil War military service records. This research yielded an article in the spring 1995 edition of the Hitch Family Newsletter where the following passage was written:

"Y.H.E. Hitch - From South Carolina, served as a Private in Company I of the 16th South Carolina Infantry and Company C of the 9th South Carolina Infantry. He was killed during the war and his body was never found."

Figure 2 - Young Henry Elkanah Hitch (1825-1864), photograph taken circa January 1863 in his CSA uniform with his Enfield rifle-musket he drew while a member of the 9th South Carolina Reserves. (Courtesy, Michael Givens, 1999)

This was the first introduction to a man who would eventually provide the impetus that compelled the writing of this book. Young Hitch's collection of writings, that comprise the Mowbray collection, date from 1846 to his death in 1864 and offer a distinct perspective of life in the southern United States at the time. At the micro-level, the collection depicts life in rural South Carolina that evolved from everyday routine of the life of a farmer in the early years leading up to the combined attributes of excitement, drudgery and tragedy of being a Confederate soldier in the later years.

The American Civil War is a very interesting and compelling time in our nation's history and it is very intriguing that many ancestors in the Hitch line have served in the various conflicts of this nation since the

1740s in the Colonial Wars[31] to the most recent conflicts in Afghanistan. However, the Civil War, or the "Struggle for Southern Independence" as Young Hitch referred to it, seems to have captivated our attention the most.

The Civil War literally pitted our own countrymen against one another in the bloodiest time of our history. This is especially evident when you leave the macro level of the War and what caused it and enter the micro level of the family and the struggles they saw during that time. In the Adam Hitch book, there are many anecdotal and historical stories about the family members who served for both the Union and Confederate sides of the conflict. All saw the horrors of the war whether it be disease in the camps, horrific deaths on the battlefield or just the extreme disruption of everyday routine to the family way of life.

The discovery of the cache of letters and other documents by Ms. Mowbray in her attic from Young Hitch and his immediate family and friends was nothing short of miraculous. To think that these fragile paper documents had survived over 150 years to breathe new life in a book speaks to the serendipity that many genealogists come to experience. It is almost as if the ancestors of the past are reaching out to us here in the future so that their story can be heard. The Mowbray collection is exceptional in its size and content and depicts the day-to-day activities of our ancestor Young Henry Elkanah Hitch from his early years as a young man to his membership in the 16th South Carolina Volunteers where he served and eventually died as part of the Civil War.

Young H.E. Hitch was the only known child of Joseph N. and Rosanna (Dalrymple?)[32] Hitch and was born August 30, 1825[33] in Laurens County, South Carolina. Young had little physical recollection of his father since he died not long after Young turned 2 years of age. Young's mother then remarried to William Brown in about the year 1828 and began raising another family of Browns, half-siblings to Young Hitch. There were five known children of William and Rosanna Brown; Emily, Lafayette, John, Caroline, and George Brown[34].

Rosanna (Hitch) Brown died sometime between the birth of son George Brown, c1845, and the taking of the 1850 census, leaving Young without living biological parents when he was just a young man of about 19 or 20 years old. His step father, William Brown, and three half-brothers and two half-sisters were there to support him, however, as was much of his extended Hitch family. Young Hitch married Mary Ann Edwards on Jan 19 1847, at about the same time his mother passed away. Young and Mary's first

---

[31] French and Indian War.

[32] Most genealogies place Rosanna Dalrymple as daughter of George and Ann (Teague) Dalrymple. The ages and years do not fit as the latter are too advanced in age to have parented a daughter of Rosanna's age. More than likely, this Rosanna is the daughter of a son of George and Ann Dalrymple or another close relative. It should be noted that one old note from Ms. Mowbray's files claims she may be a nee Clarke.

[33] The birthdate comes from an 1858 diary of Y.H.E. Hitch as some random writings of his from 1846, both are part of the Mowbray Collection.

[34] The family connections of the Brown children are proved in the census records of 1850 and 1860 EXCEPT for that of Emily Brown. She is suggested as a sister in one of the letters where she writes to "brother" Young Hitch along with Caroline L. Brown. In the 1840 Census for Laurens Co., SC, "Capt. William Brown" maintains a household that accounts for himself, his wife and all the children born by 1840 except there is an unaccounted for female age 5-10 – this is probably Emily who would have likely been born about 1829/31.

son, John Joseph Hitch was born later the same year, on Dec 2 1847. Six years later, on Jul 8 1853, the Hitches' second son, Augustus Lucian Hitch, was born.

William Brown remarried to Sarah A. (?) about 1852 and raised yet another family of Brown children through that wife; e.g., Daniel, Narcissa, Henry and Dorah Brown. Neither of these children were known blood relatives of Young Hitch but we can be confident that he probably considered them as brothers and sisters of an extended family. Later, we will see more details about where Young Hitch lived and tended to his farm.

EARLY DOCUMENTS

There are a few letters, a small diary and some random scribble sheets in the Mowbray collection that offer a glimpse of Young Hitch as he might have been in his years as a young man before his time in the War. That material is presented here in order to try and get a sense of who he was as a young man who eventually served as a Private for Company I, 16th South Carolina Volunteers in the Confederate States of America (CSA) in the Civil War.

The earliest item in the Mowbray Collection, besides the 1806-1814 school notebook of Joseph N. Hitch mentioned previously, is a three-page rambling of scribbles from Young Hitch from the summer of 1846. Young was not quite 21 years old at the time and seemed to just use those papers to write passing musings of poetry, sayings and such, maybe even to practice his penmanship. The earliest date found on those pages is Jul 5 1846 with the latest being Aug 16 1846. This is near the time his mother Rosanna (Hitch) Brown passes away. In the notes, he pens a small poem as follows:

Though I am young, yet I may die
And hasten to eternity,
There is a dreadful fiery hell.
Where wicked ones must always dwell,
There is a heaven of joy and rest,
Where godly ones with Christ are blest.
To one of these my soul must fly.
As in a moment when I die.

He also makes the following statement there (3) times on those pages, "*Young H.E. Hitch is my name and single is my station and Laurens District is my dwelling place and happy will be the girl that gets me I hope.*" Then he writes, "*My true loves name is in this letter and you may read it over and be none better then read it over and over and be none the better yet my true loves name is in this letter.*" Many of these are just random sentences, probably used to practice writing but also, providing some sense of his actual thoughts and dealing at the time.

Curiously, among what is mostly just random musings, Young writes, "*William Brown Esq a hog thief and a liar you better believe it.*" As we know, William Brown was Young's stepfather and married his mother Rosanna Hitch in about 1828. This passage makes one wonder about his relationship with his stepfather though, it could also just be random thoughts in a sentence where he was practicing writing. After all, he even writes this about himself, *"Young H.E. Hitch Esq a hog thief and a liar."* We do know from other letters in the Mowbray collection that he generally held a good relationship with all of his Brown half-siblings.

Three other random notes mention people, *"The reverend T. Robeson & H. Hit are to preach at North," "At Dover dine Geary Brown Esq. Good Christopher Finch and David Friam,"* and *"I bought a beaurau of Ribin bramblet the 11th day of July A.D. 1846 $12 Young Henry Elkanah Hitch."* "T. Robeson" refers to Toliver E. Robertson whom we will see later as he preaches for the soldiers while serving for the 1st Corps, 9th South Carolina Reserves.

Reuben Bramlett is a local man who is listed in Laurens County in the 1850 census as age 38 (born c1812) with occupation as a cabinet maker so, he probably was paid by Hitch to build a bureau of drawers. It would be nice to know where this South Carolina-made bureau of drawers built in 1846 is today as it would indeed be a treasure! This Reuben Bramlett may be the nephew or other close relative of Reuben and Sarah (Dacus) Bramlett whose sons will later serve with Young Hitch in Company I of the 16th South Carolina Volunteers. Privates James W. and William D. Bramlett will be introduced later in this book.

Hitch mentions others in his circle of friends and acquaintances including Alfred Holcombe, James B.F. Bruce, Rosanna Martin, Mary Elizabeth Martin, Martha Jane Martin, Emila L.M. Brown, Miss E. Halbert, Joseph Allen Hitch, P.P. Hitch, L.D. Hitch, and Capt. William Brown. It is unclear who Alfred Holcombe is, but there were many Holcombes in Laurens and Greenville counties at the time. James B.F. Bruce (1825-1910) is both Young Hitch's neighboring friend and adversary who will eventually marry Emila Brown, Hitch's half-sister. He will be covered in more detail in the coming pages.

The three Hitches mentioned are Young's relatives, his uncle Louther Douglas Hitch (1798-1886); son of Louther and, Young's cousin, Joseph Allen Hitch (1823-1897, son of Louther D. Hitch); and Louther's other son, Presley Pinkney Hitch (1831-1856). Capt. William Brown (1803-c186x) and Emila L.M. Brown (1831-1896) are Young's step-father and half-sister, respectively.

Not much is known of the Martin women other than it seems that Young may have had a hankering for one of them in a romantic way at one point. We do not know this for sure but there is some indication in his writings that seem to zero-in on Mary E. Martin as when he wrote, *"My true loves name is in this letter and you may read it over and be none better then read it over and over and be none the better yet my true loves name is in this letter…",* "M.E. Martyn" is the only other name written on that page! Mary E. Martin is sister to Rosanna Martin as they appear as daughters of Beverly and Priscilla (McKittrick) Martin in the 1850 census for Laurens County. Rosanna is age 20 and Mary Martin, age 18. A quick research of genealogy of this family reveals that Martha Jane Martin is also a sister to Mary and Rosanna Martin[35].

"A man wishing to gain popularity should act studiously" and *"Remember well and bear in mind that a trusty friend of wit and understanding may kiss a maid without asking,"* round out some of the more

[35] Martin family structure obtained from researching census records and an ancestry.com genealogy.

interesting musings of Young Hitch. From these early note pages, we can get a feel for the man Young Hitch was becoming. He was quite literate and articulate with excellent penmanship. He also kept up with regional events as, from the records, we know he was a subscriber to the "Laurensville Herald" newspaper in 1853. He had a mind for contemplation and he was well-acquainted with man's mortality. He had grown up a fairly conservative southern man and, as many young men do for his age, was looking around in the area for eligible women he might marry. This forms a foundation of who Hitch was and we will see in later compositions how he develops further into a man of integrity, a good farmer and business man and, eventually, a good soldier.

There is also a small diary of Young Hitch's in the collection that contains notes from Jan to Aug 1858. It contains interesting items relative to everyday life in the years in Laurens County prior to the Civil War[36]. The first item, from Jan 5 1858, states that Young *"brought from Mill the flower of 2½ bus. of wheat. At the same time the meal of 1½ bus. of corn"*. It is a nice reminder that, in those days more than 150 years ago, one could not just go down the street to the supermarket to get some flour or corn meal for baking. Instead, you had to first get the grain and then, once the grain was procured - either by growing or purchasing it - then you had to venture to a grist mill to get the grain converted to flour or meal for use in cooking.

The very next entry into the 1858 diary states, *"Saturday the 9th had Liberty shod with old shoes & ribbit put in pot hook."* A rather simple entry that is intriguing enough that Young had chosen the name "Liberty" for his horse. There is probably some subliminal meaning that can be taken from this that speaks to Young Hitch's deep sense of patriotism and love of freedom that this nation provided then and still provides to this day. By 1858, the country had emerged from its heavily patriotic Federal period and the War of 1812 and had begun to experience some deep political divisions. Divisions that would pit the northern industrial economy against the southern agrarian economy and pivotal ideas that support the two including states' rights and views on slavery. This would play out even more critically as the advent of the war approached in 1861.

The rest of the diary provides more notes of items like times that Young worked to help various people in his neighborhood. It mentions "Mr. Edwards" quite often, who was his father-in-law, John Edwards, a well-known and trusted elder in the community. We get an idea of what livestock Hitch maintained on his farm as well; for instance, *"Feb 12. We have four little lambs here"* and *"The cow called Sarah brought a young calf up Wednesday 7th of July 1858"*. We can infer that he raised chickens as well from, *"April the 14th 1858 Sold at Laurens Court House Thirty seven and a half dozen Eggs at ten cts per dozen"*, and used eggs quite often as barter for other goods and services. He also evidently raised pigs as we see him mention bacon several times in the diary.

He also remarks quite a bit about his farming and condition of his crops and orchard as, *"Sowed some stubble land today in peas for the first this season"*, *"July 7th finished laying my corn: on the same day ploughed out the potatoes"*, *"May 1st planted cotton seed and goober peas"* and, *"July 14th finished sowing peas to day P.M."*. In 1858, Young planted corn, peas, potatoes, cotton and wheat at a minimum

---

36 The diary (and the other writings from 1846-1854) also states Young Hitch's birth date written in his own hand, *"Y.H.E. Hitch was born Aug 30 1825."* The exact date was unknown until the discovery of his writings.

and probably had existing orchard trees. One time where his crops are mentioned, we get a distinct feeling for Young's innate and sometimes self-deprecating humor as is the entry, *"April 19th and not a grain of corn planted yet at Hitch's. Call him late beginner wont you yessir."* As the war commences, we will see his correspondence understandably grow a little darker in character.

As a farmer, weather was very important to Young Hitch and example entries in the diary regarding weather include, *"Feb 12 1858. Got up this morning & found the ground covered in sleet & continued falling untill night half after eight oclock"*, *"Wednesday morning April 28th a killing frost the fruit all or the biggest part of it killd I suppos"*, *"April 23rd beans kild by frost"* and *"A very warm day this but a fine growing time for all growths"*. It seems that the Hitch farm experienced a cold spring in 1858 and several late killing frosts caused problems with his early plantings.

Bartering was an important means to acquire goods and services in the south before and during the War and, in Young Hitch's diary, we get to see his acumen at bartering come to life. An entry for Jun 24 1858 is particularly enlightening:

June 24 Bartered at Greenville C.H.[37] *with Mr. Ray*	
Twenty two & half dozen Eggs	*$2.25*
Five & three fourths lbs Butter	*$0.85*

	$3.10
Thirty six lbs Bacon	*$3.60*

	$6.70
Bleaching 6 yds 10 cts per yd	*$0.60*
Linen 2½ yds 60 cts per yd	*$1.30*
Pants 1½ yds 37½ per yd	*$0.50*
Alpaca 1 yd 37½ per yd	*$0.37½*
Bottle Oil 25 cts	*$0.25*
Needles 5 cts	*$0.05*
¼ lbs pepper 20 cts per lb	*$0.05*
Soda 10 cts 1 lb	*$0.10*
½ lb Ginger 12½ cts per lb	*$0.06¼*
Pair of Scissors 37½	*$0.37½*
Four deep plates 30 cts	*$0.30*
½ lb Starch 10 cts per lb	*$0.05*
One set Knives & forks	*$0.75*

	$4.75¾
------next page	
1 ball of Shoe thread	*$0.05*
1 Gimblet 5 cts	*$0.05*
1 Box of blacking 5 ct	*$0.05*
4 yds Braid 4 cts per yd	*$0.04*

---

[37] "Greenville C.H." stands for Greenville Courthouse. 'Courthouse' was often appended to town names back in the 19th century that were also county seats and, hence, where the local courthouse was located.

2 yd Ribbon 7½ cts per yd	*$0.15*
Shirt Buttons 10 cts	*$0.10*
Bolt of Sheeting 37 yd 7 ct per yd	*$2.59*

	$3.03
	$4.75
One dollars worth of coffee	*$1.00*
7 lbs	
Fish hooks 5 cts	*$0.05*
Candys 15 cts	*$0.15*

	$8.98
	$6.70

	$2.28

"Mr. Ray[38]" was no doubt a shopkeeper in Greenville, SC in 1858 and Young Hitch brought some of the products of his farm to trade for other household items. We see from the above that he brought in $6.70 worth of eggs, butter and bacon. He then purchased $8.98 worth of sundry items like various types of cloth, needles, scissors, ribbons and braid, buttons, shoe thread, and kitchen utensils. He even picked up some fish hooks and 7 pounds of coffee. Young's final bill came to $2.28 which is the difference between his total purchases of $8.98 minus the items he bartered for $6.70 and, though, it does not say, we might assume that the difference was paid in cash. Perhaps, this shopping trip was really not much different than one would see with a modern-day grocery and shopping excursion, only in a more fundamental form.

One item, in particular from Young's shopping list catches our attention as it stands out from the rest of the list of necessities and staples – "*Candys 15 cts*". This seems to demonstrate Young's compassion as a father (and perhaps, his own sweet tooth!) as he thinks of his young sons at home; John J. and A. Lucian Hitch, at the time ages ten and four, respectively. One can just imagine the look on those boys' faces when their father returns from Greenville with a surprise treat to share with them!

The diary of 1858 is a simple, unassuming document left over many years but, one that shows the simplicity and life aspects of rural South Carolina as she approached the dawn of the Civil War. It is easy to see how these day-to-day activities, and the security they brought, would be completely disrupted once the War broke out. The soldiers, like Young Hitch, would yearn in correspondence from the battlefield to get back to the niceties of this everyday drudgery. We will see some of this in future correspondences of Young, his wife and sons and others as the war breaks out in the coming years.

---

[38] In the 1860 census, we find only one Ray in the Town of Greenville who might qualify as "Mr. Ray" – this is Samuel Ray, age 30, who is living in the same building as the Charles Merrick family, Merrick listed as a merchant. Samuel Ray may have been the grocer and dry goods merchant Hitch was writing about.

SCHEDULE I.—Free Inhabitants in ______ in the County of Laurens State ______ enumerated by me 1850 Laurens County, SC Census ______ 1850. ______ Ass't Marshal. 283

332

Dwelling No. (1)	Family No. (2)	Name (3)	Age (4)	Sex (5)	Profession, Occupation, or Trade (7)	Value of Real Estate (8)	Place of Birth (9)	
2009	2009	Wm Jones	50	M	Farmer	500	S Carolina	1
		Nancy	45	F				2
		Richard	22	M	Farmer			3
		Sarah	17	F				4
		Elvira	15	F				5
		William	4	M				6
2009	1999	John Edwards	62	M	Farmer	2500	Virginia	7
		Rebecca	42	F			Carolina	8
		Sarah	11	F				9
		Samantha	9	F				10
		Little B	6	M				11
		Eufrates	4	M				12
10	2010	Y E H Hitch	24	M	Farmer	650		13
		Mary	22	F				14
		Joseph	2	M				15
11	2011	William Brown	47	M	Farmer	1200		16
		~~Lafayette~~			Farmer			17
		John	14	M				18
		Caroline	11	F				19
		Frances	7	F				20
		George	6	M				21
		Margaret Brown	50	F				22
12	2012	Jas B F Bruce	23	M	Farmer	800		23
		Emily	19	F				24
13	2013	Frances Holcomb	46	F		1000		25
		Perreny	17	F				26
		Duff G.	12	M				27
		Martha	10	F				28
14	2014	John Bruce	26	M	Farmer			29
		Nancy	28	F				30
		Robert	4	M				31
		Jane	2	F				32
15	2015	Robert Bruce	22	M	Farmer			33
		Ann	24	F				34
17	2017	Thos Holbert	53	M	Farmer	400		35
		Lesley	28	F				36
		William	11	M				37
		Elizabeth	10	F				38
		Frances	8	F				39
		Robert	6	M				40
		Garry J.	4	M				41
		Margaret	2	F				42

*John Edwards (f/o Mary Hitch)
Rebecca (Gilbert) Edwards
Sarah Edwards
Samantha Edwards
*Little Berry Edwards
*Euphrates Edwards

*Young Hitch
*Mary (Edwards) Hitch
*John Joseph Hitch

*William Brown (Young Hitch's stepfather)
*Gilbert Lafayette Brown (Young's half brother)
*John C. Brown (Young's half brother)
*Jane Caroline Brown (Young's half sister)
*Frances Brown (Young's half sister)
George M. Brown (Young's half brother)
*"Aunt" Margaret Brown (Wm. Brown's sister)

*James B.F. Bruce
*Emily L.M. (Brown) Bruce

Frances (Word) Bruce Holcomb
*Pyrenee Holcomb
Duff Green Holcomb
Martha Holcomb

*John W. Bruce
*Nancy (Edwards) Bruce
*Robert Bruce
*Jane Bruce

Robert Word Bruce
Martha Ann (Cooley) Bruce

Figure 3 - Page 332 from the 1850 United States Census for Laurens County, South Carolina with annotations to show Y.H.E. Hitch and his family and friend neighbors. The asterisks depict people mentioned in the Mowbray collection. (United States Census, 1850, Laurens County, SC)

EARLY CORRESPONDENCE

Amongst the Mowbray collection, there is one very interesting letter that dates to Sep 30 1851 from a Mr. James B.F. Bruce to Y.H.E. Hitch[39] when Young was 25 years old. Affectionately called the "Grand Rascal" letter because this is what Mr. Bruce referred to Young Hitch within its pages. He states, "*...and to give you my opinion of you. I believe you to be a grand rascal. That's my sentiment about you...*" As one might surmise with young men of marrying age, the dispute seems to have been over a woman as, earlier in the letter, Mr. Bruce states, "*You say that your reason that you talked about me the way you did you didn't want her and me to marry. Well sir if you can help your self do it. I ask you no favors and I think that you had a very poor excuse and you say that you never talked to nobody but to Emily and it is a lie sir. Did you not come to the mill, sir, and talk to her father? You did, sir, or his family tells wrong tales and you say that when I get blood out of a turnip that you will acknoledge and not before and when you get so that you can stand on your head and shit and jump from under it, then you get my friendship but not before.*" James Bruce ends the letter with, "*So if you choose it and can make it come upright I would be glad to meet you in the field so no more at the present. Dear sir, I wrote you a friendly letter at the start and you wrote me an insulting one at the start and I wish to give you the same kind of a dost so no more.*" Those are some mighty strong words and you can practically feel the emotion in them!

In trying to identify Emily of the letter, we initially hypothesized that it was perhaps Emily Brown, Young's half-sister as she would have been about age 20 at the time and someone whom Young might be concerned with in as far as who she might choose to marry. While there is nothing that states that for certain, we decided to research more to see and to determine more about the circumstances of the letter. Mr. Bruce, in the correspondence, also claims that Young accused him of breaking "*up a match with Pyrence and Nathan Woods*" and he claimed that was a lie because Bruce states he asked Pyrence if it were true and she denied that it occurred. Just the typical daily life of young men in the mid-19th century and not much different than today! But, who indeed was this Miss "Pyrence"?

A little research shows that, in the 1850 Census records, we find James B.F. Bruce, age 23, in a household with his wife Emily Bruce, age 19, and right adjacent to the William Brown household of Young Hitch's stepfather and half-siblings (See **Figure 2**). This strengthens the case that Emily might be Young's half-sister, Emily Brown. Young Hitch's household is the next one in the census past and adjacent to William Brown's so they were all very close neighbors. In fact, the next household up from there is John Edwards, age 62, father of Mary Ann Hitch, Young's wife. Mr. Bruce states also within his letter to Young, "*You said that you never talked to nobody about me but Emily. Did you not talk to her aunt, sir? You certainly did or she has told a sorry tale. Did you not talk to Mr. Edwards, sir? If you didn't, sir, I have heard wrong tales.*" No doubt, the Mr. Edwards referenced is the John Edwards, the neighbor and Young's father-in-law and, "her aunt" was likely Aunt Margaret Brown, spinster sister to Young's step-father living in the same Brown household.

In 1860, James Bruce and wife Emily had moved to Marshall County, Alabama and had amassed a small family of a daughter and three sons; respectively, Rosannah (age 8), Jefferson (4), Harrison (3) and Christopher Bruce (0). The first child was born in South Carolina, the middle two in Mississippi and the

---

[39] See Item II in the Appendix.

last in Alabama. The fact that the daughter is named Rosannah is significant and deepens the likelihood that Emily is daughter of William and Rosanna (Hitch) Brown. By 1870, they had added three more sons, Leander, Elford and Elbert Bruce.

Further research reveals that James B.F. Bruce was born on Feb 25 1825 and died on Aug 25 1910 in Newton County, Mississippi[40]. We also see that Emily Bruce was born Mar 18 1831 and died in Mississippi in Aug 1896, her full maiden name was Emily Loretta M. Brown. James was son of Robert Bruce (c1800-c1830) and Frances R. (Word) Bruce Holcombe (1802-1900).

There were two other sons from the Bruce-Word marriage, John W. Bruce (1824-1863) and Robert Word Bruce (1828-1863). Robert W. Bruce served as a Private with Company F, 2nd South Carolina Rifles in the war and died in service.

Frances Bruce remarried to John Holcombe of Laurens County, South Carolina after the death of James Bruce's father. With Holcomb, Frances had a daughter named Frances Pyrenee Holcombe (1832-1919), no doubt the Miss "Pyrence" mentioned in James Bruce's letter that Young supposedly broke up a "*match with Nathan Woods*"! Pyrenee Holcombe was half-sister to James B.F. Bruce and lived in the Holcomb household adjacent to James in the 1850 census where she is listed as "Perreny" Holcomb, age 17 with her mother Frances (44), brother Duff G. (12) and sister, Martha (10). John Holcombe had died before the taking of the census in 1850[41].

The fact that Young kept this letter that descended with his family many years to the present day is interesting in and of itself – it must have been a notable moment in his life but, it also appears that his concern about James and his half-sister Emily as a couple were unfounded as they did indeed marry and lived long lives together and raised a large family. However, if he did break up Nathan Woods and Pyrenee Holcombe, it seemed to have stuck as Pyrenee ended up marrying a Mr. John W. Simpson so poor Nathan lost out! If one only had a time machine to go back and see all the circumstances that compelled Mr. Bruce to write this letter, it would no doubt prove most interesting.

Another letter in the collection comes from three years later, dated Jun 20 1854, from J.W. and Nan Bruce in Marshall County, Mississippi (post marked Jun 27 1854, Byhalia, Mississippi) and sent to Young and "Maryan" Hitch in Fountain Inn, South Carolina with the greeting, "*Dear brother an sister*."[42] The letter was authored by Nan Bruce and its contents are more mundane in comparison to the James Bruce letter of 1851, expressing the more everyday things people were concerned about in their lives at the time. It gives a good glimpse of what day-to-day life was like in the area in the mid-19th century south.

To research and verify the identities of the players in this letter, we again turn first to the 1850 census. As with the references in the 1851 letter where the Hitch, Edwards, Brown, Holcomb and Bruce lived very close to one another, we find the household of John (age 26) and Nancy Bruce (28) in the same

---

[40] *Findagrave.com* and *ancestry.com* provided much of the family connections for the Bruce family.

[41] Most of the information in this paragraph and the previous one was derived from the Find-A-Grave website and a genealogy of the Bruce/Holcomb family from Ancestry. These corroborate much of what we find in the primary source records stated.

[42] Appendix, Item IV.

close proximity with their children Robert (4) and Jane Bruce (2). This is no doubt the family of the letter with Nancy (Nan) Bruce authoring same. It seems as Nan was a nee Edwards, sister of Young's wife Mary Ann Hitch, who married John W. Bruce sometime around 1845. John Bruce was the brother to James B.F. Bruce of the 1851 letter. Unlike the others nearby, John and Nan Bruce owned no real estate in 1850 and, from the letter, we see they had moved to Marshall County, Mississippi by 1854.

In 1860, J.W. Bruce (age 37) shows up back in South Carolina (Anderson County) with a new wife Mary Bruce (age 27) and children John R. Bruce (Robert, age 15), Butler (8), Calhoun (4) and Frances I. Bruce (age 11 months). In fact, it appears that the John Bruce family was back in South Carolina at least by April 1858 as Young Hitch entered in his diary, the following: *"April 24th Bruce's Children came here today & left the 1st of May. John himself staid all night 1st May"*. It also appears that Nancy (Edwards) Bruce had died between late 1854 (when she penned the letter) and the taking of the 1860 census, probably after the birth of their son, Calhoun Bruce, in 1856 but before the birth of daughter Frances I. Bruce in 1859. John W. Bruce died in a hospital in Lynchburg, Virginia in 1863 while serving with Company L, 1st (Orr's) South Carolina Rifles in the Civil War.

In the letter, which is typical of many letters of the era, we hear of people's health when Nan writes; *"we air yet alive an tolarb health at this time but we hav ben sick this summer with the bowel complaint an a tuch of the flu. I was sick for three or for days that I dident set up any at tall only what time I was helping Robert to cook but he dun the most of it."* Many times, health in those days was said to be "tolerable" ('tolarb' as Nan puts it) reflecting the much higher uncertainty of sickness/health in the days before modern medicine. We will see that Young Hitch frequently refers to his health when he writes home from the War in later years. Nan refers to Robert as having, *"a large bile on his backbone an cant stoop about much tho he is peart as ever an dont complain of it much..."* and, then John *"was sick at the same time I was tho he only lost one or too days with his sickness."* Then, a general statement of the health of the community, *"Ther is a great deal of sickness about hear with the flu an bowel complaint an the cholery have ben very bad in Memphis about thirty miles from whear we live an I have hird of som few cases only a few miles of from us"*. Evidently, there had been a cholera outbreak in the area and it concerned the population, as it should have, given that it could be a lethal disease.

Also, one can see the concern with other illnesses and afflictions of the time; i.e., the flu, bowel complaints and "bile on the backbone." One might assume that the latter is some sort of large boil on his back, even though Robert was only about 8 years old at the time. His young age and health problem did not seem to prevent him from helping around the house and tend to the farm as Nan pens, *"Robert can make up doe an put down a very nice pone of bread an bake it too an he can milk very well to tho he hasnt milk any for a few days."*

Marshall County in Mississippi is in the north central part of the state bordering Tennessee, far removed from Laurens County, South Carolina and Nan Bruce was none too keen on this as she states, *"Maryan, I reckon you will want to know whether I am satisfide or not. I can tell you I aint and the reason for it is because ther aint no water hear in the summer only water is in the wells. People hav to draw water ou of ther well for all of ther stock an the women dont make no cloth an that dont soot mee. Tha by all tha war but when I git in a (__) I intend git mee a wheel and cards an loom an make our close an then we can save money to pay our dets back. Ther meany. We aim to pay you what we owe you an all the wrest of our dets if we live ever git money anuf to come back ther an pay them of. John sais if hee can ever make money anof to pay of his dets he intends to com back ther an bring mee an the children an I set a great deal by makin moey an coming back ther independent so more at present."*

Nan seems homesick for South Carolina and is looking for a means to get back there. But, the primary thing standing in the way is that they have no money and are weighed down by a considerable amount of debt – "*...dets...Ther meany*" (debts...there're many). Her objective is driven to procuring a spinning wheel and loom so that she can make clothes so the family can save money, get the debts paid off and get back to South Carolina. Also, Nan is careful to assert that they hope to get the money they owe to Young and Mary Hitch to them as well; "*We aim to pay you what we owe you an all the wrest of our dets if we live ever git money anuf to come back ther an pay them of.*" Since Nan died sometime between 1856 and 1859, we do not know if she ever got her wish to get back to South Carolina as the rest of the family had done by 1860.

The debt plight of many during those years in the south was again noted in a Feb 2 1855 letter from William P. Edwards in Lauderdale County, Alabama to Y.H.E. and Mary Hitch[43]. William uses the greeting, "Dear brother and sister," as he was an older brother to Mary (Edwards) Hitch and the primary subject of the letter is a debt he owes them. He begins by stating how depressed the prices of corn and cotton are, "*Tha corne is \$35^0 cts pur bari four \$10 dollars pur baril. Coton is worth 5 cts pur pound*" and that it is "*Hard times to get money tho I am owing rite smart and cant get eny money to pay off what I owe.*" His total debt load is \$800 "*as near as I can come to hit with thout counting up*" and that he really cannot afford to pay Young and Mary Hitch anything and hopes that they could "*make hit out of John if you coud.*" This last statement seems to be a reference to another of Mary's brothers, John B. Edwards and brother William is suggesting to get the debt paid off through him. It's a rather desperate letter showing the strained finances of many of the acquaintances of Young Hitch in the years prior to the War.

William Scruggs writes to Y.H.E. and Mary Hitch on Aug 16 1855 from Forsyth County, Georgia[44]. William is William Berry Scruggs (1826-1905) who will eventually serve with Young in Company I, 16th South Carolina Volunteer Infantry and was with him when he was fatally shot in 1864. It was he who wrote the letter home to Mary Ann Hitch informing her of the circumstances of Young's death. William Scruggs had married his first cousin Caroline Edwards, sister to Mary Hitch[45]. And, by the time of the letter, William and Caroline had three children, "*I has got too sons & a daughter that I will show with eny body*"; Young Riley Scruggs (1852-1920), John Land Scruggs (1853-1933), and Samantha Scruggs (1855-??) and, was due to have Sarah Elizabeth Scruggs (1856-1898) in just six months from when this letter was written. There is not much content to the letter here other than Scruggs saying that he had been very sick. He also mentions, Samantha as, "*Tell Samantha that I got that coat that she sent to her name sake and I though hit was purty but if she cood see her she wood think that she is purty according.*" Samantha is Mary Hitch's half-sister Samantha Edwards and she had evidently sent a coat for her "namesake" Samantha Scruggs, the infant daughter in the Scruggs family at the time. Caroline writes to Mary proudly about her; "*A little for Caroline to Mary. I hant got mutch to rite at this time. I must tel you about my*

---

[43] Appendix, Item V.
[44] Appendix, Item VI.
[45] First cousin marriages were not all that uncommon even up into the mid-20th century and an accepted relationship in those days.

little gal that I has had since I left you. She is mity little but she grose fast but she is the crass as the dayes is long."

On May 16 1856[46], we see a letter from Marshall County, Alabama from Elijah and Emily Scruggs to Young and Mary Ann Hitch addressed as "Dear Cousins". Elijah S. Scruggs (1823-1902) was a brother of William Berry Scruggs who were both sons of John Edwards Scruggs and his wife Mary (Edwards) Scruggs. Mary Scruggs was blood aunt to Young's wife, Mary Ann Hitch, making the Scruggs boys first cousins to her. Elijah Scruggs served for Company I, 43rd Georgia Volunteers (Reynolds's Brigade) and both brothers survived the War.

In the May 1856 letter, we see the customary statement of family health and good tidings in, "*embrace the present opportunity of informing you that we are yet living and enjoying tolerble health. Hoping when these lines come to hand that they will find you all enjoying the same blessing we are well satisfied with the country and neighbors.*" Then we get some family information; "*We come by Wm Scrugs and tuck dinner with them. They are all well. Caroline is the fattest I ever saw her and her children is as fat as little pigs. Caroline was as proud to see me as she could be. She talked a great deal.*" Elijah Scruggs had evidently visited with Caroline when she was the "fattest I ever saw her" during the time she was pregnant with Sarah Scruggs. This letter was composed May 16 1856. Sarah was born Feb 24 1856. So Sarah was born a little more than two months before Elijah and Emily composed their letter.

We see from these early letters that there was some draw on the people in Laurens County, South Carolina to go to Marshall County in Alabama in this time period (remember that James B.F. and Emily Bruce moved there as well by 1860). Some of the reason for this migration is explained in the letter as, "*She (Caroline Scruggs) said that she intended to move out here and be a neighbor to us. She told me that if she could not get to meeting that she wanted me to go but I hav no chance to go here for the meeting house is so fer off I cant go often. I think if Y.H. Hytch was here that he never would go back to old Carolina. I would be glad to see you come to this country for I can tell you a thousand things I cant rite.*" One might guess it was the promise of better and cheaper land, the same thing that took Louther Hitch to Laurens, South Carolina 50 years prior. But, it must have also been more rural as the church (meeting house) was quite distant causing the family not to be able to attend very often.

The rest of the letter is light-hearted and touches on three family members, "*I want you to tell cousin Anna Hughs that I am well and well satisfied and that I have not been as smart as Silvy Gilbert was. I want you to rite to me all the news you can think of and not put it of for I want to here from you all. Tell Lafayett Brown that we want him to come out here and preach for us for there aint many preachers here. Tell him there is lots of pretty girls here.*" The first is "cousin" Anna Hughes who is one of the many Hughes family members in the Laurens County area. Elijah Scruggs also mentions Lafayette Brown. His full name was Gilbert Lafayette Brown (born in 1834) who was a travelling preacher and half-brother to Young Hitch. We see the Gilbert surname show up in the Laurens County quite a bit, Elijah Scruggs' wife was nee Amelia (Emily) Gilbert and, Lafayette Brown's first given name of Gilbert comes from his mother's maiden name as William Brown had married Rebecca Gilbert after his first wife Rosanna Hitch had died. The "Silvy" Gilbert in the letter appears to be the wife of William Harvey Gilbert of Laurens

[46] Appendix, Item VIII.

County, she is the nee Sylvania Smith of that same region. We are not sure of the exact relationship, if any to Emily Scruggs but, it may be her sister-in-law.

While on the subject of Marshall County, Alabama, we find another letter in the Mowbray collection that originates from that location. It is dated May 30 1858 from Caroline L. Brown and her sister Emily[47]. Emily is the wife of James B.F. Bruce of the 1851 "grand rascal" letter. The letter is in bipartite form with the first half from Caroline and the latter half from Emily. Caroline is brief in her portion and speaks of their good health and adjustment to the climate in Alabama; *"I now take my seat to fulfill the long neglected promise of writing to you. I beg you to excuse me for not doing it before. We are all well except Frances and aunt Margrett. They have been sick but are recovering. I hope we will have good health after we are naturalized to the climate. This seems to be a great place to make grain but money is allways scarce. every one about will (__) can live (__) but they you need not think of finding refinement when they come here for the people are everything else but refined either in manners or morals. Young as you are a farmer I must tell you something about the crops. Corn looks well indeed and wheat did fair to (__) well... P.S. my beau says to ____ he is well. Caroline*" Frances, is Frances Brown, another of Young's half-sisters who would have been about age 17 in 1858 and "Aunt Margrett" is Margaret Brown, sister of Young's step-father William Brown. The final sentence relates to Young's stance as a farmer and the state of the season's crops there in Alabama perhaps offered so that he can compare to his own in South Carolina. The postscript mentions Caroline's "beau" who is well; this is William H. Lyons whom Caroline Brown will wed on Jul 14 1859.

In the Emily L.M. (Brown) Bruce portion of the letter, she mentions that it had been a long time since they lasted communicated. It makes one wonder if there were still friction left from the time the inflammatory letter of her husband in 1851 where he claimed Young tried to prevent their marriage! Nevertheless, Young's half-sister Emily seems very cordial and friendly as she relates the happenings in her family, *"It has been a long time since I have written to you but I have at (__) found time and opportunity which gladly I embrace. I have passed years without the hope of seeing father or any of my brothers and sisters. But have been blessed beyond expectation in seeing them all again and am now living here with them all and I could be very glad indeed to see you too*." We see by this time that the Bruce family had grown to include three daughters and two sons as well. She also writes a reason why we see, in the records, that the Bruce family goes from South Carolina, first to Alabama, then to Mississippi, back to Alabama, only to eventually land permanently in Mississippi when she pens, *"I was verry well satisfied in Mississippi in everything only the lands being so high father wrote to us to come hear and he would give us land. So we have come and he expects to close the trade for a place in a short time and if we get it I am set? for life*." The reason yet again was the price of land and her father William Brown was set to help them make a land purchase in Mississippi. Emily finishes her letter with *"A few lines to Mary... I am doing very we(ll with) chickens and gardening (for a?) new comer. I have wor( ) the few lines you wr(ote) when I was in Mississ(ippi) and I hope you will w(rite) again. So no more.*
Emily L.M. B(ruce)."

There are two letters from John C. Brown, Young Hitch's half-brother, to Hitch. Brown, who was about 22 years old at the time, a good 12 years younger than Hitch, had moved to Marshall County, Alabama

---

[47] Appendix, Item XII.

with his father keeping in communication with his elder half-brother. The first letter is dated Aug 7 1859 and he tells of what has happened in his life over recent months[48]. He writes:

> *"I write to inform you where I am which I ought to have done sooner, as I have been here nearly two months, but I have been too busy to write letters. I left Florida on the 8th of June and arrived here on the 14th. I was teaching a school in Maddison Co., Fla., but having a small school I concluded to abandon it, and took a notion to come back here. I traveled on foot and by a stage conveyance up to Albany, the terminal of the Southwestern railroad, took the car at 3 o'clock p.m. and at 10 o'clock found myself in the city of Macon. This is a large city and I should have liked to have spent a day here, but for the expense. At 12 o'clock I took the Macon & Western train, an against daylight I could look out at the car window and see the hills and oak woods which was a great pleasure to me after being so long in that low, level, pine woods country. Arrived at Atlanta at 9 o'clock in the morning. I thought it a very cold day, having made so sudden a change of climate, and while I was in Atlanta everybody was complaining of the hot weather, but I could not sit in the shade. After a few days, however, it seemed as hot as in Florida. If I had traveled slowly I should scarsely have perceived the difference of climate. I left Atlanta at 12 o'clock and at 4 in the evening was at Rome. I then took it on foot the rest of the way here, which took me three days. I have been that particular to give the details of my journey, only to fill my space in this letter. I have been at work for father since I have been here. I found his farm in a sad condition, he having had a good for nothing set of hands hired. I am not decided yet whether I shall continue at work or take charge of another school. I would rather have a home of my own and be a farmer, if I could get married; but that is what I can not do. I have traveled a good deal, but have never found the girl yet that would suit me. I am really afraid that I shall be a bachelor for the end of my days. I want you to write to me. Direct to Guntersville, Ala. Caroline wants you to answer her letter. Not Miss Caroline Brown, but Mrs. Caroline Lyons.*
> *Yours truly,*
> *J.C. Brown"*

John C. Brown had started out to be a school teacher in Florida but quit, indicating the school was too small. He traveled from Madison County, FL to Marshall County, AL from June 8 to 14 1859. It is interesting that he describes his whole trip, with the first leg by stage to Albany, GA where he caught a train to Macon, that leg taking 7 hours. From Macon, he caught the midnight train to Atlanta, arriving there at 9:00 a.m. the next morning. He caught another train from Atlanta at noon and arrived at Rome, GA at 4:00 p.m. The rest of his journey to Marshall County, AL (near Guntersville) was by foot where he found his father's farm and commenced working for him there.

He describes Captain William Brown's farm as being "*in a sad condition*" due to the poor farm hands he had hired. Brown is contemplating working for his father on the farm or returning to teaching there in Alabama or, better still, he would like to have a farm of his own if he could find a girl to suit him and get married! John Brown closes his letter by telling Young to write back to Caroline Brown who is now Mrs. Caroline Lyons. She had just married William H. Lyons on July 14, about 3 weeks before John Brown composed his letter.

---

[48] Appendix, Item XIII.

Another John Brown letter to Young Hitch comes from nearly a year later, on Jul 3 1860[49]:

> *Dear Brother*
> *What on earth is the reason you do not write to me? I wrote to you some time ago, I do not recollect exactly when, though it must have been early in the spring; at any rate it was since I received the last letter from you. I suppose, however, that letter never reached you. Caroline has received your letter of May 13, in which you had something to say to every one of the family and kindred, except me and Fayette, and wanted to know where we were. From your not knowing where I was and what I was doing I conclude that you had not received my last letter. I am living this year at Father's, working in the farm, and think I shall be a working man for the rest of my life. I have abandoned the business of school teaching. I intend to work, and devote only a portion of my time to scientific and literary pursuits. Fayette is traveling over the country, sermonizing and selling books, etc. You can write to him either at Guntersville or Houston, Ala. When you write to me, always direct to Guntersville, Ala. We have some very fine looking corn; but if it does not rain within a few days there will be a light crop. We have had abundance of rain this year, but none for the last ten days, and the earth is as dry as it ever gets in a month without rain in your county. We are all well We have a relative with whom you are perhaps unacquainted – a little girl by the name of Ella May Lyons. I should like very much to see you all, but as I cannot have that pleasure the next thing to it is to have a long letter from you – write often. You invited Fayette over to dine with you on slice potatoe pye. Now I think myself greatly insulted in not being invited also; for I am very fond of that sort of pye, especially if they are of Mary Ann's cooking. I am going to a fourth of July celebration to-morrow.*
> *Yours truly,*
> *J.C. Brown*
> *Marshall Co, Ala*
> *July 3, 1860*

He wonders why Young had not written him but seems to indicate that he may not have gotten his original letter to him in the first place. Young had written to his half-sister, who is John's full sister, on May 13 and has wondered where John and "Fayette" were. Fayette is referring to Lafayette Brown, another half-sibling to Young Hitch who was introduced earlier. Lafayette was a travelling preacher who was itinerant throughout the south in those years but, was primarily in Alabama in the late 1850s and early 1860s. After some words about the fine corn crop, John Brown mentions the newest addition to the family, Ella May Lyons, daughter of William H. and Caroline (Brown) Lyons. Frances Ellamay Lyons was born Jun 5 1860 and died Nov 27 1930 in Marshall County, AL.

Finally, we get a feeling for what dinner must have been like in the Young Hitch house. John Brown was "insulted" that Young had invited Lafayette over for sliced potato pie but not him. Brown states that he is most fond of that type of pie "*especially if they are of Mary Ann's cooking*." We will see that this is not the first time we will hear of Mary Hitch's excellent cooking skills in the various correspondences in the Mowbray collection.

---

[49] Appendix, Item XV.

There is one letter in the collection from Lafayette Brown to Young Hitch, dated Jun 25 1861 from Moulton, AL[50]. The main body of the letter is preaching as one might expect from a preacher but he does exchange other family pleasantries as well:

> *"Moulton Ala   June 25th 1861*
>
> *To Yong Hitch*
> *Dear brother*
> *I have writen to you several times and hav received now answer what is the matter are you yet in the land of the living or not. Hav you forgot G.L. Brown or are you determined never to write to me again. I wrote to you last fall. Shortly after I was married. And I forgit where I said for you to address me at. If you hav written to me at Guntersville I supos that some of fathers family would hav forwarded the letter to me. I now write to let you know whare I am my address etc and if you do not write me you never expect to git another line from me.*
> *Yours till death with out an answer*
> *G.L. Brown*
>
> *Well young I hav not an angel for a wif but as near so as any human being on earth but She is a good little wife I am devoting the energies of my life to the building up of a kingdom that can not be moved If you think worth while to write to me mark your letters to G.L. Brown Moulton Ala"*

Evidently, Young has not written to Lafayette since Brown had written him in the fall of 1860. In the interim, Lafayette has gotten married to an "angel for a wife." He finally closes his letter, after a long-winded discourse of preaching with, *"But I have spun this out longer than I thought I would at the start. So God bless you a your family. Let me know how your boys are growing off."*

In other early letters in the Mowbray collection, we are introduced to "Aunt Sally" Hitch. Sarah Hitch (1794-1871) was a daughter of Louther Hitch and a "spinster", meaning she never married. Like one might perhaps expect of any matriarchal aunt, even in the modern day, she related the feelings of family in a way that only a sage and elder family member could. She held no punches and expressed her thoughts and opinions at face value. These authors have grown to love and respect Sarah Hitch for her prolific correspondence and detail of her letters. In the letters that survive in the Mowbray collection, there are seven (7) composed by Aunt Sarah and they contain a great amount of detail about the family not present among the other letters therein.

Her first letter comes dated Apr 25 1856 and Sarah focuses primarily on the health of the family and the slaves and, from her report we get to hear about many in the extended Hitch family of the area[51]. She refers to Young Hitch's "*Uncle Pitts family*" as being "*greatly afflicted*" with health problems. She is referring here to the family of Henry Pitts (1792-1861) who married Mary Hitch (1794-1863), the daughter of Louther Hitch, Aunt Sally Hitch's sister and the twin sister to Young Hitch's father, Joseph N.

---

[50] Appendix, Item XVIII.
[51] Appendix, Item VII.

Hitch. The Pitts family lived in Laurens County and had ten known children; four sons and six daughters. Three of the sons (and a grandson) served in the War with various South Carolina military units. Sally Hitch began living in the Pitts household sometime in the early 1850s and stayed there throughout most of the rest of her life.

Sarah Hitch offers that John W. Pitts, Young's cousin, had been sick, "*His son John first took down and had a severe attack of the winter disease that's so prevalent in the country.*" She then mentions that "*And before he was able to see to the business out, the negroes all took down. That is the men, four of them. Pretty much the same disease. His old negro Jo had a spell before Christmas sometime. He has never got so he can labour yet and his oldest boy he raised, Jack, died of a lingering disease, something like a consumption.*" Here we find the names of two of the Pitts slaves[52], "*old negro, Jo*" who was recovering from his illness and, his son named Jack, who had died of a "*lingering disease*" similar to tuberculosis.

Aunt Sarah then turns to the family of Sarah Ann Milam (1871-1896), who is a daughter of Henry and Mary Pitts, and who married Diatrephus M. Milam[53] (1820-1895) in 1842. We know of eight children in the Milam family, of which SEVEN were girls. By the time the letter was written, six of the girls had been born and Sarah Milam must have been pregnant, for their son Robert Preston Milam was born just two months later in Jun 1856.

Isaac Boyd's family is next to be mentioned in the letter. He is Isaac Preston Boyd (1819-1905) who married another daughter of Henry and Mary Pitts, Matilda Angeline Pitts (1826-1896). The six known children in this family were four girls and two boys. All but one of the girls were born by the time of the letter in 1856. John Cooper's family is simply stated in the letter with no other explanation. He is John Anderson Cooper[54] (1824-1900) who married another Pitts daughter, Louisa Jane Pitts (1827-1913).

Next, Aunt Sally mentions Leroy Pitts' family. He is Edwin Leroy Pitts (1818-1882) who married Catherine Harris Boyd (1824-1909), sister of Isaac P. Boyd who married Leroy's sister, Angeline Hitch. Eunice Duvall's family consists of herself, Eunice Elizabeth Pitts (1821-aft 1880), another Pitts daughter, and William L. Duvall (c1821-1856), son of James and Letitia (Hitch) Duvall. At the time of the 1850 census, William and Eunice Duvall and family were living adjacent to the Pitts family in Laurens County. Finally, Young Pitts' family is mentioned, he being Young Joseph Harrington Pitts (1829-1911) who married Martha A. Anderson (1831-1907). All of the Pitts men, and those men who married Pitts daughters, seem to have some record of service in the War except of course, William Duvall who died in 1856.

---

[52] The 1850 Slave Schedule for Laurens County, SC shows Henry Pitts as owning eight slaves, ages 40 down to 10 months comprised of six males and two females.

[53] Diatrephus M. Milam enlisted as a Private in Company A, 9th South Carolina Reserves for 90 days on Nov 17 1862. However, his file states that he was "discharged before reporting". He then enlisted in 1864 with Company D, 4th South Carolina Battalion Reserves and his file states, for Nov/Dec 1864, "Detailed by Advisory Board before reporting".

[54] John Anderson Cooper (1824-1900) enlisted Dec 2 1861 for 12 months as a Private with Company C, 3rd South Carolina (Laurens) Battalion. In a muster roll for Dec 1861, it indicates that he was furloughed on Dec 15 1861 for 30 days due to sickness. In the muster for Dec 1861 to Feb 1862, it indicates that he was discharged from service on Jan 20 1862 at Camp Brooks due to disability. He became a reverend and he and his wife are buried in Union Baptist Church Cemetery, Laurens, SC.

Figure 4 - 1883 section of the Kyzer & Hellams map of Laurens County showing the location of the Hitch and Pitts households. Note that north on this map is at about two o'clock; north is to the right and about 30 degrees toward the top. (Michael G. Hitch collection adapted from an original map by Kyzer and Hellams, 1883, in the Library of Congress, Washington, DC)

The final family introduced in Aunt Sally's letter is Young Hitch's "uncle Louther". This would be Louther Douglas Hitch (1798-1886), Aunt Sally's brother, who married Catherine Lucinda Motes (1801-1857) in about 1818. The rest of Sarah Hitch's letter is devoted to preaching to Young about her opinion that he must turn his sins over to God and proclaim his faith. We will see this to be a common theme in her letters to Young Hitch in the times to come. Near the close of her letter, Sarah states, *"Your aunt Mary says she would be very glad to see you... As your father and her were it seems nearer to each other or felt as being twins than the rest of us, you therefore feel particular near to her"*. This seems to imply that Sarah Hitch was living with the Henry and Mary Pitts family at the time she wrote this letter.

It is interesting that she relates the fact that Young's Aunt Mary (Hitch) Pitts was very close in age to Young's father Joseph N. Hitch. We recall that Joseph died in 1827, not long after Young Hitch's second birthday. We know from bible records that Mary Hitch was born Oct 10 1794 and, we did not know for sure when Joseph Hitch was born until the Mowbray collection revealed the line in his 1806-1814 school book notes, *"Joseph Hitch was born October 10th Anno Domini 1794."* They were indeed twins as Aunt Sally's letter indicates. Since Young really never knew his father because of his early death, Sarah Hitch is relating that Young's Aunt Mary is very much like Young's missing father in both age and temperament and she urges him to see her more often.

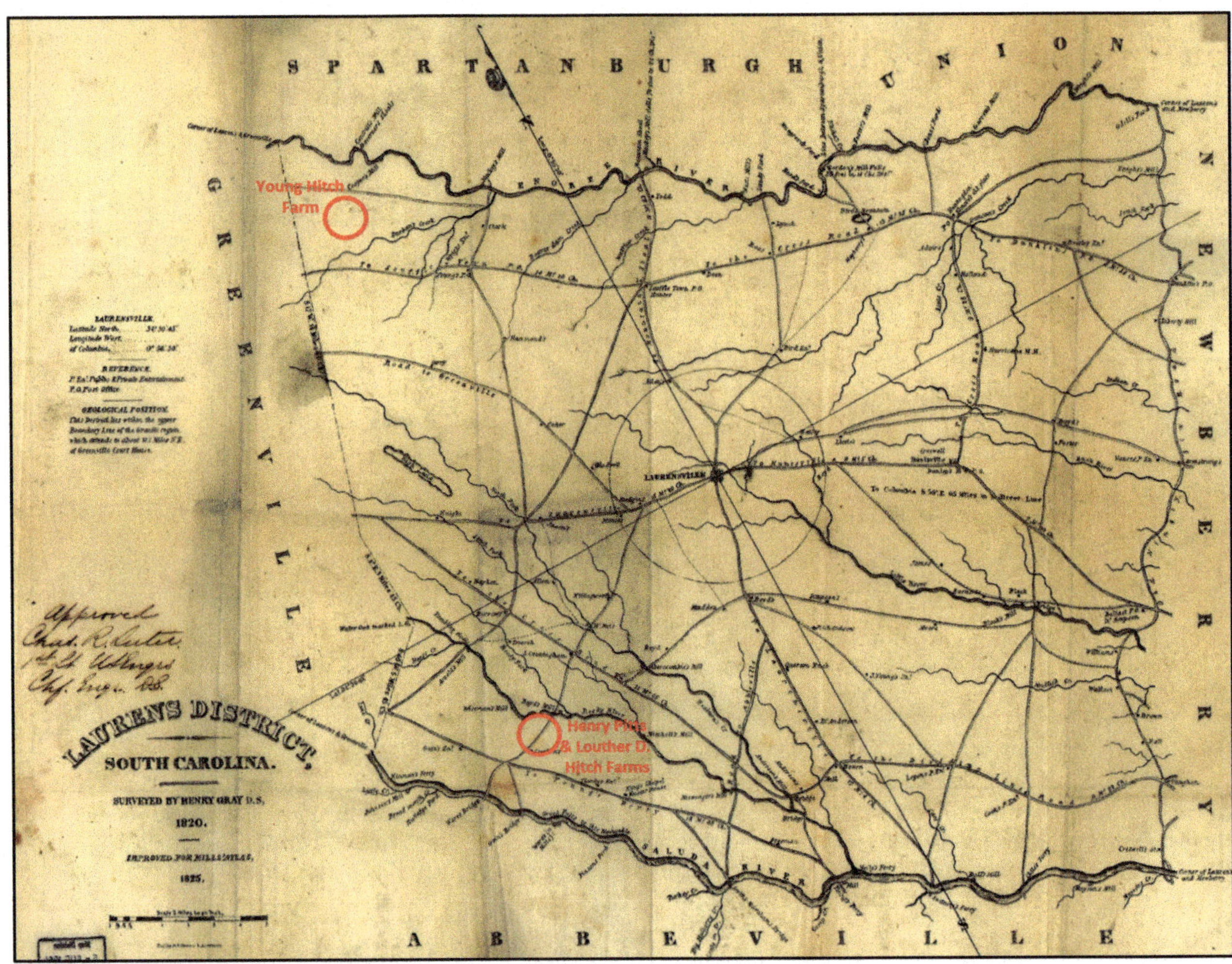

Figure 5 - 1820/25 map of Laurens County with the location of Young Hitch's farm shown in comparison with his uncles Henry Pitts and Louther Douglas Hitch. (Michael G. Hitch map adapted from an original map by Robert Mills, 1820, in the Library of Congress, Washington, DC)

Sarah Hitch writes to Young again on Mar 20 1857 with more news of the family[55]. Eleven months had passed since her previous letter and it seems that most of the family is doing much better health-wise than the year before. Sarah is still living with her sister Mary Pitts' family and tells Young that his Uncle Henry Pitts' family is doing well. However, there is some tragic news that Pinkney Hitch has died in a rather sudden and unexpected way due to a "pimple" on the side of his face that grew larger and worse over a period of five days. It is not known exactly what the "affliction" was but quite possibly a bite of an insect or spider or maybe a bacterial infection. Presley Pinkney Hitch (1831-1856) was only 25 years old at his death on Dec 12 1856, he being Young Hitch's first cousin and son of Louther D. and Catherine Hitch. Pinkney Hitch married Emily Duvall (1833-1913)[56], daughter of James and Letitia (Hitch) Duvall and had two sons, William Leander Hitch (1854-1918) and Luther David Hitch (1856-1940). Both sons were very young when their father died. Sarah Hitch indicates that "*...spent the winter or the most of it with*

[55] Appendix, Item X.

[56] Emily (Duvall) Hitch appears to be the household shown as "Mrs. E. Hitch" in the Scuffletown Township of Laurens County on the 1883 Hellams map of the area, adjacent to the household of "J.W. Duvall."

Pinkneys widow and two little children whose names are William Leander and Luther David, two lovely promising little boys".

Sarah Hitch then implores Young to visit his aunt and Uncle Pitts with his *"little family one time at least."* By this time in early 1857, Young and Mary Hitch had their two sons who were ages 9 and 3 by then. She continues her writing in this regard, *"It might be possible you might not lose anything by it. The old people and myself cannot be here many more days according to the course of nature. Its an old saying. The young may die but the old must die. Your uncle and aunt pitts wishes to see Mary-ann and the children one time as neither of them has ever seen them and in all probability if you do not visit them soon they never will see them. I myself would be so glad to see you all one time here on Reedy River."*

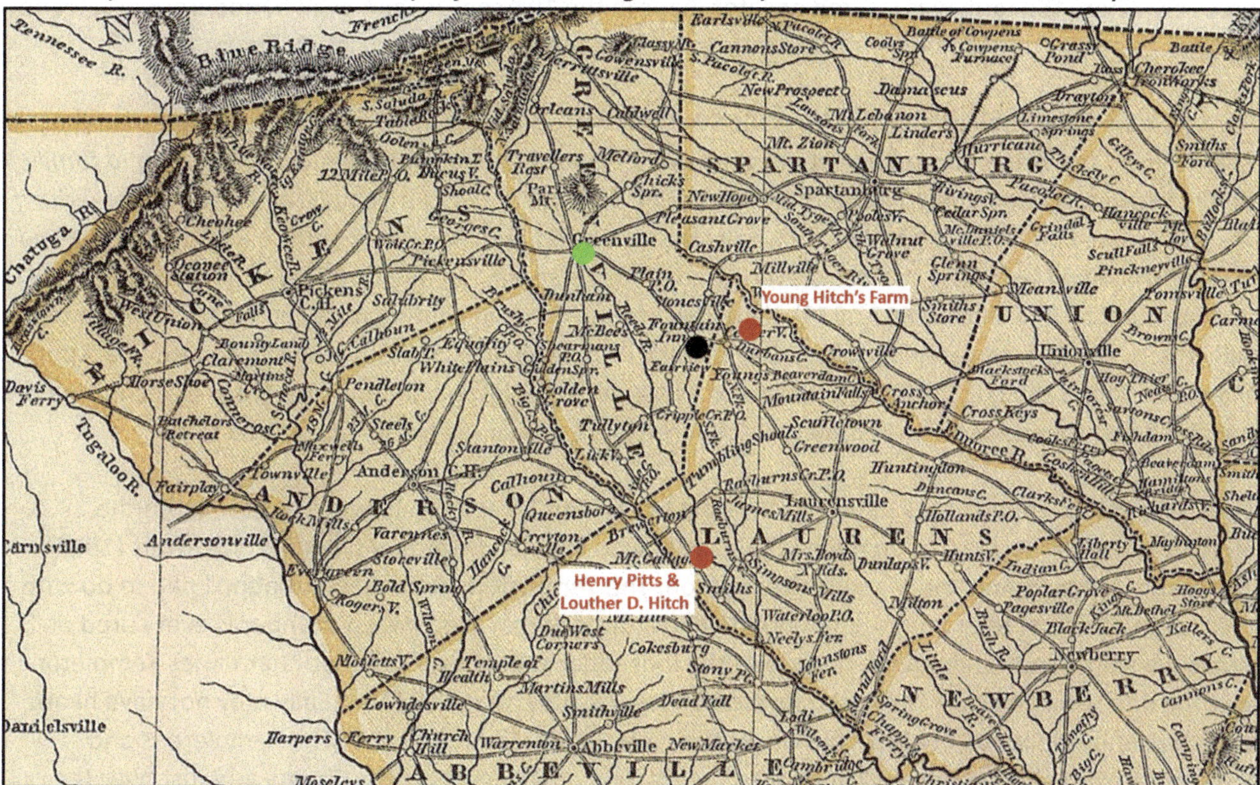

Figure 6 - Portion of an 1843 Map of South Carolina showing the "Upstate" counties. Note the approximate location of Young Hitch's farm in comparison to the Pitts and Louther D. Hitch homesteads. Also marked are Greenville (green) where Young Hitch went to barter goods and Fountain Inn (black) where the Mowbray collection of documents was found. (Michael G. Hitch map adapted from scanned copy of an original full map of South Carolina by Morse and Breese, New York, 1843)

From this passage, we get an idea of where the Pitts family was living, near the Reedy River, and, from the previous letter we know that Louther Douglas Hitch was nearby. To put this in perspective, and to show their relative location when compared to Young Hitch, we can use period maps to estimate their proximity.

Figure 4 is a map from 26 years later than the letter (1883) but it gives us a nice indication of where the Pitts and Hitch families were located that were near where Sally Hitch lived. In the figure, we see they are located near the Reedy River. E. Pitts is Edwin Leroy Pitts and J.Y. Pitts is his son James Young Pitts. We also see illustrated Joseph Allen Hitch and Louther Douglas Hitch's homesteads. Boyd's Mills is circled as two of the Boyd children married Pitts children and this is probably where the Boyd homestead originated. The map is oddly oriented in that north is the right on the image about 30 degrees up (two o'clock as they say in aviation). From the map, we can then take an earlier map of Laurens County and show where Young Hitch lived in comparison to the Pitts and other Hitch families.

Figure 5 is an 1820/25 map of Laurens County and shows the area where Young Hitch's farm was to be located and where the farms of Henry Pitts and Louther D. Hitch were situated. Note, while they are in the same county, the distance between the two is about 20-25 miles by road, almost a full day's journey back in those days. Finally, **Figure 6** provides an illustration of the entire upstate section of northern and western South Carolina in 1845. In it, one can clearly see where Young Hitch was located in comparison to the Pitts household and the towns of Greenville and Fountain Inn, SC. In chapter 7, we will see more precisely where the farm was located on later maps in the 19th century and even a modern-day satellite image.

Back to Aunt Sally Hitch's letter of Mar 20 1857 after she requests that Young Hitch visit them on the Reedy River, she writes some more about the family, *"I want to hear from James Templeton and family. I think I wrote to you one time before to tell Catharine Stewart to tell Ann Templeton I want her to write if she can to me. I have heard of Templetons distresst situation and feel to sympathise with the family and himself knowing the fewest number is ever cured of that disease*." James Clayton Templeton (1791-1857) was husband to Ann Hitch (1807-1879), daughter of John Hitch of Louther, making her a half-niece to Sally Hitch. James Templeton's brother, David Clark Templeton (1805-1880) married Ann Hitch's sister, Margaret Hanna Hitch (1813-1844). David and Margaret Templeton had four sons who served during the war; however, James and Ann Templeton's children were too young for service at that time.

Aunt Sally wants Young to tell Catherine Stewart to tell Ann Templeton to write to her. Catherine Stewart is nee Katherine Carson Hitch (1823-1898) who married Reverend Clark Berry Stewart (1813-1890) and, sister to Ann and Margaret Templeton. The Templeton's "distresst situation" had to do with the health of one of the family members who had a disease that the "fewest number is ever cured of." While we get no indication of the disease or the individual, it might be assumed that James Templeton was the one stricken as we know that he died on Jan 29 1857 at age 62. Aunt Sally may not have heard the news of his death by the time she writes the latter in March of that year. The Templetons and Stewart families all lived in the vicinity of Young Hitch in northwest Laurens County and just over the border into Greenville County.

Sarah Hitch then cordially closes her letter with, *"I shall begin shortly to draw to a close lest I should weary you with my disinteresting letter. I want you to write to me often as you can. I am always glad to see a letter come from you if it was as often as once every month. I want you next time you write send the name of your post office. I may at some time send by mail. So I remain your loving and affectionate aunt untill death. Farewell. S. Hitch to Y.H.E. Hitch."*

The next letter from Aunt Sarah Hitch in the Mowbray collection is dated Jul 25 1860, a little more than three years after the one just covered. It is another long and eloquent composition that is brimming with family information[57]. She informs her "*nephew and niece*" Young and Mary Hitch that their Uncle Henry

---

[57] Appendix, Item XVI.

Pitts and Uncle Louther D. Hitch's families are well with *"not very much sickness at this time in the neighborhood."* Then she talks about the crops in the fields; *"The crops about in this section looks solem. To look at corn fields it looks awfully discouraging. Uncle H's corn in the spring looked beautiful but in consequence of the draught it has dried up and withered so that it looks cribs will almost remain empty. Not only his but I hear it from different parts and places."* There has been a bad drought and the corn crop is failing to the point where she believes the corn cribs will remain nearly empty.

Sally then spends much time on her religion and trying to convince Young to get more serious about his:

> *"But now let us pause and think from whence comes all the blessings that we do or ever have enjoyed it looks like a scourge sent on us as a nation and for what. Not for our righteousness. But for our sins. And now my beloved nepew I want to hear from you very much if you have never yet taken up the Cross and come out on the Lords side. I wanted to have a conversation with you on that subject while I was at you house but I put it of till Sunday when going to church. I thought I would have an opportunity of talking it all over. True it is a cold and lifeless time of religion amongst Christians at this time. but my beloved nephew if God for Christ's sake hath pardoned your sins its your duty to confess him before men. For he hath said in his holy and blessed word. He that is ashamed to confess me before men him will I be ashamed to confess before my Father and his holy Angels. O Young you don't know how it would rejoice my heart to hear that you had found Him of whom moses in the law and the prophets did write Jesus of Nazareth. And had come out from the world and joined Gods Holy army to help to fight against the enemy of Gods people. For he is said in scripture to be going about as a roaring lion seeking whom he may devour. I received a letter a few days since from Katharine Stewart. She said in her letter that your old father in law had become convinced and believed it to be his duty to follow his Savior into the watry grave. O Young when I heard of it I though surely surely if Young had religion that such a sight as that would stir him up to a true sence of his duty. And now my beloved nephew can you say with a clear conscience before your God that you never have at no time felt it your duty to join the Church and be baptized. If you have now I beseech you in the name of my Master to put it not of by saying I am too mean and I am not fit you may say too. I see so many of the professed followers of Christ that act do and say things that I dare not. But my beloved nephew does that make it any less your duty to do what your Savior has commanded you to do. I think not. I have tried in my weak way to pray to my Heavenly Father for you, that he would direct and show you your duty if he never has and grant you grace and strength to perform the same. I want you to remember that the time is short when we shall all have to bid this world adieu prepared or not. So my dear nephew if you think you are not a fit subject for baptism, I pray you be up and a doing. Give not sleep to your eyes nor slumber to your eyelids till you have found Christ presious to your soul. the chiefest amongst ten thousand and altogether lovely."*

She has heard news of the family from Katherine (Hitch) Stewart that Young's old father-in-law, Captain William Brown, has found religion and she wishes Hitch would too. Brown had evidently had an *"affliction experience"* that resulted in him undergoing a *"baptism"* and she wants Mary Hitch to write and tell her of it. This is one of Sally's longest discourses about religion and trying to convince Young to be more serious about it. Sally closes with a request that Young and Mary visit her as, *"Young I do want you and Mary Ann come and see us old people one time."* We will hear more from Aunt Sally Hitch later as she writes to Young Hitch and the family during the trials of the war.

The preceding early letters from the Mowbray collection are presented not to bore the reader herein, but to lay a foundation whereby we see how Young Hitch and his family were living, working and communicating in the decade prior to the Civil War. We will see some of these same players, and some new ones, as we transition into the dawn of the 1860s and the rapidly building political strife of the times that would force the nation into civil war.

CHAPTER 4
1861 to February 1863
War Begins and the Troops are Rallied

An interesting item in the Mowbray Collection is the following receipt[58]:

1861, April 8th	Y.H.E. Hitch	Dr. to D. Boyd	
-	To Dressing & training gun		$1.00
-	To bushing same gun		$0.25
-	To repairing old gun lock		$0.75
-	To pair wipers		$0.25
-	To pair moulds		$0.50
			$2.75
Rec'd payment in full of the above			
By Mr. J.W. Bryant.		Dewitt Boyd	

Why had Young Hitch found it necessary to get his gun "dressed" and repaired and put into shape for some action? Or is this just a random, unimportant old record in a file of papers from an attic somewhere in South Carolina? Some perspective is probably in order. This receipt comes less than three weeks after Young and Mary Hitch get a letter from William P. Edwards on Mar 11 1861 from Lauderdale County, Alabama[59]. Edwards is a brother of Mary Hitch and, in the letter, he covers the usual family pleasantries before penning the following words, *"I want you to rite whither South Carolina has with severed from the union or not and what tha are doing ther. tha have caried thing big hear tho tha are sorter settling down like a warme of bees since Cing li wham has taken his seet. I don't hear mutch noyes nowe all camm as a lamb tha was a grait noyes that he shod not take his seet tho I heard that he had taken hit. Thes big men cood not get thos little men to goe and keep him from his seet."*

By carefully dissecting Mr. Edwards' writing, we see this reference to the time when South Carolina seceded from the Union as a prelude to the Civil War. He was asking for news whether it had happened and seemed to be referencing "Cing li wham" which is probably "Sydenham" Moore, U.S. House of Representatives for the 4th District of Alabama at the time. Moore had been representative for 4 years before withdrawing from his post in January 1861. What Mr. Edwards did not apparently know in March of 1861 when he wrote the letter, was that not only South Carolina had seceded but, by then, Mississippi, Florida, ALABAMA, Louisiana, Georgia and Texas had also passed their own respective resolutions of secession. So, Mr. Sydenham Moore had NOT taken his "seet", rather, he had withdrawn from Congress after his state had seceded on Jan 11 1861. Of course, South Carolina was first to secede based upon the state's resolution of Dec 20 1860 and the rest of the seven listed above followed. After that, they were joined by, respectively, by Virginia, Arkansas, North Carolina, Tennessee, Missouri and Kentucky later in 1861 to complete the formation of the Confederate States of America (CSA).

---

[58] See the back cover for an image of this receipt.

[59] Appendix, Item XVII.

So, it seems that the rather ordinary looking receipt of Young Hitch's gun repair on Apr 8 1861 was not that ordinary at all. In fact, it represents a microcosm of what many other men in the south were doing at the time – preparing for what seemed like the inevitability of war. And though William Edwards states, *"I don't hear mutch noyes nowe all camm as a lamb…"*, the "camm" was simply the CALM before a very BIG STORM to come that would plunge the nation into the struggle of its relatively young life.

William P. Edwards, still in Lauderdale County, Alabama, writes again about six months later on Sep 11 1861 and things with the War have developed considerably[60]. Tensions among the citizens are rising as Edwards describes, *"ther is two parties in this country not so mutch tho as there is in this Lyneing stat of tennisee whitch I am on the line I ben hear of devilment being done rite close by hit tis thought that hit is the younion men that dos hit Throweing down fence and puling up corne and I wod not bee badly so soprized if ther aint a little battle fought here after a while tho the most of the union men says that if tha has to fight tha will fight for the sothern confederate stats…"*. Lauderdale County is in northernmost Alabama and borders Tennessee and Edwards is relating the fact that someone is tearing down fences and destroying the corn crop and most are blaming it on "younion men." But, he then says that most of those Union men in his area say that they will fight for the Confederate States if it came down to a battle.

Next William Edwards talks about his various occupations but is feeling the call of duty[61]. He pens, "…*I have bin tending to a grocery for the last month tho I expect to quit tomorrow and hier to pull fodder and after fodder gathered I don't know what I shall doo. Mr Reynolds sed the other day that he expected he wod want me to help him till this winter and if he dont I expect I shal volunteer to protect our little confederate stats.*" As we see, his loyalty is expressly with the side of the CSA. But, he still wants to see his sister Mary Hitch again as he writes, *"Mary I might drop you a few lines to let you knowe that I hant forgot you yet and I wod bee glad to see you tho I aint able to come to see you and I will ackolege that I hant don as I ought of don or I wood of bin able to of come bee fore nowe tho if this war wod stop(?) I wod make my self able to come and I wod come tho I don't know when I ever will come or whither ever or not tho if life last long enouf I ame to come one more time if I don't goe to the ware and if I doo and live to see hit ended I will come then…"* The War and the uncertainty of its outcome weighed heavily on everyone's minds. William P. Edwards ventured back to South Carolina by 1863 when, in February of that year he enlisted in Company D of the 27th South Carolina Infantry as a Private.

THE SOUTH CAROLINA MILITIA - 1854 to 1862

There is a wrinkled envelope with a scribbled listing of names in the Mowbray collection with the embedded date of Jan 14 1854[62]. The title of the list is, "The List of Beat Camp No. 1, 2nd Battalion 41st Regt. Commanded by John D. Patten, South Carolina By Y.H.E. Hitch." Initially, it was a puzzling list as it

---

60 Appendix, Item XIX.

61 William P. Edwards enlisted as a Private with Company D, 27th South Carolina Infantry in Feb 1863 and he transferred to Company K on Jul 11 1864. Edwards was captured and taken prisoner at Weldon Railroad (VA) on Aug 24 1864 and listed on roll of POWs transferred from Point Lookout, MD to Aikens Landing, VA. One record then states he was exchanged on Sep 18 1864 after transfer to City Point, another record states he died in Sep 1864.

62 Appendix, Item III.

appeared to have nothing to do with the other letters relative to the Civil War in the collection, as the military unit mentioned was not used during that war (and, of course, the date being 1854). This seems to be some sort of militia unit but we were initially unsure. What is this list?

Doing some further research, we connected with one of the 19th century military experts in South Carolina, Rollis Smith, who provided some excellent insight. It "...is a South Carolina Militia roll and...your ancestor took the muster roll...attached. (I) believe that Beat No. 1, 2nd Battalion, 41st Regiment is part of the Second Brigade commanded by General William A. Bull. The 41st was formerly the 7th which was part of the 2nd Brigade. This brigade was composed of militia from the four districts of Edgefield, Abbeville, Pendleton, and Greenville (SC). The 41st Regiment was commanded by Colonel Adair."[63] Mr. Smith also provided a reference for more information, namely, a digest of the Militia System of South Carolina[64].

The reference adds some very interesting details regarding the envelope scribble of Young Hitch. In it, it explains laws and regulations for appointing/electing militia officers, procuring guns and ammunition, artillery items and the basic structure of the various militia organizations. The explanation of a Beat, per Act of South Carolina Dec 19 1833, is included in the following: "There shall be four Beat Companies in each Battalion as nearly equal as may be, and two Battalions in each Regiment, and to each Regiment there may be attached four Light Companies (Volunteers) and one Company of Artillery, and no more. Provided, that not more than two Volunteer Companies of Riflemen or Infantry shall be raised in each Battalion."

Beat Company Number 1, 2nd Battalion, 41st Regiment was active in Laurens County of which Young Hitch was a member as 1st Sergeant. Young writes a list of men in the Company from Jan 1854 as follows[65]:

John D. Patton, Captain	John Grumbler	William M. Patton
W.E. Garrett, 1st Lieutenant	Jeremiah Gilbert	John Edwards
J. Landrum Riddle, 2nd Lieutenant	J.T. Simmons	Jesse Godfrey Sr.
Bird Phillips, 3rd Lieutenant	T.P. Massey	Jesse Godfrey Jr.
Y.H.E. Hitch, 1st Sergeant	William Stephens	Elijah Scruggs
S.F. Riddle, 2nd Sergeant	E.A. Smith	John F. Burdette
S.K. Henry, 3rd Sergeant	U.W. Pain	Thomas Edwards
Tatiller Garrett, 4th Sergeant	James Spele?	Samuel Nelson
Richard Jones, 1st Corporal	Joseph Lang	John Massey
John Jones, 2nd Corporal	Reuben Lang	C.P. Jones
William Massey, 3rd Corporal	Newton J. Lyons	Joseph T. Burdette
Thomas Canady, 4th Corporal	Sterling Smith	Carter Holcombe
T.J. Wallace, Clerk	Stephen Griffith	E.J. Fairbairn
Alfred Sloan	Richard Compton	Ellis Riddle

63 Electronic Mail; E. Mowbray to M. Hitch forwarding correspondence with R. Smith, "List of Militia?" Apr 23 2015 11:38 p.m.

64 The Militia System of South Carolina Being a Digest of the Acts of Congress Concerning the Militia Likewise the Militia Laws of this State, Benjamin Elliott and Martin Strobel, Charleston, Printed by A.E. Miller, 1835.

65 Note that, in this table, spelling of names have been "corrected" from Young's notes in an attempt to match with family and given names known in the area from that time. Please refer to the actual transcription of the muster in Appendix, Item III, for a transcription of Young Hitch's original representation.

K____ Jones	Thomas Parks	Simeon Riddle
A_____ Ewings?	O.P. Jones	William Waddle
A_____ Holcombe	Charlie Sloan	Mansel Garrett
J. _____ Meador	Hosey Holcombe	J.F. Leopard
John Jones	James Holcombe	J.H. Templeton
J.S. Cox	B.W. Holcombe	J.F. Stewart
Dr. Lucas	Darius Garrett	

Figure 7 - Listing of Beat Company No. 1, 2nd Battalion, 41st Regiment of South Carolina Militia delineated by Y.H.E. Hitch in 1854. (Mowbray Collection)

Young's notes offer a rare opportunity to see exactly who participated in these militia units from the local vicinity as no other known musters exist from the time until about 1862 when the Civil War was commencing.

Many of the men in these militia groups eventually became the men who served in the various battle units in the Civil War. The Beat Companies were active from the time of the act in late 1833 up until the time leading into the war itself. In fact, we find a note in the Mowbray Collection to Y.H.E. Hitch from Captain S.D. Thackston as follows:

July 12. 1862.
Received of Y. H. E. Hitch
Five Dollars and 25
cents, for War Tax of the Confederate States,
under Act of Assembly of S. C., passed Dec., 1861.
War Tax,............$ 5.25
Less 5 per cent on .26
Amt. paid before 31st July, 1862, $4.99
E. Watson T.C.

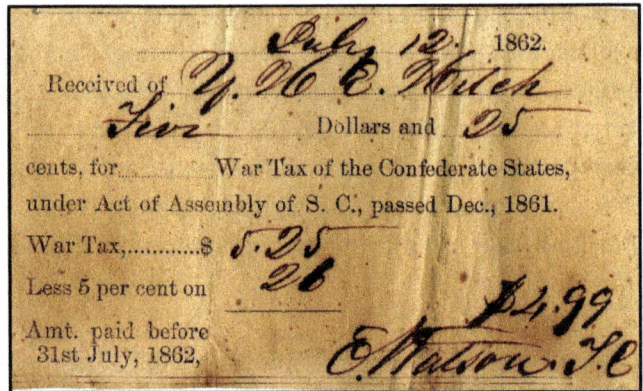

Figure 8 - Receipt for CSA War Tax paid by Y.H.E. Hitch, Jul 12 1862. (Mowbray Collection, Edward H. Nabb Center, Salisbury University)

"Mr. Y.H.E. Hitch

You are hereby appointed Capt of the patrol in beat company No. 1 with the men whose names are hereunto anexed. You will ride at least once a fortnight and make return on oath the 2 Saturday in Oct. next.

This August 16, 1862
S.D. Thackston, Capt

L.B. Edwards
J.J. Brown
Goodin Parsons
(S.D.?) Thackston

(The following is written on the back of the order)

Times we rode patrol
Monday, Sept 8
Sunday Sept 14
Thursday, Sept 25
Sunday Sept 28

Wednesday, Oct 8
Camp near Charleston S.C."

This "patrol" covered the time from Aug to Oct 1862. By the time Nov 1862 rolled around, the state government of South Carolina called into service a Corps of Reserves in which many of these men were to transition. We also see that the new Confederate government had begun to collect taxes to fund the war effort. **Figure 8** is a receipt from the collection that shows Young Hitch had paid his taxes of $4.99 on Jul 12 1862.

9th SOUTH CAROLINA RESERVES – NOV 1862 to FEB 1863

A South Carolina governmental act of Jan 1 1861 authorized the governor to receive volunteer companies for enlistments of six months. The governor could organize any companies received into battalions, regiments, brigades, and divisions. The field officers for these formations were to be appointed with the advice and consent of the Senate. This was followed by the Militia Act of Dec 7 1861 and then an Order issued by the Adjutant and Inspector General on Nov 4 1862, in response to a request from the Confederate States of America Secretary of War, G.W. Randolph, to send four regiments of militia into CSA service to reinforce General P.G.T. Beauregard for 90 days. The regiments ordered to report were the 2nd, 3rd, 8th, and 11th regiments of the South Carolina Reserves. An additional four (4) regiments; the 5th, 6th, 7th and 9th Reserves, were ordered into service on Nov 7 1862, for a total of eight (8) reserve regiments in what was called the 1st Corps of Reserves. The 4th and 10th Reserves were disbanded at that time.

The 9th South Carolina Reserves consisted of ten (10) Companies, A through K (no "J" as that designation was generally not used because of the potential confusion with the letter "I") and consisted of men from the 'upcountry'; Laurens District, the 45th regiment of the South Carolina militia (from Union and Spartanburg Districts) and the 38th regiment militia (from Newberry District)[66]. It was in service from Nov 5 1862 to Feb 17 1863. Young Hitch, with many of his local friends and family, joined on Nov 17 1862 "for 90 days". The first four (4) Companies (A through D) were mustered from Laurens County (Hitch was a part of Company C) with the following individuals[67]:

9th SOUTH CAROLINA RESERVES, COMPANY A

Officers
Hudgens, James, Captain
Glen, S.D., 1st Lieutenant
Simmons, J.A., 2nd Lieutenant
Dorroh, William M, 3rd Lieutenant

Non-Commissioned Officers
Wood, T.R.L., 1st Sergeant
Bolt, Wiley, Sergeant
Chappell, W.T., Sergeant
Garey, J.D., Sergeant
Shockley, J.M., Sergeant
Blakeley, J.K., Corporal
Bolt, Andrew, Corporal
Coleman, John, Corporal
Hudgens, J.B., Corporal

Privates

[66] South Carolina's Military Organizations During the War Between the States; Volume IV, Statewide Units, Militia and Reserves, Robert S. Seigler, The History Press, Charleston, SC, 2008; pages 175, 176.
[67] These lists come from 9th Regiment, South Carolina Reserves, *www.familysearch.org*.

Allison, L.N.
Allison, R.W.
Anderson, James
Anderson, John
Arnold, J.W.
Babb, Melmoth
Babb, Tandy
Bailey, Elijah
Bailey, W.W.
Baldwin, Vincent
Biter, James
Bolt, James
Bolt, Samuel
Boyd, Bradford
Boyd, David
Boyd, John H.
Coley, A.J.
Culbertson, Andrew
Culbertson, J.M.
Culbertson, S.B.
Davis, J.L.
Dial, Albert
Elledge, James
Fenley, Harrison
Gilkerson, J.L.
Glen, D.A.
Hammond, John
Henderson, S.E.
Henderson, W.B.
Hipps, Joseph
Holdin, Solomon
Kernels, Joel
Knight, B.H.
Knight, Dires
Lindley, James
Lindley, John
Lindley, John T.
Lyons, George
McMinch, Samuel
Meares, Eric B.
Medlock, Anderson
Medlock, J.T.
Milam, D.M.
Mitchell, William
Moloy, W.P.
Puckett, W.A.
Robison, John
Shumate, H.S.
Simmons, J.B.
South, D.L.
Sullivan, J.H.
Taylor, Berryman
Tumlin, William
Vaughn, Joel
Vaughn, Norman
Wadkins, H.H.
Wasson, J.A.
Whitlock, J.L.
Winslow, G.G.
Woods, Hugh
Woods, Kellet

9th SOUTH CAROLINA RESERVES, COMPANY B

Officers

Jones, W.J.M., Captain
Davenport, L.P., 1st Lieutenant
Becks, William, 2nd Lieutenant
Martin, Lewis, 3rd Lieutenant

Non-Commissioned Officers

Scott, William, 1st Sergeant
Henry, D.L., Sergeant
Henry, H., Sergeant
Martin, L.S., Sergeant
Smith, W.T., Sergeant
Brown, G.M., Corporal
Clardy, Reuben, Corporal
Madden, Z.L., Corporal
Martin, L.D., Corporal

Privates

Anderson, A.T.
Anderson, D.W.
Anderson, Larkin
Anderson, W.J.
Arnold, J.W.F.
Arnold, M.Y.
Beeks, Daniel
Boland, H.F.
Brownlee, J.J.
Burton, Hiram
Burton, T.T.
Burton, Thomas
Cardy, J.M.
Cook, J.C.
Cooper, Y.J.
Culbertson, R.S
Davenport, J.C.
Davis, William
Elmore, L.D.
Elmore, Matison
Finly, James
Finly, W.T.
Fowler, J.F.
Golding, J.R.
Graves, W.W.
Griffin, Newton
Griffin, Reuben
Hardy, Wiley
Hellams, J.H.
Henderson, J.F.
Hill, W.C.
Hitch, J.A.
Holcomb, J.G.
Joel, George
Joel, John
Knight, S.V.
Landress, S.S.
Madden, J.A.
Madden, Moses
Martin, James
Mates, Allen
McDaniel, Joel
McGee, L.H.
McPherson, J.M.
Milam, William
Monday, Alex
Moore, W.B.
Murff, J.M.
Nelson, David
Nelson, Josiah
Norman, John
Owens, B.L.
Owens, M.J.
Pitts, J.Y.
Redden, H.R.
Redden, Henry
Richardson, W.A.
Robertson, George
Robertson, Pierson
South, J.B.
Spoon, J.H.
Sykes, Charles
Tinsly, C.D.
Tinsly, W.T.
Ware, W.A.J.
Weathers, James
Wells, Clement
Whitly, William

Fuller, Henry
Moore, G.A.

9th SOUTH CAROLINA RESERVES, COMPANY C

Officers

Stewart, William, Captain
Johnson, H.P., 1st Lieutenant
Atwood, Melmoth, 2nd Lieutenant
Thompson, Ellis, 3rd Lieutenant

Non-Commissioned Officers

Fairbairn, Noah, 1st Sergeant
Garrett, M.R., Sergeant
Hughes, W.H., Sergeant
Prior, Joseph, Sergeant
Taylor, James, Sergeant
Cheek, Austin, Corporal
Garrett, John, Corporal
Owings, William, Corporal
Rodgers, W.A., Corporal

Privates

Abercrombie, J.H.
Adams, J.O.
Anderson, Thomas
Armstrong, William H.
Babb, John
Boll, John
Boll, Young
Bromblet, Lewis
Burditt, John
Burton, J.A.
Coker, O.H.P.
Curry, Ivory
Cury, Reason
Dial, Newton
Edwards, John
Edwards, Jonas
Farrow, L.M.
Farrow, R.M.
Garrett, A.Y.
Garrett, B.F.
Garrett, E.B.
Garrett, Pottilla
Garrett, W.E.
Garrett, Z.C.
Godfrey, Jesse
Gradan, John
Grumbles, Henry
Hand, W.W.
Hellams, William
Henderson, Richard
Henderson, Thomas
Hitch, Y.H.E.
Holcomb, Elisha
Holcomb, James
Kellett, C.M.
Kellett, Y.T.
Knight, B.W.
Knight, D.T.
Knight, Franklin
Leak, George W.
Leak, William C.
Loring, Daniel
Martin, H.H.
Newman, B.J.
Putnam, J.P.
Putnam, John
Putnam, T.R.
Riddle, Newton
Robertson Sr., Lewis
Robertson Jr., Lewis
Rodgers, L.P.
Shell, J.H.
Shockley, J.W.
Smith, Clark
Switzer, J.R.
Thomason, J.W.
Waldrop, Anderson
Wofford, R.M.

9th SOUTH CAROLINA RESERVES, COMPANY D

Officers

Jones, B.S., Captain
Wright, James M., 1st Lieutenant
Copeland, L.W., 2nd Lieutenant
Newman, T.D., 3rd Lieutenant

Non-Commissioned Officers

Sloan, W.W., 1st Sergeant
Abrams, John, Sergeant
Neal, S.H., Sergeant
Templeton, B.C., Sergeant
Winebrenner, S., Sergeant
Cunningham, John, Corporal
Farrow, W.H., Corporal
Gillam, B.B., Corporal
Taylor, A.S., Corporal

Privates

Ainsley, D.L.
Aleywine, W.H.
Barksdale, A.S.
Barksdale, S.E.
Barksdale, W.W.
Beasley, A.C.
Benjamin, J.D.
Benjamin, M.
Benjamin, S.
Duncan, R.H.
Duvall, L.J.
Fant, O.H.P.
Ferguson, E.T.
Gosset, W.A.
Hendrix, A.
Hewett, Landon
Hews, J.
Hollinsworth, W.
Neighbors, J.H.
Neighbors, N.
Newman, J.C.C.
Odle, John
Palmer, R.
Rose, W.A.
Rowland, J.J.
Simmons, N.D.
Simpson, D.D.

Butler, A.J.
Butler, M.R.
Coleman, Robert
Compton, D.T.
Copeland, G.P.
Cunningham, S.D.
Davis, John
Davis, S.T.
Day, J.G.
Deen, J.A.
Duckett, J.O.
Duncan, J.T.
Hurston, F.M.
Hurston, T.B.
Hutchinson, G.W.
Hutchinson, R.P.
Leak, J.B.
Leak, Josiah
Lyles, R.P.
Lyng, A.
McMakin, W.G.
Meadows, J.A.
Neal, D.L.
Neighbors, J.
Stewart, W.C.
Templeton, J.T.
Templeton, S.
Templeton, W.C.
Todd, N.C.
Waldrop, B.W.
Wardell, J.B.
Watson, Joseph
Workman, J.C.
Workman, W.P.

There were many connections among these men to Young Hitch. From Company A, we see Diatrephus M. Milam, who married Young Hitch's cousin Sarah Ann Pitts. From Company B, Young's half-brother, George M. Brown was a Corporal and there are also cousins Privates Joseph A. Hitch and Young J.H. Pitts. In Company C, where Young Hitch had enlisted was Sergeant Miles R. Garrett, Hitch's very good friend and future father-in-law to Hitch's son, Joseph. It also includes John B. and Jonas M. Edwards, Hitch's brothers-in-law and, his good friend Archibald Y. Garrett. Company D included Hitch's cousin Lewis J. Duvall. These are just a few of the connections we can observe when, in reality, everyone in each of these units probably knew very well most of the others therein as all were close neighbors, family and friends. They were all from the close-knit community of Laurens County and, in many instances, had either blood relations or married family relations.

The primary role of the 9th South Carolina Reserves was serving on picket duty and drilling in anticipation of a Federal invasion of Charleston. In the Mowbray collection, there are twenty letters from the time when the 9th Reserves were in service from November 1862 to February 1863. The first is dated Dec 8 1862 from Young Hitch to his wife Mary and comes four months after the patrol letter discussed previously[68]. It is probable that Young Hitch was at home tending to his farm from just after the time of the patrol in August to October 1862 to the time he was mustered into the 9th Reserves on Nov 17 1862. Hitch knew intimately of the risks of going to war and wrote and registered his will on Nov 21 1862 in Laurens County.

In the letter of December 8, Hitch indicates that he arrived in Charleston on December 6 at 3:00 pm having traveled the most part of two full days from Laurens County, stopping in Columbia along the way. He picked up his goods that day and a box he had sent to the depot the next morning and then proceeded to the camp near Charleston where he took the chill off of a cold December day by warming himself by the fires. Then he and "A.Y." (Private Archibald Young Garrett) crawled into a tent with W.H. Hughes[69] and J.M. Edwards (Sergeant William H. Hughes and Private Jonas M. Edwards[70], Jonas is Mary

[68] Appendix, Item XXII.
[69] Sergeant William Henry Hughes (1819-1897) was the son of Moses and Anna B. (Collins) Hughes of Laurens County, SC. He enlisted as Sergeant in Company C, 9th South Carolina Reserves on Nov 17 1862 for 90 days. He married Maryanna Jones Howard who was sister to Private Presley Edward Augustus Howard and 3LT John Manning Howard who would serve with Young Hitch later, for Company I, 16th South Carolina Volunteer Infantry.
[70] Jonas Meador Edwards had first enlisted in Dec 1861 at Adams Run, SC for one year as a Private with Company E, Holcombe Legion, South Carolina. After his year is up, he then enlists as a Private with Company C, 9th South Carolina Reserves from Nov 1862 to Feb 1863 and served there with his brother John B. Edwards and brother-in-law, Young Hitch.

Hitch's brother) and settled in for a good, warm night's sleep on December 6th with his Company C compatriots.

The next day, Company C captain, William Stewart, took Young and other new arrivals to see the breastworks being set up to defend the city of Charleston. They then got back in camp in time to see "Uncle Tol" Robertson preach. Toliver Robertson (1800-1878) was a wealthy landowner, slaveholder[71] and Baptist minister born in Laurens County[72]. He enlisted as a Private with Company E of the 9th Reserves for the 90 day period from November 1862 to February 1863 and would later enlist with Company E, 6th South Carolina Cavalry on Aug 18 1863.

Other than some singing of some hymns provided by Robertson and maintaining the camp, there was not much else going on in camp at the time. Young Hitch indicates, *"I haven't any news to write. I think they are looking for the Legislator to do some thing before there is any alteration made in this Regiment."* The men were "waiting on the Legislature" to see what will happen to the 9th Reserves. He gets in one little note for sons J.J. and A.L. Hitch saying he has "seen a great deal" but had no time to say any more about it at the time

Two days later, on December 10, Young writes another letter to Mary from near Charleston[73]. He writes that he could not drill that morning with the rest of the Company since he was feeling ill but felt better by evening. He states that "J.M." (Jonas Edwards) left Charleston the night before and Young sent word with him for Mary to get him a "bed tick & knapsack & haversack" and send it via John Garrett or someone else. He does tell her that he can do without them as long as his Company stays in Charleston but, he would need them if they go on the move. He also hopes Mary can send him some "butter and onions" because he had not *"tasted my butter yet (and) I have 25 or 26 cakes..."* Finally, Young relates some information about the guns in Charleston to his sons when he pens, *"Joseph and Lucian two large guns was drawn up here today eight horses each large enough for a man to put his head in the mussel."*

The next letter is a scarce surviving example from Mary Hitch to Young that is undated but probably from mid-December 1862[74] as she states, *"I want you to rite to me wether you got your bed tick and knapsack."* These were the very things Young had asked for in his letter of December 10. She then goes on to say that she will send him whatever he needs when A.Y. Garrett returns to the unit and that she needs to send *"that 20 dollars bill"* to him. Finally, some last words that show how much she misses her husband and wishes he could get some time off and come see her, *"Git off if you can do so how happy I wood be I hant ben to preaching since you left me."*

Young writes a brief letter back to her, undated, but probably mid-December 1862[75], responding to her request to come see her, *"Mary I have not tried to get off yet perhaps I will soon. I may be mistaken but I*

---

[71] The 1860 United States census indicates Toliver Robertson as a wealthy farmer owning 15 slaves. (1860 Slave Schedules, Laurens County, SC, page 90)

[72] His gravestone indicates he was a Baptist minister for 49 years and baptized over 2000 people and married over 1000.

[73] Appendix, Item XXIV.

[74] Appendix, Item XXV.

[75] Appendix, Item XXVI.

think my chance is better than it has been but if I do get off it may be after Christmas before I can leave camp. You may think that I could come as well as A.Y. Garrett but Mary, I could not of got through with that barrel of salt." He then implies that some men in the regiment get to do things through trickery ("quirking") when he pens, "*And in the next place I am not lucky as some & to act as some do I wont. I am above quirking like some. W.H. Hughes for one a good Baptist.*" However, Hitch indicates that he and William Hughes do not resort to such questionable tactics.

Young writes his next letter to Mary Hitch on Dec 20 1862 from Camp Means, near Charleston[76]. He had met that day with John B. Edwards[77], Mary's brother, and received all the news from home and mentioned that he traveled with him part of the way home. John "*insisted*" that he go home with him but he "*did not go*" promising "*to go the first opportunity.*" He is eagerly awaiting John Garrett to return from Laurens to glean some more news from the home front.

Young then offers some interesting discourse about the food available to the soldiers, "*Mary if you wish to know our fare I can give it. We get corn meal & beef a plenty. Then we get potatoes, rice and sugar vinnegar soap and candles. Our allowance of salt is rather small. We our mess had to by a quart the other day. Mary so long as we get as mutch as we have been getting we will not perish. I can boil beef & bake bread pretty well.*" It appears that the fare in the camp near Charleston was not terribly bad indeed.

Hitch then tells of regular "cold & coughs" among the soldiers but, more importantly, there is an outbreak of the measles that has hit the camp, "*We also have some measles in camp. Yesterday or the day before their was a man taken from camp to the hospital said to be a case of the measles. This morning their was another taken of one that was sitting by our fire yesterday a few moments. So if I do not get them it will be Providence providing better for me. I dread them & worst of all there is several others with myself to have them.*" Young is hoping to avoid getting sick with the measles but feels that he is probably not going to be able to escape the disease and, he is right to fear it.

Measles killed about 11,000 soldiers during the Civil War, not as many as other diseases did but, it had its fair share. With so many people gathered in such small areas this disease was able to spread rapidly and about 1 in 20 people who got it died as a result. Deaths were primarily from respiratory and cerebral (brain) involvement. The Civil War was the last large-scale military conflict fought before the germ theory of disease was developed and 2/3rds of soldiers who died in the war, 660,000 in all, were killed by uncontrolled infectious diseases. No wonder that most soldiers' letters, including Young Hitch's, are quick to include an assessment of his personal health and that of his unit.

Hitch then offers a fatherly life lesson to his sons Joseph and Lucian Hitch from afar when he writes:

> *"Dear sons myself & Capt Stewart last night went down to the Depot to see if any of our folks had come down. And while standing looking on at the passengers get aboard the Augusta train I saw an old man come along with several bundles to put them on board the car & as he was*

---

[76] Appendix, Item XXVII.

[77] John Bradley Edwards enlisted as a Private with Company C, 9th South Carolina Reserves on Nov 17 1862 to Feb 14 1863 and served with his brother Jonas M. Edwards and brother-in-law Young Hitch there.

handing them in he dropt one bundle on the ground near a young man that was sitting close by. Boys what do you think this youth did why sirs instead of his pict it up & giving it to the old man as an honest yout should he slipt it up to his feet the old man got a board the car & the youth put the bundle in his own knapsack. Dear sons you cant guess what I then thought of my thoughts was these. Is it possible that Each Either of my sons whoo I have tried to teach better should be guilty of sutch a crime. But I sincerely hope better of them. O that they may be better boys."

This passage is a nice example of the virtuous nature of Young Hitch that we see throughout most of his writings. As a father, he is trying to pass that sense of virtue on to his young sons who were ages 15 and 9 at the time. We will continue to see Young Hitch do his best at fathering his boys throughout the war, over many distant miles, through his letters.

The rest of the letter is composed of just some odds and ends of small talk between Young and his wife. He expects A.Y. Garrett to be able to bring things from home for him that he might need. He also tells Mary that he really does not need the money she offered to send in her previous letter ($20) as, he knows that the distribution of Company payroll is imminent so he expects to get paid *"in a few days or several."* Finally, he wants her to find an old knife and a fork to send him, even if the fork only has one good prong as it probably would get lost or stolen in camp anyway.

The next letter is dated three days before Christmas, Dec 22 1862[78]. Most of this letter is devoted to chatter from a father to his wife and sons. Mary had sent some items to Young via John Garrett which he was happy to receive. Then Young placates son A.L. Hitch when the nine year old wishes him to *"come & eat squirrels"* with him saying, *"...I would gladly come & dine with you if it was so that I could But as I cant come to help you you must eat my part & yours both."* He addresses his oldest son, Joseph, who has been tasked with being the man of the household while he is away and, to keep the Hitch farm up and running. Young congratulates him on his success to date, *"Joseph glad to hear that you have your grain all sowed and that your taters is sound."* He then instructs him to eat all of the potatoes he can that were harvested that year as they would be quickly going rotten.

We then see, in the letter, that Mary is hopeful for Young to come home for Christmas. However, Young replies that this is not possible, *"Mary you wish me to come home Christmas. Willingly would I comply with your request. But mary those whoo come here first all want furloughs & it would cost me at least ten dollars to visit home."* Since Young Hitch has been with his unit a shorter time than many of the others, the soldiers who had been there longer would get first dibs at furloughs. But, it seems that there are some of these soldiers that would be willing to sell their allotted furloughs for a fee as Young notes in his letter that, it would cost him at least $10 to visit home for ten days – a handsome sum in 1862. So, he resigns himself to the thought, *"Ten days & cost ten dollars is pretty tough."* He does leave Mary with some hope when he states, *"But I think if I live I will come before the time is out to see you."* His "time is out" in the middle of February 1863 when his 90-day hitch with the 9th Reserves is over. The letter was delivered to Mary Hitch by their friend Archibald Y. Garrett.

---

[78] Appendix, Item XXVIII.

Mary Hitch and Joseph write to Young next on Christmas Day, 1862[79]. Mary is very melancholy that Young is away from home and she holds nothing back from her description of the way she feels, "*Dear Young I seat mi self to drop you a few lines to let you know I am gitting along not so well. I just con eat a nuff to keap onn foot When I set down I think of Young fair I am full I go all day & don't eat as much as I aught to eat at one meal I hope the time will soon cum that mi Joy will be as grate as mi Sorrows is Now.*" She hopes that the time will soon come that her joy will be as great as her sorrows. To read these words, one can practically feel the heartbreak they describe and the loneliness that many families must have been feeling with their men away in the service.

She then relates that her father (John Edwards) has been very kind by keeping her stocked with wood to burn and will replenish the stock when it runs out. She also says that her father is eager to hear the news from the camp and asks Mary to read him Young's letters whenever he writes. She wants Young to take note of this and remember to thank his father-in-law in his next letter for the kindness he has offered to the family. Son Joseph sends a few words about the farm and expresses his sorrow that his father is away for Christmas, "*I want to knoo this is a dull Christmass with us*." Little did families know at the time but, there would be two more Christmases where the soldiers would also be away.

The next letter in the collection, the first from 1863, is dated January 5 to Young Hitch from his father-in-law and stepmother-in-law, John and Rebekah Edwards[80]. The content of the letter is rather unremarkable with the exception of the sending address where John Edwards uses, "Confederate States of America," showing the commitment and sentiment of the local population for wanting to establish southern independence. He also mentions Young's friend and brother-in-law, William Scruggs, who married Mary Hitch's sister, Caroline Edwards. William will end up joining Young Hitch as part of the 16th South Carolina Volunteers in just a few short weeks.

The next two letters are undated but most likely come from the early-to-mid January 1863 timeframe given their contents and, may have originally been sent at the same time[81]. In the first, Young tells his boys that they have drawn their guns, the Enfield rifle-musket. Young is excited and feels "*just like I could take a few pops at a Yankey with my gun. It is not near so heavy as I supposed it would be.*" This is the gun Young Hitch is holding in the photograph shown in **Figure 2** back in Chapter 3. A line from this letter, "*Write soon & let me know if you got the salt & my likeness,*" helps to date that photograph (his likeness) to the time between when Young receives his gun while in the 9th Reserves and the time he writes this letter – probably January 1863 and very probably within a few days of when he received the Enfield rifle.

The Enfield Pattern 1853 (P53) rifle-musket was a British-manufactured weapon used by both the North and the South in the Civil War, and was the second most widely used infantry weapon (only the Springfield Model 1861 Rifled Musket was used more) and, the most widely used in the South. The CSA imported more Enfields during the course of the war than any other small arm, buying from private contractors and gun runners. It has been estimated that over 900,000 P53 Enfields were imported to

---

[79] Appendix, Item XXIX.
[80] Appendix, Item XXX.
[81] Appendix, Item XXXI and XXXII.

America and saw service in every major engagement during the war. The gun was highly sought after in the Confederate ranks[82]. (See **Figure 24** in Chapter 6 for an illustration of the Enfield)

The rest of the letter is Young discoursing with his sons about things around the farm and sights he has seen while at camp, *"I have seen the largest river that I ever saw. Joseph, I visited the slaughter house Sunday evening. Saw them butcher eleven beeves in a few minutes. You see I wanted to see what sort of beef I have to eat."* Then, Young writes directly to Mary and consoles her not to believe everything she hears from the camps, especially about the food Young gets to eat (his "fare"), *"Mary if you could be here & here the lies that is told it would make you shudder just to think what tales men tell."*

Hitch then readdresses the subject of the measles cases that have gone through his camp that he discussed in a previous letter of December 20; *"Probably you think this reg is all down with the measles. To the best of my knowledge there has been three cases of the measles only & they have been taken to the hospital. I have not had them yet. I take good care of myself for fear that I may take them. Capt Stewart, Hand E. Holcombe & two or three others in this camp has never had them."* We see that he notes of only three cases of the disease thus far in his regiment and some of the people there who have never had them. And then, Hitch addresses the on-going theme of his family desiring him to join the church, though, in this letter it is indirect, *"Mary sorry to hear that you have not heard any preaching since I left you. I have been at church ever Sunday since I left home. I dont know when the opportunity may cease. I prefer going to church to sitting in camp. Mary I hope my prospects for eternity is brightening. I have nothing mutch to tell but little as it is I prize it verry high. I hope to see home once more then we can talk"*.

Young Hitch then fulfills Mary's wishes for him to thank her father for being so kind to the family so that, when she reads Young's letters to her father, he will see the praise. Young does this very directly when he pens, *"Mary you stated that your father has been verry kind to you. I am verry glad to hear & to think that someone is kind enough to assist you in my absence. I have tried to ask help for you as well as for myself. Tell Mr. Edwards I thank him kindly for his kindness to you. Allso tell him to please excuse me for not writeing to him for I have not wrote to no one but my own folks yet but I knew that he would hear from them."*

Before closing, Young asks for a few things for Mary to do for him:

> *"First to pay A.Y. Garrett for the salt he takes you & the freight on it. 2nd you may bake me some corn dodgers in the oven or a light pone of either corn or wheat. If you have any hog head and feet soused send some of it. Coffee, send me a little bunch more & one of them old knives and forks. Instead of Twenty dollars send me Ten. I hope I will not need that mutch. I have spent $7.12 cts since I left home."*

He wants her to pay Archibald Garrett for taking the salt he got for Mary (and the shipping costs). Then he asks for her to make him corn dodgers or light corn/wheat pone and, also to send some pickled hogs head and pig's feet. He rounds off his request for her to send a "little bunch" of coffee and a set of old

---

[82] Wikipedia.

knives and forks. He finally asks her to send him $10 instead of the twenty he had previously requested and, lets her know he has only spent $7.12 since he left home, over six weeks earlier.

One final word of note that explains the state of his regiment, "*We are not equipt yet & until we are we will remain here.*" So the regiment will remain in Charleston and not move until they are fully equipped with the necessary gear.

Jan 10 1863 is Young Hitch's next letter to his wife, again from Camp Means, near Charleston[83]. He states to her that on Thursday, January 7, they had some "neighbors come in," they being three (3) regiments of Georgia infantry but, there were just passing through and left for North Carolina very early on the 8th. Then, more talk of the measles and how many in the 9th Reserves were vaccinated including himself when he received the shot on January 9.

Young then turns to the prospect of going home to visit the family when he writes, "*Mary I have been thinking about coming home & I hardly know what to do. If I can't get off next week the time will be so short that I hate to be at the expense & run the risk on the road home the old cars run of so often. I would like verry mutch to see home again & hope that I may some of these days.*" We see he wants to get home but is in a quandary since his time is so short and he is afraid that the railroad cars being so "old" will be unreliable to get him home and back to camp in time.

Then we see some speculation about when his 90-day term with the 9th Reserves will end, "*Some say our time will be out the 5th of Feb. & some say the 17th of Feb. but I don't know when the time will be out. But let it be long or short, I am in for the war. Those over 40 may be out when the 90 days are out. But if I should not get to come home before the 90 days is out, I hope then I can come and stay awhile with you.*" The speculation is that they will be done their tour with the 9th Reserves by either February 5 or 17, and Young is thinking that the soldiers over 40 years of age may be out for good (Young Hitch was age 37 at the time) but he asserts, "I am in for the war." He is definitely resigned to his cause and his commitment to his country and plans to do whatever it takes to support the war effort with his presence.

One last item Young covers is this correspondence is to ask Mary to tell her father, "*that I am stationed at Camp Means one mile from Charleston...*" Various sources state that Camp Means was located on the location of the modern-day golf course of Charleston Country Club on James Island. This is where his Company of the 9th South Carolina Reserves spent the majority of their 90-day enlistment. Hitch then closes with the fact that he is "*able to eat cornbread & beef & it seems to agree with*" him to the extent that he now weighs 154 pounds!

In his next letter, dated Jan 13 and continued Jan 15 1863, Young gets right into some of his duties when he relates to her the words[84]:

> "*I am tolerable well at this time, a little sore from guard duty. Myself and eleven others were detailed Sunday to guard the Charleston jail. We went on guard half after one oclock & remained on guard until one a Monday. I stood ten hours out of 24. but the night was pleasant & I stood it*

[83] Appendix, Item XXXIII.
[84] Appendix, Item XXXIV.

> *pretty well. There is several points to be guarded. The regiment that have been guarding those points have left for north carolina. And we have to take there place. We are yet campt at the same place. The jail is about three miles from our camp. We have no drilling all guard duty now. Our regiment is small so it takes us all or near it to guard this town. Boys I spent last Sunday Evening in & around jail, locked up at that. We lay in the jailors office by a stove of fire & slept a little. Oh boys the stinkingest place you every saw, a perfect shit hole, 130 white and 40 black prisoners all our own men, no Yankees in there."*

Twelve soldiers, including himself, were assigned guard duty at the Charleston Jail, "a perfect shithole," with 170 men inside, all CSA, 130 whites and 40 blacks. Soldiers from Hitch's regiment were assigned to replace another regiment that had been sent to North Carolina. He stood guard himself for ten of the 24 hours of the assignment and came out quite sore. He jokes to his sons about being "locked up" in jail.

On January 14, it was more guard duty but, this time at the camp commissary. Then he relates another life lesson to his sons writing, *"Dear Sons I find that the man who trys to do his duty in camp fares the best in some respects. My name come in again to go on guard a Tuesday but my Capt said Hitch should not go again so soon whitch I thank him verry kindly for*." He shows how many times one can benefit in the service, and implies the same for life in general, if one tries to "do his duty" in an eager and industrious way that it pays dividends in the future. In this example, he gains the favor of his Captain who saw to it that he did not get overly chosen to stand guard since he had performed his duty well and effectively when previously ordered.

Hitch then makes a brief mention that they drew "*cartridge & cap boxes yesterday*," suggesting that the army is getting equipped slowly, but surely, for potential future action. He makes note of the opportunity to go home and is not optimistic stating, "*Capt. Stewart has tried to get of a time or tow and faild. So don't look for me until you se me... I wanted to be at home next Monday, the 19th of this ist. But fear that I cant. But the 90 days will roll off by-n-by & mabe I can come then & stay a little while at old home again*." Basically, he is saying that, if the Captain is having trouble getting time to go home, then he, as a Private, probably has a very slim to no chance of doing so! So, he focuses Mary on the fact that his 90-day enlistment will be over before she knows it and he can come home, at least for a while, at that point.

It is worth noting one other paragraph in Young Hitch's letter where he asks of friends and the farm at home:

> *"Mary, please write & let me hear from you often for I have not forgotten home & home friends. Let me know whoo shaves your father now, what Scrugs is driving at & W.E. Garrett & what has become of the Grubbs. Let me know whether your Potatos both Irish & Sweet is keeping or not. Tell me how the barley is a growing. Tell how mutch more salt you want. Please excuse this bad spelt & written letter for I am so sleepy & lazy that I cant do mutch better. Tell L.B. I rec. his letter on Sunday evening tell him I was in jail when it came to hand & will answer it soon as convenient."*

This definitely reflects that, while Hitch is devoted to his duty with the 9th Reserves, he is also missing and wondering about the people at home and his farm. He wonders how the Irish and sweet potatoes from the last season are keeping through the winter and also, how the barley is growing and whether Mary needs more salt. Then he mentions friends William Scruggs, Little Berry Edwards (L.B.), William Edwin Garrett (W.E. Garrett) and "the Grubbs," an unknown family, probably from the area near the Hitch farm. He even jokes again about "being in jail" and asks Mary to tell L.B. (Mary's half-brother) of his time there.

Three days later, Young writes to Mary again, on January 18 and he has done more guard duty and again attended the camp "preaching."[85] It had been cold weather the previous few days and frigid winds blowing in off the water as he describes the assignment:

> *"Dear Mary I am only tolerable well today. I have just returned from picket & feel verry mutch werried from losing sleep & being in the cold. We have had verry cold weather for a few days past the coldest winds I ever felt. There is not much ice here but the wind off the rivers is verry cold. Mary, I have been on guard three nights out of eight. The posts we have to guard are in town. The distance from one & a half to four miles from camp. This morning from 6 to 8 I had to guard in a house where the wind could not strike me whitch was a great favor on me."*

No sleep, frigid cold, windy and having to walk 1½ miles one way to his assigned station - this does not sound like pleasant duty and, Young states just that in his writing. He did however get a two-hour assignment in a house and out of the wind and cold of which "was a great favor on" him!

Before leaving to go "for preaching," Hitch again strongly advises that Mary get herself and their sons vaccinated for the measles. He tries to allay her fear of the needle and the painful after effects with, "*My arm is pretty sore but not bad as some yet.*" Then Young tersely addresses Mary's inquiry from her previous letter asking if he will be volunteering for a regiment after his 90 days with the 9th Reserves are over. He simply states, "*Mary you may wish to know whether I intend volunteering or not. Well I cant say what I will do yet.*" The reader can, as I am sure Mary did as well, read between the lines that Young Hitch had every intention of volunteering with a South Carolina battle unit as soon as he could. His sense of duty and national pride was just too strong.

Little did he know then, that his letter would cross in transit with one of Mary's to him on Jan 20 1863[86] that not only addresses his question of volunteering, it states, in its entirety, "*Look hear young, if you hant volunteer, dont no wa hit can benefit. don't think hard of me for writing to you to not volumeteer for I think it best from what little I can find out ther is no chance for a man that volumteer to git off. We are all well this morning the Jan 20th 1863.*" Obviously, she is not very supportive of her husband volunteering for a longer service.

Young ends his letter with a simple description of Uncle Toliver Robertson's sermon that evening, a quick statement that Mary's brother J.B. Edwards is well and then, "*I thought I would be at home*

[85] Appendix, Item XXXV.
[86] Appendix, Item XXXVII.

tomorrow the 19th but it is out of my powers to do so. But hope to see home soon." His chances of visiting home during the 90 days in Charleston are fading rapidly away.

Jan 19 1863 sees a letter to Young Hitch from his first cousin John Wesley Pitts[87]. Pitts had served as a Private in Company C of the 3rd South Carolina Battalion Infantry (Laurens Battalion). He enlisted on Dec 2 1861 in Columbia with Colonel John S. Preston for 12 months. He has a spotty record as he was more sick than not and sent home on sick furlough beginning Jun 15 1862 (and apparently on this furlough at the time he composed this letter). He never returned to his unit as he was discharged from the service on Mar 18 1863 by the Medical Examiner's Board.

Pitts was about age 31 when he writes and his attention seems to be finding a bride among the "young ladies" of the area. He has a particular fancy for a Miss Cox who caught his attention in a red dress previously. If she is not yet married, he wishes Young Hitch to tell her to wait for him to come! We can follow his exchange here:

> *"There is som young laides that I promis to come up to sea to and I never has went yet and therefore if you will co`me down when the wether gets better I will go home with you and stay a week with you and the gals up ther and I want you to rite to me when you will come and let me know whither Miss Cox is married yet or not. If not tell her to hold on till I come up. I never saw her but the one time and that was at the factory. I thought very well on her at that time and maby when I sea her again I will lover still more. I want you to give her my love and respect. She had on a red dress when I saw her."*

Pitts then tells Hitch of his mother, who is Young's Aunt Mary (Hitch) Pitts, twin sister to Hitch's deceased father. She evidently still gets around pretty well but *"she is very puny at times."* The adjective, puny, appears quite often in the letters from the 1860s and refers to a person being in a weak or feeble condition either with age or, tiredness and overexertion. Mary (Hitch) Pitts was in her 69th year of age at the time J.W. Pitts penned his letter. Then he describes dear Aunt Sally Hitch, who we know well from her letters over the years, as, *"aint Sally, she is as stout as ever most that is as she has bin for the last year."*

Pitts goes on to express the times which were typical of most southern communities then, where all the able-bodied men were occupied in some sort of service to the war effort. He also seems to lament his own sickly status which causes him not to be a part of that effort. *"Dear coson it is got to be a solem time. the men all that is able to join is gone from this naborhood and a grate many gon that will be of no service in the army & would be here at home. I am as willing to go if I was able as aney body but a camp life is no place for a sick man without he is tired of living, thar he will soon die."* Most extant genealogies show John W. Pitts as dying in about the year 1863. His words above carry a more profound and prophetic impact knowing this fact.

---

87 Appendix, Item XXXVI.

On January 24, Mary Hitch writes again to Young with some answers and replies to his previous letters[88]. The letter is very telling, again with an air of dismay that Young is thinking of further volunteering for the service as he takes to the "preaching" which he had not made much of in the past: *"Young you say you have ben to preaching ever Sunday since you left home that is more than I can say for I have not heard enny preaching since you left home I cant say when I will Young When you go to Preaching think of Mary and Pray for hear & our two souns. Young I may be Decive but I fell like if it is godds Will to call me I am prepared to go. Young I Want to know wether you aire ready ar not. Young When you rite to me aboute this matter rite hit on a pease to hit self."* The last words request that he reply to her on this subject using a separate piece of paper. This is probably due to the fact we know from earlier letters that she reads all her correspondences from Young to her father, John Edwards. Maybe Mary, expecting a terse or otherwise unsavory reply, did not want to expose that to her father. It is not known for sure, but it is an interesting request.

Mary then expresses some thoughts about her kin, "*Young pit (Pitts?) Stewart & Crugs has Never ben to See me Sence you left home. they air god brothers laws (sic, brother-in-laws?) they never have ben. they men that sed one time mary if you wont enny thin Dun I will asist you in it. Young I want you to cum home & tell me what I had better do as I Don't now whether Ginney will Git Well ar not*." The men Pitts(?), Stewart and Scruggs are all indicated as her brothers-in-law but we know of only one who fits that description for sure; William Berry Scruggs who married Jane Caroline Edwards, Mary's sister and known to her as Ginney or Jinsey. The others are probably Stewart and Pitts who would be Young's cousins. While Mary is forlorn that her brothers-in-law have not come to visit her, she does let them off the hook by indicating that if she needed them to do anything, they will assist while Young is away. She then implores Young to come home and help her make a decision about her sister as she does not know if she will get well from an apparent sickness. Mary is missing her husband terribly and she can hardly contain herself as he spends weeks away on duty.

Young Hitch's son, Joseph, next communicates with his father on January 28 and responds to Young's letter to him of Jan 21 1863 (which he had just received that day) adding some bit of news from home[89]. He reports on "Mr. Edward Hughes" whom we heard about in the John Edwards' letter on the January 5 as having recently gotten married. Joseph Hitch's letter gives more details that Hughes had married Miss Caroline Parsons and that they were living down at the "*Cusen Mansel place.*" This would be Mansel Garrett (1828-1862), a cousin to Mary Hitch, and brother to Archibald Y. Garrett who is serving with Young Hitch in Company C of the 9th Reserves. Mansel had married Martha (Cicely) Hughes and had two children by the time he died on May 24 1862, about 8 months prior to this letter. Edward Hughes[90] was brother-in-law to Mansel which would be the connection to perhaps how he and his new wife were living at the Mansel Garrett homestead. As we have seen, through the various correspondences, there are many connections between the Hughes, Hitch and Edwards families in the years prior to and during the Civil War.

---

[88] Appendix, Item XXXVIII.

[89] Appendix, Item XXXIX.

[90] Edward B. Hughes (1834-1915) and Martha R. (Cicely) Hughes (1836-1913) were children of George Tillman (1802-1876) and Lucinda Hughes who were living in Greenville County, South Carolina in 1850. 1850 Federal Census, South Carolina, Greenville County, page 232.

Joseph then expresses a rather heart-breaking notion in the words, *"PA hurry home for I am invited to Candi pullings ever Week but I hant bin to enny uv them I hant forgot my promis yet Shorly you Will Never you Cum home you Will turn Me loose for a few days PA Miss Mary Brown had a candi pulling last week and invited me to it but I did not go to it."* We must remember that Joseph was age 15 at the time and still a boy. But, he had made a promise to his father to be the man of the house while Young was away doing his duty with the 9th Reserves. Here, we get a glimpse of the stress it made for Joseph to take on the full responsibilities of the household and farm at a young age and, how it interfered with the everyday life of being a young teenage boy at the time. Candy pullings were big social events for young men and women at the time and Joseph was missing out and longing to attend them but, like his father, would not even consider shirking his duty and promises. Joseph writes this to his father, *"PA I never have left MA nairry Night Senc you left home and if I can bea at home with Ma I Will bea hair."*

Joseph gives us two more bits of information of life at home in Laurens while Young is away. First, his uncle Jonas M. Edwards and Aunt Clarissa stayed with the Hitches on the night of January 27 with *"ther 2 least sons..."*; that is, their youngest sons, John C.C. (age 7) and Elihu E. Edwards (age 6), Joseph's young cousins. Uncle Jonas helped Joseph cut wood the morning of the 28th after a snowfall that night.

Secondly, Joseph makes a comment about the high price of regular household items. In a previous letter, Young has mentioned that he thought it a very high price to charge 30 cents for "paper and needles" but, Joseph indicates that such a price is cheap compared to home where the same is selling for $1.00! Joseph Hitch writes, *"PA you Sed A.Y. Garrett give 30 cts for a paper and needles but you think that is a big price a paper and needles hear is A Dollar a paper."*

Here, we see how normal and customary household items were beginning to get scarce due to lack of manufacturing in the south. Additionally, the Union blockade of southern ports was preventing such items from getting to market. With high demand and decreased supply (and monetary inflation), these items skyrocketed in price, if they were even found available at all. However, southerners made do in enterprising ways. We see this even in the correspondence in the Mowbray collection where paper was recycled by using twice – once to send a letter and then to get back a response on the same paper. Also, **Figure 23** in Chapter 6 depicts an envelope in the collection that was re-used by folding inside out for recycling to send a second letter. The following briefly shows how costs of some key household items became outrageous in the southern states after the outbreak of the Civil War:

> *After the initial months of the war, the South was plagued with shortages of all kinds. It started with clothing. As the first winter of the war approached, the Confederate army needed wool clothing to keep their soldiers warm. But the South did not produce much wool and the Northern blockade prevented much wool from being imported from abroad. People all over the South donated their woolens to the cause. Soon families at home were cutting blankets out of carpets.*
>
> *Almost all the shoes worn in the South were manufactured in the North. With the start of the war, shipments of shoes ceased and there would be few new shoes available for years. The first meeting of Confederate and Union forces at Gettysburg arose when Confederates were investigating a supply of shoes in a warehouse.*

> *By the end of the Civil War, Confederate money wasn't worth the paper it was printed on. Money was another problem. The South's decision to print more money to pay for the war simply led to unbelievable increases in price of everyday items. By the end of 1861, the overall rate of inflation was running 12% per month. For example, salt was the only means to preserve meat at this time. Its price increased from 65¢ for a 200 pound bag in May 1861 to $60 per sack only 18 months later. Wheat, flour, corn meal, meats of all kinds, iron, tin and copper became too expensive for the ordinary family. PROFITEERS frequently bought up all the goods in a store to sell them back at a higher price. It was an unmanageable situation. FOOD RIOTS occurred in Mobile, Atlanta and Richmond. Over the course of the war, inflation in the South caused prices to rise by 9000%.*[91]

We see evidence of this throughout the letters in the Mowbray collection. Young Hitch and his family are not only concerned with the price of "needles and paper" but also staple necessities like shoes, salt, and food. In Joseph Hitch's letter, we see the increase in price for the needles and paper from 30 cents to $1.00 in a very short period of time in early 1863. This would get much, much worse as the war wore on for another 2+ years. It was a very trying time indeed.

This thought is continued in a letter from Mary Hitch to Young on January 29 where she expresses dismay about the scarcity of needles and pins and the cost to replace them, "*Young Please bye me Some needles for I hav not got but one that I can soe with. I cant git then. A thought paying one dollar for a paper a paper of pins is three dollars*." She is reduced to only one needle to sew their clothes and cannot purchase them near their home[92]. In the same letter, Mary wants Young to try and get some camphor for she needs it badly, "*...git me Some camfer for I need some Verry bad...*" Camphor oil was used as a topical liquid to prevent infection and itching back in the mid-19th century. During the war, it was needed on the battlefields for both sides and became very scarce and, to obtain it on the home front was next to impossible.

The rest of Mary's January 29 letter concerns mostly household news and health. Son Lucian has been sick as has been Mary, herself. Her sister Ginney Scruggs is getting better as she had been eating more. Mary writes that she is sorry she did not send Yong anything to eat but she was "*...was looking for you home but you have not return yet but I hope you will soon...*" Lucian adds a few words at the end of the letter for his father, "*I receive your letter the 28 Young Me & J.J. has a ruf time feeding. Our lot is shew mutch deep in mud & snow. PA dont shoot all your powder away at a pine(?). Cum home & kill me a Mes of squirrels for they air verry plenty.*" He notes that the boys are finding it tough to get enough food to eat with the weather causing issues with deep mud and snow. He then longs to have his father home to hunt for squirrels as they are "plenty." No doubt that this bestows a double meaning in that it would solve their food problem and get their father home for a long overdue visit.

Joseph continues his lament to his father in an undated letter probably from late January 1863[93]. He reports that the health of him, his brother and mother are okay by not well. He hopes to see his father again – either in this life or "*in that world whare wee wont part no more whare thir will bee no war nor*

[91] This excerpt from *www.ushistory.org*, 34d. "The Southern Homefront", ©2008-2014.
[92] Appendix, Item XL.
[93] Appendix, Item XLI.

toiling and grief and pain." Joseph then mentions that "*...you air in the army struggling while others is at hom doughing nothing Me and Mother al in the field working and toiling for to make sum thing to eat and live on..."* He is referring to those men who had not joined the service just and how he felt that to be unjust to those who are serving like his father. Joseph Hitch is still struggling with his father being away and leaving him in charge as the "man of the house."

The next letter in the Mowbray collection that occurs in the time that Young Hitch is part of the 9th Reserves comes again from Camp Means, South Carolina[94]. It is dated Feb 9 1863 and is only six days from when he believes his tour with the unit will be over, *"It is thought that we will be disbanded on the 15 inst if so we will be at home the first of next week if we are spared to be alive & able to make the trip*." There is also his expectation that he will be home soon as he writes, *"Mary you need not write again untill you see or hear from me again. I hope to see you soon. I have ben home three times since I came to camp but when I awoke it was all a dream..."*

He writes of his own health which he says is not very well at the moment and is still fearful of contracting the measles even though he had been vaccinated, *"...I am not well today. I have a very severe cold. And maybe takeing the measles but I think it is just cold. I got verry cold the other night & suffered that night severely with the headache. Last night the latter part of it suffered badly with the back and limbs aching. Today I have lain the most of the day*." Then Young relates one of the trials of life in close quarters with others (besides the propensity to spread sickness) when he states, *"Since dinner today I have washed myself & put on clean cloths. I have bin to that old jail until I have got some of them nasty lice on my clothing. I want to have the cloths that I pulled of washed & maybe it will kill the nasty things*." Somehow, he has contracted lice, which he says came from guarding that "old jail" and, he is so disgusted with it that we wants to get his clothes washed to hopefully rid himself of the infestation! Then, he offers a quick note that J.B. Edwards (Mary's brother) and A.Y. (Garrett) are not well before closing the letter with, *"So I bid you farewell. Look not until you see me at the gate*."

The letters from the time Young was camped with the 9th South Carolina Reserves offer unique insight into what was happening in the camps in South Carolina and on the home front in the period from November 1862 to February 1863. We know from the official records that Young Hitch and his fellow 9th Reservists end their service on Valentine's Day, Feb 14 1863. We also note from the records that Young enlisted with the 16th South Carolina Volunteers with Company I, the day before his time with the 9th ended, on Feb 13 1863. His term of enlistment for the new unit? "FOR THE WAR..." Much to his wife's chagrin, Young Hitch was committed to seeing through his cause and the cause of the Confederacy, through to the end, whether that be a southern victory or loss or the point where he could not fight anymore due to sickness, injury or death.

---

[94] Appendix, Item XLII.

CHAPTER 5
March to December 1863
"...the Yankeys...have Jackson in their possession & may get Vicksburg..."

Young H.E. Hitch enlisted as a Private with Company I of the 16th South Carolina Regiment on Feb 13 1863 in Adams Run, SC "for the war." However, from a later letter in the Mowbray collection, we know that Hitch left home for good on his adventure with the 16th on Mar 27 1863. So Mary Hitch in one way received her wish to have her husband home but, in another, only had to give him up again to the war effort after about a brief 6-week stay at the farm.

We need to digress a bit here to see how the 16th South Carolina was created as, it existed for almost a year before Young Hitch came into its ranks. It was commanded by James McCullough (1824-1892), first as a Captain of Company E and, later as Colonel McCullough, commanding the entire regiment. He was born Feb 20 1824, about 25 miles south of Greenville, South Carolina. "Old Beeswax" as he was sometimes affectionately called, initially organized a company of soldiers of a regiment (Company E) that Charles J. Elford was granted to raise in the autumn of 1861 by South Carolina Governor Francis W. Pickens. The regiment consisted of Companies A-K (no "J" because of its handwritten confusion with "I") and all, except for I and K, were mustered into state service on Dec 12 1861 for twelve months. Five months later, the entire Confederate army was reorganized on Apr 28 1862 and the regiment was re-mustered for three years "or the war."

Charles Elford, a Greenville lawyer, newspaper editor and mayor, and original organizer of the regiment, was elected its colonel in November 1861, defeating T.S. Arthur. At the same time, James McCullough was elected lieutenant colonel, defeating John M. Jones. After the army-wide reorganization, another election was held on Apr 29 1862 and McCullough supplanted Elford for command of the regiment. Elford left and went on to become colonel for the 3rd South Carolina Reserves in late 1862 and 1863. Wallace B. Ioor defeated D.I.J. Chandler for the rank of major in the elections in November 1861 and was elected lieutenant colonel in the reorganization on Apr 29 1862 while, Charles C. O'Neill was elected major at that time[95].

The 16th regiment was originally called the Greenville Regiment and, more informally sometimes, the "Greenville Boys," but would eventually be labelled the 16th South Carolina Volunteer Infantry (SCVI) when it converted from a state-level of service to national service for the Confederate States of America (CSA). The 16th had the honor of being the only South Carolina regiment where every company was comprised of men from the same district. It was the 16th SCVI by April 1862, 10 months prior to when

---

[95] An excellent historical background of the 16th SCVI can be found in the book, South Carolina's Military Organizations During the War Between the States; Volume III, The Upstate, Robert S. Seigler, The History Press, Charleston, SC, 2008; pages 167-177. Some of the content here is taken from this reference.

Young Hitch joined in February 1863. A listing of all Company I members from its inception to the end of the war follows[96]:

NAME			RANK		ENLISTED			PLACE	NOTES
LAST	FIRST	MID	IN	OUT	YR	M	D		
Adair	George	W	Pvt		1864	1	22	Greenville, SC	
Allison	Andrew	Jackson	Pvt		1862	1	24	Camp Hampton	captured 12/16/1864 near Nashville, TN.
Armstrong	J	D	Pvt		1863	3	3	Adams Run, SC	Paroled 4/26/1865.
Austin	John	T	Pvt		1863	3	3	Adams Run, SC	died Caldwell hospital, Griffin, GA 7/16/1864 from wound received at Kennesaw Mt.
Austin	Thomas	Jeremiah	Pvt	2LT	1863	5	1	Adams Run, SC	Elected 2LT 12/7/1863. Had typhoid fever and may have died from it in the summer of 1864.
Austin	William	A	Pvt		1862	3	27	Camp Leesburg	Discharged 3/27/1863 end of service.
Babb	Newton		1LT	Capt	1862	1	24	Camp Hampton	Promoted to Captain on 7/30/1862. Died 11/6/1863 at Murrays hospital, LaGrange, GA.
Baldwin	Jeremiah	C	Pvt		1862	1	24	Camp Hampton	Died 10/21/1863
Bozeman	Toliver	L	Pvt		1862	3	30	Camp Leesburg	Was Captain of Co. E, Hampton Legion from 6/12 to 7/16/1861 when he resigned due to health reasons. Shows as AWOL on rolls here.
Bramlett	James	W	Pvt		1863	4	1	Adams Run, SC	Purportedly died in a hospital in Franklin, TN, 11/30/1864
Bramlett	William	Dacus	Pvt		1864	2	11	Dalton, GA	$50 bounty due.
Brown	Jerry	Jackson	Pvt		1863	3	12	Adams Run, SC	Discharged 3/28/1864 due to hearing loss from protracted case of typhoid fever.
Burditt	Benjamin	William	Pvt		1862	1	24	Camp Hampton	Paroled 4/26/1865.
Burditt	David	Wilcot	Pvt		1863	7	1	Jackson, MS	Wounded 11/30/1864 with gunshot fractured left ulna upper 3" and front left thigh. Captured Franklin, TN 12/18/1864, sent to Louisville, KY 1/17/1865, sent to Camp Chase in Nashville 1/18/1865. Transferred to Point Lookout 3/26/1865. Took Oath of Allegiance and released 6/9/1865.
Chaplain	Josiah		Pvt		1862	3	27	Camp Leesburg	Discharged 3/27/1863 end of service.
Cheek	Austin		Pvt		1863	2	13	Camp Hampton	
Curry	Wilburn	A	Pvt		1862	2	7	Camp Hampton	
Divier	J	Y	Pvt		1862	3	30	Camp Leesburg	
Edwards	Little	Berry	Pvt		1863	2	11	Camp Hampton	Paroled 4/26/1865.
Farrow	R	M	Pvt		1863	2	13	Camp Hampton	
Forester	Andrew	J	Pvt		1864	2	11	Dalton, GA	$50 bounty due.
Forester	John	E	Pvt		1862	3	27	Camp Leesburg	Captured by enemy near Kennesaw Mt., GA 6/19/1864, sent to Louisville, KY 6/26, then Camp Morton, IN 6/27. Died of pneumonia at Camp Morton 3/20/1865.
Forester	William	L	Pvt		1862	3	27	Camp Leesburg	
Forester	I	B	Pvt		1863	9	1	Chattanooga, TN	Paroled 4/26/1865.
Forrester	Isaac		Pvt		1862	3	27	Camp Leesburg	Paroled 4/26/1865. (may be the same as I. Forester)
Forrester	John		Pvt		1863	2	13	Camp Hampton	Captured by enemy near Kennesaw Mt., GA 6/19/1864, sent to Louisville, KY 6/26, then Camp Morton, IN 7/14. Released after taking Oath of Allegiance on 6/12/1865.
Fowler	George	R	Pvt		1862	1	24	Camp Hampton	Captured at Battle of Lookout Mountain near Ringgold, GA 11/27/1863. Died of chronic diarrhea at U.S. Field Hospital in Nashville, TN on 12/16/1863.
Fowler	J	W	Pvt						Mislabeled? Co. F?
Fowler	W	Joseph	Pvt		1863	5	1	Adams Run, SC	
Garrett	Erasmus	Newport	Pvt	2LT	1862	1	24	Camp Hampton	Promoted to 2nd LT on 7/30/1862. Resigned 5/2/1864, asked to be xfered to Co. F, Hampton Legion SCV.
Garrett	James	Matthew	Pvt		1863	2	11	Camp Hampton	Died of chronic diarrhea, Lauderdale, MS on Aug 20 1863 or Sep 1 1863[97].

[96] The listing in the Table is compiled by the author from Confederate Civil War Military Service records, National Archives, Washington, DC.

[97] The service records for J.M. Garrett show him deceased in one instance on Aug 20 and another on Sep 1 1863. Since Young Hitch writes a letter on Aug 21 1863 indicating that Matt Garrett "may go home," this researcher would tend to accept the September 1 version of the death date as more accurate.

NAME			RANK		ENLISTED			PLACE	NOTES
LAST	FIRST	MID	IN	OUT	YR	M	D		
Garrett	Miles	Rainwater	Pvt		1863	2	13	Camp Hampton	Died in Clayton hospital in Forsyth, GA on 9/30/1864 of c. diarrhea.
Gary	W	S	Pvt		1863	9	1	Chattanooga, TN	Killed near Decatur, GA on 7/22/1864.
Gault	John	W.P.	Pvt		1862	6	27	Camp Leesburg	
George	Fielding		Pvt		1864	2	11	Dalton, GA	
Goldsmith	Thomas		Pvt		1863	2	13	Camp Hampton	paroled 4/26/1865
Goodwin	Henry	T	Pvt		1863	2	28	Adams Run	Died 11/16/1863, Rome, GA.
Goodwin	John	Franklin	Pvt		1863	1	28	Camp Hampton	Died 9/23/1863, Greenville, SC.
Goodwin	Johnson	William	Pvt		1863	2	13	Camp Hampton	
Goodwin	William	Davis	Pvt		1862	3	27	Camp Leesburg	
Goodwin	Westly	W	Pvt		1862	1	24	Camp Hampton	Discharged 5/24/1864 for sickness.
Graden	John		Pvt		1863	2	13	Camp Hampton	Went to Co. E in Nov 1863. Wounded 7/22/1864.
Greer	John	B	Pvt		1862	3	27	Camp Leesburg	Nurse in Regt Hospital. Died 10/21/1863 in Demopolis, AL of chronic diarrhea.
Greer	James	Manning	Pvt		1862	3	30	Camp Leesburg	
Greer	John		Pvt		1862	3	27	Camp Leesburg	(may be a duplicate of John B. Greer above)
Hamby	Green	Smith	Pvt		1863	9	1	Chattanooga, TN	Paroled 4/26/1865
Hamby	John	T	Pvt		1862	4	7	Camp Leesburg	Paroled 4/26/1865
Hamby	Stephen	R	Pvt		1862	3	27	Camp Leesburg	
Harrison	John	R	Pvt	SGT	1863	4	15	Charleston	Paroled 4/26/1865
Hawkins	Alfred	J	Pvt		1862	3	27	Camp Leesburg	Transferred to Palmetto Battalion Light Artillery on 5/1/1863.
Hawkins	James	H	Pvt		1862	3	27	Camp Leesburg	
Henderson	James	M	Pvt		1862	2	3	Camp Hampton	Regimental Waggoner. In hospital with syphilis on 1/29/1863, bronchitis in Feb 1865.
Higgins	George	P	Pvt		1862	1	24	Camp Hampton	Transferred to Aikens Partisan Rangers on 10/31/1862.
Hitch	Young	H. E.	Pvt		1863	2	13	Camp Hampton	Killed on picket duty at Kennesaw Mt., GA on 6/19/1864.
Hodges	W	L	1LT		1864	2	11	Dalton, GA	Paroled 4/26/1865.
Holcomb	Hosea	K	Pvt		1863	2	25	Greenville, SC	Killed Kennesaw Mt., GA on 6/28/1864.
Howard	Augustus		Pvt		1862	3	27	Camp Leesburg	Detailed to commissary Jul 1863.
Howard	J	M	Pvt		1864	2	11	Dalton, GA	collected $50 bounty
Howard	John	Manning	3LT		1862	3	27	Camp Leesburg	Probably is the same as J.M. Howard above.
Howard	Presley	E.A.	SGT	Pvt	1862	1	24	Camp Hampton	Discharged Jan 1863, end of service. Re-enlisted 2/11/1864 at Dalton, GA and collected $50 bounty.
Howard	W	P	Pvt		1862	3	27	Camp Leesburg	Wounded 8/15/1864.
Howard	Young	O	Pvt	SGT	1862	1	24	Camp Hampton	Promoted to SGT on 8/4/1864, killed 8/24/1864 at Atlanta.
Huff	John	H	Pvt		1862	3	27	Camp Leesburg	
Hurt	Riley	W	Pvt		1862	1	24	Camp Hampton	Detached as blacksmith to Pioneer Corps by Gen Walker in Nov 1863. Paroled 4/26/1865.
Hyde	James	H	Pvt		1862	3	27	Camp Leesburg	Died 2/15/1864
Johnson	James	P	Pvt	SGT	1862	3	16	Camp Hampton	Promoted to SGT on 8/4/1864.
Jones	J	W	Pvt		1864	2	25	Dalton, GA	Killed near Decatur, GA on 7/22/1864. $50 bounty due.
Jones	James	L	Corp	Pvt	1862	1	24	Camp Hampton	Discharged due to expired service Jan 23 1863.
Jones	James	M	Pvt	3LT	1861	12	12	Camp Leesburg	Re-enlisted 3/27/1862 at Camp Hampton. Elected LT 8/9/1864.
Jones	John	M.H.	Corp		1862	2	26	Greenville, SC	
Kellett	J	A	Pvt		1863	9	1	Greenville, SC	Transferred from Palmetto Battalion Light Artillery on 6/16/1864. Paroled 4/26/1865.
Kellett	W	M	Pvt		1863	9	1	Greenville, SC	Transferred from Palmetto Battalion Light Artillery on 6/16/1864.
Knight	D	T	Pvt		1863	2	13	Adams Run, SC	
Knight	Jesse		Pvt		1862	1	24	Camp Hampton	
Lee	J	B	Pvt		1862	12	17	Greenville, SC	$50 bounty due.
Linder	Simpson	B	Pvt		1863	12	15	Spartanburg, SC	Transferred from Palmetto Battalion Light Artillery on 6/16/1864. Killed near Decatur, GA on 7/22/1864. $50 bounty due.
Linder	Willis	Lee	Pvt		1863	3	1	Spartanburg, SC	Transferred from Palmetto Battalion Light Artillery on 6/16/1864. Paroled 4/26/1865.
Locke	George	W	Pvt		1862	3	27	Camp Leesburg	
Locke	Jesse	James	Pvt	3LT	1862	5	16	Camp Leesburg	Elected 3LT 12/23/1863. Died at home of disease 6/4/1864.
Lyon	George	W	Pvt		1862	1	24	Camp Hampton	Died 3/27/1864 in hospital at Dalton, GA.

NAME			RANK		ENLISTED			PLACE	NOTES
LAST	FIRST	MID	IN	OUT	YR	M	D		
Mahaffey	Madison	Roland	Pvt		1862	2	7	Camp Hampton	Captured by the enemy near Kennesaw Mt., GA on 6/18/1864. Rec'd as POW in Louisville, KY on 6/26 and sent to Camp Morton, IN on 6/27/1864. Transferred for exchange 3/4/1865.
Mahaffey	Hoyt	Jackson	Pvt		1863	5	1	Adams Run, SC	Paroled 4/26/1865.
Mahaffey	James	L	Pvt		1863	3	3	Adams Run, SC	
McCrary	James	A	Pvt		1862	2	7	Camp Hampton	Died 12/22/1862 in camp near Wilmington, NC.
McCrary	William	K	Pvt		1862	4	16	Camp Leesburg	Paroled 4/26/1865.
McHugh	William	A	Pvt		1862	3	27	Camp Leesburg	Discharged 3/27/1863 at end of service.
McKinney	James	T.J.	1SGT		1862	1	24	Camp Hampton	Died in hospital on 8/8/1864 of wound received on picket duty in Atlanta.
McKinney	Newton	J.A.	Pvt		1862	4	19	Camp Leesburg	Died 2/23/1864 in Dalton, GA.
McKittrick	Samuel		Capt	LT	1864	2	11	Dalton, GA	Company I was originally named Capt. Samuel McKittrick's Co. in 1861/62. He re-enlisted in 1864 as a PVT and was elected LT 6/28/1864. Killed near Decatur, GA on 7/22/1864. $50 bounty due.
Nash	Young		3SGT	Pvt	1862	1	24	Camp Hampton	Discharged 1/23/1863 end of service.
Nelson	T	B	Pvt		1863	2	13	Adams Run, SC	
Nelson	W	B	Pvt		1863	2	13	Camp Hampton	
Nix	William	W	Pvt		1862	3	27	Camp Leesburg	Discharged 2/21/1863
Nunly	Francis	F	Pvt	SGT	1862	2	14	Camp Hampton	Re-enlisted 4/16/1863 at Camp Leesburg. Promoted to SGT 8/24/1864 after SGT Howard was killed. Paroled 4/26/1865
Owens	John		Pvt		1862	2	7	Camp Hampton	Died 8/1/1862 of typhoid fever at Adams Run, SC.
Peden	John	McVey	Pvt	Corp	1864	6	16	Charleston, SC	Transferred from Palmetto Battalion Light Artillery 6/16/1864, promoted to Corp 8/4/1864.
Peden	James	Scipio	Pvt		1863	12	1	Greenville, SC	Transferred from Palmetto Battalion Light Artillery 6/16/1864. Died 7/28/1864 in hospital of wound received near Decatur, GA on 7/22/1864.
Peden	Thomas	Carlisle	Pvt		1862	3	27	Greenville, SC	Transferred from Palmetto Battalion Light Artillery 6/16/1864.
Phillips	Claibourn		Pvt		1862	1	24	Camp Hampton	
Rea	Samuel		Pvt		1862	3	30	Camp Leesburg	
Richards	J	A	Pvt		1862	6	27	Camp Leesburg	Discharged 11/20/1862
Roberts	Edward	G	Pvt	Capt	1862	3	20	Camp Leesburg	Elected 2LT 8/21/1862. Elected Capt 4/7/1864. Was clerk for Regimental commissary. Paroled 4/26/1865.
Robertson	Berry	W	Pvt		1862	3	30	Camp Leesburg	
Robertson	George	W.T.	Pvt		1862	3	27	Camp Leesburg	Captured by the enemy near Kennesaw Mt., GA 6/19/1864, sent to Louisville, KY, then to Camp Morton, IN 6/27/1864. Transferred for exchange 2/26/1865.
Robertson	John	Thomas	Pvt		1862	5	28	Camp Leesburg	
Scruggs	William	Berry	Pvt		1863	2	11	Camp Hampton	Paroled 4/26/1865.
Sheffield	William		Pvt		1864	2	11	Dalton, GA	$50 bounty due.
Simmons	John	Hiram	Pvt		1862	1	24	Camp Hampton	Wounded 7/22/1864. Paroled 4/26/1865.
Smith	James	H	Pvt		1862	4	7	Camp Leesburg	
Smith	Matison		Pvt		1862	3	30	Camp Leesburg	
Step	John		Pvt		1862	4	16	Camp Leesburg	Captured by enemy 11/27/1863 near Missionary Ridge (Ringgold, GA), sent to Louisville, KY 12/9/1863 then to Rock Island, IL 12/11/1863. Died 2/4/1864 of diarrhea.
Stewart	W	Henry	Pvt		1862	1	24	Camp Hampton	Discharged 1/24/1863, end of service. Re-enlisted 2/11/1864 at Dalton, GA, $50 bounty due. Wounded 7/22/1864. Paroled 4/26/1865.
Stewart	W	W/M	Pvt		1864	7	10	Greenville, SC	$50 bounty due. Died 12/1/1864 chronic diarrhea, Clayton Hospital, Columbus, MS.
Stewart	William		Pvt		1863	2	13	Camp Hampton	
Taylor	David	S	Pvt		1862	4	16	Camp Leesburg	
Thackston	J	S	Pvt		1862	7	26	Camp Hampton	Transferred from Aikens Partisan Rangers 10/31/1862. Brigade wagoner & ambulance driver. Sent to hospital wounded 6/28/1864.
Thackston	J	F	Pvt		1864	2	11	Dalton, GA	$50 bounty due. Furloughed from hospital 60 days 8/8/1864, wounded.
Thackston	Thomas	M	Pvt		1863	3	15	Adams Run, SC	

NAME			RANK		ENLISTED			PLACE	NOTES
LAST	FIRST	MID	IN	OUT	YR	M	D		
Thackston	William	S	Pvt	1LT	1862	1	24	Camp Hampton	Promoted to 1LT 7/30/1862. Resigned due to health 10/1863.
Vaughn	Henry	G	Pvt	1SGT	1862	1	24	Camp Hampton	Promoted to 1SGT 8/4/1864 when SGT McKinney was killed.
Vaughn	Paschal	D	Corp	3SGT	1862	1	24	Camp Hampton	Died Franklin, TN ~3/1865.
Vaughn	Toliver	R	Pvt		1862	1	24	Camp Hampton	Killed Kennesaw Mt., GA on 6/20/1864.
Verdin	Allen		Pvt		1862	4	7	Camp Leesburg	Discharged 4/7/1863 end of service.
Verdin	Paul	J	Pvt	SGT	1862	3	27	Camp Leesburg	In hospital, wounded 8/17/1864. Paroled 4/26/1865.
Waldrip	Little	Berry	Pvt		1863	4	13	Greenville, SC	Transferred from Palmetto Battalion Light Artillery 6/16/1864.
Waldrip	William	M	Pvt		1863	5	22	Greenville, SC	Transferred from Palmetto Battalion Light Artillery 6/16/1864. Wounded 8/15/1864.
White	Absalom	Abner	Corp		1863	2	9	Columbia, SC	Promoted to Corp 8/4/1864. $50 bounty due.
White	Anthony		Pvt	2LT	1863	5	1	Adams Run, SC	Elected LT 8/6/1864. Killed on picket duty 8/7/1864 in Atlanta.
White	John	Jones	Pvt		1863	3	3	Adams Run, SC	Brigade/Division wagon driver. Paroled 4/26/1865.
White	Solomon	A	Pvt		1863	5	5	Laurens, SC	Died of disease 1/28/1864 in Augusta, GA. $50 bounty due.
White	William	H	Pvt		1862	7	25	Columbia, SC	Was Co. E from 3/6/1862. Died 4/2/1865 in NC.
White	Young	Moses	Pvt		1862	2	3	Camp Hampton	Killed in Franklin, TN Nov 30 1864.
Wood	N	J	Pvt		1863	2	13	Camp Hampton	Wounded in foot 8/29/1863.
Wood	Nicholas	Joseph	Pvt		1862	3	30	Camp Leesburg	Wounded 9/26/1863. (probably the same as N.J. Wood)

The preceding table gives name, rank when the soldier entered service, rank eventually reached before leaving service (if different from entry), date of enlistment and location and, any special items of note from the service files. A company in the Civil War period usually consisted of 100 men and this list contains a total of 134 which accounts for people leaving and new ones joining due to discharge, transfer or becoming a casualty. Probably at no particular time did Company I have its full contingent of 100 men but was closest to that number when it was first formed. More details regarding the service and families of many of these men are presented at various points throughout this book.

We see the thrust of enlistments taking place in three (3) locations: Adams Run (Feb-May 1863), Camp Hampton (Jan-Jul 1862) and Camp Leesburg (Mar-May 1862), all in South Carolina. Adams Run still exists in modern day by its original name and is approximately 25 miles almost due west of Charleston, SC and, is near where the Civil War camp was located. Research indicates that Camp Hampton was located just outside of Columbia, SC and, with the other two, was a primary staging area for troops from the upper part of the state[98]. Camp Leesburg was located not too far from Adams Run in modern-day Colleton County, SC. Besides a few random enlistments elsewhere, the only other site noted for a more general influx into Company I is Dalton, GA in February 1864. This was a later recruiting effort conducted to replenish the depleted 16th regiment and included a $50 bounty for volunteers who joined at that time.

We need to go back to 1862 to see how Company I of the 16th regiment began. Company I was originally being assembled as Captain Samuel McKittrick's Company in early 1862 as the embryonic units of the 16th South Carolina began to come together. He was organizing his forces at Camp Hampton, near Columbia in the winter of 1862 but, McKittrick's Company dissolved into Company I sometime in the spring of 1862 when the general reorganization of the army took place. Captain McKittrick did not join Company I at that time but did as a Private on Feb 11 1864 in Dalton, GA. Like those of Young Hitch,

---

[98] While the exact location of Camp Hampton is not known, most historians believe that the camp was located on a site very near where the SC State Archives sits today (2015).

quite a few of McKittrick's letters survive and can be researched as most are in the files at the Kennesaw Mountain National Battlefield Park (KMNBP) in Georgia. Here are a few excerpts from McKittrick's letters denoting key times in the early days just before Company I came into being:

> *"Camp Hampton near Columbia January 26, 1862*
>
> *Dear Wife*
> *I now seat myself to let you know that I am well and have been same ever since I left home we got to camp on Friday night about dusk about 15 companies in camp we struck up camp that night on the next morning each man drew his rations. ...I had not been at Columbia for some 11 or 12 years, when, I found myself in soldiers uniform ... We have agreed to go into the Greenville Regt. I am going down on the night train to Charleston to see how things are going on I expected to visit the Regiment, my company is not full. I cannot therefore go into the Regt, formed here. The government promises to give me time to recruit up he says it is to large a company to disband ... I hope to be able to comp up this week to fix up things and recruit my company. ... We have a very peaceable time in camp."*

We observe that, by Jan 26 1862, McKittrick's Company has agreed to be a part of the Greenville Regiment which became the 16th South Carolina. But, his company has not fully formed by that time as he writes "my company is not full," and needs to conduct more recruiting to get it up to size. He is caught in a place where his company is too large to disband but not large enough to join a regiment. Three weeks later, on Feb 17 1862, he has still not assembled a full company as we see in the following excerpt:

> *"Columbia, S.C. Feb. 17, 1862*
>
> *Dear Wife,*
> *...When I came home I found a letter from Col. Elford stating that if he could get up our list to 55 men he would make on the roll and also get a letter from Cap. I. Shumate proposing for me try and get those men in Laurens Dist. The 28 men spoken of in his newer Regt. of Laurens are not returned. General Gist has written to the Col. of that Regt., this is not Moseleys Regt. from what I can find out that Regt. has finished its quota or at least they cannot be got at. I went this morning to Col. Chestnutt I told him the condition of the company and showed him Elfords letter he directed the letter and the situation of the company to sent to General Gist at Charleston. So within a day or two we will know what is to be done. I now think the chance pretty fair for a company. The boys are anxious still Col. Chestnutt told me there would be a call for five regiments for the war the call he said would be made within about 2 weeks. So all hands may pitch in this in no joke I had it from Chestnutt himself and others also. I think this will help my company."*

We see here that it has become official to try and raise five regiments "for the war." McKittrick needs to get his company strength up to 55 men to be able to join a regiment and, hopes to try and get those men from the Laurens District. McKittrick's next letter comes six days later with more information of the progress he is having:

Figure 9 - Colonel James McCullough, Commander of the 16th South Carolina (Michael G. Hitch files)

"Columbia, S.C. Feb. 23, 1862

Dear wife
... I have this morning received marching orders from the Sec. of War we are going to the Greenville Regt. to fill out our Regts. And the ranks and be like other folks. My boys are busy cooking their four days rations. Each man has drawn a haversack canteen and old musket. So we leave tomorrow at six o'clock the boys seem tired staying here, we pleased with the idea of getting our company. It seems there has been luck in leisure this time. Col. Chesnutt told me he would not disband my company I had been industrious to get it up ... When you write direct your letters to Adam's Run, 16th Regiment, Captain McKittrick ... Tell my dear children I am gone to war now, ... So farewell my dear wife."

McKittrick's company has been recognized and, if filled, will indeed become a part of the Greenville Regiment that, as of the date of this letter, is officially called the 16th regiment. McKittrick also refers to himself as "Captain" now that he has been "industrious" to form a company beneath him. Three more weeks pass, and we get some interesting information from McKittrick in the following excerpt from a March 12 letter:

"Camp Greenville March 12, 1862

Dear Wife
... there is great excitement here now about the last call for volunteers some are talking of volunteering and (some) are not. I do not wish to discourage others in this matter. But in my situation I do not feel inclined to volunteer for the war. I have volunteered twice if that will not do I believe I will stand a draft before I will go it again. The men of this Regt. are placed on equality with those at home. There are efforts making here to get this Regt. to volunteer for the war. I think that I will stand my draft first. I will take my hand with them at home. I think it unfair to draft men for 3 years or during the war. I would like to have your opinion on this subject I do not think near all the boys will go it for the war. My company cannot go as a company because it is not full. If we all would volunteer we would have the chance to recruit but as we are we cannot for a less term than 3 years or the war. A regt. can go as a Regt. or a company as a company. I could not recruit for 12 months in Georgia, I cant see how I could for the war. I wish you to keep this letter secret for a while at least.... I will let you know shortly (what) the Regt. will do I think I know what I shall do. Your affectionate husband until death,
Saml. McKittrick"

Captain McKittrick has still been unable to raise enough men to form his company. The option for his men is then to volunteer but, there is a lot of consternation within the camp that the government wants the volunteers to sign up for "3 years or during the war." McKittrick is not happy about that and states that he could "stand the draft" better than commit to such a long term of service. The decision of the regiment is pending. By April 1, things are progressing further:

"Camp Leesburg April 1, 1862

Dear Wife
... My company have elected Newton Babb 1st Lt. Babb ... So we are to be mustered in next Wednesday with a full company I hope. We can every day or night hear the enemy's guns they are bombing the coast near us. When I came down we expected a battle every day but it has not come on yet, and think likely will not here. We had the Governor to review us the other day and give us a fine speech he is anxious for the Regt. to go into it for the war but this it will not do now. I do not think that were the officers themselves all willing we think that we are doing well enough... Your affectionate husband. S. McKittrick"

McKittrick still has not raised a full company though they have elected a first lieutenant in Newton Babb. He notes that the regiment will NOT volunteer for the full war even at the behest of the Governor's request. Finally, by late April 1862, a resolution is found:

"Camp Leesburgh, April 22, 1862

Dear Wife,
...My dear wife I can tell you there has been a perfect Revolution taken place within one week. You know the change Congress has made namely all men 18 and over 35 years are to be discharged within 90 days or perhaps sooner. I have been at a stand to know what to do. But after considering my condition over, and everything between duty and Interest I just say to you that I am coming home as soon as I am honorably discharged, this means now (this news) no doubt is gratifying to you, you and my dear children lay nearer my heart that the captaincy of a company The company were anxious for me to go as their Captain. I could be elected without any opposition. But I just told them I could not go the war. I am sorry and so are they but I do not feel bound to go under the circumstances. I suppose I will be able to go home as soon as the Reorganization takes place and that I suppose will be within a few day, or perhaps it may be within a month or over yet. I think that nearly all the men over 35 will go home. Capt. Roberts and Hodge and I think several other Captains and many other officers and Privates will go home the opinion here is that the men ought to go home. ... There is great canvassing for office, there is to be a change from Col. to Lieut. John Howard and Nicilus Wood are coming home. Newton Babb is not old enough yet. Elford and McCullough for Col. Ioor and some body else for Lieut. Col. and some 3 or 4 I think for Major. I have advised my company and they are anxious to select them a man that will make them an officer... Your affectionate husband until death.
Saml. McKittrick

This letter describes in detail a general reorganization of South Carolina units in 1862 as units convert from state to national service. All of the older officers and men are sent home where many will return to the Reserves before re-enlisting for active service with other units. We also see in the letter how there will be changes in the command of the regiment from Colonel down to Lieutenant. Babb, who was just elected for the latter was evidently not old enough to even serve at the time. Elford and McCullough are vying for the colonel position and this will soon be decided in the favor of James McCullough. Wallace B. Ioor will become the regiment's lieutenant colonel. John Taylor, in his well-respected pamphlet on the history of the 16th, states[99] about this period of time, "*On the 28th of April, 1862, the Regiment was reorganized and changed from State to Confederate States service for 3 years or for the duration of the war. At this time a new election was held and James C. McCullough was elected Colonel, W.B. Ivor (*sic, Ioor*), Lieutenant Colonel and C. C. O'Neall (*sic, O'Neill*), Major*." This is the point where the 16th South Carolina Regiment really comes into being as a viable and official unit of the Confederate States of America and, along with it, the men from Company I, to eventually include Young H.E. Hitch.

Samuel McKittrick, for his part, in a small autobiographical sketch written almost a year later in March 1863, states[100]: "*In December 27th, 1861, (The United States being in Revolution) I volunteered in defense of my county I was elected Captain of a company and on the 24th of January 1862 I left the comforts of home to endure a soldier's life. I remained in service until the second of May, 1862 at which time the 'Conscript Act' went into effect. Having a dependant family I refused the position of Captain in the reorganization in the 16th Regt. to which I belonged and went home.*" So, McKittrick goes home from his failed attempt to raise a company of his own where he enlists as a Sergeant with his old friend Charles Elford in the 3rd South Carolina Reserves and serves from June 1862 to January 1863. Next, he becomes a Private in Company B, 1st Battalion South Carolina Sharpshooters, then as a Captain in Company K, 1st South Carolina State Troops from August 1863 to February 1864. He eventually returns to Company I of the 16th regiment as he signs on for $50 bounty on Feb 11 1864 in Dalton, Georgia. We are indebted to Samuel McKittrick to preserving this eyewitness account of the historical formation of Company I from his initial attempt to assemble McKittrick's Company, 16th SCV. We will see more of him in the later chapters of this book when he does indeed return to the 16th South Carolina Regiment.

Advancing to the spring of 1863, while there are no letters or other documents from Young Hitch's time at home from Feb 15 to Mar 27 1863, we can assume that he was spending much-needed time with his wife and family and getting the springtime chores done around the farm to help them get through the days ahead when he would again be absent. On March 27, he set out with Company I and arrived in Camp Croft, South Carolina on March 30from where he writes his first letter the next day.

16th SOUTH CAROLINA VOLUNTEER INFANTRY – MARCH TO DECEMBER 1863

Young Hitch's first letter as a member of Company I, 16th South Carolina Regiment comes Mar 31 1863 and is very brief as he seems caught up with his unit's preparations of getting outfitted and finding his own bearings within it[101]. He writes, "*I arived at this place yesterday. I stood the trip pretty well and found the boys generally well. I have nothing very strange to write. I am going to the run to see Mr. Hughes as I did not think to hunt him up as I came by the run yesterday. I will get him to bear this to you. The boys drawed their guns last night. I have not the time to write today. I will write soon & give you the*

[99] Pamphlet, "Sixteenth South Carolina Regiment CSA from Greenville County, SC"; John S. Taylor, Greenville, 1964.
[100] "A Biographical Sketch of S. McKittrick; Camp Haywood, Pocotaligo Beaufort Dist. So.Ca. March 12th 1863," Samuel McKittrick
[101] Appendix, Item XLIII.

news. Please write to me." The only news of note is that the company were given their guns the night before, on March 30th.

Young's next letter to Mary comes from April 5 when he is at Camp Roberts, South Carolina[102]. He complains about the men in his mess, in general, but gives credit to a few. He says, "*Mary the mess we have are some I can tell you if Jerrey can be beat I don't want to see the boy. Mat will sorter do. Berry is a very good boy. Billy is our main dependence for cooking & getting things done. The boys will do anything if you can catch them at the right time & place, but that is very seldom I can tell you, And some can eat like dogs. That is any thing that is good to eat. Billy tells me that sugar they can not keep for they eat it as pigs do corn all at once and then do without until they draw again*." Here we get a feeling of what it was like to adjust to the diversity of new people in a little community in the service. We know that "Berry" and "Billy" are Mary Hitch's half-brothers Little Berry Edwards[103] (age 18) and Billy Edwards (about age 17), respectively. "Jerrey" is Jerry Jackson Brown who was also age 17 at the time and "Mat" is James Matthew Garrett[104] who is age 18. No wonder Young refers to these soldiers as "boys" since they are all so young, especially compared to Hitch, who was 37 at the time. Of them, he rather likes Berry and Billy and is okay with Matt but, he definitely does not seem to care for Jerry! We will hear more about Jerry Brown and Matt Garrett and the other "boys" later.

Then, to add to Hitch's frustration, someone has stolen his brandy, "*Mary my little bottle of brandy has done me but little good some rogue got half of it but they was neighborly; they left me a little, probably a half tumbler full. I had treated two or three before the rogue came along. So when the measles git hold of me I will not have any of my own.*" He had planned to use it as a medicinal remedy to help others and himself should he get the measles. In this letter, we see the testier side of Young Hitch which we do not often experience throughout many years of his writings and letters. He is no doubt disgusted with the "boys" wreaking havoc through the camp and a "rogue" who absconded with his brandy.

Hitch also notes that Miles R. Garrett has a lock-box at his disposal to keep their sugar under lock and key. Sugar is one of those key commodities that became increasingly scarce during the war. It became very valuable, almost like money and, hence, the need to protect it. He also is self-rationing the provisions he brought from home on March 27, "*I have half of my pone of bread We have all our flower* (flour) *yet & the most of my meat. I have all my fruit and some of the potatoes.*"

The next letter is written to Joseph J. Hitch from Little Berry Edwards dated April 6 from Camp Roberts[105]. Little Berry is only 18 years old when he pens this letter and, serving in the same unit as Young Hitch, he is Mary Hitch's half-brother. It is a rather mundane letter but it does tell us a little of what is happening with the 16th regiment, "*I have nothing to write more than we have move again and we have drand new guns and I hav shot mine three times and I think that hit will dought to depend on.*" They have been issued new guns and he seems pleased with them. Next he tells Joseph about the

---

[102] Appendix, Item XLIV.
[103] Little Berry Edwards enlisted with Company I, 16th South Carolina Volunteers on Feb 11 1863 for three years. He is shown as present on all muster rolls from Jan 1863 through Aug 1864 except when sick in the hospital on the May/Jun 1863 roll. He became part of Company D, Consolidated 16th and 24th Carolina that formed on Apr 9 1865.
[104] Matt Garrett (1844-1863) is the son of William Edwin Garrett, "W.E. Garrett" in Hitch's letters.
[105] Appendix, Item XLV.

excitement he has recently had, *"J.J. I have seen a rattle snake five feet long hit had eleven rattles and a button. I tell you what hit was one."* Ah, the fascination of teenage boys and snakes!

Young Hitch's next letter is addressed to his sons, dated Apr 13 1863 from *"Camp Robberts Slands Island, So. Ca."*[106] From its initial content, we gather that Young had promised to have a subscription of a newspaper sent to Joseph but had not been able to get it taken care of quite yet. He writes, *"The paper that I talked of ordering for you I have never attended to. I stopt but a short time at Columbia. If I knew exactly how to write to the Editor I would try to get it sent to you. You ask Mr. McNeely to write to the Editor to send you the paper. You ask ma to give you the money for it. You must send the money before you can get the paper. And if the Cola. does not grant you the favor let me know & I will then see what I can do. I hope you will try to read all you can in them. Hannah Moors Tracts they are verry good to read."* He is introducing Joseph to more worldly events rather than just those surrounding his immediate environs near the Hitch farm in Laurens County. He seems to be directing him especially to a regular column by a writer named Hannah More. More (1745-1833) was an English woman who wrote on moral and religious subjects, and as a practical philanthropist.

More and other members of a group of literary individuals in Clapham, England produced the *Cheap Repository Tracts*. These were a series of readable moral tales, uplifting ballads, and collections of readings, prayers and sermons. Hannah More was to write and edit many of the tracts, while others raised the money for printing and distribution (the tracts were sold at a little under cost). The first was published in March 1795 – and last some three years later. The tracts were published monthly – and overall sold in the millions – with over 100 total that were produced – fifty of them by Hannah More[107]. In this instance, Young Hitch is either referring his son to reprints of More's articles in the newspaper or to a book of More's tracts. This fits within Hitch's propensity to instill moral education to his sons as he writes from the camps, to suggest reading of an author who promotes such values.

Next, there is some news about activities around camp, *"I was detailed this morning to chop firewood with two other men from company I & by being so detailed it clears me from drill untill dress parade this Evening. We was gone about two hours only but the gnats allmost eat us up. I had to work to keep them from Eating me entirely up. Lucian I have drawed a pair of shoes today the moste of the men drawed shoes today."* Chopping wood was the chore of the day and it relieved the men who helped with it from having to participate in the daily drilling but, it did not excuse them from an evening parade in their dress uniforms. Also, we see familiar indications of April in the south as the gnats and flies become major pests!

The subject of the letter then shifts to what could be any typical American father giving instruction to his sons on life, *"...Above all use no bad words, Joseph, and ask your brother to do the same if he loves his Pa...Hurah Boys & be little men if you are left to shift & no one to assist you. I hope if you both do your duty as you should that you will be blessed with help from on high. So be industrious & good as fare you know how & are able, if you are not able immediately you will be some day."* Sound advice that would

---

106 Appendix, Item XLVI.

107 "Hannah More: Sunday schools, education and youth work," *http://infed.org/mobi/hannah-more-sunday-schools-education-and-youth-work/*, 2015.

surely rather have both parties experience in-person, instead of absent over a distance, during a time of war.

The next letter comes on April 18-19 from Young to his wife, Mary Hitch and son Joseph[108]. The bulk of the letter is about the health of himself and his unit:

> *"...today finds me rather unwell but up. The pains pester me a great deal last night & today. Scruggs & Mat are both well. Berry is grunting with his leg. M.R. Garrett is not well but better than he has been. J.J. Brown was taken sudenly sick the other day & was taken to the hospital. I have not heard from him today...I heard from Jerry Brown yesterday. He was verry bad but the doctor thinks there is some little hopes of him recovering. I thought yesterday awhile that I was about to have a severe attack of the bowel complaint. But fortunately for me it has stopt for the present. My mess are all on foot but Brown. I dont know how long it will remain."*

We see that most are well or with fairly minor complaints except Jerry Brown (his "*mess are all on foot but Brown*"). Hitch describes him as "*suddenly sick*" and "*very bad but the doctor thinks there is some little hopes of him recovering.*" Today, we can find out more from the official records about what became of Jerry Jackson Brown. He was the son of Oliver Perry Brown (1822-1855) and Amanda E. Hughes[109] (1824-1913) and born in Laurens County in 1845. The O.P. Brown family is listed in the 1850 in and among the community of Scruggs, Garrett, Gilbert, etc. and, would be very familiar to Hitch and his family as well.

He enlisted as a Private, Company I, 16th South Carolina Regiment, on Mar 12 1863. In the muster records, he is listed as absent almost immediately in the muster rolls from March 1863 and lasting through March 1864 when he was discharged due to disability on Mar 24 1864. At that point, he owed the Confederate States $100.37, which he paid. His Mar 4 1864 discharge papers state he was age 18, 5'-8", blue eyes, fair complexion, and light hair. He had lost all hearing due to a protracted case of "typhoid fever of 9 months duration" and, he had no education and was declared unfit for duty anywhere in the service. Indeed, as Young Hitch described in his letter, J.J. Brown was in "very bad" health.

Young Hitch continues his letter on April 19 to address his son, Joseph, and provide counseling to him about the farm:

> *"Glad to hear your wheat & rye is looking well. I hope it may please God to spare you & your ma & brother so as to get it saved, if it should not meet with no accident before the time to save it. If your wheat comes good it will be a great help out to you in the bread line. Your barley to will make you coffee. That I have tried done fine I tell you. That will save your bread for you can not eat that in bread & anything to save bread. Joseph the eggs you spoke of come pretty safe. There was about a dozen broke but not lost. There was a few broke so ar to be of no use. But I had a good look to what Mr Vaughn had. He got to camp a Tuesday evening & his boxes landed today*

---

108 Appendix, Item XLVII.

109 Amanda (Hughes) Brown is sister to William H. Hughes who served in various capacities with Young Hitch over the years.

> *in a verry bad condition. Mr Vaughn toted out about as mutch pies and chickens as he could in his arms & threw it a way. His eggs was broken up shockingly."*

"Mr. Vaughn" is mentioned in this correspondence for the first time and he and his wife will appear in several more letters in the future. This is referring to Richard Harrison Vaughn (1812-1894) and the Vaughns were very close neighbors of the Edwards and Hitch families in Laurens County and two of his sons, Toliver and Paschal Vaughn, were serving with Hitch in Company I[110]. Next, we see Young and his son trading ideas and thoughts about the farm. The wheat and rye, while in trouble earlier in the season due to weather, seem to be recovering. An oddity in Hitch's words comes when he writes, *"Your barley to will make you coffee. That I have tried, done fine I tell you."* Not much used as such in the U.S. in modern times but, coffee substitutes were often depended upon when real coffee was not available. In the south during the Civil War, coffee was very scarce and so other means were used to make a similar beverage. In this case, Young instructs his son to use barley for his coffee and he has "tried (it), (and) done fine (with it,) I tell you." Coffee was just another commodity that had become scarce during the war, especially in the south, and prices skyrocketed so the coffee lover was forced to find suitable substitutes:

> *"In 1832 President Andrew Jackson ordered coffee and sugar substituted for the daily liquor ration in the military, thereby introducing into soldier's lives a habit that helped them through the difficult times of the Civil War. During the war, speculators bought up all the coffee for Northern armies in order to charge the U.S. government a high price, but agents in England purchased ship-loads and prevented the action. A Southern woman described the shock in home life when President Lincoln blockaded Confederate seaports on 19 April 1861. By 1862 coffee supplies were exhausted. Coffee prices escalated, often higher in areas densely populated, invaded or occupied by the Union. Price per pound in 1861 was $3.00; in 1862, $1.50 to $4.00; in 1863, $5.00 to $30.00. By 1864, coffee was going for $12.00 to $60.00! ... Acorns,* ***barley****, beans, beets, bran, chestnuts, chicory, corn meal, cotton seeds, dandelion, okra seeds, sweet potatoes, peas, peanuts, persimmons, rice, rye sorghum molasses, sugar cane seeds, watermelon seeds and wheat berries were parched, dried, browned or roasted to make ersatz coffee."*[111]

Note, from this reference, that coffee prices increased dramatically from $3/pound in 1861 to upwards of $30/pound in 1863 and, compare that with Young Hitch's grocery list from 1858 earlier in this book when he bought 7 pounds of coffee in Greenville for $1.00! No wonder people were looking for substitutes. In the Savannah (Georgia) Republican newspaper of Nov 27 1862, we see a whole article on substitutes for coffee that are claimed to be "perfectly counterfeited...except in its stimulating qualities":

---

[110] Private Toliver R. Vaughn (c1840-1864) was son of Richard Harrison and Mary Ann (Garrett) Vaughn of Laurens County, SC. He was brother to fellow Company I soldier, Sergeant Paschal D. Vaughn (1842-1865). According to census records, the Vaughn's lived in very close proximity to the Edwards and Hitch families in 1850 and 1860. The "Mr. and Mrs. Vaughn" that Young Hitch refers to in several of his letters are Richard and Mary Vaughn who had the two sons in Company I (Hitch writes on one of his letters, May 1 1863, "Favord by R.H. Vaughn"). Sgt. Henry G. Vaughn of the unit was probably a relative as well, but the exact connection is unknown.

[111] "The Cape Fear Civil War Round Table, That Indispensable Civil War Coffee!" Ann Hertzler, *www.cfcwrt.com.*

> *"Practical Hints for Hard Times.*
> *"What man has done, man may do."*
> *NO. IV.—FOOD.*
>
> *13. SUBSTITUTES FOR COFFEE.—Except in its stimulating qualities, and its peculiar and delicate aroma, coffee can be so perfectly counterfeited as to defy detection, by mixing together [illegible] the following substitutes in such [illegible] that the coffee taste of all of them shall predominate, and the peculiar flavor of no one of them shall be perceived: viz: Rye, wheat, barley (scalded and then parched,) okra seed, rice (parched black, but not ground,) sweet potatoes (cut into ribbons, or into dice, dried in the sun and then parched,) corn grits (parched to a dark brown,) sweet acorns, chiccory (parched brown, then broken and ground.) These should be parched separately, and then combined in about equal proportions, or in such proportion as experiment shall decide to be necessary. If possible, a little coffee should be combined, simply for truth's sake. The best critic can scarcely distinguish between the spurious compound and the real coffee."*[112]

Here we see that Young Hitch's barley coffee would be made from grain that has been "scalded and then parched" before grinding and being brewed and Hitch liked it very well, it seems. Americans and their coffee cannot be separated even during hard times, and if not available, their ingenuity will arise to find suitable alternatives until times get better!

Young writes again, immediately, to his wife on Apr 19 1863 from Adams Run[113]. Some pleasantries ensued in the early part of the letter and Hitch seemed to be in a very good mood due to having feasted on a substantial dinner. He writes almost jokingly, "*After eating a verry hearty dinner of chicken & dumplings & then standing two hours immediately afterwards, you may guess that I am very warm at the present time. Yes, me and Tol Vaughn got a splendid dinner & have all but M.R. Garrett eat verry hearty of it. What will be the result of our feast I don't know. But I hope nothing serious.*" He and Toliver Vaughn partook of the feast but Miles Garrett did not, presumably because he was still ill. In Hitch's description, one can practically smell the "rib-sticking" chicken and dumplings dinner as it must have smelled on that warm mid-spring day in South Carolina.

After a brief snippet about the warm and dry weather, Hitch then tells us of the latest happenings with his unit in camp:

> *"...It is said the Yankeys are leaving for some other point. Some think that we will leave after a while for some other point. And some think differently, that we will remain on the coast whitch looks reasonable. Enough. it is said furloughing will begin soon, probably by the 1st of May next. We have drawed nothing but guns and (_rings) & some shoes. We have new harness out & yet(?) so fare we have no knapsacks or canteens yet. if we had them we would be harnesst in full."*

---

[112] Savannah Republican (Georgia), November 27, 1862, page 1, column 3.
[113] Appendix, Item XLVIII.

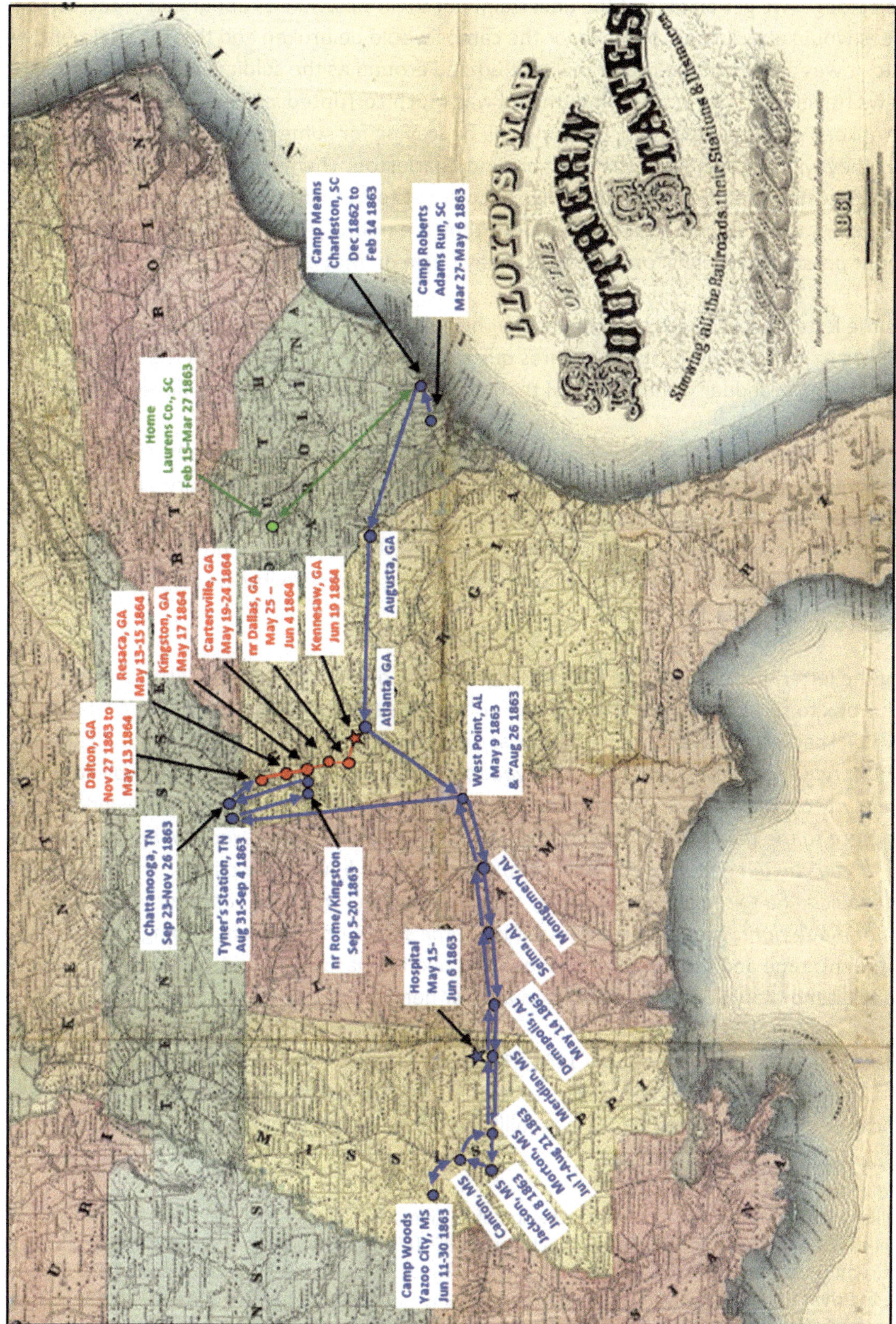

Figure 10 - Route of Young H.E. Hitch and Company I, 16th South Carolina Volunteer Infantry, 1862-1864, as depicted on a portion of "Lloyd's Map of the Southern States", 1861. Blue lines are 1863 and red are 1864 up until the time Hitch dies in battle. (Michael G. Hitch map, adapted from the Lloyd's map, 1861)

From this passage, we get an idea of the uncertainty of the times. Stories abounded in the camps that the Yankees would attack soon, or move, or the camps would be broken and the 16th regiment would march, etc. It was all part of the rumor mill that buzzed around as the soldiers waited in their camps where news traveled fast by word-of-mouth and was much corrupted in the process. Hitch has heard that the Yankees will leave and then, his camp will be leaving for some other unknown destination. But, others say they will stay to defend the coast around Charleston. Then, with a terse "*Enough*," he seems somewhat disgusted that there is no definitive answer yet to their destination, after which, he resigns that they are not ready to move yet anyway since they are not fully equipped. Hitch also adds a few words about possible furloughs for leave which may begin on May 1.

He closes the letter quickly since he exclaims that his tent is getting hot and he wants to lie in the shade before he has to go on guard post. He inquires quickly about Mary's garden and the corn and asks her to notify her father ("grandpa," John Edwards) that his son, Berry Edwards, is getting along well.

Young writes to Mary next on Apr 25 1863 from Camp Roberts and first informs her that his health has been rather feeble the past couple of days but "not serious."[114] He has read Mary's letters from April 20, 21 and 23 (these do not survive) and was excited to hear from her except for the fact that she had not been feeling well either. He expects Lieutenant (William S.) Thackston[115] to be heading home soon and wanted to get a letter to her via him. He then pauses his letter to see what he can get into "the box" that will be delivered to her via Thackston.

Resuming the letter, he tells Mary he has put leggings, one pair of shoes and a "little bunch" of sugar for her into his box to send home. He also states that "*Scruggs & Edwards(,) Nelson*[116] *& M.R. Garrett*," along with LT Thackston, have items in the box as well. He describes why he is sending the shoes and leggings, "*Mary, I send these shoes to you for you to swap or make the most of them you can. They are badly made, my old ones will do me more service than those. If you could se see (a) Taylor he can by putting a piece to the toe of those leggins, make you a nice pair of guaters lace them up on the inside of the ankle. If you can get enough soles to bottom them you can have a nice pair for yourself & the shoes besides. If you can go to see Lieut. Thackston, he can show you some that has been made in camp but they are not made right. They should be sowed up at the side & open in front.*" Things are very scarce in the south at this time and the recycling of shoes and textiles was paramount to survival. Young closes by saying he will send Mary $65.00 via Thackston and for her "*to do the best you can with it.*"

Six days later, on Friday the first of May 1863, Hitch writes to his wife from Camp Roberts "Slands Island, So. Ca."[117] These researchers have had very little luck trying to identify the location of "Slands Island." Even the experts of South Carolina Civil War military history do not know for sure. There is some

---

[114] Appendix, Item XLIX.

[115] 1LT William S. Thackston (1839-1910) was the son of William Jesse Turner and Harriett G. (Howard) Thackston of Greenville, SC and brother to Thomas M. Thackston (1839-1896), also of Company I. Harriett (Howard) Thackston remarried after William J.T. Thackston died in 1840, to Richard Baldwin who died in 1853. She married a third time to Private Andrew Jackson Allison, fellow Company I soldier with her two sons, William and Thomas!

[116] Of these four men, we know William Berry Scruggs, Little Berry Edwards and Miles Rainwater Garrett but "Nelson" is new to Young Hitch's correspondence. In the list of Company I soldiers, we find Privates W.B. and T.B. Nelson, probably one of which Hitch is referring.

[117] Appendix, Item L.

conjecture about its location but the exact spot seems to be lost to time[118]. Young had been fairly seriously sick with gastro-intestinal ills causing bleeding and severe pains. But, he has gotten better as of the morning of May 1. Not much news of the unit is forthcoming except that there had been a general inspection the day before. News about the possibility of leave furloughs has diminished from hopeful to not very promising as Hitch indicates only one "well man" got one and he believes that is because the man's father was not well and he had not been home in over nine or ten months.

Young also believes that fellow Company I soldier, Richard Farrow, will get a sick furlough and maybe even a discharge. Farrow's health had been *"verry bad & no likelihood of its being much better."* The records show Private Richard M. Farrow of Company I as being "sick in hospital" in the muster rolls for May/Jun 1863. He is then shown as "absent without leave" for the Jul/Aug and Sep/Oct musters. However, he returns to "present" status for the Nov/Dec 1863 musters. After another brief stint in the hospital in late February 1864, he shows as present for the remaining musters through August 1864. Richard was born in 1830 and lived to after 1900[119] so he survived his bad health during the war and lived a long life.

No other news of his unit is offered in this letter but, Hitch does give us a description of the food he is having and it seems rather good, *"Mary, the provisions you sent got to us yesterday Friday in time for dinner all right or near it. We took dinner of the hen and corn pone. Supper of eggs boiled with butter and corn pone and coffee. Today breakfast fried corn pone and coffee. Dinner fried shellots & light wheat pone, a most excellent mess."* Wheat and corn pone and shallots for carbohydrates with eggs and chicken as protein – as Young describes, *"a most excellent mess."* Young closes his letter with a couple of "Hurrahs!" to encourage his sons to work the farm well and *"get your bread honestly."* He particularly tells Joseph not to lose heart as his corn will not grow as fast on the old land where it was currently planted as it would if the land were fresh. This is classic Young Hitch acting as a long distance farmer and using his sons as his own hands to tend his land from afar.

Young writes another letter "Confidential" to Mary dated May 1[120], evidently to inform her of a letter from April 28 that he received from A.Y. Garrett[121] which does not survive. Garrett is planning to run his liquor still that summer and he wants to either buy the fruit for it from the Hitch farm or, barter for it by sharing the proceeds from the still. Young leaves the final decision to Mary Hitch but, he explains in more detail what is being offered and what benefit the family might gain:

---

[118] Rollis Smith, Lieutenant Commander of Camp 36, 16th Regiment SC Volunteers and Life Member, Sons of Confederate Veterans writes in 2015, "My research shows that Company I was at Camp Roberts between March and April of 1863. Two possible locations for this Camp are Sand Island, Georgetown County, South Carolina. This location is on the ocean about halfway between McClellanville and Georgetown. The other possibility is Sandy Island, South Carolina located near Murrell's Inlet. It will require more research to define which location is correct. Records do show Company I at Camp Roberts but so far I have not seen any document that narrows the location."

[119] He is probably the R.M. Farrow who died Sep 15 1904 and is buried in Pelzer Cemetery, Anderson County, SC.

[120] Appendix, Item LI.

[121] Archibald Young Garrett had served with Hitch in the 1st Corps, 9th South Carolina Reserves. He had left the service in February 1863 when Hitch joined the 16th SCVI. He did rejoin the service but not until Aug 1 1863, so he would have been home in Laurens County at the time Hitch and he exchange correspondence here. In Aug 1863, Garrett enlisted as a Private with Company I of the 5th South Carolina State Troops where he served till Jul 1864 when he left and hooked up with Company E, 4th Battalion South Carolina Reserves, serving there till Dec 31 1864.

> *Mary I rec. a letter the 28th of this Inst. from Mr. A.Y. Garrett. I see from that letter he is aiming to still this summer. He proposes to by your fruit & do all the gathering, or still on the share, and wishes to know of me whitch way I had rather do. he says that he wants to still all that he can for it's about all the chance to make money now. Mary, I want you to do what you think to be the best. I can't tell you now what would be best. Only this fare if there is money to be made you and the children should have the best right to it. If the fruit should be good and you could, you ought to try for it will be valuable and your pigs can eat a heap of them. My notion is that the fruit has been so injured with frost that it will drop off. But I shall not tell Garrett what I will do until I get an answer from you & you need not be in a hurry untill you can see whether there is any fruit to dispose of. He proffers to pay ten dollars per stand. And if I had that big jug here, I could get more than ten for one quart. I haven't the least dout of it getting $50.00 per gallon to retail it out. Mary, don't treat everything that passes for it is too costly. If you can sell any & wish to do so at a good price, do so, but keep some for yourself untill you see if there is any new made."*

Hitch then takes the time to say a few good words about Mary's half-brother, Billy Edwards, "*Mary, Billy is doing tolerable well. His health is very good. You may tell his wife that I found Billy more of a moral man than I expected to. Also tell her that I don't recollect of hearing him swear any since I come to camp. But there is a sight of profane language used here.*" Camp life is full of profanity as one might expect but Young Hitch does not like it and Billy Edwards does not partake of it, at least not around Hitch. Hitch also tells Mary that he now knows who stole his brandy, the "rogue" from a few letters back, though he does not name the person directly in his letter. He is evidently still stewing over that event.

In other news, Young relates to Mary, for the first time, his trip to camp after being home between his stints with the 1st Corps, 9th Reserves and mustering in with the 16th regiment. He writes:

> *Mary, I don't think that I ever told you of paying my fare from Greenville to Columbia. The reason was Capt. Stradly had given orders to the conductors not to rec. transportation unless printed and the fare was $4.25 and that the quartermaster would refund it over to me. But unfortunately, being green on the road, I did not have him to endorse on the back of my paper. Then I neglected to cut the part at the top off from the other. So when the second conductor came around and waked me up I handed the paper to him and he took both the first and second part. The third past me from the Citty to the run. The error was all in the first part and if I had been smart that should not happened.*

This was the time from Mar 27-30 1863 and he had paid a fare to ride the train from Greenville to Columbia of $4.25, expecting to get reimbursed by the army. However, since he was not familiar with "*being...on the road*," he forgot to keep his receipt and have the conductor sign his papers. So, he is thinking that he might not get reimbursed for the first leg of his journey back to Adams Run. All told, for his fare and cargo, he paid $6.30, part of which he hopes to get refunded from the unit's Quartermaster and a part from a gentleman for whom Young carried a "box."

Hitch then tells Mary about what has happened to two of his Company I colleagues. The first is about John Graden[122], *"who has had the luck to get everything burnt night before last... Graden was his house and home that got burnt leaving wife & children out of doors."* Evidently, a collection was taken up in the Company to help offset some of Graden's costs and Hitch gave 50 cents to the cause. However, Jesse Knight[123] was not so rewarded when he *"made him a little smoke to keep the gnats off & went to sleep & dropt his pocket book or rather it shift out of his pocket into this little fire whitch burnt pocket book and sixty dollars he said burnt."* There was no charitable collection for Jesse, however, as *"Knight will not get any mad up for they say he won't send hardly any to his wife."* Jesse must not have been too popular with his Company I mates. Hitch then shares some religious epiphany he has been having:

> *Confidential*
> *Mary, I have never dreamed of seeing you or of being at home since I come in to service this time. Mary, you say you pray for me dayly. I hope you will continue to still pray on for me. I try to pray for my self & my family. The past week has been a trying one with me for I have suffered severely. But, Mary, I have the New Testament to read and the more I read it the more I delight in reading of it. I find in it sutch rich promises. It appears more plain the more I read it. I see in that little volume that it is best that we should have trials and difficulties to undergo, whitch I believe. Mary, I believe that the war and my afflictions will be an advantage to me in a coming day. Difficulties and trials cause us to feel more sensibly our dependence in the Almighty.*

One almost feels guilty reading this very personal passage that Young Hitch shares with his wife. But, it does tell more of the trials of life in the camps and being away from the family that many soldiers were feeling at the time. His renewed interest in the Bible is strong and to him, *"It appears more plain the more"* he reads it. He also notes that the Bible expects us to have *"trials and difficulties"* and Young sees that his trials away at war will be an advantage *"in a coming day."* Hitch ends the letter with a note to his son Joseph who has been despairing over wanting to see his father, *"Joseph, gladly would I comply with your request if I could see any chance. You surely do not want to see Pa worse than he wants to see you. It is said distress furloughs have started. If so I hope well furloughs will start soon but the whole company will get off before me, but perhaps I, if no accident, will get to come the last of the summer or first of the fall."* We see that Hitch misses his family as much as his family misses him but, there seems little chance for a visit to the farm until at least the end of the summer or early fall 1863.

May 3-4 and 6 bring two more letters from Hitch to Mary, the first from "Coleton District" (sic, Colleton County, SC) and the second from Camp Roberts[124]. He has not moved from his location so this gives more indication where Camp Roberts was situated – near Adams Run but in Colleton County. Young is still having some health issues, so badly that he has *"done no duty since last Sunday morning untill this morning I went out on company inspection."* When he wrote those words, it was Sunday, May 3, so his

---

[122] This is John D. Graden (Graydon), son of Sterling and Elizabeth Graden. In the 1860 census, John Graden is listed in Dublin, Greenville County, SC as age 30 with wife Jane (age 24) and son John (age 3). In 1850, he is listed as age 17 in Laurens County, putting his birth year at 1830/33. By the time his house burns in 1863, John Graden is supporting a wife and at least one son.

[123] Jesse Knight was son of Benjamin (Berry) and Elizabeth (Vaughn) Knight of Laurens County. Not much else is known of him other than he was born in about 1840 in South Carolina.

[124] Appendix, Item LII and LIII.

absence from duty had been a whole week. With most of his issues being bowel troubles with bleeding, it seems he has been dealing with dysentery which was the number one disease that produced fatalities during the Civil War. The following segment discusses the causes and impacts of disease during the war.

DISEASE DURING THE CIVIL WAR

By many estimates, there were over 680,000 who died during the Civil War. Of those, about 2/3rds, or over 400,000 died of disease. Besides the more primitive medical and hygiene practices at the time, the reasons many soldiers became afflicted with disease include[125]:

- Poor hygiene – soldiers didn't get a daily shower and, they often used the same few pots to cook food and to boil lice-infested clothing.
- Garbage in the camp – trash accumulated around the camps and, with it, the unhealthy conditions it would bring.
- Filth in camp sinks – Latrines/outhouses were often dug too close to streams, which also happened to be the camp water supply. Water contamination was the source of much disease.
- Overcrowding – consistent, close contact with other soldiers caused diseases to spread rapidly
- Exposure to weather – limited shelter in times of extreme hot and cold; rain, sleet, snow, dust and mud. Exposure to the elements lowers the body's ability to resist disease
- Improper and inadequate diet - staple foods were hardtack for Union soldiers and cornbread for Confederates. Fresh fruit and vegetables were rare. Soldiers received some meat, but, often, it spoiled or too full of preservatives to eat.
- Bugs - Flies, mosquitoes, ticks, lice, maggots, and fleas were abundant and carried disease.
- Lack of medical knowledge - people did not yet know about "germs" and how they were spread. Doctors didn't wash their hands before operating, or clean tools after each patient.
- Lack of doctors/surgeons - There were too few surgeons to handle the huge numbers of sick and wounded.
- Lack of immunity to diseases - many rural soldiers became sick because for the first time they were in a large group of people and had no immunity to diseases such as chickenpox, smallpox, scarlet fever, measles, mumps, and whooping cough so, these epidemics ran rampant through many regiments.
- Impure water – water was usually provided from nearby streams or springs which could be contaminated with camp waste of just contain parasites or other matter that would cause disease.

From the above, we can see many of the conditions that Young Hitch would have faced during his time in the camps and on the battlefield. At this particular time, in 1863, he was stationed near Adams Run, SC which was situated in a low, swampy area ripe for catching a disease of some sort or another from insects or other soldiers in close proximity. A soldier might get the disease transmitted by a mosquito or flea and then, being in close quarters, the disease would rapidly spread among the men who would have low immunity since they had not been exposed to those pathogens in the past in their more typical rural setting, spread out and away from others.

---

[125] This list is adopted in part from *www.civilwar.org* and the National Museum of Civil War Medicine.

This was a time when vaccinations were still very much in their infancy as a medical tool so, in general, the soldiers were at the mercy of whichever "bug" was going around the camps at the time. Common diseases in the camps were dysentery, typhoid fever, yellow fever, ague[126], malaria, pneumonia, consumption (tuberculosis), small pox, chicken pox, scarlet fever, measles (rubella), mumps, whooping cough, etc. Dysentery, the illness Young Hitch seems to be suffering from here in early May 1863, is caused by a bacterial infection and practically every soldier contracted it at one time or another. Accounts vary but, statistics seem to indicate that upwards of 10% of the soldiers who suffered with dysentery, died from it.

Returning to Young's letters of May 3-6 1863, he informs Mary that he is sending his trunk home with "Mr. Vaughn" containing the items, "*...Williams flask with four other bottles, tickets on them. Also one pair of drawers to work up as you think proper. If you have no other use for them, you can hang them up and put seed beans this fall in them. Be sure you save them*." He then asks his wife to send back "*a patch or two to patch with after awhile. I don't need them now but will by & by.*" It is interesting and common that the soldiers would send a "box" or trunk back and forth to home and exchange items with their families as required. In this case, Hitch is sending some bottles and old underwear and asks his wife to return some patches, presumably to repair his clothing, when she gets the chance. He indicates that she can use his old underwear to dry and store "seed beans" if they are good for no other use to Mary!

By May 6, we see that Young's health has gotten much better as he is "*Enjoying tolerable health at this time*." It is timely because the 16th regiment and others in the camp are packing and ready to move. They will be taking the train to Vicksburg, Mississippi.

Some background of the impending Vicksburg campaign is in order here. In late April 1863, the Federal forces under General Ulysses Grant conducted a surprise landing along the Mississippi River south of Vicksburg at Bruinsburg, MS and even waged a small battle with Confederates at Port Gibson on May 1. Before going to Vicksburg, however, he headed towards Jackson, MS to attend to General Joseph Johnston's Confederate forces that had been instructed to approach from the east in an effort to aid General John Pemberton caught in the city of Vicksburg. This is why Young Hitch and his compatriots were headed to Vicksburg as he states in his letter of May 6 1863. He was part of Johnston's Army of Relief to come to the rescue of Pemberton.

By May 9, Young Hitch writes another letter to Mary as they were on the move, from West Point, Alabama "*at or on the Ala. side of the Chattahoocha River*."[127] His health is better but he is still worn out from being sick and then embarking on a long traveling expedition. He explains to Mary his itinerary so far in his train journey and, what is to come:

> *"Last Wednesday 3 p.m. we left Camp Robberts for Vicksburg, Miss. We got aboard the car at the run after a warm march of seven miles about dusk. Arived at the Savannah Depot, Charleston about 11 or 12 o'clock the next day. We marched over to the So. Car. Depot & at 4 p.m. we left*

---

[126] General definition of ague is fever and the chills, can be accompanied with malaria.

[127] Appendix, Item LIV.

> *for Augusta Ga, arived there 11 a.m. and left there at 2 p.m. for Atlanta, Ga, arived there at day break this morning Saturday. Left in an hour or two for West Point 2 p.m. at whitch point we are at. We have put up our tents. How long to stay I can't tell. If we go on to Vicksburg there is two other regiments to go before ours. The 24th South Carolina Regt of Volunteers and 46th Ga Volunteers are here at this place. I heard it said since we got here that there was as good a chance to get to go back to Augusta as to go on to Vicksburg or Jackson, Miss. Where we will go and when we will go, I can't say. Our regt. all are opposed to going to the west."*

We note that Hitch mentions the 24th South Carolina and the 46th Georgia infantries with the 16th at West Point, AL. At this point in time, all three of these regiments, plus the 8th Georgia and T.B. Ferguson's South Carolina Battery of Light Artillery, were part of States Rights Gist's brigade. In May 1863, Gist and Brig. Gen. William H.T. Walker were commanding two brigades of South Carolina troops to reinforce Confederate forces under General Joe Johnston as he pressed westward towards Vicksburg[128] (photographs of Johnston, Walker and Gist are presented in Chapter 6). After arriving in Mississippi, Walker was promoted to major general and Gist's brigade was placed in Walker's division and this is where Hitch and the 16th South Carolina Regiment were situated in the order of battle at the Vicksburg campaign as part of Johnston's Army of Relief.[129]

We again hear from Young Hitch on May 14 1863, this time from McDowell's Landing, AL, very near to Demopolis, AL[130]. He takes the time to tell Mary and the boys of his trip to that point, "*When I wrote to you last I was at West Point. On Monday last we left there for Montgomery at 10 a.m., arived at Montgomery at dark there at 12 p.m. Took the steamboat down the Coosy River to Selma, arived there 8 or 9 a.m. There took the car for Demapolis at 3 p.m.*" Train, steamboat and train again in a relatively short period of time, a very coordinated logistical movement of the southern forces towards Mississippi. He details the journey even more, with mileage traveled:

> *"We are in one hundred and fifty miles of Jackson, Miss...*
> *Joseph and Lucian, I will give you the places where we stopt and shifted cars and boats.*
> *Charleston to Augusta 136.*
> *Augusta to Atlanta 171*
> *Atlanta to West Point 86*
> *West Point to Montgomery 87*
> *Montgomery to Selma 110*
> *Selma to Demapolis 50*
> *Selma to McDowels Landing 4*
> *We are now 644 miles from Charleston If I could see you I could tell you a heap more than I can write to you. Whether I ever shall have the pleasure of conversing with you God only knows..."*

---

[128] The 16th and 24th regiments joined up on May 19 1863 in Canton, MS; Ref: South Carolina's Military Organizations During the War Between the States; Volume IV, Statewide Units, Militia and Reserves, Robert S. Seigler, The History Press, Charleston, SC, 2008; page 86.
[129] National Park Service, Vicksburg National Military Park website, "Order of Battle – Confederate."
[130] Appendix, Item LV.

This was the most distance Young Hitch had traveled at any time in his entire life to date and he was eager to share it with his sons by letter. He was also impressed with the rich farmland in the area and made sure his sons knew of it, *"Boys, I have seen some verry rich land in the Ala and south corn fields I never did see. I have seen hundred of acres of corn that the corn was as high as your shoulders, A.L., and green as poisen. & wheat that will do to cut next week. If it is a good crop year there will be an abundance of bread stuffs made this year, no cotton being planted hardly."* It is notable that Hitch observes that cotton was not being planted. Cotton production had steadily suffered during the war due to Union blockades (no place to ship it to produce revenue). In 1861, cotton production was about 4.5 million bales, in 1862 it had dropped to 1.5 million and, by 1863, barely 0.5 million bales.

Hitch was excited that, apparently, the journey would not be for naught as he states, *"A part of our regt. is gone on & the rest of us should of been gone if it had not of been for a little accident...From what I can learn we are going where there will be something to do. Great fighting expected to come off soon in the State of Miss."* At the time, the regiment and what was then called the Army of the Department of Mississippi and Eastern Louisiana, commanded by General Johnston, was expecting to fight Grant's Federal forces from behind as he approached Vicksburg. Hitch realizes that, if they do get into a fight, then he may not come out alive when he pens, *"There is nine chances to one for me never to get home, yet I still hope to be spared to see you all again on earth."*

Young mentions the fact that he has encountered some Yankees in his travels as well when he shares with the boys, *"Boys, I have seen lots of the Yankey but they was all prisoners. We meet them every day, bring them to Atlanta & Augusta, Ga. I have heard them talk. Some of them say we will whip them while others say we never will."* No fighting yet, but Yankee prisoners seen, nonetheless. Note that, this being May 1863, it was before the infamous Andersonville POW camp opened in Georgia in February 1864 and, prisoners were being detained in Atlanta and Augusta, GA. Hitch also relates to his youngest son, *"Lucian, yesterday I saw a little Yankey boy hardly as large as you sitting by the side of his pa eating of a cracker and a piece of raw meat that one of our men give to him. Him and his pa was pasengers on a boat when they was taken prisoners,"* and this prompts him to get into his father mode once again:

> *"Boys, I hope you will be good boys in every respect. Always keep it in your mind that you have to die & leave this world & there is a hell for you to shun & heaven to seek for. So if you wish to go to heaven, you must be good boys. Work & do the best you can for your ma as your pa is deprived of helping of her. Be good to her. It is your duty to do so & I hope that you both love your ma so as to honor & respect her as long as you all live."*

Finally, we note Hitch's trouble with riding "the cars." He had a rough time of it on a train on his passage from McDowell's Landing, AL to Meridian, MS as he writes, *"Our traveling on the train yester & last night was the roughest I ever had. The road was rough & they stald frequently."* The railways were very important during the Civil War for the logistics of getting troops and supplies around to locations where they were most needed. The northern army was always pulling up track, destroying rail cars and just generally trying to disrupt rail service for the south in any way possible. The following from the Civil War Trust describes the railroad situation in the South during the war very well:

"The Civil War is the first war in which railroads were a major factor. The 1850s had seen enormous growth in the railroad industry so that by 1861, 22,000 miles of track had been laid in the Northern states and 9,500 miles in the South. The great rail centers in the South were Chattanooga, Atlanta, and most important, Richmond. Very little track had yet been laid west of the Mississippi...the Confederate government was slow to recognize the importance of the railroads in the conflict. By September 1863, the Southern railroads were in bad shape. They had begun to deteriorate very soon after the outset of the war, when many of the railroad employees headed north to join the Union war efforts. Few of the 100 railroads that existed in the South prior to 1861 were more than 100 miles in length. The South had always been less enthusiastic about the railroad industry than the North; its citizens preferred an agrarian living and left the mechanical jobs to men from the Northern states. The railroads existed, they believed, solely to get cotton to the ports... Once the war began, the Union blockade of the Atlantic and Gulf ports was very effective in shutting off that supply. Locomotives and tracks began to wear out. By 1863 a quarter of the South's locomotives needed repairs and the speed of train travel in the South had dropped to only 10 miles an hour (from 25 miles an hour in 1861)."

This matches what Young Hitch had observed in May 1863 that the railroads were in bad shape. Additionally, travel by rail was not the luxury we tend to think of as most modern-day trains offer. The quarters for southern troops on a train were meager and very cramped. In 1863, there was a derailment in Mississippi west of Meridian of a train carrying many Confederate troops that caused many injuries. **Figure 11** shows a lithograph of the 1863 train derailment in Mississippi and the cramped quarters to which troops were subjected when riding in the "cars."

However, the railroad remained of paramount importance during the war on both sides and both armies would continue to sabotage and capture what they could from the other throughout the conflict. In 1863, when General Johnston abandoned Jackson, MS, the Union captured 90 locomotives and hundreds of railroad cars in his wake, probably some of the very same equipment Hitch had ridden on to get to Mississippi in the first place[131].

At some point in time after Young wrote the preceding letter and the time he writes the next two on the very next day, he has traveled 60 miles by these rickety old trains and enters "Hospital Ward 5" near Meridian, MS. He is troubled with the "bowel complaint" again. In his first of two letters from May 15, he relates that his regiment is getting confusing information about where they will be going next, *"A portion of our regt. is gone on to Jackson or in that direction. Whether they reached there or not I don't know. We are waiting for further orders. What they will be I can't tell you now. It is a pretty noisy time, a heap of lies afloat."*[132] Part of the 16th regiment has already gone to Jackson but his group is awaiting what to do next.

In the second letter of May 15 1863, more information has become available with, *"Only just now I hear that Johnson and Loreing are at Jackson, their Headquarters at the citty of Jackson."* Generals Joe

[131] Civil War Trust, "Railroads of the Confederacy," *www.civilwar.org*.

[132] Appendix, Items LVI and LVII.

Figure 11 – Train derailment in Mississippi. ("The Civil War in America: Train with Reinforcements for General Johnston running off the tracks in the forests of Mississippi." Source: Illustrated London News, August 8, 1863, pg. 128)

Johnston and William W. Loring[133] are headquartered in Jackson but still no word on what Hitch's regiment will be doing once they get there themselves. Then, he makes a quick digression to the high inflation of food prices, "*Boys, I bought a dozen hen eggs yesterday. I paid one dollar for the dozen. I have eat two of them. Eatables are verry high in this state. Sutch sweet breads as your ma bakes in the little baker would be worth one dollar & upwards here. Some grumble at their fare. As for my self, I can do pretty well.*" Young, as he always indicates, will seem to make do with whatever fare he gets. In fact, he again shows some entrepreneurial spirit when he thinks of the possibility of selling Mary Hitch's "sweet breads."

Next, Young Hitch conducts many "father-to-son talks" with his sons via the mail and this correspondence provides another example. Nothing special, but the warmth and caring in his words dictate that they be presented here in their completeness. Heartfelt words and a fatherly feeling perfectly expressed even if they are words on paper delivered from over 700 miles away from his boys:

> *"Boys, our nurse's little son whoo is not as big as you, Lucian, road eight miles to stay all night with his pa & I thought it would please me to see one of you coming to see me. I want you on Sundays if you can, to go to church. If you cant go to church, get your books and learn all you can. Whatever you do keep off the creek with rude boys who might cause you to do more than*

[133] Johnston is commanding the "Army of Relief" with Loring under him commanding Loring's Division. "Order of Battle – Confederate," Organization of Confederate Forces, Army of Relief, Vicksburg National Military Park website, U.S. National Park Service.

you would if you was alone at home. I hope to hear from you soon. If not let us try to be prepared to meet in Heaven....Lucian I hope you are well & a doing well & hope that you are a good little boy to your mother. Allso I do hope that you will use no bad words in your conversation whatever. Lucian men hear whoo are looking more like they would die than live swear the hardest you ever heard. Don't get mad, son, at good advice from one who wishes you well both for time and eternity. I hope to be able to see you again on earth, if not let us try to be prepared to meet in Heaven where we will never be separated again...take good care of Brutus and Toby Pig...Joseph, I hope you are well and doing well. Allso I hope you will not get out of heart at trifles and little accidents. You may expect many crosses in your life. Tell me in your next how your steers are getting on..."

Hitch writes again the next day on May 16 to wife Mary Hitch from the same place, Meridian, Lauderdale County, Mississippi[134]. The letter is lengthier and covers the fact that is health has deteriorated rather dramatically, so much so that he and five others (unnamed) of Company I are *"at a hospital in two miles of a little town called Meridian."* Then, he describes the hospital where he is staying:

"Mary, you can't think how I hated to leave my company and come here but the soldiers have to do as they can, not as they wish. There is something over 100 men in this hospital, not all in one house, but they are in three or four houses all situated in the woods. The water drinks pretty well but a great ways off well water the most of it. One good spring between hear & the town. All of us that are well enough to walk to the table, go. It is as fare as I want to go. It's about 300 yards from where I stay to the eating house. There is seven men & myself in the room that I stay in, about the same number in the adjoining room & in another little house close by there is some twelve or fourteen. Four of our company are in the little house & me in the big house with strangers but so long as I can get up and walk about, I can go in the other house to see my friends. I have just been to the well to get some coal water the best that I have drank lately by a good deal, but it made me swet to get it. If I understand it right the men whoo are able to wait on themselves are sent to this house."

This gives a good indication showing how the hospital conditions at the time were not optimal. Eight men to a room in a house is very cramped and not sanitary. Hitch does say that the water available is *"the best that I have drank lately by a good deal"* but not easily accessible because of the distance needed to walk to get to it. Young then gives some interesting information regarding the 16th regiment and tries to separate rumors from facts the best he can. He begins on May 16 and finishes up with more information he has learned by May 17:

"Mary, I suppose you have heard a great many tales. Probably you have heard that our regt. has been cut off. I think that to be a false rumor. True our regt is divided but I was told just now that the rest of our regt started this morning to join the rest of our regt some fifty miles from hear. That portion of the regt that went on first must be in 30 or 35 miles of Jackson. It is said that Jackson has been retaken by our men, as to the certainty of it I can't say... Mary, I learn this

---

[134] Appendix, Item LVIII.

> *morning, Sunday the 17 of May that the Yankeys who have Jackson in possession have burnt the principal buildings & preparing to leave the town. But it is said that our army is closing in on them on three sides of them. From what I can learn there is either something verry bad or verry good just a going to hapen for us. Notwithstanding the enemy have Jackson in their possession & may get Vicksburg, it may all be for the best for us at last. This is said to be the boldest attack that the Yankeys have ever made here. They are getting further out from their gunboats. Some are expecting the enemy to be here soon at this town. It is said that we fellows at the hospital when discharged from here will be assigned to the nearest regt, let it be what regt it may be. I don't know that that rule will work for the men. All will want to join their own companys again soon as able so to do. There is one thing I don't like, that is our troops can't get transportation as I think they should. We were 9 days traveling 644 or 50 miles. Something wrong in the conductors, I think. We should of been to Jackson by the time that we got to this place. It may all be for the best for us."*

Rumors had been swirling that the 16th regiment had been cut off by the enemy. However, this turned out to just be a rumored corruption of the facts that the regiment had been divided due to issues with train transportation. They are traveling to merge their parts as soon as practical as they approach Jackson to the west of Meridian. On Sunday, May 17, Young Hitch then tells Mary of the word that "*...the enemy have Jackson in their possession & may get Vicksburg*."

Hitch was reporting on the Battle of Jackson that had occurred primarily on May 14 1863. We know that General Johnston had arrived in the city on the 13th, from Tennessee, when he learned that two army corps from the Union Army of the Tennessee (the XV Corps, under Major General William T. Sherman, and the XVII, under Major General James Birdseye McPherson) were advancing on Jackson, intending to cut the city and the railroads off from Vicksburg. When Johnston consulted with the local commander, Brigadier General John Gregg, he found out that only about 6,000 troops were available to defend the town. Johnston then had no choice but to order the evacuation of Jackson, but instructed Gregg to defend Jackson until the evacuation was completed.

By 10:00 a.m. on May 14, both Union army corps were near Jackson and had engaged Gregg's forces and slowly but surely pushed him back. By mid-afternoon, Johnston informed Gregg that the evacuation was complete and that he should retire and follow. Soon after, the Yankees entered Jackson and had a celebration, hosted by Major General U.S. Grant who had been travelling with Sherman's corps. They then burned part of the town and cut the railroad connections with Vicksburg. Johnston's evacuation of Jackson was a tragedy because he could have, by late on the May 14, had 11,000 troops at his disposal and by the morning of May 15, another 4,000[135]. The reinforcements of which Hitch and the 16th South Carolina regiment were a part of, arrived just a little too late to help keep Jackson out of Union hands.

Even with the loss of Jackson, there is some confidence that the southern forces will prevail among the ranks as Hitch states that the word about the federals is that the "*...army is closing in on them on three sides of them*." However, the overall tone of his letter is resignation that Jackson is lost and Vicksburg

---

[135] "Civil War Battle Summaries, Jackson - Grant's Operations against Vicksburg (1863)," United States National Park Service website, *www.nps.gov*.

may be next. Young closes the letter with some conciliatory words for his two sons, words that speak for themselves about the life on the road during the war and, need no further explanation:

> *"Well Boys, you may want to here from your Pa by this time my opportunity to write has not been as good as you may suppose, and I can't write all that you probably would like me to write to you. I have seen a great deal, some things that was not very pleasant but expect if I last long, to see a heap of things that is not pleasant. Boys, you make think that Pa is starving but that is not so. I get as mutch as I want at present. I have been for some time that I care nothing for anything strong. I get as much bread & coffee as I want & we get beef & some bacon with a little rice. I hear a heap of grumbling about our fare. This morning at breakfast I heard one remark that if a man could just live through this war that there would not be any danger of his diing afterwards. I must close in short."*

It is May 21 1863 when Young Hitch next writes to his wife[136]. He is still in the hospital near Meridian, MS and he has not heard of what has happened to the 16th South Carolina regiment since he was separated from it on May 15. He also has no real news from the "seat of war" as he is rather isolated in his hospital setting and, news he does get is primarily rumor. He gets *"news but a great deal is false so that when the truth does happen to come I don't know that it is truth."* The letter does not contain much else except some salutations to his friends A.Y. Garrett and J.J. Brown, his father-in-law John Edwards and Mary's half-brother, Euphrates Lafayette Edwards.

Official records indicate that the 16th regiment had reached Jackson on May 19 and, finally caught up with the brigade the next day near Canton, MS. They bivouacked near Cordt's Pond, MS from May 21-30 1863 before marching to Yazoo City on May 31. The brigade left Yazoo City on June 14 and marched two days by way of McNamara's Ferry on the Big Black River to Vernon, MS[137].

On May 24-25 and again on June 2-3 1863, Hitch writes to Mary from the same hospital location[138]. In the first correspondence, he is still hearing some news of the immediate war but does not know what is true or not. The fellow soldiers from Company I with Young in the hospital are itching to get out and rejoin the regiment. Hitch writes, *"I hear a heap of news; sometimes hear the enemy have whipt, then hear that our men have whipt the enemy. It is said that Johnson is at or near Vicksburg but has not yet formed a junction with Pemberton. The other men whoo come with me here are with me yet. They say as soon as they can get the chance to get to there regt they are going on."* The rumor that Johnston is at Vicksburg is false, as history tells us he evacuated Jackson and retired to the north. But Grant then abandons Jackson in favor of bearing down on Vicksburg where he has General Pemberton trapped within its city limits. Pemberton did repel two federal assaults there on May 19 and 22 1863. After the failed assaults, General Grant laid back and began a long siege beginning May 25 where he would force Pemberton's surrender almost six weeks later, on Jul 4 1863.

---

[136] Appendix, Item LIX.

[137] South Carolina's Military Organizations During the War Between the States; Volume III, The Upstate, Robert S. Seigler, The History Press, Charleston, SC, 2008; page 174.

[138] Appendix, Items LX and LXI.

Young spends 2/3rds of the first letter devoted to his renewed interest in hearing the "preaching" and bemoans that some soldiers have lost their way in this regard as he pens,

> *"Mary the steward told us at breakfast that he wanted us all that was able to be present after dinner to hear preaching. Whitch orders pleased me verry mutch. I hope to be able to attend for I want to hear some preaching once more. Mary this is a lonesum place to stay although it is quiet a pleasant place. The wether is beautifull dry & not very hot. Well Mary I have been to preaching & have heard a good sermon & prays & the preacher gave us some tracts to read the first that I have seen since I left home. I think text Hebrews 4 chapt & 9th verse. There remaineth therefore a rest to the people of God. Mary, I hope these troublesum hard times have not had the same effect upon you that it has on the soldiers. It seems to me that the most of our men have forgotten that they ever have to die & appear before their Maker to render an account for the deeds in life. Mary look forward. Don't give over. But pray that you may get strength from God to ennable you to bear with your trials and troubles. And please remember Young in your petitions."*

By the time Hitch writes his June 2-3 letter to Mary, his health has improved substantially except for the "*rheumatism & hip pain as you know I am subject to and was before I left home*." He had been in the hospital about 19 days at that point and still did not know when he would leave it, just "*when the doctor says go*." Hitch notes that this is the fourth letter he has written to Mary and gotten no response back from her. No doubt, this is because he is in the hospital and her letters are being directed to his regiment that is stationed to the west near Jackson at the time. Young realizes this possibility as he relates, "*Mary pleas write to me I want to hear from you bad. I will again tell you where to direct your letters to. Direct them to Meridian P.O. Lauderdale County Miss. Hospital ward no. five. 16th regt, So. Ca. V. so if I should be here when a letter comes I can get it. If with my regt the letters will be sent on after us to our regt please write & give me all the newes that you have*."

On June 3, Young offers more information about what is transpiring with the war in his neck of the woods:

> *"June 3rd a.m.*
> *I hear this morning that General Johnson is moving on toward Vicksburg. The certainty of it I don't know. We can get but little news here from the seat of war that is reliable. It is thought by some that the struggle now on hand at Vicksburg will be the deciding struggle. Someone has prophesied that it would be decided in the great valley of the Miss & we all hope it may be settled soon and hope it may be decided in our favor."*

The "*struggle now at hand at Vicksburg*" that Young Hitch mentions is the siege that the federal forces had begun nine days earlier. Johnston was not moving towards Vicksburg at the time and Pemberton was alone to defend the city and endure the long siege. Whether Vicksburg would be the "deciding struggle" as Hitch foresees, we know that it was indeed one of the defining moments of the Civil War. When Vicksburg fell in July, the Confederacy was cut in half and the Mississippi River was placed fully into the hands of the Union. Even the though the war would be waged for another 21 months, Vicksburg, "*in the great valley of the Miss.,*" was indeed one of the deciding points in the overall "struggle" for southern independence.

Hitch then turns to the more mundane again in the June 3 letter as he focuses on his clothing:

> *"The weather is warm & my clothing to heavy to toat on a march. I have been offered eight dollars for the coat that I brought from home. I believe if I can get that for it I will sell it. My plain pants are getting a little slick & thin. I shant mind throwing of them away so bad. My uniform is as good as new. It has not been worn but a few days. I may try to make it convenient to loss my roundabout coat & keep my other coat although the roundabout will suit the summer the best. My jeans pants is verry good yet. I will hold on to them as long as possible. I have a verry pretty fitting uniform. The first things I aim to dispose of will be my bedtick & the plain pair of pants & one haversack. The next one of my coats, my jacket I don't know what I may do with it. But two shirts, two pair of drawers, three pair of pants, two coats, one vest, one bed tick & two blankets & other trappings is more than I can carry through the heat of this summer, I fear."*

With the hot and humid Mississippi summer weather upon the troops at the time, Young Hitch is looking to off-load some clothes to keep cool and not to have so much to lug around on marches. He looks to keep his "roundabout coat" but maybe sell his coat he brought from home if he can get $8.00 for it. The roundabout or "shell" coat is the typical coat one sees in illustrations of Civil War soldiers both north and south and, for the latter, were medium gray in color. It typically was lined, made of 100% wool with one inside breast pocket and seven (7) brass CSA buttons (See **Figure 13**). Hitch closes the letter with some words for his sons that he wishes he were home to help them take care of their wheat and wants them to make their own "bread" if it is within their power.

Figure 12 - Jacob D. Mock wearing his Southern Cross of Honor c1910.

The next three letters are bunched together for June 4, 5 and 8 1863 from Young Hitch to his wife Mary and sons, Joseph and Lucian[139]. The June 4 and 5 letters are to sons Joseph and Lucian, respectively, with Mary receiving a few words at the end of Lucian's letter. They are short notes to the boys and just address things Young misses around the farm with his sons, *"Joseph, let me know how your stock is getting along, your steers in particular and your milk cows, whether old Sarah is alive or not. Tell me how J.J. Brown is getting on and I wish to hear from your granpa. Also tell how J.D. Mock is or whether he has ever got home. Tell old Mr. Mock Howdy for me"* and, *"Lucian, I dreamed last night of seeing your dog Brutes and I called him by his name as I thought. And he did not know me and you do not know how it hurt me to think that he did not know me. I have dreamed of seeing your ma and Joseph. But have never dreamed of seeing A.L. Hitch."*

It is interesting how he dreams of Lucian's dog, Brutus, who did not "know him." These may be some subconscious thoughts Young is having about being away from his sons for so long that they are forgetting about him. He also expresses to his son to let him know his friends the Mocks are doing. "Old Mr. Mock" is John Mock (1807-1897) and "J.D. Mock" is his son Jacob Dillard

139 Appendix, Items LXII, LXIII and LXIV.

Mock (1845-1926), neighbors to the Hitches in Laurens County[140]. Jacob Mock was just 16 years old when he enlisted as a Private with Company E of the 14th South Carolina Infantry in December 1861. He was wounded on Dec 13 1862 at Fredericksburg, VA and never fully recovered from his wound. He was discharged from service on Jan 8 1864 in Columbia, SC. Hitch must have heard of Private Mock's wounding by the time he writes this letter in Jun 1863 and wonders whether *"he has ever got home."* **Figure 12** is a photograph Jacob D. Mock in later years.

Then, Hitch offers a few words to his wife about how it has been in the hospital and how he feels about it:

> *"Mary, I have been at this hospital three weeks today. Mary I am able to be up & nock around & has never faild to be able to go down to the dinner house to get my meals. True I have not been able for duty since I came here. Mary, there is but little honor in lieing in a hospital, but there is a heap of dishonesty going on in this war. And if I don't try to take care of myself, no one else will. I have not reported able for duty yet neither is it worth while for I would just be sent to meridian as others have been that reported able for duty."*

Figure 13 - Reproduction Confederate Roundabout Coat

He seems willing just to stay in the hospital until there is something worthwhile for him to do outside of it. Three days later, he writes that he was finally discharged on Saturday, June 6, and caught the train the next day for Jackson that was now back in Rebel hands as the federal forces had left and were busy with the siege of Vicksburg. He had arrived there on the evening of June 7 and was traveling with "Forrester" from Company I and another unnamed man from some other unit. Since there were several Forresters in Company I, we cannot be sure to which one he is referring but it may have been Isaac Forrester. A later letter shows that he had traveled with Mr. I. Forrester but, "I" and "J" are sometimes hard to discern in 19th century handwriting but it does appear that Hitch wrote an "I" (for Isaac) in that later letter.

The group of three men are to catch the 4:00 p.m. train from Jackson to Canton, MS to try and catch up with their command *"if they have not left lately."* He then exclaims, *"Pretty stiring times here. Something to be done I think from what I can see. It will be some two days or more before I can reach my company."* Hitch is back in the thick of it now that he has left the hospital and is reminded of his own mortality and he expresses this to Mary as:

---

[140] John Mock is buried with his second wife, Elizabeth (Compton) Mock (1828-1906) in the Durbin Creek Baptist Church Cemetery in Fountain Inn, SC. Jacob Dillard Mock married Rosanna Malinda McHugh (1853-1901) and they are both buried in the Laurens City Cemetery, Laurens County, SC. Rosanna is the daughter of Private Thomas Simeon McHugh (1834-1892) of Company A, 16th South Carolina Volunteers.

> *"This leaves me tolerably well at the present I want you to write to me, the 30 of April was the last letter I got from you. Direct your letters to Jackson, Miss. So I wish you & children well Both for time & eternity. Mary, as this may be the last letter that you may ever get wrote by me to you, if it should be my lot to get killed or die, I want you not to grieve after me at all for I hope when I am no more here on Earth that I will be at rest in heaven. Mary I may be deceased but I hope you will still pursue your course as you have been doing. Let us try to be prepared to meet God in peace. So I bid you farewell."*

With the above, Young has taken the time to create a multicolored pen and ink drawing of a woman, finely dressed, and enclosed it in the envelope. Presumably, this woman is his remembrance of how Mary looked as he left her at home. Commonly called a "doodling," it is a nice example of a Civil War soldier's drawing that was based from memory where he might be thinking of his home, wife, or children and would compose a picture. **Figure 14** shows the drawing Young Hitch created on Jun 8 1863.

June 12 finds Young Hitch near Yazoo City, MS, *"Enjoying moderate health But verry mutch fatigued from my march. I footed it forty miles in about two days."*[141] He had not seen his Company in almost a month and describes them as looking bad, *"I found the boys (*in*) my mess all but M.R. Garrett in moderate health. Garrett is sorter puny. Our men generally look bad. They seem to be verry mutch worn down."* We see Hitch has found his friend Miles Garrett still in poor health but, even the rest of Company I is worn ragged too from endless weeks of marching, traveling, sickness, poor diet, weather and other stresses of being at war. Nevertheless, Hitch seems very glad to be back with his unit. He mentions Mr. Forrester again and then his Captain, *"Mr. I. Forrester was the only one of Com (I) that went on with me from the hospital. I got with Capt. Babb yesterday morning."* Again, we see I. Forrester who is probably Isaac Forrester and "Captain Babb." The Captain is the Newton Babb we encountered earlier. He was originally elected Lieutenant in the old failed McKittrick's Company in April 1862 but was later determined too young to serve at the time. He eventually becomes part of Company I as a 1st lieutenant and then a captain soon thereafter. Babb will end up dying of disease in a Georgia hospital on Nov 6 1863.

Young Hitch does not have much decent to say about Yazoo City saying it is *"undoubtedly must be the Stern End of Miss."* – a less than glowing review of the area! Company I and the rest of the 16th SCVI are camped 3 miles west of there on Short Creek, about 30 miles northwest of Vicksburg but, *"With the exception of a pretty shade, it is surely the roughest country that you ever saw, although verry rich."* Hitch is a little disappointed that he has not gotten more letters from Mary other than one from May 22 that was waiting for him when he arrived at the camp. He writes, *"I was verry glad to meet up with him but would have been more so if he had brought me a letter. Mary I rec a letter from you bearing date May 22nd I got the letter from the boys when I got to camp. It is the only letter that I have got since the one that Mr. Brown brought to me. I have wrote to you regular as mutch as once a week & expect to as near as I can. The Capt said when I first come up with him that he thought he had a letter for me but if he did he has lost it on the way."* It seems Captain Babb may have misplaced one or two of Mary Hitch's letters to Young!

---

[141] Appendix, Item LXV.

A letter from Jun 15 1863 comes next, from Young in Camp Woods, MS (postmarked Canton, MS) to wife Mary[142]. It is a short one with some news that they are about to go on the move, "*We have just been*

Figure 14 - Young Hitch's drawing included with his Jun 8 1863 letter. (Mowbray Collection, Salisbury University)

[142] Appendix, Item LXVI.

stript of our knapsacks and all the baggage that we can spare. The weather is warm & hard marching to be done. Where I don't know. I have brought my turn down to one blanket, one oilcloth, shirt, pants, drawers, socks and gloves besides the suit on my back. Probably I yet have more than I can carry. You need not think strange if you do not get letters from us soon as the communication will be stopt." Then a brief note that Little Berry Edwards and Mat Garrett are doing fine but Miles Garrett has gone to the hospital.

His next letter to Mary is written the very next day, June 16, from Madison County, MS, probably near the town of Canton and the 16th regiment is not yet moving but Hitch expects they may by June 17[143]. "*Dear Mary I will write a few lines to you this morning perhaps I may not have the opportunity of writeing again soon. We may start to march tomorrow. Where I can't tell but maybe to Vicksburg. If so, we will have several days marching to do. And probably some fighting to be done before we can get thare.*" Vicksburg was in its 23rd day of a long siege and word was probably swirling around the camps that they would be setting out to relieve the citizens there and Pemberton's army.

Young provides more details of the 16th SCVI and the camp he is in near Canton, MS; "*The 16 has not yet come up with any Yankeys yet but I fear that they will in the course of ten, fifteen or twenty days. We come here last Sunday Evening we may leave here tomorrow it will not be many days before we leave at most. This country is alive with our soldiers. The face of the hole earth all most covered with men waggons horses mules and beefs.*" He was among and viewing General Johnston's whole army there at the time which consisted of Breckinridge's, Loring's, French's and Walker's divisions as well as Jackson's Cavalry division. Hitch and the 16th were part of Walker's division, under Gist's brigade. With all the army gathered, the soldiers must have been convinced they would see regular fighting action within days.

The food in the camps while on the road has paled in comparison to the good fare that Company I had gotten while in the camp near Charleston. Hitch gives us a look at what they are eating:

> *"Mary, no doubt but you think that we are liveing verry hard. Yes we are living hard, indeed we are. Our fare at Charleston was a feast to our fare here. We get a plenty of corn meal and beef. The meal is so coarse it is allmost impossible to turn a hocake. I have found several whole grains of corn in the bread. The only chance to get any of the brand & silks out is to get the meal in a pan & shake it until the brand & silks rise to the top & then blow them off. Probably when we get on the march we will get some bacon. I hope those times will not continue as they now are. I think there will be a change soon, either for the better or the worse. I hope it may be for the better for us. Although there may a many a noble fellow fall before it is decided. I have wrote to you concerning our fare not to trouble you but just to let you know. Our water is standing pon water, the creek at home would be mutch better. The water is the worst thing we have to contend with."*

Corn meal is the staple part of diet on the road for the soldiers and, it seems they are getting plenty of beef as their protein with the army supporting cattle as it marches. The corn meal has gotten pretty poor lately as Young relates, it is poorly and coarsely ground and includes the byproducts of corn silks

---

[143] Appendix, Item LXVII.

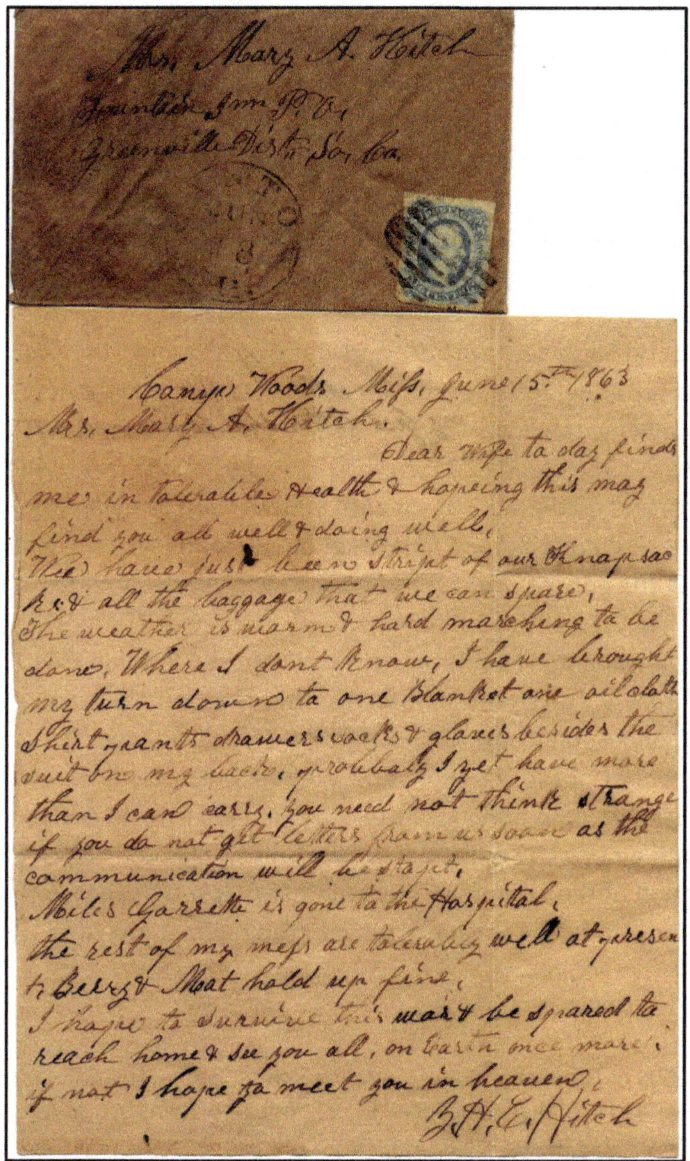
Mrs. Mary A. Hitch
Frontier [illegible] P.O.
Greenville Dist. So. Ca.

Camp Woods Miss. June 15th 1863
Mrs. Mary A. Hitch
Dear wife to day finds me in tolerable health & hopeing this may find you all well & doing well,
We have just been stript of our knapsacks & all the baggage that we can spare,
The weather is warm & hard marching to be done, Where I dont know, I have brought my turn down to one blanket one oilcloth shirt pants drawers socks & gloves besides the suit on my back, probably I yet have more than I can carry, you need not think strange if you do not get letters from us soon as the communication will be stopt,
Miles Garrett is gone to the Hospittal,
the rest of my mess are tolerably well at present L. Berry & Mat hold up fine,
I hope to survive this war & be spared to reach home & see you all, on earth once more, if not I hope to meet you in heaven,
B.H.E. Hitch

Figure 15 - Young Hitch's letter to Mary A. Hitch dated Jun 15 1863 from Camp Woods, MS. Note the franking on the letter of the 10c Jefferson Davis CSA stamp with June 18 Canton, MS postmark. (Mowbray Collection, Nabb Center, Salisbury University)

and bran. Water is not very good either as they are using stagnant pond water instead of healthier and better tasting spring or flowing creek water. Hitch exclaims that the "*water is the worst thing we have to contend with*" and he is correct is more ways than he knows. Not only is it bad tasting, but it harbors disease and parasites as well and is a major source of illness among the troops.

By Jun 22 1863, Hitch writes another letter to Mary and they have remained in Madison County, MS[144]. With time on his hands while they await their next move, Young pens a longer letter with interesting information about his camp and even the hospital where he was confined while in Meridian a month earlier. Hitch is now fearful again of contracting the measles as Little Berry Edwards has been stricken with them and Hitch is in close proximity to him day and night – even sleeping directly next to him. Here is some of the news directly from the words of Young Hitch:

> *"My health is not as good as it has been. I have taken some medicine this morning & hope to be better soon. I have a severe cold & may be taking the measles. But it is not time for me to take them from L.B. yet. But if I don't take them from him, I don't know how I will take them for I lay by his side last Thursday night & he had a high fever & severe cough. L.B.'s case is the only case of measles that I know of in camp. I (__) talked in camp today that there is some probbability of us being sent back to So.Ca. soon but I fear it will not be our lot to be so fortunate to get back so near home. Our regt would shout at the order to start back to Adams Run. As me it would please me verry mutch, then I could hear from home oftener & see people from home."*

At this point, the talk around camp includes the possibility to get stationed back in South Carolina as the urgency to march on Vicksburg seems to have passed. While Hitch and the rest of the 16th regiment would clearly invite the relocation back to Adams Run, he sincerely doubts they will go. Young also

---

144 Appendix, Item LXVIII.

relates some idea of what goes on in the camps with his fellow soldiers, *"Mary, we have all sorts of amusements in camp. Just right close to me are three bunches of men playing cards, some reading the scriptures, some cooking, some eating, some sleeping, some shoe mending and the rest doing nothing."* We often hear of the major battles and fighting of the war but we forget that the vast majority of the time, the soldiers were either traveling or stuck in the camps with not much to do besides their official duties of drilling and manning guard posts. We can just imagine, as Hitch is sitting to create this letter, his head panning around and observing what is going on in the camp surrounding him and, then putting his image into words on Jun 22 1863 from where he was then located in central Mississippi.

Hitch tells Mary that he received a letter from her on Saturday, June 20, and was glad she and the boys were "all alive." She had evidently related in that letter, which does not survive, news that their honey bees had produced lots of honey that spring, *"Hurrah with your bees & be sure to save the honey & eat it & not do as we did last year let the worms eat them out instead of yourselves."* In that missing letter, she had also expressed that she would love to sit with and take a walk again with her husband as evident in Young's reply, *"Mary truly would I comply with your request & hope it may yet be our lot to take the walk you speak of. I often think of our home the yard & the garden that I set so mutch by."*

Hitch also tells Mary who, in Company I, were his companions while in the hospital near Meridian; *"As you wish to know who went with me to the hospital I will give their names. Augustus Howard*[145]*, Isaac Forrester*[146]*, John Simmons*[147]*, James Bramlet*[148]*, John Gault*[149]*, Joseph Fowler*[150] *& a ga. man, myself, Forrester & Simmons (torn paper) of the seven that has got to the regt yet."* We finally can confirm that the "Forrester" and "Mr. I. Forrester" Hitch had spoken of in previous letters was indeed Private Isaac Forrester. All the other men are Privates and listed among the enlistments for Company I in the Table presented earlier in this chapter, with the exception of the unknown "Georgia man." It seems that Forrester and Simmons are with Hitch and that they had not yet caught up with the regiment at the time.

---

[145] Private Presley Edward Augustus Howard (1823-1891) of Greenville County, SC, was son of Samuel H. and Mary (Jones) Howard. He married Margaret Locke (1839-1903) in c1856 and they had 10 children who lived to adulthood. She was the sister of Lt. Jesse J. and Private George W. Locke of Company I. It is also notable that Presley Howard's sister, Maryanna Jones Howard was wife of William Henry Hughes who was close friends with and served with Young Hitch in the 1st Corps, 9th Reserves. Private P.E.A. Howard was also brother to 3LT John Manning Howard (1821-1896) of Company I. Their sister, Harriett G. Howard was married to another Company I soldier, Private Andrew J. Allison (see later notes on them).

[146] Private Isaac B. Forrester (born 1825) of Greenville County. He is likely the brother of fellow Company I soldier, Andrew Forrester, as they live very close to each other in 1850 and both, sons of Isaac and Elizabeth (Justice) Forrester. These two may also be brothers to, or very closely related to, Private John Forrester.

[147] Private John Hiram Simmons (1844-1913) of Greenville County, was son of Martin Luther and Nancy Edwards (Miller) Simmons. He married Rosa Jane Wood.

[148] Private James W. Bramlett (1833-1864) was son of Reuben and Sarah (Dacus) Bramlett of Greenville County. He married Elizabeth R. Holland Private Bramlett died in a hospital in Franklin, TN on Nov 30 1864. He was the brother of Company I's Private William Dacus Bramlett (1820-1875).

[149] Private John W.P. Gault (1835-1900) of Greenville County was son of James and Jane (Woodside) Gault and, he married Pernesey Babb in c1856, sister to Company I's Captain Newton Babb (1830-1863). Pernesey and Newton are children of Abner and Elizabeth (Kellett) Babb of Laurens County. Private Gault and his wife are buried in the Fountain Inn Municipal Cemetery, Fountain Inn, SC.

[150] Little is known about the identity of this Joseph Fowler.

Young Hitch then turns his attention to his sons, Joseph and Lucian and, even though we cannot see what the boys had written to him, we can get an idea of what it was from Young's response:

> *"J.J. Dear son you can't think how it pleased me to get a letter from you. I expected to hear that you was not well but glad to hear that you was not confined to a sick bed. Glad to hear that your stock are all alive or so near it. Glad to hear that (__) well & hope you may get (__) seasons so as to make your breads. Glad to hear that you can plough so well. Hurrah Joseph support yourselves if you can. I hope if you will act your part that God will bless you...A.L. Dear son glad to hear from you but sorry to learn that your health is like mine not good I would be glad to come home & se you & would be glad to have an opportunity to help you to Eat your union. You say you think of your pa when you Eat unions & wonder if you shall see him any more. Lucian I hope to be able to see you again but God only knows whether I shall or not. Dear Son be a good boy do your duty towards your Ma."*

Hitch tells Mary that, even though she might be lonesome, it is better than it would be if the army were near the farm, "*Mary, you & the children notwithstanding that you are left in a sad condition and in a verry lonsom one to, you need to be verry thankful that there is not an army near you. You have no idea what a misfortune it would be to have (___)* (paper torn and words are missing)." In the Civil War, family farms near where the army was located, or marching by, were generally scavenged and picked clean of all food and livestock to help feed the masses. Hitch tells Mary to be glad this is not the case for their farm. He closes with a remark that he is pleased that the family is "*shod with shoes for the winter*" and that his own old shoes are holding out well.

There are no other letters in the Mowbray collection until about six weeks later, on Aug 11 1863, and sent from Young Hitch in Scott County, MS to wife Mary Hitch[151]. Scott County is adjacent to, and southeast of, Madison County from where Hitch wrote his previous letters. He was probably near Morton Station, MS at the time and from where he will write his next letter in a few days.

By August 11, the siege of Vicksburg had ended with the surrender of 30,000 troops of Pemberton's army in addition to 172 cannon and 50,000 small arms. The army there and the citizens faced incredible hardships during the siege with widespread disease and starvation and they were given no choice but to surrender, which they did on July 4. Johnston did not attack Grant at Vicksburg from the rear as Young Hitch and others in the army had expected because, by June 14, the Federal forces had been bolstered by 27,000 troops in addition the 50,000 Grant originally had at his disposal. It would have been military suicide to try and conduct such a move when southern forces were outnumbered 5-to-2. There had been a Confederate effort to cut Grant's supply line, when units under Major General John G. Walker attacked Milliken's Bend up the Mississippi on June 7. But the attack eventually failed and left Pemberton in Vicksburg with no hope for relief but from the cautious General Johnston who was hopelessly outnumbered.

---

[151] Appendix, Item LXIX.

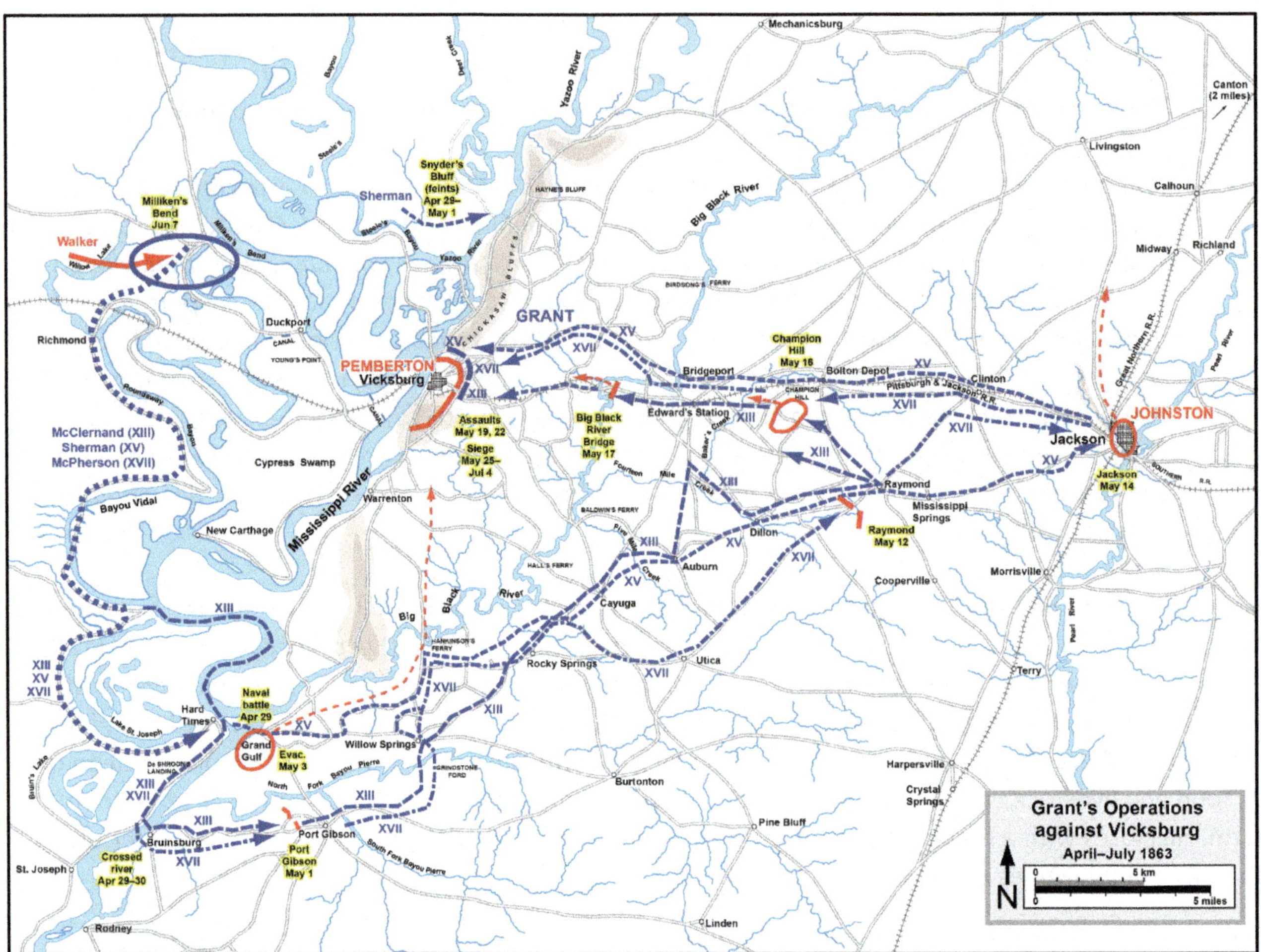

Figure 16 – Operations in and around Vicksburg, MS in April to July 1863. Young Hitch and the 16th SCVI did not see any action here but were sent in with Johnston's Army of Tennessee in a failed attempt to support from the east. Vicksburg fell to General Grant on July 4, 1863 and with it, General John Pemberton's Confederate army of nearly 30,000 men, 172 cannon and 50,000 rifles. (Map by Hal Jespersen, *www.cwmaps.com*)

After Pemberton surrendered, Grant chose not to take all 30,000 of his army prisoner due to logistics of feeding and transporting to POW camps. Instead, he offered to parole all of them on Jul 6 1863. Considering their destitute state, dejected and starving, he never expected them to fight again and, hoped they would carry home the stigma of defeat to the rest of the Confederacy. He also realized that it would have occupied his army and taken months to ship so many prisoners to the north. As it turned out, most of the men who were paroled on July 6 were exchanged and received back into the Confederate Army on August 4 in Alabama and actively served throughout the rest of the war.

The 16th regiment and Gist's brigade had left the Vernon, MS area on July 1 and began marching towards Vicksburg to help alleviate some of the pressure there but, with Vicksburg surrendering on July 4, it turned back around and headed to Jackson, arriving there on Jul 8 1863. With Vicksburg defeated, Grant turned his attention back to Johnston's army and ordered General W.T. Sherman to advance on the Confederates and retake Jackson, from which they had retired back in May. Johnston resisted the federal attack on Jackson from July 10 to July 16 when, fearing entrapment, he evacuated the city to Sherman. At this time, the 16th regiment was based in Canton, MS and, the Vicksburg campaign ended when Sherman and his forces occupied Jackson on Jul 17 1863. Gist's brigade had evacuated the area on July 16 and marched east to Morton Station, MS where they rested for five weeks.[152]

Returning to Hitch's August 11 letter to Mary; in it, he informs her that he has contracted the measles while on the march to Vicksburg on a very hot day of Jun 30 1863. He had to be transported in a wagon for a while and then an ambulance in the hottest portion of the day. It must have been a miserable experience being sick with the measles and broiling in the hot southern summer sun. His words do better justice to the experience than any other description might:

> *"I seat myself to write a few lines to you to inform you that I am yet alive. I am not well but am well to what I have been. I was very unwell with pains when I took the measles & we were on the march to Vicksburg & the weather was awful hot. The first day on the march I got to ride in an ambulance. The next, the first of July, I had to get on a loaded waggon with nothing to shelter me from the broiling hot sun shine. It was a day to be remembered by me for it seemed to me that it was all that I could do to sit up without being exposed to the hot sun & being jolted as I was on the second of July. I got to ride in an ambulance two or three miles when we came to the house where I was left. Mary, you have no idea how thankful I felt when I was told that I could get to stop & get some kind of a shelter."*

Even though Hitch was very ill, we get an idea of where the soldiers had trekked in the time since he composed his letter of June 22:

> *"The doctor gave me blue pills before we left Vernon and after I got to Mr Odoms the doctor came back & cald in to see us. He gave me another blue pill & my Bowels then runing off severely. The water where I stayed was the verry strongest of limestone spring water whitch did not agree with me at at all. It kept my Bowels runing off all the time. And they never got any better until after I left Mr Odoms. Mary you can form no idea my feelings for the first two weeks after I was left. It was but a few days after our army passed on to Vicksburg until I heard that they was retreating back. They passed by Brownsville within six miles of where I was & the Enemy pushing them closely. I could heare them fighting at Jackson. There was one week that I expected every moment that the Yankeys would step in & get me but if they had they would not of got mutch for I felt more like diing than living just at that time. But the Enemy retreated back the same road that they come & never give the neighborhood where I was a call."*

They were in the vicinity of Vernon and Brownsville, MS, first heading in the direction of Vicksburg, then retreating towards Jackson. Brownsville is about 11 miles northwest of Jackson and 17 miles northeast of Vicksburg, between the two cities. Hitch mentions being given "blue pills" by a doctor at "Mr. Odom's"[153] for his illness. These pills were commonly used on both sides in the Civil War. Sometimes

---

[152] South Carolina's Military Organizations During the War Between the States; Volume III, The Upstate, Robert S. Seigler, The History Press, Charleston, SC, 2008; page 174.

[153] Hitch mentions "Mr. Odom" several times in his letters. It is unknown who exactly this is but, research shows a family headed by "M.J. Odom," age 38 and born in South Carolina, in the 1860 census for Brownsville, MS. This is probably the family with whom Young Hitch stayed and received help when he contracted the measles on the way to Vicksburg. Later letters seem to confirm this as well.

called "Blue Mass pills," they were a popular period medication prepared from chalk and mercury, which could be mixed with licorice, rosewater, or honey. Like many "patent medicines" of the day, they claimed to cure just about anything; depression, toothache, constipation, dysentery and tuberculosis among other things. The mercury content of these pills was up to 9,000 times the amount considered safe by modern standards, so the medicine may have caused more issues, even deaths, than it prevented!

In the Confederate retreat back towards Jackson, the Federal forces were pushing them hard to the east and Hitch was caught in the middle while he convalesced from the measles. We will see that he acutely feared he would be taken prisoner, which often happened to soldiers in hospitals as lines of battle and positioning of the armies ebbed and flowed. But the Union army never came directly to area where Young was located. Hitch then gives some more clues of the activities in the information void between his letters of June 22 and August 11:

> *"The negros in the section have a great many of them left and gone to the Yankeys & the Yankeys have taken a great many horses from the Miss. & pretty well all there meat & chickens. Me & J.M. Garrett started for our regt 1st of this inst & reached our regt 7th five days traveling 60 miles & got to ride 23 miles of the 60. we only was out two dollars on the road. I paid two for our breakfast one morning. J.M. is not verry well. he has had a bad spell & ot not to started so soon. L.B & W.B are tolerably well. M.R. Garrett is in camp well as common. Tell E.L. Edwards that I got his letter when I got to camp & was verry glad to see it. It was dated July 8th I think. Mary I have no news to give. It is said that we will be sent to some other place soon, some say back to Charleston, some say to Savannah & some say to Mobile or Tennisee. So I think it uncertain where we go to. But hope that we may rec orders to go back to Charleston soon."*

In this area of Mississippi, where the Union forces had been very active, most of the slaves had gone and the Yankee army had picked all the farms and homesteads clean of horses and food, especially "meat and chickens." Young Hitch and J.M. (Matt) Garrett had left the sickbay to catch up with Company I on August 1 and had, by August 7, traveled five of the days for a total of 37 miles by foot and 23 by ride of some sort, 60 miles in all. Hitch treated himself and Matt to breakfast one morning for $2.00 total. Young reports that Matt Garrett is not well but that Little Berry Edwards, William Berry Scruggs and Miles Garrett are all pretty well. The only news Hitch has learned upon catching up with his Company is the uncertainty of their next destination – Charleston, SC; Savannah, GA; Mobile, AL; or Tennessee. It will soon be known that the latter will be the destination of choice.

Young Hitch, as did many soldiers, had the continuing challenge to try and manage his finances while on the road and in the camps. Payroll draws occurred only very infrequently and, the prospect of getting separated from their units due to sickness and threats from the enemy, added to the need to keep some funds available for use at all times. Hitch does a good job of helping us understand this as he explains to his wife on Aug 11 1863:

> *"Mary, I had just 38 dollars and 50 cents when I was left at Mr. Odoms & a pack of envelopes, some of them had stamps on them. I don't remember how many now but several. When the Yankeys come in so close I slipt $20 into one of my suspenders. So when I went to leave I just had*

> *$18.50 in my pocket book. I told the gentleman it was not worth while to ask him his charge, that I would pay according to my pile so he took $13, whitch left me $5 in my pocketbook. I now only have 22 dollars. I did not get here in time for the last draw & the capt would not draw for me & Mat not knowing when we would come up. Mary, I haven't got any letter from you in a long time. There has come several from you to me in my absence from the regt and in the fight at Jackson they destroyed them just as I would of done myself had I had anybodys letter in my hands."*

Young also informs his wife that some of the letters she has sent recently were purposely destroyed in the battle at Jackson before he could rejoin his regiment and read them. This was a common policy because, if the enemy were to have captured those letters, they may have gathered intelligence about soldiers and their units that might prove detrimental. For this reason, anyone carrying letters for other soldiers were instructed to destroy them if a threat arose like a battle or other situation where the enemy might have an opportunity to gain possession of them.

Nine days pass before Hitch writes his next letter and, this to his son, Lucian[154]. He is still located in Scott County, MS (Morton Station) and his health has again taken a turn for the worse as he is back in the regimental hospital, having gone there on August 18. He writes in more detail how, in his earlier bout with the measles, he was acutely afraid of being captured by Union forces:

> *"Dear son,*
> *I take this opportunity of droping you a short letter to inform you where I am and how I am a getting along. I am in the hospital at the regiment. This is the third day I have been in this hospital. Dear Son, I have suffered a great deal since I saw you last. I suppose that you heard of me having the measles and me being left behind allmost right amongst the Yankeys. Lucian, Pa fared rough with the measles. I thought one week that I could not live. But for sum cause God has spared my life a little longer. Lucian, I calculated on being captured by the Enemy while I was sick. The Yankey passed in six miles of me on their way to Jackson & they returned by the same road. I was about halfway between Jackson and Vicksburg. The people where I staid treated me as good as I deserved probably but not as good as they could of done. I paid him $13.00 & would of give him as mutch more if they had acted more gentlemanly with me. My health a little better today."*

Hitch describes himself as having been "*about halfway between Jackson and Vicksburg,*" and this fits perfectly with the time he had the measles near Brownville and was tended to by "Mr. Odom." Brownsville fits between the two cities but is a little north of the direct route between the two. Hence, while the Union army was indeed trekking back and forth between the two cities, Hitch would have escaped detection, being somewhat north of their activity. While he does not refer to Odom by name in this letter, it is with little doubt that he is whom Hitch is writing of when he states, "*The people where I staid treated me as good as I deserved probably but not as good as they could of done. I paid him $13.00 & would of give him as mutch more if they had acted more gentlemanly with me*. So, Odom was

[154] Appendix, Item LXX.

hospitable but not overly so and, perhaps, in the process missed out on getting paid double by Hitch for his troubles.

Hitch completes his letter to Lucian on Aug 21 1863 with some interesting insight into the various food stuffs available for purchase with their wildly inflated prices:

> *"August 21 – Lucian, you ought to be here to see how fruit & watermelons, cakes, pyes and sutch like are selling. Peaches & apples $1.50 to $2.00 per dozen. Mellons from three to twelve dollars a piece, ginger cakes from $1.00 to $2.00 a piece. Small fruit pyes, sutch size as your ma frys $1.00 to $1.50 a piece without shortening, spice or anything but flour & fruit & sometimes a little salt in them. Biscuits six to the dollar. Bacon $1.50 to $2.00 per lb. Flour $1.00 per lb. Lucian, I would like to be at home to help you to eat Irish taters & unions & some stewed chicken & dumplings of your Ma's cooking & some of our eggs. I got some verry good bacon and beans, squashes and collards at Mr. Odoms. Lucian, I have eat peach pye made out of rye meal & fritters too. And have eat wheat meal not batted, just sifted. Both does fine. Save all your rye for it does fine to make fritters. It's worth $10.00 per bushel Lucian, let me hear from you. Let me know how your dog, Brutus, and Tompy are getting on…"*

By this time, Lucian Hitch was still only ten years old but his dad is teaching him about the economics of the day. He gives examples of the prices of many items that would be available around the Hitch farm to perhaps spur his interest in how he can gather income for the family. He especially focuses on the rye for making "fritters" and possibly to sell the grain at "$10.00 per bushel." We also see that Young had eaten very well at Mr. Odom's house of bacon, beans, squash and collards but, he would rather be home *"to help you to eat Irish taters & onions & some stewed chicken & dumplings of your Ma's cooking & some of our eggs."*

Young encloses a second, short, letter for August 21 addressed to his wife from Morton Station, MS, where he explains in more detail about his ill health[155]:

> *"Dear wife*
> *I seat myself to drop you a few lines to inform you of my health. Mary, I am not well. I have been here in the regimental hospital some days. How long I will remain here I don't know. I am not able to drill. I just can poke about. My legs is stiff & I cant use them sufficient to drill. They may send me off to the hospital unless I improve soon. If I am sent to the hospital I may get better soon. I can't improve lying here on the hard ground with the disease that I have. Garrett may come home soon. I don't know whether you need to try to send any thing more than a letter to me for its uncertain about me being with the others but I hope to be. Mary the last few days nothing sets well on my stomach. I took calamel & oil the other day & then lay upon the hard ground which is against my disease. Mary I hope to see you again but God only knows whether I shall or not. I wish you well. Mary, please excuse me for writing on old paper. I pict this up after losing my stamps. I have not had the chance to get any more is the reason why your letters are*

155 Appendix, Item LXXI.

> *not paid. I supose you can pay for them. Mary if I am spared today I will write you a confidential letter soon."*

Hitch is still quite sick and unable to drill with his unit. Young also states that (Matt) Garrett may "come home soon" as his health has gotten much worse. Other than the detail above, the most interesting part of this letter is that it is written on paper that had evidently originally been used by the hospital staff for some sort of record keeping. On the back of the latter, Hitch writes between the lines of a partial list of soldiers in the 16th South Carolina Regiment regimental hospital, their Company designation, and their illness (the latter of which is mostly cut off the letter). The list follows:

John H. Rice 929	*C*
S.F. Clary 930	*G*
F.T. Trammel 931	*H*
John Kelly 932	*"*
W. Bryant 933	*"*
Th. Morris 934	*A*
W.B. Lock 935	*"*
W.M. Burton 936	*D*
Augustus Howard 937	*I*
W.W. Goodwin 938	*"*
E.R. Yeargin 939	*B*
James Holcomb 940	*H*
W.P. Smith 941	*F*
Jessie James 942	*"*
R.I. Vaughn 943	*"*
T. Vaughn 944	*"*
P.B. Watson 945	*"*
James Wiganham 946	*G*
T.W. Johnson 947	*"*
H.D. Coleman 948	*"*
J.A. McCreary 949	*I*

The list is interesting and we see three (3) members of Company I; Augustus Howard, Westly W. Goodwin[156] and James A. McCrary. The numbers presented next to the names remain a mystery as to

---

[156] Private William Wesley Goodwin (c1842-1911) of Greenville County, SC was son of John Hamlin and Catherine Goodwin. He was brother to fellow Company I soldiers, Privates Henry T. Goodwin (1840-xx) and John Franklin Goodwin (c1843-xx). Wesley Goodwin would have recurring bouts with disease causing him to eventually get discharged from the army on May 24 1864. Henry died in the hospital in Rome, GA on Nov 16 1863. John would die in Greenville on Sep 23 1863. Two sons in this family lost within a 7-week period and a third debilitated with disease later in the war. It is unknown, but probable, that the other two Goodwin's in Company I, Johnson and W.D. Goodwin, are related to this same family. Private Johnson William Goodwin (1823-1913) is son of Harris and Celia Goodwin and, buried with his wife Caroline (Richards) Goodwin (1817-1892) in the Clear Spring Baptist Church cemetery, Simpsonville, SC. Private William Davis Goodwin (1844-1915) is son of John H. and Louisa (Hodges) Goodwin and, is buried with his wife Jennie (Lake) Goodwin (1848-1930) in the Christ Episcopal Church Cemetery, Greenville, SC.

what they indicate but they may just be a unique designation to identify the soldier by the hospital. The paper Hitch was using was old, recycled stationery from the hospital. In this case, at least nine (9) months old as service records indicate that J.A. McCrary died on Dec 22 1862 in camp with the 16th regiment near Wilmington, NC before Young Hitch had even become a part of the unit[157].

Young Hitch's health had improved by the time he composes his next letter on Sep 7 1863 and, the 16th regiment was then located "three miles west of Rome," Georgia[158]. They had taken a rather long and circuitous route from Mississippi to Georgia via Tennessee as Hitch indicates, "*...we have been traveling a great deal of late. I have seen a good deal of the country but could of seen a heap more had I of been well and sound. We left Miss for Ten. & went there and stayed five or six days only when we got orders to leave there for Rome, Ga. So we landed here yesterday.*"

Regimental records show that the 16th South Carolina regiment left Morton, MS by rail on August 25 and arrived at Tyner's Station, TN, near Chattanooga, on the 31st of the month. There, they joined the Army of Tennessee then commanded by General Braxton Bragg. Five days later, they left there by rail and arrived in Rome, GA on September 5 to support the cavalry on the extreme left of the Confederate lines in Georgia/Tennessee. For Gist's brigade, the 16th regiment and most of the 46th Georgia were temporarily stranded near Rome waiting for another train as the rest of the brigade; the 24th South Carolina, the 8th Georgia Battalion, Ferguson's Battery of Light Artillery and a small remaining part of the 46th Georgia, headed by the first train to Ringgold, GA on Sep 18 1863. The 16th was therefore detached at Rome when the Battle of Chickamauga played out on September 19 and 20 and was only able to rejoin the brigade on the 23rd as it marched towards Chattanooga. It then camped at the foot of Lookout Mountain to the left of the Confederate line during the siege of Chattanooga from September 23 to November 23[159].

Hitch tells Mary of the news of his friends in Company I and it is generally not very good, "*Mary, we had to leave Scruggs at West Point sick have not heard from him since. Mat Garrett is dead as you know. M.R. Garrett is not verry well. L.B. Edwards is tolerable well.*" Little Berry is still doing well but William Scruggs was left in the hospital back in Alabama. The worst news of all is that one of the "boys," Matt Garrett, has died. Service records indicate conflicting dates for when he died; August 20 or September 1. Since Hitch writes about Matt in a letter on August 21, the correct date when he passed was probably the Sep 1 1863 as in the records. Private Garrett had just reached his 19th birthday on August 24.

Young shares a few bits of small talk about the different locations he has seen, "*This is a verry good farming country, this & Ten both...*" and says that an engagement with the enemy may be in the offing, "*We are sorter expecting to meet some of our Enemy soon & it would not surprise me mutch if we don't see them this time.*" He adds, "*Mary, I would write to you about some clothing but things are in such an*

---

[157] Private James A. McCrary (c1838-1862) was son of Matthew McCrary. He died in camp near Wilmington, NC on Dec 22 1862 and his belongings were given to his brother there, also of Company I, Private William K. McCrary (1838-1915). William McCrary is buried with his wife, Polly, in the Clear Spring Baptist Church Cemetery, Simpsonville, SC. The two brothers may be twins as they are listed as the same age in the 1850 census.
[158] Appendix, Item LXXII.
[159] South Carolina's Military Organizations During the War Between the States; Volume III, The Upstate, Robert S. Seigler, The History Press, Charleston, SC, 2008; page 174-175.

uproar at present that I will wait awhile before I write. It may be that I have Enough or more than I can carry." He sees that things are rapidly reaching a flash point in northern Georgia and southern Tennessee and, history tells us that he is indeed correct. The Battle of Chickamauga is less than two weeks away, one of the bloodiest fights of the Civil War.

Like the previous correspondence, this letter was also written on recycled paper from the regimental hospital and the following list was included on the back page:

N.A. McKinney	*Private*	*16th*	*(page torn)*	
W.A. McHugh	*"*	*"*	*(page torn)*	
G.W. Lyons	*"*	*"*	*(page torn)*	
E.H. Boles	*Lieut.*	*"*	*G*	
A.J. Howard	*Private*	*"*	*"*	
W. Brown	*"*	*"*	*F*	
S.E. Smith	*"*	*"*	*"*	
S.P. Mims	*Sargt*	*"*	*A*	
H.T. Fisher	*Private*	*"*	*D*	
H.M. Bishop	*"*	*"*	*"*	
Jerry Fowler	*"*	*"*	*"*	
M.C. Cantrell	*"*	*"*	*H*	
J.H. Stansil	*"*	*"*	*E*	
James Hunt	*"*	*"*	*C*	
John Crafford	*"*	*"*	*E*	*otitis*
C.R. Twitty	*Sergt*	*"*	*A*	
John Wallace	*Private*	*"*	*A*	*Diarrhea*
T.M. Cox	*"*	*"*	*A*	
I.L. Henning	*Corp*	*"*	*A*	
I.G. Barton	*Private*	*"*	*A*	*Diarrhea*
L.C. Collins	*"*	*"*	*D*	*Dysentery*
F.M. Lenderman	*"*	*"*	*B*	*Catarrh*
C.W. Bridges	*"*	*"*	*B*	*Constipation*
James Hester 971	*"*	*"*	*K*	*Enteris Fever*
H. Springfield 972	*"*	*"*	*G*	*Dysentery*
H.W. Clayton 973	*"*	*"*	*C*	*Surditas*
George Shannon Green 974	*"*	*"*	*F*	*General debility*

In this month are recorded four names which count in 974, then discharged as being on sick report.

From this list, even though the page was torn and the Company not indicated directly, we know that Privates Newton A. McKinney,[160] William A. McHugh[161] and George W. Lyon(s)[162] were in Company I with Young Hitch. McKinney and Lyon would eventually die of illness before the war is over. Like the previous list, we do not know the date that this list was generated, perhaps many months earlier than the date Hitch writes his letter. Hitch then closes by writing between the lines of the above list, *"Tell me who thrashed our wheat for you, whether Hughes or Stone. Mary, direct your letters to Rome, Georgia. If I am spared, I will write again soon. Lucian, I have seen a heap of big towns in my travels but wish that I could see your little home in Laurens. Joseph, let me hear how you come out in pulling of your fodder."* A Mr. Hughes or Stone harvested the wheat on the farm and Hitch is inquiring about who it was exactly.

Young Hitch pens his next letter on Friday, Sep 18 1863 from Kingston, GA where the 16th is soon to be heading back to Tennessee[163]. Hitch states that the regiment is expected to leave at 12:00 that day for Tennessee but other records of the movement of the 16th indicate that they did not arrive back in Tennessee until September 23. Hitch writes:

> *"Dear Wife, I seat myself to drop you a short note. My health is as has been for some time. We are here at Kingston this morning on our way back to Ten. We came here yesterday and I suppose we will leave at 12 today for Ten. A great many soldiers passing this place. Troops from Virginia are rolling in. The 3rd regt of South Carolina passed last night. I saw Simeon Thackston & talked awhile with him. He was well and in high life. Sim said O.H.P. More was on bord but I did not see him."*

The entire Army of Tennessee was in the area of northern Georgia and across the state line into Tennessee with more troops still arriving from Virginia. Hitch had also run into his friend Private Simeon R. Thackston[164] of Company G, 3rd South Carolina infantry, who had rolled through the area. Thackston

---

160 Private Newton Jefferson Allen McKinney (1833-1864) was son of James McKinney of Greenville County and brother to Company I compatriot, Sergeant James Thomas Jefferson McKinney (1830-1864). Newton died of disease in a Dalton, GA hospital on Feb 23 1864 and his brother died less than six months later, on Aug 8 1864, of a wound received while conducting picket duty. The McKinney brothers married Wood sisters. Newton's wife was Mary Wood (1828-1895) and James married Keziah Wood (1832-1898), both daughters of Joseph and Mary (Garrett) Wood of Greenville. To make the family connection even more interesting, Private Nicholas Joseph Wood (1825-1895), also of Company I, was a brother to the Wood sisters and, therefore, brother-in-law to the McKinney's. Newton McKinney is buried in the Clear Spring Baptist Church Cemetery, Simpsonville, SC and his brother, James, in the Stonewall Confederate Cemetery in Griffin, Georgia. Nicholas Wood is buried in the Bellview Baptist Church Cemetery, Woodruff, SC.

161 Private William A. McHugh (1833-xx) had been discharged on Mar 27 1863 due his coming to the end of his service. Little more is known of this man.

162 Private George W. Lyon (1822/25-1864) died in a hospital near Dalton, GA on Mar 27 1864, about five weeks after his "mess" mate, Private Newton McKinney, dies in the same place. Not much else is known of Lyon except that he was a single farmer in 1850.

163 Appendix, Item LXXIII.

164 Simeon Robert Thackston (1839-1925), son of Nathaniel and Arza (Garrett) Thackston, enlisted as Private in Company G, 3rd South Carolina Battalion on Apr 14 1861 at Laurens Courthouse for 12 months at age 22. He re-enlisted on May 13 1862 for two years. Muster rolls show that he was wounded near Richmond, VA on Jun 29 1862 and sent home for furlough where he remained until at least Feb 1863. Then he shows as "present" in the May-Aug 1863 rolls when he was again wounded near Knoxville, TN sometime in Nov/Dec 1863 and remained in the hospital

was a veteran of action, having been wounded at Richmond, VA in June 1862. O.H.P. Moore, whom Young Hitch mentions, is Oliver Moore who was a member of the 3rd South Carolina (Laurens) battalion[165], by this time as a 2nd Lieutenant. Ironically, LT Moore would be killed two days after Hitch writes this letter, on September 20, during the Battle of Chickamauga[166].

Even though the 16th South Carolina regiment missed the action at Chickamauga on Sep 19-20 1863, some words about the battle are needed here. While Chickamauga was a decided Confederate victory, the results of the battle were staggering. There were over 16,000 Union and 18,000 Confederate casualties and, Chickamauga reached the highest losses of any battle in the Western theater. Although the Confederates had driven General Rosecrans from the field, they had not succeeded in General Bragg's objectives of destroying Rosecrans's army or reoccupying Chattanooga. Fighting would resume after about a two month siege and then battle for Chattanooga.

Besides the mention of Hitch's friend O.H.P. Moore above, who was killed in the battle, one of Young's relatives saw action and was wounded at Chickamauga, H. James Duvall. Like Moore, Duvall was also a member of the 3rd South Carolina (Laurens) battalion, Company C, and was wounded badly enough to have been absent from service until he was able to return in May 1864. It is also notable that another cousin of Young Hitch, John Wesley Pitts, had been a Private in the 3rd South Carolina battalion from Dec 2 1861. However, Pitts was discharged on Mar 18 1863 by the Medical Examiner's Board due to debility. Lastly, Major Robert Marcus Hitch of the 30th Georgia Volunteer Infantry and, another Hitch cousin, saw action at the Battle of Chickamauga but was not injured.

Young reports on the food and weather and his two friends, William Scruggs and Little Berry Edwards, *"This morning is quite cool. Last night it clouded up and sprinkled rain a little and is yet cloudy & wet. I haven't heard from Scruggs since we left him at West Point. Berry is tolerable well. He has cold & pretty bad cough but is better of that. We got us some sweet potatoes last night & have eaten hearty of them and some gingerbread whitch was very good. We have spent 3 dollars at this place for tater cakes."* He then turns to the activities of his unit with, *"I don't know where to say for you to direct your letters now as we are on a march but it don't matter mutch for letters come sometimes directed to no certain point. We can't go as far on railway as we did before on account of the bridges being burned. Probably we may have a heap of marching to do."* With railroad bridges being strategically destroyed by both the Union and Confederate forces, it was more difficult to get around and, many times, the only way to get from one place to the other was to march.

One more tidbit of information is forthcoming in Hitch's letter that offers a feel for the inflation that has hit the Confederate economy by late 1863; *"Mary, you may want to know if I have any money. I only*

---

until Feb 1864. He shows as present in the rolls for May/Jun 1864 and then as paroled on May 2 1865. (Confederate Service Records, National Archives, Washington, DC)

[165] Note that the 3rd South Carolina Regiment Infantry is an entirely different unit from the 3rd South Carolina (Laurens) Battalion.

[166] Oliver H.P. Moore (1828/29-1863), son of Harrison and Susannah Moore of Laurens County, enlisted as Private in Company E, 3rd South Carolina (Laurens) Battalion on Jan 2 1862 at Camp Hampton for 12 months. He shows as "present" in the Jan-Apr 1862 rolls and is elected 3rd and then 2nd Lieutenant later in 1862. He was killed at the Battle of Chickamauga on Sep 20 1863 (Ibid.)

have 12 dollars. I have not made arry draw since May. I have a half dollar in silver whitch is as good as five dollars of Confederate money. I am a most oblige to spend some and can get but little ever thing is so high." He remarks that 50 cents in silver being as good as $5.00 in CSA currency which is probably fairly accurate at this stage of the war.

This is the final fully readable letter from Hitch that survives from 1863. Hitch does compose letters on November 6 and 15 and December 19 that are in the Mowbray collection but largely unreadable[167]. The paper they are written on is poorly preserved and the ink has faded so to make them largely illegible. It is unfortunate because this is the time when the Battles of Lookout Mountain and Missionary Ridge in Tennessee occurred. We can still fill in the three month "hole" in the records of Young Hitch by examining the limited number of his legible words in the surviving letters and by providing information from other records from other sources.

The first of the barely readable letters comes on Nov 6 1863 from "Near Chattanooga, Tenn." The only information we can glean from this letter is that Hitch had been in Georgia until November 4 and left from where he was positioned for Atlanta at 1:00 p.m. that day and, subsequently, left Atlanta at 9:00 p.m. for Chattanooga. From there, he went to find Company I where he reunited with before revelry on November 5. Unfortunately, there is not enough decipherable information in the rest of the letter to tell us why he was away from his unit in the first place. However, Hitch's service records show that, in the muster rolls for September and October 1863, he was "sick in the hospital," so he probably was returning from sick bay. There is one titillating line from the November 6 letter of which the only readable thing is, "*I hear since I come to the camp of the Death of two...*" The rest of the letter is unreadable so, we do not know who the two people were; but, we do know from the records that Privates Jeremiah C. Baldwin[168] and J.B. Greer[169] both died of disease on Oct 21 1863 as had Private John F. Goodwin[156] on Sep 23 1863. Hitch may have been writing about two of these men of his fellow Company I "mess" mates. Additionally, Private Nicholas J. Wood[160] was wounded in the foot in the action after Chickamauga on Sep 26 1863[170].

Also, although Hitch probably would not have known of this by the time he wrote the letter of November 6, Company I's Captain Newton Babb died in the hospital on Nov 6 1863[171]. Practically nothing of note is discernable from Hitch's November 15 letter except that he mentions his friend, William Scruggs, and fellow Company I soldier, Private Young Howard[172].

---

[167] Appendix, Item LXXIV, LXXV and LXXVI.

[168] Private Jeremiah C. Baldwin (1827-1863) was son of Benjamin Franklin and Sarah Baldwin of Greenville County. He is buried in the Clear Spring Baptist Church Cemetery, Simpsonville, SC.

[169] Private John B. Greer (1838-1863) was son of Isaac and Mary A. (Snow) Greer of Greenville County. It is unknown whether he is related to Private James Manning Greer (1826-1900) who was son of John and Sarah (Hawkins) Greer of Greenville. While it is uncertain where John Greer is buried, James M. Greer is buried with his wife, Mollie (Tarver) Greer (1824-1889), in the Ebenezer United Methodist Church Cemetery, Greer, SC.

[170] Confederate Military Service records, National Archives, Washington, DC.

[171] Ibid.

[172] Private Young O. Howard (1842/43-1864) was son of Stephen S. and Mary (Goodwin) Howard of Greenville County. He was killed in the action around Atlanta, GA on Aug 24 1864.

In the final letter from 1863, dated December 19, not much of importance is readable either. Hitch comments about (Little) Berry Edwards as "*...a hog & lazy to kill. He is a full brother to Billy Edwards. He is verry (__) & sullen with the boys in talking. He is not as well liked now as he was when he first came to the regt. Me & him gets on fine. Please read & burn this. I don't wish to start up a fuss.*" We do not know what has prompted Little Berry to get this description attached to him by Hitch but he does not want it to get out and cause a "fuss," instructing Mary to burn the letter (which she obviously did not).

As Young Hitch caught up to, and reunited with, his unit on November 5, not much had happened with the 16th regiment since late September. After the Battle of Chickamauga on the 19th and 20th of that month, the regiment camped at the base of Lookout Mountain from September 23 till November 23 as the Confederate siege of Chattanooga was underway[173].

Probably unbeknownst to Hitch at the time, his cousin, Young Joseph Harrington Pitts, had joined as a Private in Company D, 19th South Carolina regiment on Nov 3 1863. Three weeks later, he was taken prisoner, having been captured at Missionary Ridge. He is listed as being admitted sick to a U.S. field hospital in Nashville, TN on Dec 13 1863 and then sent on as a POW to Louisville, KY on Jan 6 1864. From there, Pitts gets processed out to the U.S. POW camp at Rock Island, IL and listed as "for exchange." He was apparently exchanged and discharged from Rock Island on Jan 17 1864[174].

Another cousin, Henry Tyler Templeton, a Private in Company A, 3rd South Carolina infantry, had also been taken prisoner near this time. Templeton had been "left behind" on a march from Knoxville, TN and was captured on Dec 4 1863 and sent to Camp Chase, OH on December 15 and on to Rock Island on December 31. But, unlike Young J.H. Pitts being exchanged, Private Templeton was confined in the POW camp at Rock Island for the rest of the war, only being freed after he signed an Oath of Allegiance on Jun 22 1865[175].

SIEGE OF CHATTANOOGA: Some more historical background of the general war action in northern Georgia and Tennessee in the autumn of 1863 is helpful here. After their disastrous defeat at the Battle of Chickamauga, the 40,000 men of the Union Army of the Cumberland under Major General William Rosecrans retreated to Chattanooga. Bragg's Army of Tennessee besieged the city, threatening to starve the Union forces into surrender. The Confederates established themselves on Missionary Ridge and Lookout Mountain, both very strategically positioned with excellent views of the city, the Tennessee River flowing through the city, and Union supply lines. Lookout Mountain is actually a narrow plateau that extends 85 miles southwest from the Tennessee River, terminating in a sharp point 1,800 feet above the river. From the river the end of the mountain rises at a steep angle and at about 2/3rds of the way to the summit it flattens, forming a ledge, 150–300 feet wide, extending for several miles around

---

[173] South Carolina's Military Organizations During the War Between the States; Volume IV, Statewide Units, Militia and Reserves, Robert S. Seigler, The History Press, Charleston, SC, 2008; page 86.
[174] Before his service with the 19th SC regiment, Pitts had earlier served as a Private with Company B, 9th South Carolina Reserves from Nov 17 1862 to Feb 14 1863. (Confederate Military Service records at the National Archives, Washington, DC).
[175] Private Templeton's Oath of Allegiance describes him as age 23, fresh complexion, dark hair, grey eyes and 5'-8" tall. (Ibid.)

both sides of the mountain. Above the ledge, the grade steepens again into a 500-foot face of rock called the "palisades."

Confederate artillery atop Lookout Mountain controlled access by the river, and Confederate cavalry launched raids on all supply wagons heading toward Chattanooga, which made it necessary for the Union to find another way to feed their men. The federal government sent reinforcements to try and alleviate the issue. On October 17, Grant received command of the Western armies (designated as the Military Division of the Mississippi), moved to reinforce Chattanooga and replaced Rosecrans with Major General George H. Thomas.

Thomas launched a surprise amphibious landing at Brown's Ferry on October 27 that opened the Tennessee River by linking up Thomas's Army of the Cumberland with a relief column of 20,000 troops from the Eastern Theater's Army of the Potomac, led by Major General Joseph Hooker. Supplies and reinforcements were thus able to flow into Chattanooga over a supply artery now known as the "Cracker Line." In response, Bragg ordered Lt. General James Longstreet to force the federals out of Lookout Valley, directly to the west of Lookout Mountain. The ensuing Battle of Wauhatchie (October 28–29) was one of the war's few battles fought exclusively at night. The Confederates were repulsed, and the Cracker Line maintained.

On November 12, Bragg placed Major General Carter L. Stevenson in overall command for the defense of the mountain, with Stevenson's own division positioned on the summit. The brigades of John K. Jackson, Edward C. Walthall, and John C. Moore were placed on the bench of the mountain. Jackson later wrote about the dissatisfaction of the commanders assigned to this area, "Indeed, it was agreed on all hands that the position was one extremely difficult to defense against a strong force of the enemy advancing under cover of a heavy fire." Although Stevenson placed an artillery battery on the crest of the mountain, the guns could not be depressed at low enough an angle to reach the bench, which was accessible by the Union forces from numerous trails on the west side of the mountain.

Sherman arrived from Vicksburg, with his 20,000 men of the Army of the Tennessee in mid-November. Grant, Sherman, and Thomas then planned a double envelopment of Bragg's force, with the main attack coming from Sherman against the northern end of Missionary Ridge, supported by Thomas in the center. Hooker would support by capturing Lookout Mountain and then move across the Chattanooga Valley to Rossville, GA to cut off any attempt at a Confederate retreat southward. Grant later withdrew his planned support for a major attack by Hooker on Lookout Mountain, intending the mass of his attack to be by Sherman. On November 23, Sherman was ready to cross the Tennessee River. Grant ordered Thomas to advance halfway to Missionary Ridge on a reconnaissance to determine the strength of the Confederate line, hoping to ensure that Bragg would not withdraw his forces and move in the direction of Knoxville, TN, where Major General Ambrose Burnside was being threatened by a Confederate force under Longstreet. Thomas sent 14,000 men toward a minor hill named Orchard Knob and overran the Confederate defenders.

Surprised by Thomas's move against Orchard Knob, and realizing that his center might be more vulnerable than he had thought, Bragg quickly readjusted his strategy and recalled all units within a day's march that he had recently ordered to Knoxville. He began to reduce the strength on his left by

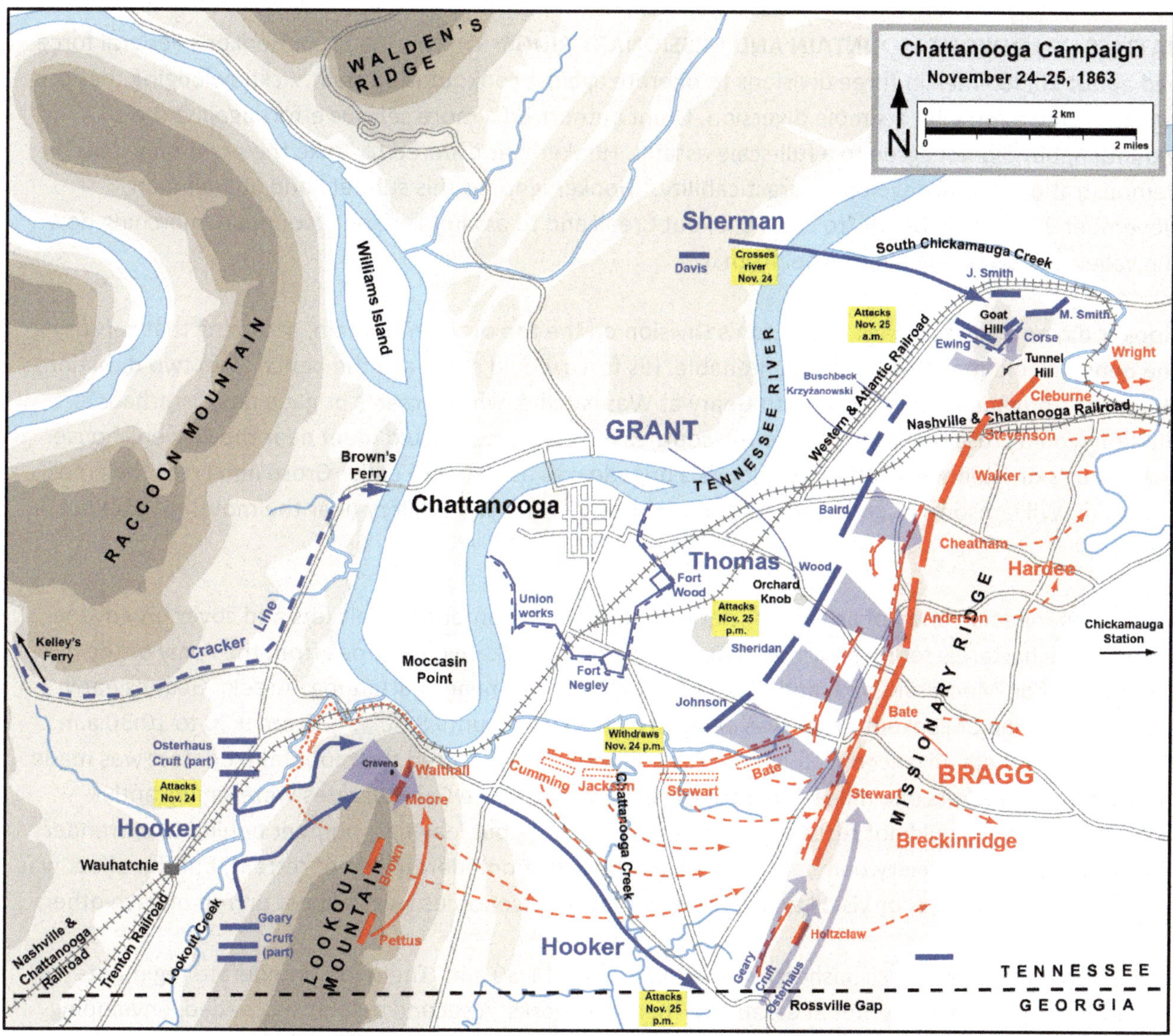

Figure 17 - Wide depiction of the Battles of Lookout Mountain and Missionary Ridge, Nov 24-25 1863. (Map by Hal Jespersen, *www.cwmaps.com*)

withdrawing Walker's division (and the 16th SCVI) from the base of Lookout Mountain and placing them on the far right of Missionary Ridge. He assigned Hardee to command his now critical right flank, turning over the left flank to Carter Stevenson. Stevenson needed to fill the gap left by Walker's division from the mountain to Chattanooga Creek, so he sent Jackson's brigade of Cheatham's Division and Cummings' brigade of his own division into that position. Stevenson deployed Walthall's brigade of 1,500 Mississippians as pickets near the base of the mountain, withholding enough for a reserve for Moore's brigade, which would defend the main line on the bench near the Cravens house.

The Union side also changed plans. Sherman had three divisions ready to cross the Tennessee, but the pontoon bridge at Brown's Ferry had torn apart and Brigadier General Peter J. Osterhaus's division was stranded in Lookout Valley. After receiving assurances from Sherman that he could proceed with three divisions, Grant decided to revive the previously rejected plan for an attack on Lookout Mountain and reassigned Osterhaus to Hooker's command to help with that effort. A battle was in the offing.

BATTLES OF LOOKOUT MOUNTAIN AND MISSIONARY RIDGE: On Nov 24 1863, Hooker's Federal force had about 10,000 men in three divisions to operate against Lookout Mountain. Acknowledging that this was too large a force for a simple diversion, Grant authorized a more serious effort against the mountain, but did not agree to a full-scale assault. Hooker was ordered to "take the point only if his demonstration should develop its practicability." Hooker ignored this subtlety and at 3 a.m. on November 24 ordered Geary "to cross Lookout Creek and to assault Lookout Mountain, marching down the valley and sweeping every rebel from it."

Hooker did not plan to attack Stevenson's Division on the top of the mountain, assuming that capturing the bench would make his position untenable. His force would approach the bench from two directions: Whitaker's brigade would link up with Geary at Wauhatchie, while Grose's brigade and Osterhaus's division would cross Lookout Creek to the southeast. Both forces would meet near the Cravens house. Osterhaus's division was in support: Woods's brigade was assigned to cover Grose and cross the creek after him; Williamson's brigade was assigned to protect Hooker's artillery near the mouth of Lookout Creek.

Hooker arranged an array of artillery batteries to fire at the Confederate pickets and cover his advance. He had nine batteries set up near the mouth of Lookout Creek, two batteries from the Army of the Cumberland on Moccasin Point, and two additional batteries near Chattanooga Creek. Geary's early morning crossing of Lookout Creek was delayed by high water until 8:30 a.m. From 9:30 to 10:30 a.m., Geary's skirmishers advanced through the fog and mist that obscured the mountain. Contact was made with Walthall's pickets one mile southwest of Lookout Point. The Confederates were significantly outnumbered and could not resist the pressure, falling back but leaving a number behind to surrender. Hooker ordered an artillery bombardment to saturate the Confederate line of retreat, but the effect was minimized because of poor visibility and the fact that the two forces were almost on top of each other.

The Union pursuit of the skirmishers was halted around 11:30 a.m. The two Confederate regiments repulsed Ireland's first attempt at assaulting their fieldworks. A second assault succeeded, enveloping and outnumbering the Confederates 4-to-1. Despite Walthall's attempt to rally his men, he could not prevent a disorderly retreat and, the Union brigades kept up their pursuit past the point and along the bench. As Geary's Union forces appeared below the point around noon, Candy's brigade advanced across the lower elevations of the mountain, clearing the enemy from the east bank of Lookout Creek. Hooker ordered Woods's and Grose's brigades to begin crossing the foot bridge over the creek. Woods moved east at the base of the mountain, Grose moved up the slope. These movements isolated part of Walthall's Brigade and the entire 34th Mississippi was forced to surrender, along with 200 men from Moore's picket line

When Stevenson on the summit heard the fighting between Walthall and Geary, he ordered Pettus to take three regiments from the summit to assist Jackson. By this time, Moore's Alabamians were moving up amidst Walthall's retreating men, and they fired on Ireland's New Yorkers from 100 yards. Unable to see the size of the force resisting it through the fog, the Union men retreated beyond a stone wall. Moore's 1,000 men took positions in the rifle pits facing the wall and waited for the inevitable counterattack. Ireland's men were too exhausted to make an immediate move. As Whitaker's brigade

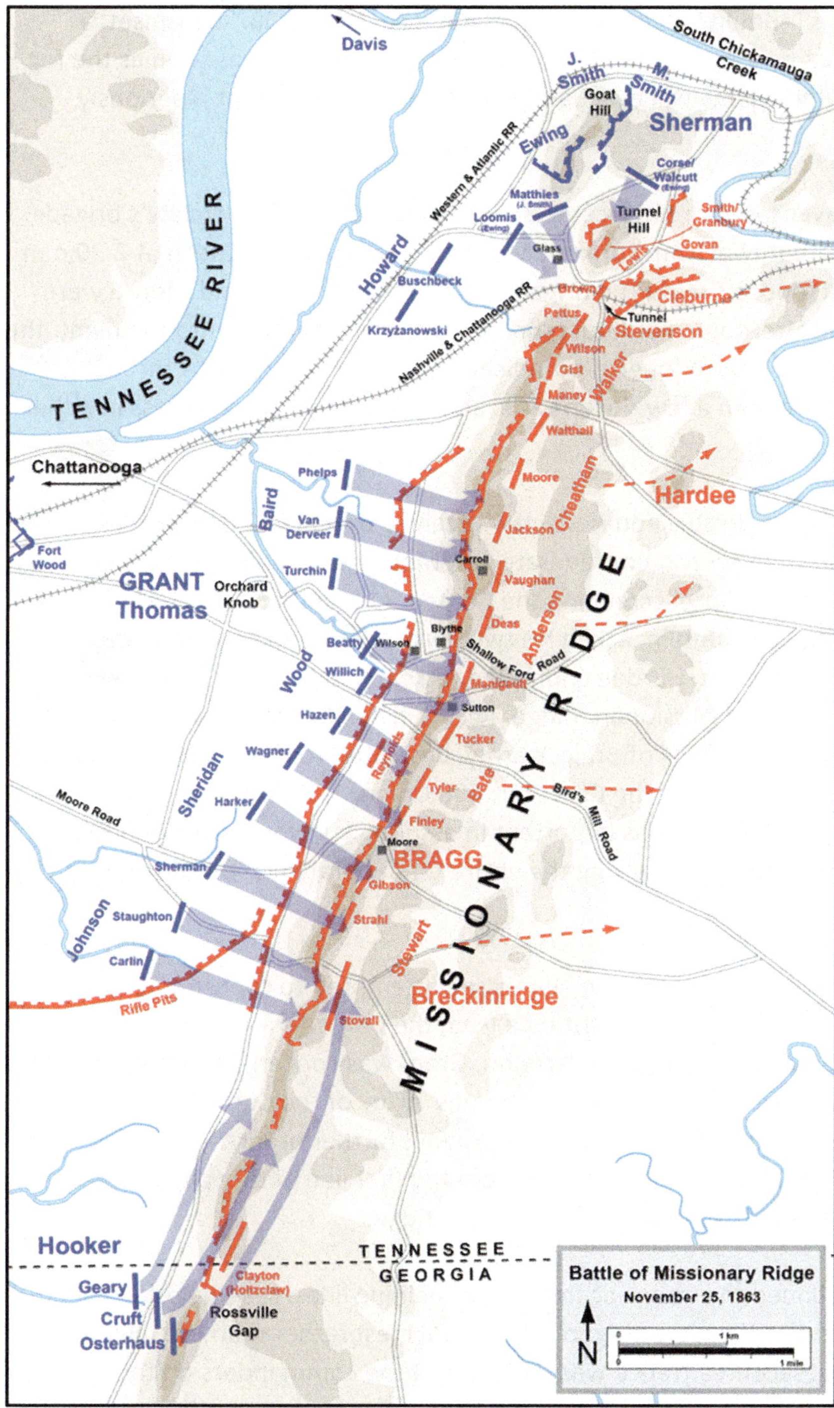

Figure 18 - Close-up of the action at Missionary Ridge on Nov 25 1863. (Map by Hal Jespersen, *www.cwmaps.com*)

arrived after 1 p.m., they stepped over Ireland's men and rushed into the attack. Candy's brigade was moving up the mountain side on Whitaker's left, followed by the brigades of Woods and Grose. Moore could see that he was being significantly outflanked on the right and chose to fall back rather than be surrounded.

All of the Union brigades, including Ireland's tired men, began the pursuit. Hooker was concerned that his lines were becoming intermingled and confused by the fog and the rugged ground and they were tempting defeat if the Confederates brought up reinforcements in the right place. He ordered Geary to halt for the day, but Geary was too far behind his troops to stop them. Hooker wrote, "Fired by success, with a flying, panic-stricken enemy before them, they pressed impetuously forward."

Moore's brigade was able to escape in the fog and Walthall had adequate time to form a rough defensive line 3–400 yards south of the Cravens house. His 600 men took cover behind boulders and fallen trees and made enough of a racket to dissuade Whitaker's men from moving against them. By this time Pettus' brigade of three Alabama regiments had descended from the summit and came to Walthall's assistance after 2 p.m.

Hooker sent to Grant alternating messages of concern and confidence. At 1:25 p.m. he wrote that the "conduct of all the troops has been brilliant, and the success has far exceeded my expectations. Our loss has not been severe, and of prisoners I should judge that we had not less than 2,000." By sunset, a confident Hooker informed Grant that he intended to move into Chattanooga Valley as soon as the fog lifted. He signaled "In all probability the enemy will evacuate tonight. His line of retreat is seriously threatened by my troops."

Bragg responded to a request by Stevenson for reinforcements by sending Col. J.T. Holtzclaw's brigade to be used to cover a Confederate withdrawal from Lookout Mountain, ordering Stevenson at 2:30 p.m. to withdraw to the east side of Chattanooga Creek. The brigades of Walthall, Pettus, and Moore were ordered to hold on for the rest of the afternoon. For hours through the afternoon and into the night, the six Alabama regiments under Pettus and Moore fought sporadically with the Union troops through dense fog, neither side able to see more than a few dozen yards ahead nor make any progress in either direction.

By midnight, Lookout Mountain was quiet. Pettus and Holtzclaw received orders at 2 a.m. to march off the mountain. Postwar writings of both Union and Confederate veterans refer to a brilliant moon, which slipped into the blackness of a total lunar eclipse, screening the Confederate withdrawal[176]. That night Bragg, stunned by the defeat on Lookout Mountain, asked his two corps commanders whether to retreat from Chattanooga or to stand and fight. Hardee counseled retreat, but Breckinridge convinced Bragg to fight it out on the strong position of Missionary Ridge. Accordingly, the troops withdrawn from Lookout Mountain were ordered to the right flank of Bragg's army. Casualties for the Battle of Lookout Mountain were relatively light by the standards of the Civil War: 408 Union, 1,251 Confederate (including 1,064 captured or missing). The action was important in assuring control of the Tennessee River and the railroad into Chattanooga and endangering the entire Confederate line on Missionary Ridge[177].

The next morning, November 25, Sherman's Army of the Tennessee attempted to capture the northern end of Missionary Ridge, but were stopped by fierce resistance from the Confederates, specifically Cleburne's, Walker's, and Stevenson's divisions. In the afternoon, Grant was concerned that Bragg was reinforcing his right flank at Sherman's expense. He ordered Thomas' Army of the Cumberland to seize a Confederate line of rifle pits on the valley floor, and stop there to await further orders. The Union soldiers moved forward and quickly pushed the Confederates from the first line of rifle pits but were then subjected to a punishing fire from the Confederate lines up the ridge.

At this point, the Union soldiers continued the attack against the remaining lines, seeking refuge near the crest of the ridge (the top line of rifle pits were sited on the actual crest rather than the military crest of the ridge, leaving blind spots). This second advance was taken up by the commanders on the spot, but also by some of the soldiers who, on their own, sought shelter from the fire further up the slope. The Union advance was disorganized but effective; finally overwhelming and scattering what ought to have been, as General Grant himself believed, an impregnable Confederate line. In combination with an

[176] There was a full lunar eclipse visible over the entire United States on the night of Nov 25 1863. (*eclipse.gsfc.nasa.gov/LEhistory/LEplot/LE1863Nov25P.pdf*).
[177] "Battle of Lookout Mountain," wikipedia.com, Mar 23 2015.

advance from the southern end of the ridge by divisions under Hooker, the Union Army routed Bragg's army, which retreated to Dalton, Georgia, ending the siege of Union forces in Chattanooga, TN[178].

The 16th South Carolina Regiment, as part of Gist's brigade, had evacuated their position at the foot of Lookout Mountain on November 23 and marched to a position on the right on the Confederate lines on Missionary Ridge. See **Figure 18** for an illustration of the Confederate line on Missionary Ridge and the position of Gist's brigade in the center of Walker's division on the right side of the line. The regiment was under fire but only lightly engaged on November 25 as the battle played out. They acted as rear guard for Hardee's corps on November 26 as the Confederate forces withdrew. Companies B, E and K were detached to support Ferguson's Artillery battery on that same day in the rear at Graysville, GA and most were captured, along with three of four cannon in the battery. The 16th stayed in reserve for rear guard action at Ringgold Gap, GA and then arrived in Dalton, GA on November 27. There, they set to constructing winter quarters which they completed by Dec 15 1863[179].

Company I of the 16th regiment shows only two casualties from the battles at Lookout Mountain and Missionary Ridge: Private George R. Fowler[180] was listed as captured on Nov 27 1863. He would later die in a U.S. Army field hospital of disease (chronic diarrhea) in Nashville, TN on Dec 16 1863. Private John Stepp[181] was also listed as captured on November 27 near Missionary Ridge and sent to Louisville, KY on December 9, then on to the POW camp at Rock Island, IL on Dec 11 1863. He died there on Feb 4 1864 of disease[182].

The northern army, under General Grant, had effectively driven the Confederate forces out of Tennessee at the battles of Lookout Mountain and Missionary Ridge in November 1863. The Army of Tennessee, then commanded by General Braxton Bragg, fell back to northern Georgia, where Bragg would be replaced by General Joseph E. Johnston. In the immediate aftermath of the retreat from Tennessee, the defensive-minded Johnston arranged his force along the imposing Rocky Face Ridge near Dalton, GA. This is where Young Hitch and his Company I compatriots were as we begin the year 1864.

---

178 "Battle of Missionary Ridge," wikipedia.com, Mar 10 2015.

179 South Carolina's Military Organizations During the War Between the States; Volume III, The Upstate, Robert S. Seigler, The History Press, Charleston, SC, 2008; page 175.

180 Private George Riley Fowler (1830-1863) was son of George and Catherine (Cox) Fowler of Greenville County.

181 Private John Stepp (1840-1864) was son of John and Esther (Payne) Stepp of Greenville County.

182 Confederate Military Service records, National Archives, Washington, DC.

CHAPTER 6
1864
"It is made my painful Duty to inform you that your Dear husband is no more…"

By 1864, the war had worn on so long that the citizens in the North wanted peace so badly that they were willing to replace the Republican incumbent, President Abraham Lincoln, with a Democratic choice who would repudiate their pro-war and anti-slavery policies[183]. So, the feeling at the time was that, if the South could hold out until the presidential elections in the Fall of 1864 without being defeated, then they could break the will of the North, get Lincoln ousted as President and, set the stage to be recognized as an independent entity.

In order not to lose the Union, Lincoln and the Republicans realized that, as 1864 dawned, the Union must set forth to put an end to the war by soundly defeating the Confederates and at least show that the war could be won by the Union before the election of 1864. To do this, Lincoln appointed Ulysses S. Grant to the newly created rank of lieutenant general on Mar 9 1864. Grant had proven his worth by capturing whole Rebel armies at Fort Donelson and Vicksburg and routing another at Chattanooga.

Figure 19 - General Joe Johnston, commander of the Army of Tennessee. He replaced General Braxton Bragg after the Tennessee battles.

To accomplish Lincoln's objectives, Grant devised a plan to go at the South in a two pronged approach. One would be to advance and try and take Richmond and the state of Virginia while a second focus would be to capture the economic hub of the South at Atlanta. For the latter, Grant chose his good friend Major General William Tecumseh Sherman to lead the effort. Grant chose Sherman not so much on his abilities as a General but more so his standing as a friend he could trust to carry out his orders and strategic plan[184].

Also, in the month previous to his appointment of Grant to the Union Army's highest rank, Lincoln issued a call for 200,000 additional troops in February 1864 to augment the 300,000 he had summoned the previous October. A force of a half million new soldiers would be more than the Confederacy could muster altogether!

The South's strategy by early 1864 had sought to "win by not losing" and forcing the North to lose its will to continue fighting an unwinnable war. So, this became the strategy of the Confederacy, it must absolutely deny the Union victories in Virginia and Georgia. Jefferson Davis would rely on General Robert E. Lee to secure Virginia and keep the Union out of

---

[183] "Kennesaw Mountain and the Atlanta Campaign", text by Albert Castel, National Park Civil War Series, copyright 2014 and published by Eastern National, page 2.
[184] Ibid., page 3

Richmond, the capital of the Confederacy and the very symbol of its independence. Much confidence was given to Lee by Davis to carry this part of the strategy to successful completion.

When the Union drove the Confederates out of Tennessee at the battles of Lookout Mountain and Missionary Ridge in November 1863, the Army of Tennessee, then commanded by General Braxton Bragg, fell back to northern Georgia. Davis replaced Bragg with General Joe Johnston, who took command on Dec 27 1863 in Dalton, Georgia. The defensive-minded Johnston, after Bragg's retreat, arranged his force along the imposing Rocky Face Ridge near Dalton, a town that was directly situated on the Western & Atlantic Railroad to Atlanta. The railroad would be a key mode for supplying both armies as the Atlanta campaign played out.

Figure 20 - Lt. General William J. Hardee, commander of Hardee's Corps where the 16th South Carolina served in the Atlanta Campaign.

Davis *"considered Johnston to be vain and selfish as a man and as a general more inclined to retreat than to fight, to defend rather than to attack, and so recalcitrant in implementing the wishes of the government with regard to military operations as to border on the insubordinate."*[185] Johnston got his command just after Chattanooga, more because he was the only available officer with the training and tenure and not because he was well-liked by President Davis. Davis could only hope that Johnston would be more aggressive and cooperative in his strategy in northern Georgia in order to keep the Confederacy alive.

We will let the reader research the campaigns in Virginia between Grant and Lee as a separate subject. For this book, we now focus on the campaign in Georgia as it drifted out of Chattanooga in late 1863 and into northern Georgia in the very early part of 1864. This was the preface to the Atlanta campaign which began in May 1864 but was set into motion officially when Grant sent Sherman his instructions on Apr 4 1864 to *"move against Johnston's Army to break it up, and get into the interior of the enemy's country as far as you can, inflicting all the damage you can against their war resources."*[186]

Sherman replied on April 10 that his mission was to *"knock Jos. Johnston, and do as much damage to the resources of the enemy as possible."* He wanted to drive the Army of Tennessee back to Atlanta and eventually take the city. Sherman had about 110,000 soldiers to try and accomplish his objective. 65,000 of these were the infantry and artillery of the Army of the Cumberland commanded by Major General George H. Thomas. 23,000 more of these soldiers belonged to Major General James B. McPherson's Army of the Tennessee[187]. Next in size was the Army of the Ohio consisting of 11,000 men of the U.S. XXIII Corps commanded by Major General John M. Schofield and a few soldiers of Major

---

[185] Ibid, page 3.
[186] Ibid, page 5.
[187] Note that the Union's Army of "the" Tennessee is distinctly different from the Confederate Army of Tennessee. The North typically named their armies after rivers where, the South named theirs after states or parts thereof.

General George Stoneman's cavalry. The balance of soldiers at Sherman's disposal were an artillery of 254 cannons and 11,000 cavalry troopers.

For the Confederate side, Johnston had a comparatively small army of about 50-55,000 troops and 144 cannon[188]. The infantry consisted of two corps commanded by Lieutenant Generals William J. Hardee and John Bell Hood, respectively. The cavalry, included in the above total, consisted of about 8,500 men commanded by Major General Joseph Wheeler. By June 1, the estimated number of men participating in the Atlanta campaign for the Union army was about 113,000 and, for the Confederate side, 70,000 infantry and cavalry, as General Leonidas K. Polk's corps had reunited with Johnston and increased his total by about 16,500 infantry.

In the Atlanta Campaign, Young Hitch and the 16th South Carolina regiment would serve in Hardee's Army Corps under Major General William T.H. Walker's Division and Brigadier General States Rights Gist's Brigade. Hardee's Corps was the largest of Johnston's army with about 22,000 men. With the 16th in Gist's brigade, were the 8th Georgia Battalion, the 46th Georgia and the 24th South Carolina. The 16th South Carolina regiment was still under the command of Colonel James McCullough[189]. The stage now set, we follow Young Hitch and the 16th South Carolina Regiment through the correspondences of Hitch and his family as the year 1864 unfolds and, they embark with the Army of Tennessee on the Atlanta Campaign.

Figure 21 - Major General William Henry Talbot Walker (1816-1864), commander of Walker's Division for which the 16th South Carolina served in the Atlanta Campaign. Gen. Walker was killed in Atlanta on Jul 22 1864.

JANUARY and FEBRUARY 1864

These correspondences cover the period in early 1864 before the big push by Sherman that would become his campaign to take Atlanta that officially began on May 7 1864. The letters in the Mowbray collection from this period offer various tidbits of information about life in the camps, health conditions and supplies. They also provide insight into the families trying to conduct family business with the men away from home tending to the war.

The first letter from 1864 in the collection is dated Jan 19 1864 from near Dalton, Georgia[190]. Hardee's Corps, along with the rest of the Army of Tennessee had left Chattanooga in late 1863 and headed into Georgia and had camped near the town of Dalton for a few months. Little did they know at the time that

---

188 William R. Scaife reports an effective strength, as of April 30, 1864, just before the start of the Atlanta Campaign, of 110,123 total for the Union and 54,500 infantry for the Confederates; The Campaign for Atlanta, William R. Scaife, McNaughton & Gunn, 1993.

189 "Order of Battle, Federal and Confederate Forces Engaged in the Campaign for Atlanta, May 7 to September 2, 1864", William R. Scaife, Atlanta, GA, published by McNaughton & Gunn, 1992.

190 Appendix, Item LXXVII.

this was the dawn of Sherman's Atlanta Campaign that would have General Johnston's Army of Tennessee slowly drifting backwards along the path from Chattanooga as Sherman and his Union forces looked to capture the economic hub of the South at Atlanta. **Figure 26** shows the eventual progression from near Dalton, Georgia in early May 1864 to the Battle of Kennesaw Mountain on Jun 27 1864 (remembering that the 16th South Carolina regiment and Young Hitch are part of Hardee's Corps).

Young Hitch's letter of January 19 came during a relative lull time before the big push towards Atlanta, and its associated battle action. The letter is special in that Young writes to Mary Hitch on their 17th anniversary of their marriage (hence, the reason this letter is affectionately called the "Anniversary Letter"). It is a poignant bit of prose and probably one of the most fascinating letters in the entire collection for it shows deep feeling and emotion and Young's melancholy lament over having been at war and not with his wife and family for many months.

He also shows a compassionate and tender side not often exposed in his other correspondences with an undertone sense that he will not survive the war to enjoy life with his wife again. He writes, rather sadly, *"True we are hopeing for this war to close so that we may have the pleasure of being at home together and enjoying life together again. But our hopes I fear will never be granted."* And then Young waxes poetically a heartfelt yearning to see his wife and home and experience the intimacy that he misses while away at war:

> *"Oh how happy I would feel if I could have the privilege of starting this evening to see you. I would feel proud indeed. I should not know how to contain myself until I could get home. The cars*[191] *would not run fast enough for me. Mary it has been a long time since I have had a hug and kiss. I would not say go away to you now I don't think as I have often done. But I hope that you will forgive all sutch offences. Let them pass by."*

Figure 22 – Brig. General States Rights Gist, the commander of Gist's Brigade of which Young Hitch and the 16th South Carolina were a part during the Atlanta Campaign. He was killed at the Battle of Franklin (Tennessee) on Nov 30 1864.

This passage speaks for itself and we, as readers of Young Hitch's mindful prose, can get a sense of feeling what it must have been like being so far from home for so long in a situation that was growing ever more desperate as time passed. Young Hitch's final march had begun.

Young writes to his wife again six days later on January 25[192]. This letter is more mundane and covers mainly the difficulties in the camp of getting items from home and keeping his clothes in good working order. The problem that many soldiers endured in getting and maintaining useable things to wear is explicitly expressed in Young's writing as, *"True my clothes are good sutch as they are and do verry well so long as (__ing) at this place ever get socks, gloves and a cap. I have pants some three weeks before Christmas but if I had not taken care of them they would (not?) of last. They would have had the seat worn out by now."* Evidently, Mr. Garrett

[191] "Cars" are referring to the train cars that transported the soldiers.

[192] Appendix, Item LXXVIII.

(probably Archibald Y. Garrett or perhaps, Miles R. Garrett), who had delivered news and the letters to Mary Hitch had also told her of the bad shape his clothes were in!

Garrett also must have related some troubles that had cropped up in Young's Company I as he pens, *"Garrett landed here yesterday evening Sunday. He brought me some letters only nothing else. Mary if their has been any falling out in our mess I know nothing of it. What hapened while I was absent I cant tell. Scruggs quit our mess while he was on patrol guard because he had to be there all the time or nearly so. But they have broken up that guard and he comes back to camp. He has not been more than three hundred (__) us all the while. He thought I suppose that he could have some chance (__) over there."* From this we see that there must have been some trouble in Young Hitch's "mess" but it had happened while Young was absent and not apparently continuing by the time he writes the letter. However, it appears that "Scruggs" (no doubt, William Berry Scruggs, Mary Hitch's first cousin) was sufficiently dismayed with the "mess" that he quit because he was forced to be on patrol guard nearly all the time. But, with his new "guard" being "broken up", he was forced to return to Young's camp.

Finally, the letter talks about the possibility for Mary Hitch to come out to visit Young in his camp in Dalton, Georgia. He relates to her, *"Mary if you think you can stand the trip out and wish to come to see me I want you to use your own choice in the matter provided you can get Mrs. Vaughn and Mr. Vaughn to come with you or some person that you can depend upon. If I understand you hant put in the little things in the trunk for me. If you do come be sure to wrap yourself up in clothing. Bring me a coat and pair of pants. If it is cold you can put my coat on and wear it. You need not put buttons on. I will furnish them. If you don't leave and Vaughn comes let him bring the coat and pants. Mary I...* (there are about 3 more sentences here that are unreadable)*...Mary I think hard of some but not you in the least you start with money enough ... & if you have a small trunk you could bring a jug ___ by packing it ____ with clothing & other things."*

This passage is interesting in several ways. First, it covers Young's concern that Mary not travel alone but to come with Mr. and Mrs. Vaughn or someone that can be depended upon. He also instructs her to dress warmly in the January chill. Secondly, though he asks Mary not to worry about his clothes earlier in the letter, he instructs her to bring him a coat and pair of pants. In fact, even if she does not come to visit, he wishes her to send these items via the Vaughns when they come, this again showing the dire need for proper clothing in the camps. He also asks her to bring a jug of something - unfortunately, the contents of the jug requested is not readable in the letter but one can surmise that it might be some sort of spirit to help stave off the cold of winter while in the camp.

Finally Young ends the letter with a short note to his son Augustus Lucian Hitch telling him to take good care of his "wound" and, in the next breath, telling him to "try the timber again." Lucian had evidently injured himself cutting timber and was on the mend and his father was proffering sage advice to heal and get back at it as soon as practical.

The next letter from the Mowbray collection is one from Aunt Sally Hitch to Young on Jan 31 1864[193]. We offer it here in its entirety since it provides much good information of the people and environs in

---

[193] Appendix, Item LXXIX.

Laurens County in early 1864. Her letter is in response to one that Young Hitch had written to her and that she had received on January 30. She writes:

So.C. L. Dist.
Jan 31st 1864

Dear Nephew, I received your kind unexpected letter on the 30th inst. It found me enjoying as good health as I ever expect to have. Through a kind and merciful God I have been enjoying as good health for a year or two except a spell I had last summer as I have for a number of years. I feel sorry truly sorry to hear of your afflicted situation but the good word says all things shall work together for good to them that love God. I hope and trust that God will spare your life to return to your beloved family again and that you may have the opportunity of offering yourself to the Church and be baptized and go on your way rejoicing. O my beloved nephew you don't know how glad I was to hear from you and to hear that you had a hope that when you was done with this troublesome world you would have a resting place in heaven. O glorious thought that there is a resting place for the weary traveler where there will be no more parting with friends and relatives. You said you asked me to remember you in my prayers. O my dear nephew I don't think I shall forget you. I thought for a long time you had entirely forgotten me. The last letter I wrote to you you gave me no answer. I waited and looked for a long time for one but it never came. I wrote to Ann Templeton to know of her if she knew what was the matter that you did not write to me. She said Adellar saw Mary Ann at meeting at Clear spring Meeting House and she said she said she could give no reason but through neglect. I then gave up on a writing to you any more till you wrote to me. I have wrote to them that is Katharene Stewart and An Te when they heard from you when I would write to them. I had just lately heard you was in the Camps. It is a hard task for me to write. It takes me so long to write a letter. I will begin now and tell you a little of my troubles since I saw you last for it would take me a long time to tell you all. Your Uncle Henry you know is no more. And John W. Pitts also is no more. And worst of all your Aunt Mary is no more. She died the last day of Oct last. And o the trouble I have seen and felt in consequence of the conduct of that spoiled child emeline. She got so after the death of her father that she wanted to make me leave there. And would abuse me in the shamefulest manner you ever heard and would threaten to hit me if I did not keep out of her way. She would urge her mother to make me leave. I saw no satisfaction when I was there. I staid at Eunice Duvalls the most of my time but when I would go back there again I would have to bear the same abuse again or worse. It would trouble her mother very much. She would tell her frequently to hush and then she would abuse her mother. Her mother said to me one day maybe you had better go to uncle Louthers or somewhere awhile and stay a while and so I did. I went down to Duncans Creek to Susan Duvalls last Jan. and staid six months and came back and it was no better but still worse and worse. She wanted no one to stay with her mother but herself so she could have the whole rule and control of every thing in and out. Her brother John had to leave his mothers and go to eunices and die on the account of the abuse that she gave him while at his mothers. Em was always a teasing of her mother to make a will and will all or the most of her property to her but she never could get her to do it till within a few days of her death and there is but few that believes it to be her mothers will but her own making. The rest of the children except Isaac Boyd is a trying to break it and the reason he is not is because em has promised to give something to him. O my beloved nephew this is a world of trouble and distress. I am at this time at eunices but rather expect I shall live at D.M. Milams the man that married Sarah Ann Pitts. Em is a living at the same old place where her father and mother died a keeping house her and the negroes such a keeping of house as it is.

She has but little company only of men and negroes. Leroy P and family and John Cooper and family, Eunice D. and family and uncle Louther and family are all well at present as far as I know. Marian Duvall went to Virginia and staid I think something over a year and became diseased and came home and died some few weeks ago of the brain fever. And now my dear nephew I do hope that God permits you to return home again. You will not fail to do your duty lest a worse thing come upon you. You say you have suffered affliction. It may be because you did not your duty that God had required at your hand before you left home and he has followed you as he did Jonah of old and has been a chastising you with his rod of affliction. I hardly know how to leave of but I must come to a close by saying to you I want you to writ as often as you can. Now I heard from you I shall want to hear from you worse than ever. If you get home be sure to write. So no more at present but remain your loving aunt till death. So fare you well to Y.H.E. Hitch.
Sarah Hitch"

Aunt Sally Hitch has outdone herself with this letter to her nephew! She received what she believes to be a long overdue letter from him on Jan 30 1864 and is eager to write back the very next day. However, she says that she had resigned to never write again if she did not get a letter from him first! Shes minces no words in her assertion: "*I wrote to Ann Templeton to know of her if she knew what was the matter that you did not write to me. She said Adellar saw Mary Ann at meeting at Clear spring Meeting House and she said she said she could give no reason but through neglect. I then gave up on a writing to you any more till you wrote to me.*" "Adellar" may be Ann (Hitch) Templeton's daughter Adelia Templeton who would marry James M. Thackston in 1865.

Remember that Aunt Sally is sister to Young Hitch's deceased father and she has always been the primary news source for this part of the family. She writes with sad news of her sister Mary (Hitch) Pitts who had passed away on Oct 31 1863, she the wife of "Uncle" Henry Pitts and twin sister of Young Hitch's deceased father. Sally is greatly fired up about one of Henry and Mary's daughters, Emeline Pitts, who has been up to no good it seems. Before her mother died, "Em" Pitts was after her to write a will to leave most everything to her and, it seems that did not happen – at least until Mary Pitts' final hours when a will appeared as such. But, the family thinks that Emeline made the will herself and is trying to contest it, that is, everyone except Isaac Boyd, whom Emeline is supposed to have promised some of the booty. Boyd is husband to another sister, Mary Angeline Pitts.

This indeed seems to be a confounding family situation! "Em" Pitts even threatened to hit Aunt Sally and was so mean, it forced her to move out to stay nearby with Eunice Duvall for a time and then, from the Reedy River area in Laurens County over to Duncan's Creek with Susan (Hitch) Duvall, her niece, daughter of Louther D. Hitch, where she stayed for the first half of 1863. Eunice (Pitts) Duvall was a widowed niece of Aunt Sally Hitch and another daughter of Henry and Mary Pitts. Sally Hitch even states that the situation was so bad that Emeline's own brother, John W. Pitts, had to move out "to Eunice's to die" on account of the abuse she subjected upon to him. We saw earlier that John Wesley Pitts had enlisted to serve in Company C, 3rd South Carolina battalion in December 1861 but immediately fell ill and was discharged Mar 18 1863. We do not know exactly when he died but it was sometime in the latter half of 1863. What an awful woman Emeline Pitts was – at least from the viewpoint of Aunt Sarah Hitch.

At the time Aunt Sally writes this letter, she is staying with Eunice Duvall but seems to be planning a move to the D.M. Milam household, "the man that married Sarah Ann Pitts." Sarah Pitts is another niece of Sally and another daughter of Henry and Mary Pitts. Sarah Milam's sister, the estranged Emeline Pitts, is left at the old Pitts homestead near the Reedy River to tend to it herself with her group of "negroes." Sally even contends that her only company was "men and negroes," not a nice thing to say about her niece, no matter how contemptuous she might have been!

Aunt Sally closes her letter with a quick run through of the family and their health. Leroy Pitts and family were well, Leroy had married Catherine Boyd, sister to Isaac Boyd whom Emeline Pitts was supposed to have been in cahoots with. John Cooper and family are also well, his wife was another sister, Louisa Jane Pitts. Eunice Duvall is also well, with her family. One of Eunice's sons, Private H. James Duvall, was home convalescing as he was wounded on Sep 22 1863 at the Battle of Chickamauga while serving for Company C of the 3rd South Carolina infantry. He wound return to service in about 5 months. Finally, Louther D. Hitch and family were well. There is another bit of sad news to report that Francis Marion Duvall, who was husband of Susan T.E. Hitch, had died at home after being in Virginia. Private Marion Duvall served for the Holcombe Legion Cavalry in Company C. Records show that he had died of brain inflammation on Jan 11 1864, just 20 days before Aunt Sally had written this letter.

After reading this one letter, one might think they have lived a whole lifetime with the South Carolina Hitch family! It is written well, with excellent penmanship, and is a fine example of the contrasts seen in the south during the Civil War. We get the regular family "drama" and health and such and, we also get to see the realities of the impacts the war is having to daily life. It is a nice juxtaposition from the image one gets of Young Hitch in the camps as a soldier through his letters. God bless ol' Aunt Sally Hitch!

We get back to the regular course of business in early February when Young Hitch writes again to his wife, this time on February 2 from Dalton[194]. It generally describes more of basic life in the camp and the day-to-day activities along with news of his health and the weather; *"Dear wife I take this opportunity of writing a few lines to let you hear from me again. I have no strange news to give particular. My health is tolerable. I have been verry bad off with cold but I hope that I am getting over it. I have had a powerfull caugh but it seems to be getting better. I hope when this comes to your hand that it may find you all doing well. We have beautiful weather now."* Here we see that the good weather actually has him somewhat concerned because, *"If this weather should hold as it is I fear the enemy will cause us to have to head out from our little town. The roads are improving verry fast so that the enemy can begin to travel again. And it will go pretty hard with us to have to leave our shantys and turn out all at once."* He reflects that the army will be sorry to leave their cabins where they wintered in Dalton.

Next, we hear of Hitch and his clothes and performing regular duties in purchasing necessary items while in the field:

> *"Mary, I have just bought half a square of this sort of paper. I give two dollars for it. And I just bought me a new pair of socks. I paid a five dollar bill for them. And I have just six dollars fifty cents of money in hand at present. Mary, I dismissed my old shoes yesterday morning Feb. 1st.*

[194] Appendix, Item LXXX.

> *they have been faithful old friends to me and have carried me over many a rough mile of rocks. The shoes that I have on are not worth mutch but they did not cost me a thing. They were a pair of the donation shoes. Mary, today has been wash day with me. I washed two pieces, a shirt and pair of drawers. Got them clean & white too."*

The subtle humor Young Hitch has been noted for in many of his letters comes out well as he tells his wife that he "*dismissed my old shoes yesterday morning Feb. 1st. they have been faithful old friends to me and have carried me over many a rough mile of rocks."* He then lets on to Mary how proud he is with his clothes washing abilities for he has washed his drawers and shirt and "got them clean...too." Hitch then changes the subject to what is happening with his Company:

> *"Our men are getting off to come home occasionally. John White left the other day and Lieut. Austin today. Mary I have wrote to you in answer to the letter that Lieut. Garrett brought. I hope you have got my letters to you may know better what to do about coming to see me. I have wrote to you to come if you wished to & could get the right company. If you do come you should try to get here pretty soon as wee may have to leave soon. True wee may have to leave in a few days or weeks. And we may be allowed to remain here until April next. But I dont think it."*

There seems to be some break in the ability to get furloughs as John White and LT Austin have headed home for a visit. John White is Private John Jones White, LT Austin is Thomas Jeremiah Austin, and LT Garrett is Erasmus Newport Garrett, all three of whom we will hear more of later. Hitch is hoping still that his wife can visit but thinks probably not as they "may have to leave soon." The next portion of the letter states:

> *"Mary pleas tell me in your answer what you do your hauling with. I want to know whitch you haul with, the mare or the steers. You speak of hauling this, that & the other. But don't say what with. Mary when you write let me know whether you did start Mr. Mocks trunk to me or not. Berry says that the keg that was sent to him is frate's keg."*

Evidently, Mary had written Young, in a letter that does not survive, that she had been "hauling this, that & the other." Hitch wants to know how she had done the hauling, by using the mare or the steers on the farm?! He also wants to know whether Mr. Mock's trunk is on the way to him (this is, again, probably John Mock, neighbor to the Hitches in South Carolina). Finally, he states that Little Berry Edwards received a keg that was "frate's keg." "Frate" is Euphrates Lafayette Edwards, Little Berry's younger brother. Young then wants to know more from home, "*Mary tell Joseph I thank him verry mutch for his present that I have read it different times. Mary, pleas tell me who your preacher is this year at Cedar Grove. Let me know if any body has joined since S.R. Thackston."* After a quick word to Mary to tell Joseph thanks for sending him some reading material, he wants to know who the preacher is now at Cedar Grove Baptist Church back home. He also wants to know if anyone else had joined the church since S.R. Thackston (Simeon Robert Thackston, whom we met previously). Such is just regular chatter of Young trying to stay in touch with things at home. Hitch concludes his letter as follows:

> *"Scruggs has a severe fresh cold at present. But up and baken bread & boilen beef for our supper. You can hear a heap of new about the 16 regt. I would repeat but you must not believe it. (next*

line is impossible to read) wicked set of men you may believe it all. Mary there is but little difference between a professor & the worldling here in camp. I shall have to come to a close as my paper is short. Mary don't forget your husband when you try to pray. Write soon as you can."

He states that his good friend William Scruggs has a cold but is up baking bread and cooking the beef! Then Young again warns his wife not to believe the things she may have been hearing about the 16th regiment as, evidently, some stories have been circulated by a "wicked set of men." The army life is a great equalizer as there is "little difference between a professor and a worldling" in camp. A lengthy and very interesting letter comes to a close.

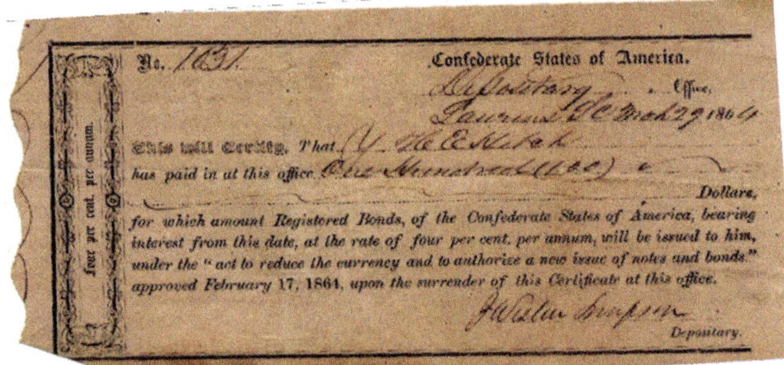

No. 1631 Confederate States of America.

Depository Office,

March 29 1864

This will Certify, That Y. H. E. Hitch

has paid in at this office One Hundred (100)

Dollars,

for which amount Registered Bonds, of the Confederate States of America, bearing interest from this date, at the rate of four per cent. per annum, will be issued to him, under the "act to reduce the currency and to authorize a new issue of notes and bonds" approved February 17, 1864, upon the surrender of this Certificate at this office.

Depositary.

Four per cent. per annum.

Figure 23 - CSA War Bond Receipt for $100 paid by Y.H.E. Hitch on Mar 29 1864. (Mowbray Collection, Edward H. Nabb Center, Salisbury University)

There is an undated letter in the Mowbray collection from Young to his son A.L. Hitch[195]. It is on the same type of note paper as the known January 1864 letters and the subject matter follows the theme of the injury implied by the letter of January 25. In it, Young tells Lucian, who was age ten at the time, that he has received his notes from January 26 and February 1 and that he is *"Sorry to hear of you being so puny & being so crippled up but you must (*next line illegible*) good care of your foot & (__) perhaps it will soon be well again"*. This is obviously a continuation of conversation about the 'wound' A.L. evidently received from cutting timber as mentioned in the January 25 letter and, with the letter mentioning that Young had received A.L.'s letter of February 1, then it is estimated that this letter is probably dated sometime around February 7-10, 1864.

He also tells his son that he would like to be *"home to help your ma eat biscuits and honey"* but that would not be possible for perhaps *"twelve months if I live that long"*. Then Young seems to answer a question that Lucian had asked about his appearance since it had been a long time since he had last seen his father. Young responds somewhat interestingly, *"You want to know how fat I am and how my hair & beard is. I think I am about as fat as I was I had my likeness taken & my beard is about as it was that time. The hair is not near so thick on my head. last July when I was sick my hair pestered me so I got Mr Odom to shear my hair... in Oct. my hair shed out almost as bad as when I had the fever. I had it cropt the long leathering? hairs before Christmas and it is thin enough now for me to comb with a fine comb without a course comb. So if you want to see me just get my likeness you will see me. Only my hair is ____, my beard is about the same"*. The "likeness" Young Hitch is referring to is likely the photograph shown earlier in this book in **Figure 2**. This and the brief description in the letter of his father's current appearance must have come to young Lucian as only a very pale consolation to actually seeing his father in person, something that would never again come to pass.

[195] Appendix, Item LXXXI.

Young ends the letter with a final, terse reference to the war: *"Lucian, you want to know if I think the war is near at a end. I have been afraid that we were whipt. But we are not quite defeated(?) yet."* The statement reflects both the weariness of Young Hitch and, some despair that the Confederate cause might already be lost. But, it also reflects a final sentiment of hope that the cause will eventually prevail.

On Feb 8 1864, Young Hitch writes to his other son, J.J. Hitch, who was age sixteen at the time[196]. In this letter, we see Young relate some advice for his oldest son on preparing the farm for the springtime. He advises, *"Joseph I have just rec. your letter by Thos. Mchugh*[197] *glad to hear from you but sorry to hear of you all being so unwell. Also I got J.C. Browns letter & one from Uncle Jonas Edwards. I will send you a letter that I got from Aunt Sally Hitch if I can think of it when I go to mail this letter. Joseph you wish me to be at home to advise you about your farm. I have been thinking of giveing you a letter on the subject but have not time at present. But the best thing for you to do is to hurrah and get your land broke as you can. Your mare you must not push to hard but keep steady a looking. I fear your land that you have to tend this year will be hard for you to manage. But the main thing is to get it in a good fix before you plant it. Break your land as good as you can ___ stiff part of the bottom don't break it too deep the first time to make it cloddy. Take as good care of your mare as possible & mabe she will pay you for your trouble. Hurrah work & do the best you can let others do as they please."*

So Young tells him, it will be hard but to plow the land and not too deep into the soil, otherwise it will be harder to work due to dirt clods. Fatherly advice that ends with "do the best you can", something you might expect from a caring father to his son at home tending the farm as he writes as a soldier from the battlefield. Son, Joseph Hitch, feeling the pressure of not having his father home and from having all the responsibility to tend the farm resting upon his own shoulders, writes on the back on one of the Young Hitch letters on Feb 28 1864, *"Well this is the losoms iss Day that I ever Past I think sholey Feb 28 1864."* Next, Young Hitch relates to Joseph some interesting soldiering information for his son:

> *"I have just come off of Battalion drill this morning ... we have to drill twice a day and attend a big review one day out of every week. The two last Fridays we had to go to Dalton to the review. Last Friday I saw the most men that I ever saw at one sight I am verry sure. It was supposed that their was 35 or 40 thousand men their. It was said that there was 32 brigades there. I saw as many men on the days of the missionary ridge fight. But never saw so many at one look. They was situated in an open field so that they could be seen to an advantage. There was three strings I think about a mile & a half long. It was so long that it took General Jo Johnson a good while to lope his pretty bay mare around. It is three miles to Dalton & we went to the other side & then back to camp something near ten miles."*

From this we see that Young Hitch, as part of the Army of Tennessee, probably viewed the better part of General Joseph Johnston's entire army! We know Johnston had about 55,000 infantry and Young Hitch

---

[196] Appendix, Item LXXXII.

[197] Private Thomas Simeon McHugh (1834-1892) of Company A, 16th South Carolina Volunteers, was the son of Elisha and Cassandra (Westmoreland) McHugh of Greenville, SC. Private McHugh enlisted on Dec 30 1861 with Colonel C.J. Elford at Camp Moore, SC. He was sick for the better part of 1862 and early 1863 and was on a 30-day furlough beginning Jan 27 1863. He was detailed to the Division Quartermaster as a carpenter for March 1863-February 1864. He is buried in the Clear Spring Baptist Church Cemetery, Simpsonville, SC.

guesses that he saw "35 or 40 thousand men" and, "It was said that there was 32 brigades there." A brigade consisted of four (4) regiments and each regiment theoretically held 1,000 men so, 32 brigades could have a total of 128,000 men. However, by this point of the war, many regiments were severely depleted due to sickness and battle casualties so, it is quite possible that Young witnessed the entire portion of Army of Tennessee "last Friday" (which would have been Feb 5 1864) that were Hood's and Hardee's corps (Polk's corps was still in Mississippi defending Meridian).

Hitch states that he saw as many men on the days of the fighting at Missionary Ridge (which was back in late November 1863) but, "never saw so many at one look". We also see that Hitch observed General Johnston himself there reviewing the troops from "his pretty bay mare". William R. Scaife, in his The Campaign for Atlanta, writes, "Johnston instilled a new spirit de corps among the troops with frequent reviews of the army on parade and hundreds of spectators rode up from Atlanta to watch those events. Brigadier General Arthur M. Manigault of South Carolina described one such review held at Dalton: *'On one occasion a review was held by General Johnston, in which 36,000 men were under arms with 120 guns...It was a fine spectacle...'*"[198] It is quite possible that Manigault was relating his experience with the very same event that Young Hitch observed on Feb 5 1864. Whatever the case, it must have been a very impressive sight, just as Young related it to his son in his letter home!

Young had evidently also gotten correspondence from "J.C. Brown", his half-brother John C. Brown, and Jonas Edwards. Though these letters do not survive, one can only imagine their content. Jonas M. Edwards was Mary Hitch's brother and had served for the Confederates earlier in the war for the Holcombe Legion and then for the 9th South Carolina Reserves. By February 1864, he was 50 years old and does not appear to be in the service. John C. Brown served in some capacity but the records are incomplete exactly when and how.

The letter also mentions Miles R. Garrett twice. He is Young Hitch's old friend from the days of the Beat Company in the South Carolina militia and then the 9th South Carolina Reserves before they both joined Company I of the 16th South Carolina. Neither man would survive 1864. Miles will die of cholera in a Forsyth, Georgia hospital on Sep 30 1864. Posthumously, Miles Rainwater Garrett would become Joseph J. Hitch's father-in-law when Joseph marries Margaret J. Garrett in about 1870.

In mid-February 1864, the 16th regiment and Company I saw an influx of new recruits who joined to collect $50 bounty money. The records indicate the following men joined, their rank and their dates of enlistment

W.D. Bramlett[199]	PVT	Feb 11 1864
Andrew J. Forester[146]	PVT	Feb 11 1864

[198] The Campaign for Atlanta, William R. Scaife, McNaughton & Gunn, 1993.
[199] Private William Dacus Bramlett (1820-1875) was son of Reuben and Sarah (Dacus) Bramlett of Greenville County. He married Martha E. McCrary (1825-1905). The Private and Mrs. Bramlett, and his parents, are buried in the Bethel United Methodist Church Cemetery, Simpsonville, SC. He was the brother of Company I's Private James W. Bramlett (1833-1864).

Fielding George[200]	PVT	Feb 11 1864
W.L. Hodges	1LT	Feb 11 1864
J.W. Jones	PVT	Feb 25 1864
Samuel McKittrick	PVT	Feb 11 1864
William Sheffield[201]	PVT	Feb 11 1864
J.F. Thackston[202]	PVT	Feb 11 1864

The entire 16th regiment was replenished in this wave of recruits and Company I benefited by gaining eight (8) fresh members. It makes one wonder how the new men acclimated into the regiment since they were collecting bounty money when the others who had been there much longer got no special consideration.

BATTLE OF DALTON, GEORGIA ON FEBRUARY 24-25, 1864

On Feb 24 1864, northern forces under General George Thomas attacked the Confederate forces near Dalton, Georgia. History tells us that this was the Union testing General Johnston's defenses for signs of weakness. Thomas stopped his offensive on February 25 but gathered intelligence that the North would apply during the Atlanta Campaign that would begin soon after. Part of Sherman's army had originally been diverted to Mississippi for a campaign against Meridian, a major supply center and that forced Johnston to send part of his army to reinforce Leonidas Polk, who was defending Meridian against Sherman.

When General Grant became aware of this, he ordered Thomas to probe Johnston's defenses in search of weakness amid the depleted southern army. The Union enjoyed initial success but soon found that rebel troops were strong, and the reinforcements diverted to Mississippi were no longer needed after Polk abandoned Meridian, so they returned to bolster Johnston's forces near Dalton. The skirmishes that began on February 24 showed that Rocky Face Ridge and Mill Creek Gap were well defended. On February 25, the Union's 39th Indiana Mounted Infantry attacked Dug Gap, just a few miles south of Mill Creek Gap. Also on February 25 at Crow Valley, Union troops almost turned the Rebel right flank, but ultimately it held. On the 26th, Brigadier General Hiram B. Granbury's brigade drove the 39th Indiana out, and on February 27, the Northern army withdrew, after realizing that Johnston had established a stronghold and was ready and able to counter any assault. This discovery by the Union was to be significant in the Atlanta Campaign in May 1864 when Snake Creek Gap would become their objective.

---

200 Not much is known of Private Fielding George (c1820/24-aft 1880) except that he was born c1822 in Spartanburg County, SC.

201 Nothing more is known of Private William Sheffield. There is only one index card in his service file at the National Archives.

202 Private J.F. Thackston is probably James Ford Thackston (1826-1907), son of William Bell and Melinda (Ford) Thackston of Greenville County. James F. Thackston has a shield on his older gravestone denoting service in the war. He is buried in the Reedy River Baptist Church Cemetery, Greenville, SC. James Ford Thackston had a brother John Starling Thackston who is probably the Private J.S. Thackston listed in Company I as was wounded Jun 28 1864 after the Battle of Kennesaw Mountain.

The Battle of Dalton casualties were light relative to Civil War standards. Thomas' army suffered less than 300 men killed, wounded, or captured, while Johnston lost around 140 troops. The Union did learn that a direct attack against Rocky Face Ridge near Dalton would be foolish. Sherman used this intelligence later when he sent a portion of his army further south to Snake Creek Gap that was not well defended by the southern forces, paving the way for a Union victory at the Battle of Dalton.

The next letter in the Mowbray collection is dated Feb 28 1864 from Young Hitch to wife Mary and comes just after the action of the First Battle of Dalton[203]. In the interim of time that had passed from his last letter, Company I compatriot, Private James H. Hyde[204] has died while home in Greenville, SC. Nothing in the records indicates how he died but, most likely, it was from sickness and he passed while home on furlough. Hitch does not mention him in his letter of February 28 or subsequent letters.

On February 28, Young Hitch does not hesitate to tell his wife the news of the fight happening around them, "*Well Mary we have just got back to our cabbins again this morning. Wee left on Tuesday last & went out to Dalton and fortunately for us we got to ly there untill this Sunday morning when we returned back to our old camp. You probably will get a truer account of the fight than I can give. We were near enough to hear the small arms verry distinctly. Thursday last they put their shots in like hail all day long. What has been done I can't say now report say that we lost 110 men killed dead, the loss on the enemys side I don't know. Fortunately for our brigade we did not get hitcht in. If they had of come on wee would of got in as we had one road to guard that the enemy were a coming. But as it was we had a verry pleasant time the weather was dry and not so verry cold. We have found all of our huts a standing as wee left them. How long we will get to stay in them I don't know for we may have to leave before tomorrow morning again. All around here looks sorter like home. I had rather stay here untill the winter is over.*"

Here we see Young Hitch describe returning to their "*cabbins*" after "*the fight*" and that the "*huts a standing as wee left them.*" Young's unit, the 16th South Carolina, saw no direct action as they were assigned to defend a road that the enemy never came to. However, they were close enough to hear the action not far away consisting of rifle and pistol fire (evidently with the absence of artillery/cannon). On "Thursday last", which would have been February 25, Hitch describes the bullets flying "like hail all day long" as the Battle of Dalton raged. His account of 110 Confederate killed parallels well with the official account of 140 casualties for the South. While Hitch did not hear of the enemy lost, it seems that the North lost more than twice as many men in the small battle.

Since the 16th regiment had not seen any action of note thus far in the war, there seems to be some people questioning their will as Young Hitch pens the following words to his wife[205], "*Mary from what I can learn there has been a heap of slurs throughd at the 16th regt. I should like to know what we have*

---

[203] Appendix, Item LXXXIII.

[204] Private James H. Hyde (1833/34-1864) was son of Jacob Harlan and Mary (Cox) Hyde of Greenville County, SC. By the time of the 1860 census he has wife, Martha, and three young children in his household; Catherine, Mary and William.

[205] The 16th South Carolina was sometimes called by other units, the "Bloody 16th" in 1863, a derisive reference to the fact that it had not been heavily engaged up to that time. (South Carolina's Military Organizations During the War Between the States; Volume III, The Upstate, Robert S. Seigler, The History Press, Charleston, SC, 2008; page 167.)

done that they should talk about us so. We have not done any fighting I know. But whoos fault has it been tell me will they. There is one thing I do know & that is that the 16th has done as mutch hard marching as any of them. She has generally reported when ordered so far as I know... I do hope that peace may be made without the 16th fireing a single gun but enough on that subject." Hitch seems rightfully frustrated at the "slurs throughd (sic, thrown) at the 16th" and counters with the assertion that the unit has marched as hard, or harder, than other units and always reported to duty as ordered. Even though Hitch hopes that "peace may be made without the 16th fireing (sic, firing) a single gun", this will not come to pass and their lack of seeing any action will change greatly in the coming weeks.

Returning to Young's account of returning to their "cabbins" and "huts" – this appears different from what one might expect of an encampment in the Civil War where we tend to think of life in tents. However, the Army of Tennessee was camped near Dalton, Georgia for an extended period and had time to construct more permanent living quarters than the tents that would typically be utilized in a more mobile setting. Although Young Hitch does not describe the particulars of their cabins, there are other accounts from the time period that do. For instance, consider the following:

> "Our brigade, Gen. John K. Jackson's, Maj. Gen. William H.T. Walker's division, Lieut. Gen. William]. Hardee's corps, was encamped about two miles east of Dalton on a slightly elevated plateau sloping generally in every direction, thus affording good drainage. Our cabins were built of split logs, the cracks being "chinked" during the severest weather with red clay, thus making a very comfortable house indeed. An ample chimney was constructed of sticks "chinked" in the same manner as the house; and when the fireplace was piled up with wood and set going, we had as comfortable quarters as to warmth as one could wish. Our bedsteads were four posts with end and side pieces nailed to them, and boards were placed so as to give us room to fill in with straw, and over this our quilts and blankets were spread. I occupied a cabin with my brother Charlie, who was adjutant of the sharpshooters, 2nd Georgia Battalion. We were as comfortable as the proverbial bug in a rug." *Frank S. Roberts, 2nd Georgia, CSA*[206]

Here, we see Private Frank Roberts was in a sister brigade (Jackson's brigade) in Walker's Division to Young Hitch's Gist's brigade. Roberts was part of the 2nd Georgia Sharpshooters under Brigadier General John R. Jackson and most likely camped very near to where Young and the 16th South Carolina regiment were camped near Dalton. Roberts's description of his cabin must have been very much the same as the cabins in which Young and his 16th SCVs and the rest of the Army of Tennessee were quartered.

There was even a brief mention of these "huts" in Colonel Ellison Capers' report from May 1864, he being the commander of the 24th South Carolina regiment and actually part of Young Hitch's Gist's brigade[207]. He states, *"During the winter of 1863-64 we were comfortably quartered in huts, located on the Spring Place road, about two miles east of Dalton."* The troops, it seems, were living in decent shelters near Dalton, Georgia while waiting for General Sherman and the Northern Army to make its move, which it began to do with the demonstration at the Battle of Dalton on Feb 24-25 1864.

---

206 "In Winter Quarters at Dalton, GA, 1863-64," Confederate Veteran, Volume. XXVI, Civil War Trust Blog, 2014
207 The Winter at Dalton, Resaca or McGinnis Ferry, and Calhoun; May 5, 1864 through May 17, 1864; Report of Ellison Capers, Twenty-fourth South Carolina. *www.oocities.org*.

Within the Feb 28 1864 letter, we see Hitch speak of his frustration of not receiving a letter from home in quite a while and mentions some of his colleagues in Company I again:

> *"Mary nary letter have I got since by Mchugh. It seems strange that I can't get letters. Edwards & Scruggs are like myself only get a letter now and then. M.R. Garrett scarcely ever miss a week without getting a letter from home. If Henry Stewart comes surely I will get a letter from you. I want to hear from you all badly. I have wrote once a week or about so to you I don't know whether you get my letters reggular or not. Yesterday eleven months ago since I saw you I hardly I can think how you look & the same by the boys. I can come nearer seeing how Joseph looked than any of you. I wrote in my last for the boys to send me there weight and hight. You don't know how bad I want to see my boys. I see a heap of boys but not Joseph and Lucian."*

It had been 11 months since "yesterday" since he last saw his wife, that would be Mar 27 1863 and he misses home terribly and even wonders how Mary and his sons now look. He asks them to send information about the boys' height and weight so he can at least get a mental image of how they might have grown over that eleven month period. He even forlornly states that he sees lots of boys around but none like his sons Joseph and Lucian. This is a rather heart-breaking passage from a soldier who is a father that has been away at war for an extended period of time, yearning to see his family. Hitch mentions that Little Berry Edwards, William B. Scruggs and Miles R. Garrett get a letter every week yet, he does not as he has not gotten one since (Thomas) McHugh[197] returned from home on February 8. He hopes that, when Henry Stewart[208] gets back to his unit, there will be a letter from his family forthcoming.

MARCH 1864

Young Hitch's next letter comes on Mar 6 1864 to his wife, Mary, again from near Dalton with an accompanying letter to son J.J. Hitch dated Mar 7 1864[209]. Things had calmed dramatically since the action of late February and Young has returned to writing of the more mundane aspects of life in camp during the war. He had been on guard duty on a very cold night in early March and he had not felt well even before the assignment; however, he was feeling well enough by the time he composes the letter to Mary. In his letter, he has returned to the boredom and drudgery of sitting in camp that is occasionally interrupted with the frantic activity of marching and preparing for a fight. He writes, "*Mary I have been in the army long enough to be getting verry lazy & you know that I was lazy Enough before I left home. But I think if I was at home I could get your firewood. But hearty as I am I cant chop nor toat a great deal my back never has been as well since I had the measles as it was before. It may be if I could work steady & not be out in the night or bad weather that I could do more. There is a heap of the time that wee are doing nothing. Then again run like all the world.*" He has also returned to his forlorn thinking about the

---

[208] Company I Private Walter Henry Stewart (1826-1899) was son of John and Adeline (Pitts) Stewart of Laurens County. Adeline Pitts was brother to Henry Pitts who married Young Hitch's aunt Mary Hitch, twin of Hitch's father, Joseph N. Hitch. John Stewart was half-brother to Rev. Clark Berry Stewart who married Katherine Carson Hitch. W. Henry and wife Temperance Caroline (Jones) Stewart (1841-1906) are buried in the Duncan Chapel Methodist Church Cemetery, Greenville, SC.

[209] Appendix, Items LXXXIV and LXXXV.

war and the politics that have driven it, *"Our people appears to be growing more wicked Every day. I sometimes think that times will never be any better for us not in our time no how. If wicked has brought this war on us I fear it will not End soon. It seems that all is aiming to make a speck some way. And some is not particular how they make it."*

In Young Hitch's letter to son J.J., the topic again switches to helping his son run the farm from afar. He speaks of how Joseph has done well with the plowing of the land and instructs him to break the ground up well and, *"if you have good luck & seasons you will make corn."* Then he longs to be with his son in that pursuit, *"I wish I could be at home to help you to plant it to lay off the rows anyhow."* Hitch then mentions the new colt on the farm and tells his son he may want *"to raise you a mule colt"*. While the practicality of having a young mule on the farm exists, there seems to be an ulterior motive for getting the mare in foal as *"it might save your mare from being taken from you next winter. They will not want a mare that is in fold."* The army desperately needed horses and mules at that time and all farm animals were at risk of being proffered into service. However, Young notes that, if the mare is with colt, she would not be taken.

Hitch ends the letter to his son with a written conversation about Joseph being baptized and joining the church. He encourages his son to join the church and be baptized because, *"You know that you have to dy & after death appear before your Creator."* But, this is not all that is on Young Hitch's mind as Joseph Hitch had then reached an age of 16½ and was quickly approaching the age that he would be joining the army. So Young Hitch says, *"You may soon have to leave home for camp. And if so you will find camp a poor place to try to get religion. So I hope that you will have yours before you leave home & then try to hold on to it."* In other words, Young instructs his son to join the church at home before it becomes something that he has to do in a unit on the battlefield or at camp[210].

Mar 13 1864 is the date of the next letter from Young Hitch to Mary, his wife[211]. This letter is one of two that are not in the Mowbray collection but rather are in a collection of Mr. Michael Givens of South Carolina, he being a descendant of Young Hitch through his son Joseph J. Hitch. The subject of this letter, again from camp near Dalton, is devoted almost entirely to Hitch's clothing, or lack thereof, that are useable. One major item of apparel that most soldiers seemed to be lacking was shoes as they wore out through constant marching. Young had worn out another pair that were now *"thin & rather tight"* and he got a new pair that were a bit big but, he indicates he *"can wrap my feet up with rags & keep them warm."* He was also running low on socks and asks Mary to send him some, "cotton ones", if she can. Mary had evidently expressed to him that she was concerned about his clothing and he replies, *"Mary you may rest easy about my clothing, the way everything has turned out I have done pretty well, as we have had cabbins to stay in most of the winter and the winter has not been as hard as some winters."* Again, we see that the soldiers had the relative luxury of spending the winter in cabins rather than tents and fared rather well as the weather was rather temperate over the winter season in northwest Georgia

---

[210] Joseph J. Hitch never had to serve during the Civil War even though he reached age 17 during the time it was being waged in late 1864. His obituary from 1915 includes the following excerpt: *"During the war between the sections, Mr. Hitch offered his services but was refused. He weighed only 65 pounds."*

[211] Appendix, Item LXXXVI.

in 1864. Finally, he requests Mary to get his box from H.G. Vaughn[212] for her to send him a little care package; "*...fetch it (so) you may send me a little honey & brandy for I could sell the brandy & get something to eat.*"

By Mar 20 1864, Young has written another letter, this time to his son, Joseph Hitch. In it, he relates more of camp life around Dalton[213]. He is not pressed for food as he pens, "*Joseph I weighed the other day, I weighed 158½ the most I think that I Ever weighed before. So you see that I am fat or well stuffed. The stuffing is mostely cornbread & water. This morning I had a good breakfast good hoecakes, cornbread & boild fat beef & some rice. And for dinner I had some pancake of the flower & meat that your ma sent me but it is nearly out.*" Cornbread and water seemed to be the main staples in the camps but some beef protein and fat were on the menu as well with the only 'treats' being those that survived the trip from home in old trunks and boxes.

There is also discussion of the day-to-day activities where a religious revival in the army has been happening, "*I have just come in from preaching. I saw the M.E.[214] take the sacrament today. There appears to be a revival of religion in this army. This Evening half after three oclock there will be preaching in our regt*" and the regular training and inspections common to army life, "*But I may have to be on guard.... This morning wee had inspection as wee always do on Sunday morning. Wee have a heap of big kickups of late. Wee get to go to Dalton Every two or three days to have a division drill or sham battle or some review.*"

Finally, the letter turns to a "few words" to his son A.L. (Lucian) Hitch, "*Dear Son it maybe that you may have the pleasure that you speak of sometime this summer. It may be if we don't have to go the Kentucky, Tenn or some where else that I can get to come sometime this summer. if furloughing is kep up as it has been for a few weeks my turn will come after awhile. I hope to live to se it. I may get to see you all. I would of wrote to your ma to tried to get me a recruit if I had known of ary one to get. But I cant pay sutch prices like some are for a ten days furlough. Me & Garrett like to of quarreled on the subject last night. He is wanting to see home Enough worse than I do. So do all that have been home lately. Dear Sons I hope this may find you all well. So fare you well. If wee never meet on Earth let us try to be prepared to meet in heaven.*" This portion of the letter is rather melancholy as Lucian has apparently asked in a letter that does not today survive whether his father could visit with him soon and Young's reply is not at all optimistic. But he hopes that his turn for a furlough comes "after a while". He even suggests the possibility of purchasing a 10-day furlough from a recruit but he just "can't pay such prices" and ends the letter with a resigned tone that they may never again meet on earth so to be prepared to meet in heaven.

THE GREAT SNOWBALL BATTLE OF 1864

---

[212] SGT Henry G. Vaughn was born c1834 in South Carolina. It is unclear if and how he is related to brother Toliver and Paschal Vaughn of Company I. The on-line site, batsonsm.tripod.com states H.G. Vaughn died of wounds in November 1864 near Franklin, TN.

[213] Appendix, Item LXXXVII.

[214] M.E. stands for Methodist Episcopal, a protestant denomination.

On Mar 24, 1864, Young Hitch replies with a letter to respond to his wife's letter of March 13 (which does not survive)[215]. This gives some indication of how long it took to receive a letter in 1864, on the battlefield and, in this case, it took nine days from Laurens County, South Carolina to Dalton, Georgia. The content of the letter reflects on a more delightful event of being in the camp during the war in the late winter of 1864 – a series of snowball fights that grew large enough that it was widely reported by many soldiers on both the Union and Confederate sides all along the east coast.

Evidently, a late winter storm hit that affected everyone on the east coast during late March 1864. Eyewitness accounts show that about 5" of snow fell near Dalton on March 22 and more fell over the next day. Further up the east coast, 18" fell in Orange County, Virginia. Here is one account from the Dalton area:

> *On March 22, 1864, near Dalton, Ga., the troops from Arkansas found 5 inches of new snow, and a spontaneous snowball fight erupted all across the camp. The men of Cleburne's Division from Lucius Polk's Brigade attacked Gen. Daniel C. Govan's Brigade. Here the famous Irish Gen. Cleburne suffered the embarrassment of capture, twice. This Georgia battle became a total melee. One Arkansas soldier recalled, "Such pounding and thumping, and rolling over in the snow, and washing of faces and cramming snow in mouths and in ears and mixing up in great wriggling piles together."*
>
> *When it was all over, Cleburne authorized a ration of whiskey for all the troops, who huddled around huge bonfires singing and yelling "at the top of their lungs." More snow fell the next day and the snowball war continued. Rainy, snowy weather continued until March 31, when another huge engagement erupted. Commanding Gen. Joe Johnston organized an attack involving Gen. William J. Hardee's Corps. Cleburne's and Gen. William B. Bate's divisions battled the troops of Gen. Benjamin Franklin Cheatham and Gen. William H.T. Walker. A small audience of ladies who had driven out from Dalton were delighted by the sheer joy of the scene…*
>
> *More snow fell on the 23rd of March, provoking yet another snowball fight and rain and snow continued through the rest of the month. On the 31st a more serious sham battle occurred when Joe Johnston organized a mock engagement involving Hardee's Corps. Cleburne's and Bate's Div. Squared off against those of Cheatam and Walker. It was a fine weather for a charge, and the troops entered the spirit of the drill, firing off a blank cartridge each, thrilling the small audiences of ladies who had driven out from Dalton to watch. One veteran recalled, "The noise was terrific and the excitement intense, but nobody was hurt . . . except perhaps one of the cavalry men who was dismounted while charging a square of infantry." That night, back in camp, it was peaches and cornbread again for dinner.*[216]

Some research finds that snowball fights within the ranks during the war were not all that uncommon and usually recalled with levity amongst the letters of the soldiers that observed and participated in

---

[215] Appendix, Item LXXXVIII.

[216] Rebel and Yank Snowball Wars: Fighting Winter Boredom; John E. Carey

them. The snowball fights seemed to break the drudgery of camp life and increased morale and camaraderie among the troops.

We get a small glimpse of one of the snowball battles through our own Young Hitch's eyes as he writes about one to Mary Hitch in his letter of Mar 24 1864:

> *"Mary you have often heard of snow balling. If you had been here yesterday & the evening before you could of seen the biggest one you ever did sure. Tuesday evening Jacksons Brigade made an attackt on ours & I am sure I never saw snow fly before. And yesterday I never saw & heard the like it was not just a few men it was hundreds against hundreds. One Brigade would charge another & fight until the ones they had charged would get to hard for them when they would break for home & the others after as hard as their heels could carry them. And then sutch whooping you never heard. Each side would take prisoners all they could. I was on post a part of the time & then on my line and on each side they did not aim their missiles at me at all but I was in the hot place, one army on the one side & the other on the other. Their balls flew around me thick & heavy. I did not take any part with them for I was on guard & would not no how."*

What fun this had to have been amid the monotony of camp life and the duties it brought! Hitch's fascination and muted enthusiasm betray the general conservatism of his writing of the incident. The snowball fight probably exhibited particular glee among the Confederate soldiers since they were natives of the south where snowfall was a rare or non-existent event! This is an excellent account of a much-needed light moment within the Confederate ranks of 1864. It was a good experience for Young Hitch as the realities of war would soon creep back into the fore in the days ahead.

The final letter from March 1864 is dated the 27th from Dalton to wife Mary[217]. It is notable in that it is the one-year anniversary date of when Young left home for good for his time in the service and he speaks of "*I have seen & felt aheap since I left home more than I ever thought of liveing to see*." Not much else of note except that Hitch is still trying to get the things from his wife in a trunk that gets raided as it makes its way to him over the distance and the food it contains regularly spoils. The trunk is then sent back to Greenville bearing the name E.L. Edwards[218]. In it, he sends his wife some old shoes, leather straps and buttons and a buckle for use by her and their sons. He ends the letter with a rumor he had heard about possibly going to Virginia, "*Some talk of us going to Verginy*." Of course, this is just rumor as history tells us that the Army of Tennessee will be quite occupied with the Atlanta campaign in Georgia for the approaching months of 1864.

APRIL 1864

The month of April finds Young Hitch still camped near Dalton, Georgia as he pens four (4) letters from there; one to an unknown woman named "Ellen", two to his wife, Mary, and one to sons Joseph and

---

[217] Appendix, Item LXXXIX.

[218] This is Euphrates Lafayette Edwards (1846-1916), Mary Hitch's half-brother, or "Frate" as he was called by the family. Records show that he ends up serving with Company E, 4th South Carolina Reserves in 1864 but gets transferred to Provisional Army on Oct 14 1864.

Lucian[219]. During this time, on April 6, Lieutenant Edward G. Roberts was promoted to Captain of Company I[220]. Hitch's letter to Ellen is dated Apr 21 1864 and, though it is unknown who exactly "Ellen" is, it may be a sister of Mary Ann Hitch or some other close relative. Whoever it is exactly, she must not be able to read as Young instructs his son to do the following, *"Joseph read this to Ellen if you please."*

Figure 24 - An envelope in the Mowbray collection addressed to "Y.H.e. Hitch" in Dalton, Georgia franked with a postally-used CSA ten cent stamp. Note that it includes his unit named as "Gists Brigade 16 reg. Com I. So C. V." The handwriting on this envelope for the address portion is that of Aunt Sally Hitch whom Young states on April 21st sent him a letter on April 16, 1864 (the actual letter is missing, however). It is notable that this envelope was folded inside out to be reused at a later date given the scarcity of paper. (Mowbray Collection, Edward H. Nabb Center, Salisbury University)

Young expresses to her, as he often has to his wife, how food is frequently sparse in the camps, *"I have seen some sorry times since I left my home and Expect to see worse if I live. But I hope there will be some way provided better than I can see. As to perishing you don't I hope know anything yet. Wee don't get Enough here wee say, yet we are fat Enough. Ellen I hant perished yet but I have eat a many a meal off of corn bread and water. Time of the Lookout Mountain fight I picked a chunk of corn dodgers up in an old camp that had been throughed out eat it & thought good. And I saw some men on the retreat bring some bacon skins out of a meat house and broil them to eat. The other day I seen a man with about 15 inches of a cows tail skind to eat."* Again, we see "cornbread and water" to be the main staple of the soldier's diet within the Army of Tennessee though, there are times where there might be a "delicacy" available like some bacon skin or a skinned cow's tail!

---

219 Appendix, Items XC, XCI, XCII and XCIII.

220 This is not mentioned in any of Young Hitch's letters but it obtained from the Confederate Military Service records at the National Archives.

Note, that Hitch recalls the "Lookout Mountain fight" (in Tennessee) where they found some good corn dodgers to eat. If not from the south, one may not be familiar with what a corn dodger actually is, but according to official definitions, it is a stiff or fried bread made of corn meal. The ingredients are similar to hushpuppies but dodgers are a flat "cake" where hushpuppies are roundish balls. That stated, the two are sometimes referred to interchangeably in the south today. Though dodgers seem very plain, a soldier who had subsisted on only cornbread and water would view a dodger as a welcome treat. Young then closes by noting that it is his night to get wood to cook the meal as the "old man" (unknown person, maybe Ellen's husband or maybe Young himself?) is on guard duty as well as is (William Berry) Scruggs who will be coming back into camp soon.

On the same day, Thursday, Apr 21 1864, Young writes to his wife and gives some interesting details about his duties and that of the 16th South Carolina regiment over the past few days:

> *"A Sunday night I was on guard & it was a rough time to be out. Tuesday wee had to go to Dalton on a big review a heap of doublequicking to do whitch give me out I tell you. Yesterday our regt were ordered out near Dalton on the Cleaveland Road to work. The work was throwing up a battery to place cannon & rifle pitts and sutch like. The 16th done the biggest days work that she has ever done since I have been with it. Every three men has so mutch to do there was no slideing out. But this morning I feel better than I expected to after sutch tramps. Mary on Tuesday at one time I was so mad when they was runing us so that I felt like I could of throughed hot shot at them. Mary the Enemy & our Headquarters are only 14 miles apart. The Enemy is at Ringgold. Ours at Dalton. There may be fighting done hear about Dalton."*

This was the time when the Atlanta campaign was about to begin in earnest, in about three (3) weeks' time, and Young's assessment of the increased activity within camp at the time reflects that. Hitch spent the night of Sunday, April 17, out on guard duty and "it was a rough time to be out". Then, on Tuesday the 19th, the regiment did a review in Dalton in "double quick" time which proved very strenuous, so much so that Young became so angry that he could have hurled "hot shot" at his superiors! Then, the next day, on the 20th, more hard work was required as they were detailed out to Cleveland Road near Dalton (modern day Georgia State Highway 71) to construct a cannon battery and rifle pits, so much work that Young describes it as the "*16th (SC) done the biggest days work that she has ever done since I have been with it.*" No doubt, the Army of Tennessee was expecting imminent action and Hitch verifies this by mentioning that the Union headquarters and that of the Confederates are only 14 miles apart, the former being at Ringgold, Georgia and the latter in Dalton and that "*There may be fighting done hear about Dalton* (soon)."

We now know that the Union army in Tennessee and Georgia under Sherman was beginning to push towards Atlanta. The army that Young Hitch cites as being at Ringgold was a subset of Sherman's whole, the Army of the Cumberland, commanded by General George Thomas. The Federal Army of the Tennessee under General James B. McPherson headed south to the west of Thomas and General John M. Schofield's Army of the Ohio headed southward to Thomas' east to prepare for a May 1864 confrontation with the Army of Tennessee under General Joe Johnston.

After the news of himself and his unit, Young Hitch returns to writing about family matters and mentions a letter from Aunt Sally Hitch from Apr 16 1864 (this letter does not survive but the envelope does as shown in **Figure 24**). She had indicated that she was then staying with the family of (Edwin) Leroy (Pitts), who is her nephew and speaks of "the Milam's" (who is her niece's family, Diatrephus M. and Sarah (Pitts) Milam) as a place where she thought of residing but that could not evidently fit all her wares (e.g., her "plunder") in their house! Consequently, Aunt Sally would like to move in with Mary Hitch and the family. Young, in a bit of husbandly diplomacy, leaves that decision up to his wife on that matter. There is no indication in the records that Aunt Sally ever moved in with Young Hitch's family but it was not because not trying. Such was the life of the spinster aunt and acting family matriarch in the days of the War Between the States!

Finally, Young addresses the ever-increasing interests of the soldiers in finding religion as he writes, *"Mary wee have good preaching here & pretty good attention. Some are joining the Church. There is a little warmth of religion of late in our camp & I am glad to see it. There is service a moste every night when the weather is suitable near our cabin. Prayer is offered for mouners they have from three to six I believe generally when I have been out."* As the war has worn on, Young Hitch has noted a higher level of interest in the church and "preaching" amongst the troops and he is "glad to see it."

Additionally, there is another letter from Apr 21 1864 from Young Hitch to his sons, J.J. and A.L. Hitch. Hitch reiterates to his boys what he had written to his wife about the "double quick" drills of Tuesday, April 19, *"Boys we have plenty of drilling to do we had a big review Tuesday last it come the nearest wearing me out of arry one that we have had yet, but I was in a poor plight for it for I was old guard & had a bad cold & pains to kill allmost seemed to me."* He also mentioned the work of April 20 where the unit had to build cannon batteries and rifle pits, *"yesterdays work did not hurt me near so bad although I had to use a pick & shovel."* Young Hitch then gets into an interesting discussion about his gun and his prowess at keeping it clean:

> *"Boys I must tell you of there takeing our Enfield rifles from us and giveing us the Austin rifles whitch are a rough looking gun at best. And you may know that I was not pleased with the swap. My Enfield had kept me off of the guard lines six weeks hard going and one week besides & had I been allowed to keep it I could of got the premium the next Sunday morning. But the second Sunday after getting our new guns me & another man tied so we had to draw for it & I lost it but it was said that my gun was the cleanest. If nothing happens I will make some of them rub for the premium next Sunday morning. Col. Ioor said to me the first Sunday after we drew the Austin rifles that he believed I always would have a clean gun. Some say to me that they won't work on a gun like I do. But they bought sandpaper & wore it out on there guns & I beat them without any sandpaper then I laugh in my belly good. It pays mighty well to keep a clean gun sutch weather as we have for there is no fun in standing twenty four hours in bad weather."*

Evidently, Young was made to give up his Enfield rifle-musket, much to his dismay, in favor of a "rough looking" "Austin" rifle[221]. It seems that a "premium" was given in the camp for the cleanest gun with the

---

[221] Young Hitch's "Austin" rifle was no doubt really an "Austrian" rifle-musket common in the Civil War. This was the Lorenz Rifle, invented in 1854 by Austrian Lieutenant Joseph Lorenz. It was similar in design to the Enfield rifle-

reward being to be excused from guard duty and Hitch received this reward six weeks running plus another week in-between (See **Figure 25** for a photograph of the Enfield rifle-musket). But Hitch states that the new guns are rougher and harder to clean so he competed into a tie with dressing it with another soldier. The tie was subsequently decided by drawing straws and Hitch lost but others had said his gun was the cleanest anyway. Young is rightfully proud in his ability to keep his gun in top shape and he is so confident in his abilities that he will use no sandpaper against someone who does and still win every time and, in the process, get to be excused from 24-hour guard duty! He even gets noticed by Col. Ioor[222] for his efforts.

The undated letter in this four-letter series is from Young Hitch to his sons and no doubt comes from April 1864 based upon its content. To his oldest son, Joseph, Hitch writes that he should be thankful that they are relatively well off. He relates that things could be a lot worse in wartime when he writes, *"We have to be thankful that we are as well off as we are. Suppose your ma had no meat at all and your whole dependence for something to eat was in the milk and butter from your cow. And think soldiers was to come and drive her off and kill her for beef. Leave you nothing to eat but a little dry bread. Just sutch a case took place near this camp. No, don't you think you see hard times but wait until the army comes along, they will steal the last thing that you have to eat."* Things like this were happening in northern Georgia where families were impacted by the marauding armies and were left with nothing on their farms to eat or with which to make a living and, he reminds Joseph Hitch to count his blessings in that regard. Young also compliments his son for taking good care of the farm, *"got a letter from A.Y. Garrett speaking of the late spring and the neighbors being behind with their work. He said you were ahead of the neighbors with your work."* Joseph no doubt was glad to have made his father proud.

In the second portion of this letter, Hitch addresses his youngest son, Lucian, *"I have just come from preaching and eat my dinner. I saw several baptized or sprinkled. And they are now gone to the river to baptize them that joined the Baptist. I felt to lazy to walk to the river. Berry is gone I think. Scruggs is on guard."* More preaching and more baptizing were the order of the day in camp with the 16th South Carolina. He mentions that Little Berry Edwards has gone to view the baptism ceremonies at the river but that he was too lazy to attend! Private William Scruggs was on guard duty at the time. Hitch then laments to his young son how he was beaten again with the gun cleaning, *"I lost the premium today again. Had I of worked on my gun as the man did on his this morning who beat me, I would of beat him. I generally clean mine on Saturday so it rained last night and I done as good as nothing to mine this*

---

musket, using a percussion lock, had a similar length, and had three barrel bands, like the Enfield. While, it was originally .54 caliber, many were bored out to .58 caliber so that they could use the same ammunition as the Springfield and Enfield rifle-muskets. The quality of Lorenz rifles was not consistent. Some were considered to be of the finest quality, and superior to the Enfield where, others, especially those later in the war, were described as horrible in both design and condition. Many of these poorer quality weapons were swapped out on the battlefield for Enfield rifle-muskets whenever one became available.

[222] The identity of Ioor from Hitch's letter was a mystery for some while. In his writing, it looks as if he has written Col. Toor or Joor. Knowing that J's and I's looked very similar back in the 1860s, we might assume the name to be "Ioor" but still the mystery lingered until research in the records index of the National Archives shows that the 16th SCV had a Lt Col. Wallace B. "Ivor" among the ranks. He was appointed Lt Col. under Col. McCullough on Dec 2 1861 and assigned Apr 29 1862 at Camp Leesburg, SC. However, further research still in the actual primary records there and, the letters of others like Samuel McKittrick, show that the index is incorrect and the correct name of the Lt. Col. is indeed "Ioor" as Hitch spells it in his letter.

morning but I make them work. I don't spend a great deal of labor on my gun." But, he makes sure to let Lucian know that he keeps his gun in good working order nevertheless.

The final April letter is dated the 25th from Young Hitch to his wife from Dalton[223]. He expresses that he is not in the best of health (mainly back and leg pains) after having come off guard duty from the morning before but had nothing to do on the day he writes *"until dress parade this evening."* The camp is rather

Figure 25 - Civil War Enfield rifle-musket much like Young Hitch took to war with him.

deserted as *"moste of our regt are gone to Dalton for Provoste guards, two companys and a piece[224] left in the camp."*

Hitch also expresses to his wife the bad news that there will be no more furloughs available in the near future, *"the stoping of furloughs. If the furloughing had kept on I would of got to of come home this summer. But as it is God only knows when or whether or ever or not. But I trust there is a better day a coming soon."* But, even though he seems frustrated and tired with the war and its troubles, he is not ready to give up as others around him seem to be, when he states, *"Mary I feel like that if we could just humble ourselves all of us both soldier and citizen and ask the Lord to assist us and aid in the Battling with the Enemy, I do think we could have peace in our land again. Mary I want to come to see you bad but not bad enough to run away to get to see you yet. Mary I am tiard of soldiering but I cant say what*

---

223 Appendix, Item XCIV.

224 It is unknown whether the reference to "piece" means a cannon or simply a portion of a company as in "two companies and a piece (of one)."

some say. That is peace any way just give them peace. They dont care whitch side gains just so they get out of the war. I know that I have never been in a battle but I have been near Enough to see a good deal. But I am not willing to stop just on any terms as some speak of...Mary was it not for being so troubled with rhumatism I could enjoy myself in the army fine. Wee soldiers should recollect what we are fighting for & try to be content even if wee do have a heap to undergo."

Here, we see that he is not willing to accept peace just for the sake of peace; he wants to see some gain for the Southern cause for all the effort they have put into the war. In fact, we see in **Figure 23**, a receipt in the Mowbray collection dated Mar 29 1864 where "Y.H.E. Hitch" paid $100 for a 4% War Bond in the Confederate States of America. This was just 4 weeks before he writes in this letter the words, *"Wee soldiers should recollect what we are fighting for & try to be content even if wee do have a heap to undergo."* Young Hitch had put his proverbial money where his mouth was.

MAY 1864 – THE ATLANTA CAMPAIGN COMMENCES

May 1864 opens for Young H.E. Hitch still located in Dalton, Georgia with another letter to his wife on the first day of the month[225]. He is replying to an April 26 letter she had written to him which unfortunately does not survive; however, it was a *"most kind and loveing letter."* He further states, *"I was truly proud to get a letter from you. I had not recd ary letter since the one by Vaughn. Glad to learn that you was all well. I was afraid that you were all sick by me not getting no letters."* In this letter, Young pines for home since some of the *"men that have just come in from Greenville say that the trees are greener here than at Greenville. But I suppose it about the same"* and it appears that he is reflecting on some of things Mary had written in the letter we do not have. He says:

> *"Mary you say for me to come home & you will give me something to eat. I will try to comply with your request as soon as possible. It may be some time before I can get off though. Mary I often think of home & the past & gone by days of pleasure that I have spent with you. I hope that I may live to get home again & that we may Enjoy a few more days on Earth together. I want to see my old home again verry bad. I would be glad to see the old chicken coop or the sheep house. And I would love to see them pretty shade trees & the rose bushes in the month. Tell me if the wodvine and the big monthly is yet alive & standing. To come home would be a treat to me sure at this time."*

It is a rather sad discourse and the pain in Young's heart is obvious from his words as he misses his home and family dearly. We can, however, get a very good visual of his farm from what he writes such as the "old chicken coop and sheep house," the "pretty shade trees & rose bushes" and the "woodvine and big monthly(?)." He would consider it a treat to see these things just for a few more days on earth.

The only news on the activities of his unit with regard to the war directly are when he pens, *"...Friday last there was some appearance of a fight. I was at Division Headquarters on the road & the Couriers flew a round in a hurry. The cannonading was pretty heavy. I don't know the result yet But hear that the enemy have retiered* (sic, retired) *back to Ringold. We are in our old holes yet it will soon be five months*

[225] Appendix, Item XCV.

since we came to this camp. We have got to stay a heap longer than I expected when we come here." "Friday last" would have been April 29 and there was fairly heavy cannon fire and some major commotion that resulted in the enemy retiring back to Ringgold, Georgia. While this was probably just a little skirmish, we now know that, on Apr 29 1864, Sherman issues orders to his Generals Schofield, McPherson, and Thomas, to have their forces ready to move against the Army of Tennessee at Dalton by May 5[226].

Finally, Young closes this letter with more mention of the influx of religion into his camp, especially his brigade which he calls out by name of the four (4) separate regiments of which it is comprised, "*Mary there is a great revival of religion going on now in this Brigade mostely of the 24 SC v and some of the 46 Ga & eighth Ga Battalion. There has some few joined of the 16 SC reg.*"[227] He even inquires about the churches he left at home in Laurens County, when he requests of Mary Hitch to "*let me know how Cedargrove Church is getting on of late & if any have joined of late. Also the same from old Durbin.*"

The next letter in the Mowbray collection is a surviving correspondence from Joseph J. Hitch to his father, Young, also dated May 1 1864[228]. When we last heard about J.J. Hitch, it seemed that he was weighed upon heavily over the responsibilities of caring for the family farm, but that was tempered by his father's note that Joseph was ahead of all the other farms in getting its spring work completed. In this latest letter, Joseph seems quite confident and proud of what he has been able to accomplish there during the spring of 1864. He writes about the condition of the farm specifically and his tending of it as,

> *"...wee air dun planting corn. Wee finished the 30 of April. Wee got all the bottom planted. Father that old bottom is a going to bee cloddy the loar end of the rows. I Bedded the ends of the rows in the old Bottom and onn the other side of the branch the ends of the rows. Well now the Wheat, the Wheat looks sorter small. I think that wheat will bee late to save and I am afrade that the rust will ketch it and ruin it all together. Oh daddy cum home and help us set out cabedge plants. We have got sum Just as purty as you ever saw. Wee want to set out sum as soon as it rains and I think that in a week I will have sum tobacco plants big Enuff to set out. The rye and barley looks very bad indeed it has ben Sutch a bad winter on it until it like to of killed all the barley. Father as ruff a winter as it has been your birveany is yet alive and a blooming out verry pretty and Mother has got the best Stand of Beens that you ever saw in the garden for they air as thick as you ever saw beens and Sum peas they have got Sum blooms onn them now and Sum cucumbeirs up and Shallots wee have plenty of them too and Sum ounions and a Sallet bed and the irish potatos I don't now what they will do but they air cuming up verry pretty and our potato patch it will be Just where you told us to have it last year below the garden. wee had our potato patch thair last year and this year again in the same place. Pa cum home and I will give you a big mess of Eggs rite brand new ones. I have got four ar five duzen rite at this minit in the cubard and that wont be all that wee will give you to Eat for I think Ma wood kill a hin and stuff hir besides the eggs friers grows as fast you ever saw a colt in your life."*

---

226 "The American Civil War 150 Years Ago Today", for Apr 29 1864.
227 Note, this corroborates with known history that the 16th and 24th South Carolina and 8th Georgia Battalion and 46th Georgia were the four regiments that made up States R. Gist's Brigade.
228 Appendix, Item XCVI.

We see that Joseph, as the eldest son, is attending to the role of caretaker of the farm quite well and managing things very efficiently. He will need to continue this in the future as the farm responsibilities will fall upon him in his father's absence. We see he has planted and is tending corn, barley, wheat, cabbage, beans, cucumbers, shallots, onions, Irish potatoes and some tobacco. He is also tending chickens and having good luck getting eggs from them. He wishes his father were there to see his success and, so that *"Ma wood kill a hin and stuff hir"* for his dinner. Joseph Hitch has taken the reigns to run the farm quite ably and Young Hitch was no doubt proud of him as he read this letter in his camp in Dalton.

In the final portion of this letter, Joseph takes the opportunity to return the favor that Young did in his letter to the boys explaining his appearance by offering a good description of himself and his brother Lucian, *"Well father now my hight and wait. Five feet one inch and a quarter, I way ninety lbs. Now A.L.'s wait and hight four feet five inches and a quarter and ways sixty 2 lbs. I am just about as high as Ma. I recken you know how high Ma is."* Joseph Hitch, just before he turns age 17, is 5'-1¼" tall and weighs 90 pounds and Lucian is 4'-5" tall and 62 pounds. We even find out that Mary Hitch was about 5'-2" to 5'-4" as she was just a little taller than J.J. according to him. We see that Joseph Hitch was quite small for his age, even for mid-19th century standards. We can see why his physical stature caused him to be refused entry into the army when he reached the proper age which he could join, a few months after this letter was written.

The next letter in the collection comes from May 7 1864 penned by Young Hitch to his sons J.J. and Lucian[229]. May 7 happens to be the date the Atlanta Campaign officially begins with the Battle of Rocky Face Ridge just to the west of Dalton. The 16th regiment had just left their snug winter quarters in Dalton the day before and marched to Mill Creek Gap on Rocky Face Ridge[230]. Young had not yet received the aforementioned letters of May 1 from Mary Hitch and the boys (*"Joseph please write to me. I rec. a letter from you & your ma on Wednesday last of the 15 April"*). In Young's letter, it appears that the hostilities have not yet broken out but they are imminent, as he writes,

> *"the Enemy is said to be advancing on us slowly. They are coming on the Cleveland Road. We are still preparing for them. The Ladys have been ordered to leave hear. Wee had a fly round Tuesday & Wednesday last out to the Spring Place some ten or twelve miles. My company was sent out on pickette that night. But we saw yankeys. In a few minutes after wee got back to camp there come orders to be ready to leave at a moments notice. And we keep our crust ready baked for a tramp."*

Spring Place, Georgia is east of Dalton by about 10 or 11 miles and, at that place, Young got more of a taste of active picket duty. In Civil War terms, a picket is defined as follows:

> **PICKET** - An advance outpost or guard for a large force was called a picket. Ordered to form a scattered line far in advance of the main army's encampment, but within supporting distance, a picket guard was made up of a lieutenant, 2 sergeants, 4 corporals, and 40 privates from each

---

[229] Appendix, Item XCVII.

[230] South Carolina's Military Organizations During the War Between the States; Volume III, The Upstate, Robert S. Seigler, The History Press, Charleston, SC, 2008; page 175.

> regiment. Picket duty constituted the most hazardous work of infantrymen in the field. Being the first to feel any major enemy movement, they were also the first liable to be killed, wounded, or captured. And the most likely targets of snipers. Picket duty, by regulation, was rotated regularly in a regiment.[231]

It is interesting to note that picket duty might even be considered more hazardous than being in battle. This is simply because there were relatively few men on picket at any given time and they were fully exposed to the enemy out in front of their own combat units. Enemy snipers and sharpshooters took pot shots at picket soldiers regularly and many of those soldiers were killed or wounded while conducting such duty. We see here that Company I of the 16th South Carolina was assigned picket duty in Spring Place, Georgia on Tuesday night/Wednesday morning, May 3 and 4, and encountered Yankees. They have also been kept on high alert since returning to their camps in Dalton as Young Hitch states to Joseph, "*There will no doubt be a great battle fought near Dalton soon. How it will turn out time will only tell. I cant help but dread it for I know that some will be sure to fall & I may be one of them.*" An eerie message indeed.

Finally, in his discourse with Joseph he mentions, "*I hear today that wee have gained a great victory in Virginia. I hope it may be so.*" Even though he is skeptical of its truth, Young is no doubt hearing early word from north of him at the Battle of the Wilderness in Virginia in which the South did achieved a big victory in action on May 5 1864. In it, the Union suffered nearly 20,000 killed, wounded and missing while the number for the Confederate side was about 11,000[232]. The victory would provide little consolation ultimately as the North, with superior numbers and an overwhelming amount of men in its forces, continued to press the campaign toward Richmond while Young and his fellow soldiers to the south defended Atlanta in the North's campaign against that city.

A sidebar here on another member of the 16th South Carolina regiment, Company I. Second Lieutenant Erasmus Newport Garrett resigned on May 2 1864 "instead of facing a Board of Examiners" and asked to be transferred to Company F, Hampton Legion, South Carolina. Hitch never specifically mentions him in any of his correspondence but he is nephew to Hitch's good friend Archibald Y. Garrett who is mentioned often[233].

Young adds some words in the letter for his other son, Lucian. Besides the regular discussion of the weather and his health and some reiteration of going to Spring Place, Young finishes with some words of

---

[231] "Historical Times Illustrated Encyclopedia of the Civil War" edited by Patricia L. Faust and "The Civil War Dictionary" by Mark M. Boatner III.

[232] The Wilderness, May 5-7, 1864, Spotsylvania and Orange Counties, Virginia, *www.civilwar.org*.

[233] 2LT Erasmus Newport Garrett (1834-1914) was son of Thomas M. and Nancy Wade (Vaughn) Garrett of Greenville County, SC. He is buried with his wife, Mary Frances (Jones) Garrett (1842-1882), in the Durbin Creek Baptist Church Cemetery, Fountain Inn, SC. His veteran's gravestone, placed in the modern day, incorrectly states that he was a Private for Company E of the 16th Regiment SCV as, apparently someone incorrectly researched his service record when applying for the stone from the U.S. Veteran's Administration. Nevertheless, we give credit to Mr. Garrett as a Lieutenant of Company I in these pages! Young Hitch's good friend, Archibald Young Garrett, was brother to Thomas M. Garrett. While LT Garrett asked for a transfer to the Hampton Legion, no records can be found whether the transfer was actually completed. (Confederate Military Service records, National Archives, Washington, DC. Genealogical information from the author's personal records in conjunction with ancestry.com.)

wisdom for Lucian and his brother, *"when you need advice you must go to some old person for it. I know you feel at a great loss often times. I am away from you so as to be no help to you atal. But while you are struggling to make something to live upon your father is struggling hard to gain our independence & freedom. And I do hope that we may yet gain our independence though I may fall in the struggle. I hope you two sons may reap some of the benefit of our independence*." It is a profound, prescient statement and sums up Young's never waning drive to achieve the final objective of what he is fighting for: Southern Independence. And, in his correspondence, he has never expressed to his family any ideological premise for wanting this independence except in this statement here, "I HOPE YOU TWO SONS MAY REAP SOME OF THE BENEFITS OF OUR INDEPENDENCE." He simply wants what most fathers want for their children; a good life with abundant opportunity for their future.

In an undated letter from Young Hitch to his wife Mary, but probably from May 1864, we get more idea of how hard it was for farm families to make do during the latter part of the war[234]. Hitch writes:

> *"Mary you speak of your visitors. My advice is for you to shun company all you can. I think it right for its not for your benefit that they visit you. Its for their own interest and after you are eat out they will stop coming to see you & tell Joseph to feed light & if they don't like it, it will take the less to do them. You know nothing yet about folks. You had better shell your corn as fast as you can & if no better pile it up in the little room and box up your bacon & put it upstairs. Mary take good care of everything that is to eat. You will have to be verry stingy. Let the people say what they may. Be sure you & the children eat a plenty your selves."*

Here, Hitch is responding to a letter he has received from Mary but that does not survive today. She has evidently been having a lot "visitors" of late who seem to want to eat their food, which is becoming very scarce. Young instructs her to actually hide the bacon and corn so that they will not know it is there. He tells her she must be very "stingy" with the food and if they do not like it then so be it. Hitch is looking out for his family from afar and wants to make sure they are taking care of themselves first and foremost during these trying times and to not worry about others and, "let the people say what they may." A final few words from Hitch that will soon amount almost as a premonition when he writes, *"But I suppose when the war is over I will be discharged, probably before by death. If so God grant that I may be prepared for Eternity, Death and Judgement oh that I may be ready."*

Aunt Sally Hitch is next to write to Young when she composes a letter dated May 9 1864[235]. By this time, lots of skirmishing and fighting have occurred in and around Young's camp in Dalton. The Battle of Rocky Face Ridge is still playing out, having begun on May 7. Of course, Aunt Sally would probably not have known that at the time she had written her letter. She is age 68 by this point and, as is typical of most of her letters, she provides Young with news of the entire extended family.

In her last letter that is part of the Mowbray collection (Jan 31 1864), Sally was trying to figure out where she would be living, but she was staying with her nephew Leroy Pitts' family at the time. Here in May, it appears that she has settled in to stay in the E(dwin) L(eroy) Pitts household for *"the rest of my days."* In

[234] Appendix, Item XCVIII.
[235] Appendix, Item XCIX.

this latest correspondence, she indicates that she had received a letter from Young Hitch on May 8 (this one does not survive) and was glad to hear that he *"was still in the land of the living."*

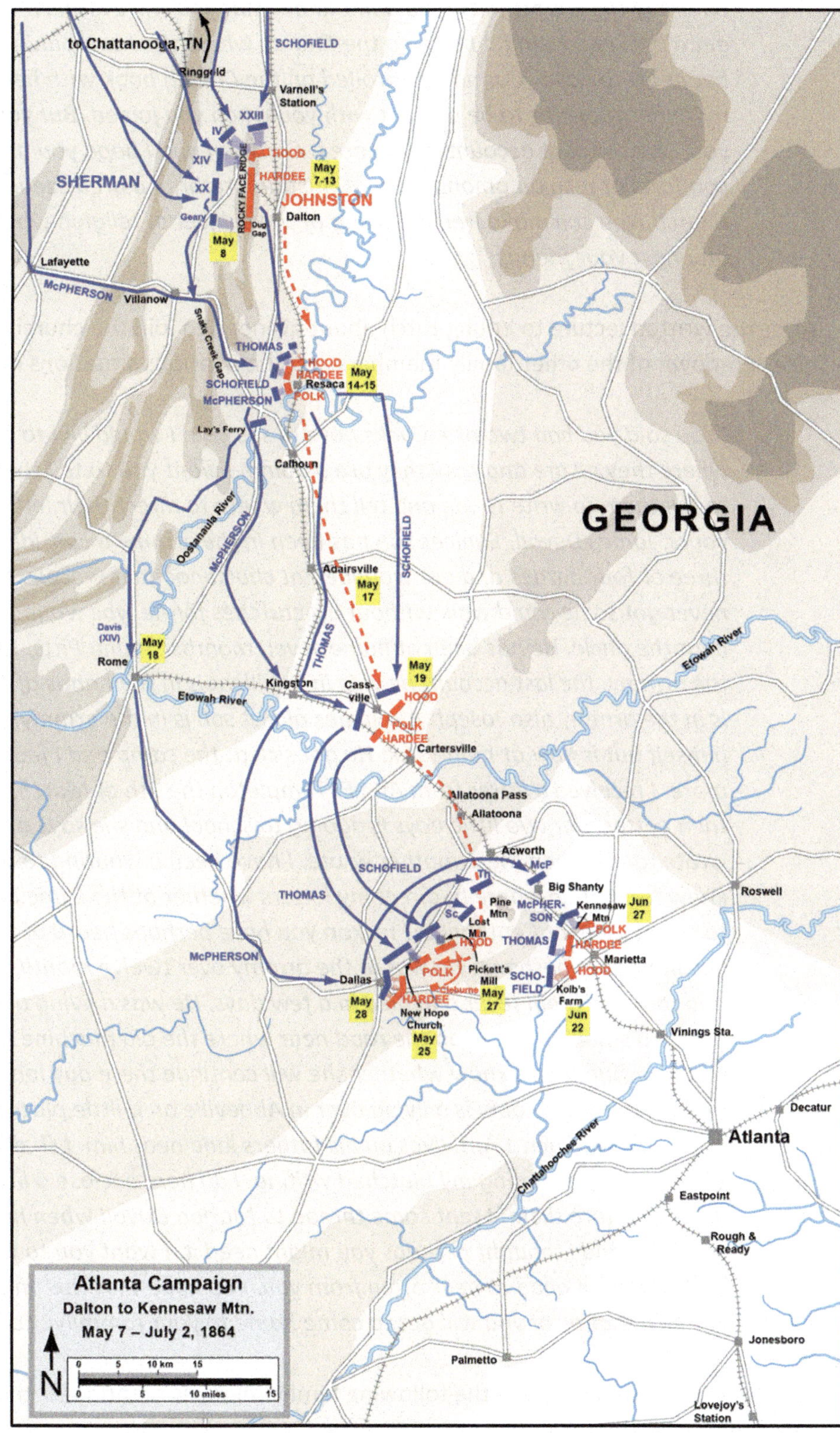

Figure 26 - Atlanta Campaign map for the Dalton to Kennesaw portion that occurred from May to July 1864. (Map by Hal Jespersen, *www.cwmaps.com*)

She then continues in her theme to Young as she has done in the past for him to join the church and be on *"pleading ground with your God"* as he had related to her the proclivity of many of the other soldiers to take up religion more seriously. She then invokes the fact that Mary Hitch, his "companion", would like to see his name amongst the church rolls along side of hers. She writes in more detail:

> *"You say you are having a good time there amongst you in religious meetings. You say they are a joining the Church out here and now my beloved nepew try to do your duty as others are a doing. You said in your first letter you sent me you was not satisfied in not offering yourself to the Church while at home and now you have the same priviledge as others have to join the Church and I would advise you as a friend you would*

embrace the opportunity. you don't know that you will ever have a better opportunity and then get a letter and send it home to the Church where your companion is. No doubt it would rejoice her heart to have your name enrolled on the Church book with her own although it would be more desirable for to be present with you when you joined. But you should not neglect doing your duty on that account. If you are a Christian and I hope you are you will enjoy your self in the comforts of religion amongst your Christian brethren a great deal more than you do out of the Church. You can make free in talking of the subject of religion what you can out of the Church amongst your friends."

After the written lecture to Young Hitch about his need to join the church, Aunt Sally then embarks on a nice run-down of the other family members and their various situations in the war time as follows:

"You said you had two of J. Cooks boys to see you. I would like to hear from them all and to know where they all are and how they are a doing. I want you to tell them if you should see them again to tell them to write to me and tell them where to direct their letters to direct them where you do yours. James Duvall, Eunices son has been in the armmy a considerable time. He has been in three or four battles and got wounded at chattanooga if I recolect right and came home and has never got so he could walk without his crutches for he was wounded in the ancle or in the leg near the ancle. He has been at home seven months. Young Pitts, Leroys brother is somewhere in the armmy. the last account he was in the illenois in the hands of the yankeys. Leroys oldest son is in the armmy also Joseph A. Hitches oldest son is in the armmy. Joseph A.H. has been in it himself but is now at home sick. He got sick at the camp and I fear he never will get well any more. I received a letter from Ann E. Templeton the 1th of March. They had all been sick but was then better. Her two little boys is agoing to school and she says a learning very fast. They both wrote to me when there mother wrote. I have been a wanting to write to Mary Ann but did not know for certain where to direct my letters whether at the same post office or not where I used to direct them at Centerville. I reckon you have perhaps heard of the death of Marian Duvall, Susan Hitches husband. He was in the armmy over twelve months and came home on a furlough and took the brain fever and died in a few days. He was a living at his fathers old place. He had put up a small house up on the road near where the old machine stood and susan is a living there this year but I don't know whether she will continue there any longer than this year or not. Pinkney Hitches widow is a living over in Abbeville on a little place she has rented and her two little sons with her. J.A.H. lives on his fathers land near him. I shall begin to draw to a close lest you get tired a reading my blotched writing. I do here enclose a little thread to mend your cloths when you tare them. I sent some thread to Marian Duvall when he was in camp and he was very glad of it and I thought perhaps you might need it. I want you to write every chance you can get for it does me good to hear often from you. I do hope that this unholy war will shortly come to a close so that all of you will get to come home to your fammilyes one time more"

In this long discourse, we see the following family relatives mentioned, most relative to things associated with the on-going war:

1. "J. Cook's Boys" – This is Jesse Spencer Cook (c1812-1880) who married Mary E. Hitch (1820-1852), daughter of Louther Douglas Hitch, and she, being Young Hitch's first cousin. The family

lived in Alabama at the time and at least one of their sons, Jesse Madison Cook was serving for the Confederate cause with Company E of the 25th Alabama infantry, Loomis' Battalion.

2. "James Duvall, Eunices son" – This is H. James Duvall, son of William L. Duvall (c1821-1856) and Eunice Elizabeth Pitts (1821-aft 1880). Eunice was daughter of Henry and Mary (Hitch) Pitts[236], anther first cousin of Young Hitch. James Duvall was serving as a Private for Company C of the 3rd South Carolina infantry. He had been wounded at the Battle of Chickamauga on Sep 22 1863 (not Chattanooga as Aunt Sally "recollects"). Evidently, his wound left him significantly disabled in his lower leg so he still needed crutches to walk. However, official war records show that he did return to service in June 1864.

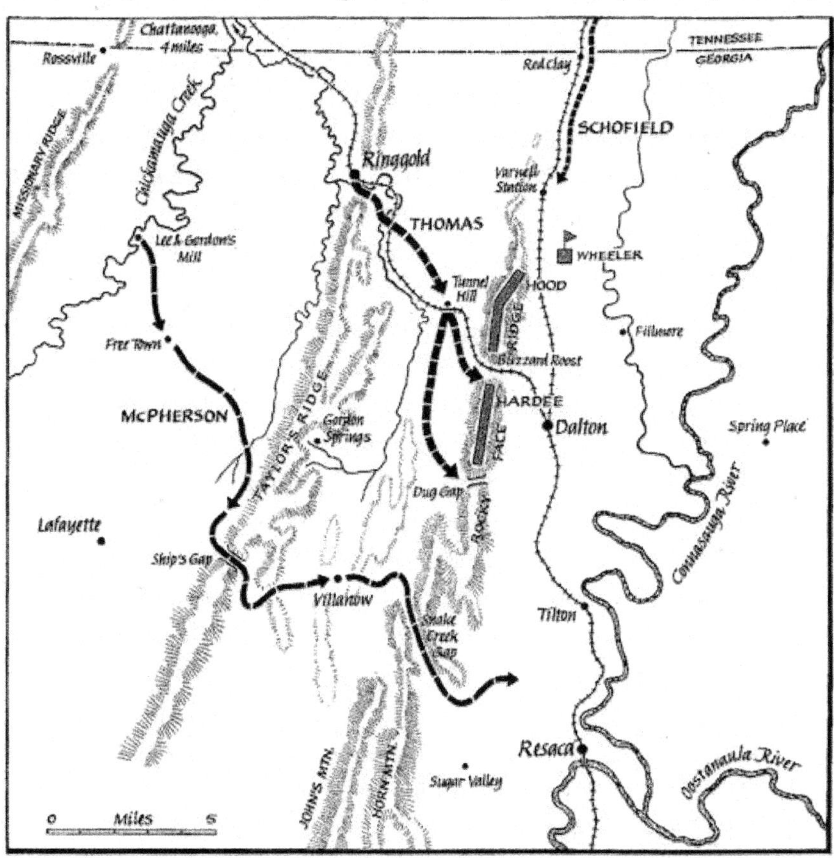

Figure 27 - The Battle of Rocky Face Ridge, May 7-12 1864. Also note the area called Spring Place where Young said he had tramped in the days before May 7th and where Company I of the 16th South Carolina conducted picket duty. (Public Domain Map, *www.americancivilwar.com*)

3. "Young Pitts, Leroys brother" – This is Young Joseph Harrington Pitts, brother to Edwin Leroy Pitts and son of Henry and Mary (Hitch) Pitts. He is another one of Young Hitch's first cousins. Young Pitts was serving "somewhere in the army" according to Aunt Sally but we know he was engaged as a Private with Company D of the 19th South Carolina infantry. In the muster records of Nov/Dec 1863, he was indicated as "absent" since Nov 25 1863 "supposed to be a prisoner of war." In the musters of Jan through Apr 1864, he is listed as "absent" saying he had been captured at Missionary Ridge (Georgia) on Nov 25 1863. But, another note card is his official service files shows him as captured at Chickamauga, Georgia on Nov 27 1863 and he appears on the rolls of POWs when he was forwarded to Louisville, Kentucky on Jan 6 1864 and indicated as available "for exchange." He then appears as discharged from POW status at Rock Island (Illinois) on Jan 17 1864. So the official records are confirmed with Aunt Sally's statement in her letter that *"the last account he was in the illenois in the hands of the yankeys."*

---

236 Mary (Hitch) Pitts was born October 10, 1794, a twin of Young Hitch's father, Joseph N. Hitch.

4. "Joseph A. H., J.A.H., Joseph A. Hitch" – All of these refer to Joseph Allen Hitch, son of Louther Douglas Hitch (1798-1886) and Catherine Lucinda Motes (1801-1857), another first cousin to Young Hitch. Joseph A. Hitch was age 41 at the time and serving as a Private for Company D of the 5th South Carolina State Troops and then Company B, 9th South Carolina Reserves. His service dates extend from Aug 1863 to Feb 1864 so it appears that he was out of the army as Aunt Sally states but, he lived till 1897 so her worry that "he never will get well any more" was apparently unfounded. In 1864, according to Aunt Sally, J.A. Hitch was living on his father's land near him.
5. "Ann E. Templeton" – This is Ann Elizabeth (Hitch) Templeton (1807-1879), daughter of Aunt Sally's half-brother, John Hitch (1773-1849), and Katherine Hanna (1783-1851). Ann Templeton was wife of James Clayton Templeton Jr. (1791-1857). Her sons, Perry Franklin and Clayton Walker Calhoun Templeton, were only ages 13 and 11, respectively, at the time so too young to have served in the Civil War.
6. "Marian Duvall, Susan Hitches husband" – Francis Marion Duvall who married Susan T.E. Hitch, daughter of Louther D. and Catherine L. (Motes) Hitch. He enlisted on Jul 1 1862 with Company C of the Holcombe Legion Cavalry of the South Carolina Volunteers. Muster records show a record of sickness after he was listed as "present in Jan/Feb 1863. From Mar to Oct 1863 he is listed as "absent" and intermittently in the hospital in Richmond, Virginia. He had a recurring fever as the records show he was admitted to the General Hospital in Richmond on Jun 4 1863 with "int. fever" and discharged on Jun 19 1863. But he again had "debilities" and was readmitted to the Hospital in Richmond on Jul 3 1863 and put in Jackson Hospital in Richmond on Aug 10 1863. He was returned to duty on Sep 7 1863 but again fell sick and was admitted Sep 21 1863 to Hospital 9 in Richmond and then placed on sick furlough from the brigade hospital for 30 days beginning October 17th. Finally, the official records dated Apr 4 1864, indicate, "F.M. Duvall" appears on claims of deceased by widow "S.T.E. Duvall" stating that he died in Laurens District, South Carolina on Jan 11 1864.
7. "Pinkney Hitches widow" – Presley Pinkney Hitch was reported as died by Aunt Sally back in her letter of Mar 20 1857. His wife was Emily Duvall, daughter of James and Letitia (Hitch[237]) Duvall. Pinkney and Joseph A. Hitch were brothers and sons of Louther D. Hitch (1798-1886). Aunt Sally indicates that Emily (Duvall) Hitch was, in 1864, living in Abbeville, South Carolina with "her two little sons" (William Leander Hitch and Luther David Hitch) who were ages 9 and 7 at the time.

Sally Hitch closes her letter with reference to a little "care package" she has sent Young with her letter, *"I do here enclose a little thread to mend your cloths when you tare them. I sent some thread to Marian Duvall when he was in camp and he was very glad of it and I thought perhaps you might need it."* Finally, she even fits in a few words about the war that indicates it is wearing heavy on the general population in the South when she pens, *"I want you to write every chance you can get for it does me good to hear often from you. I do hope that this unholy war will shortly come to a close so that all of you will get to come home to your fammilyes one time more."*

[237] Again, note that there is uncertainty over whether Letitia was actually a Hitch, daughter of Louther Hitch (1750-1838).

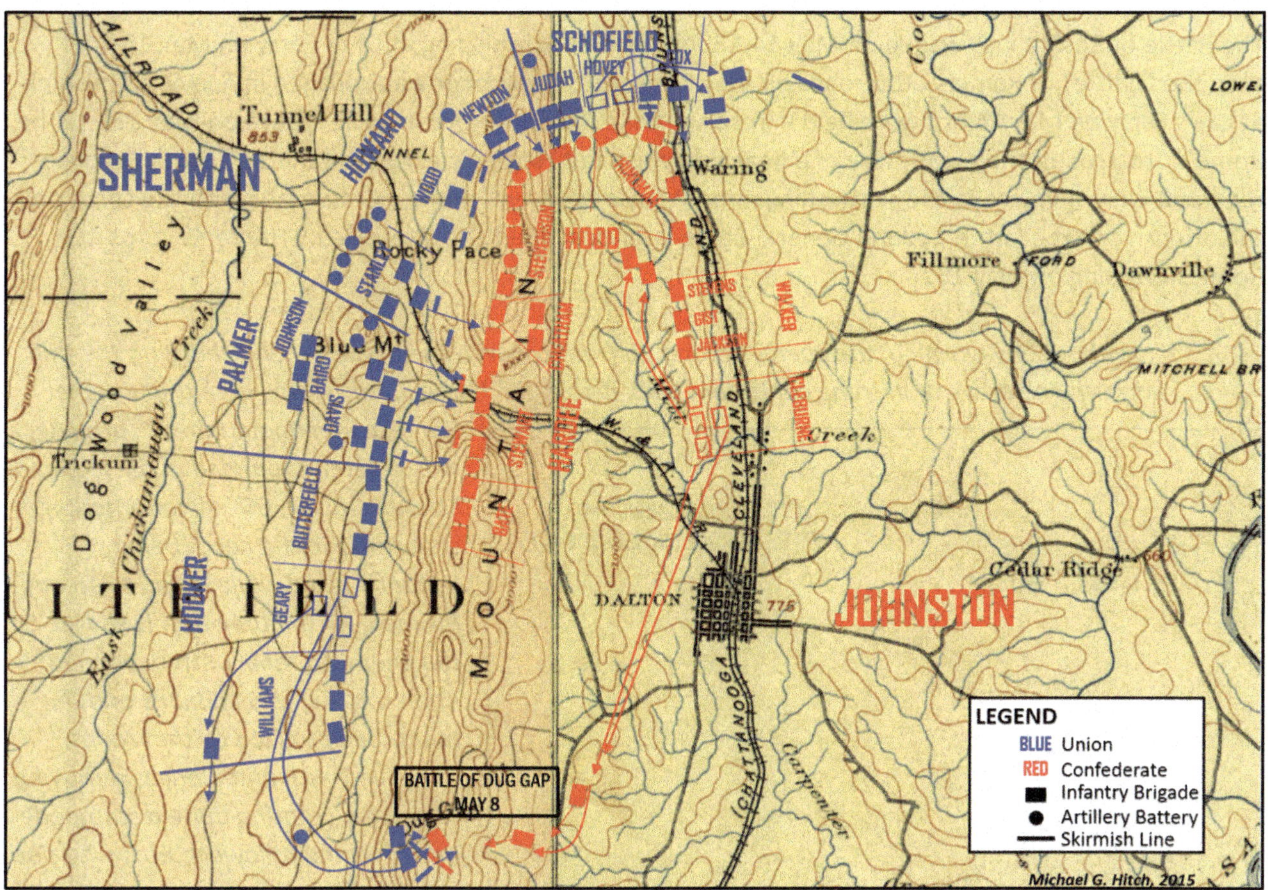

Figure 28 - Battles of Rocky Face Ridge and Dug Gap near Dalton, GA. Note the position of Gist's brigade (including the 16th South Carolina and Young Hitch) occupying the center of Walker's Division. They are situated atop Hamilton Mountain and out of the main lines of battle. (Michael G. Hitch map, 2015).

There is one remaining letter dated from May 1864 in the Mowbray collection, another from Young Hitch to his wife, Mary[238]. The letter is dated May 22 and, notably, Young Hitch is no longer in Dalton, Georgia for the first time in many months – instead, he writes from *"Cass County Ga near Cartersville."*

The Army had moved southeastward towards Atlanta after various confrontations with the enemy in early-to-mid May 1864 and since Young's letter to Mary on May 7. Within this time, the Battle of Rocky Face Ridge had occurred on May 7 and Dug Gap on May 8 1864. In **Figure 28**, we see illustrations of Rocky Face Ridge and Dug Gap with the Confederate line perched all along the brim of the ridge. The Dug Gap action was a small affair with Rocky Face Ridge much larger and, used as a decoy to allow McPherson's army to sneak through Snake River Gap. In the Figure, we can see where Young Hitch and the 16th South Carolina were located with Gist's brigade, on Hamilton Mountain to the rear of the primary action and did not see much of the direct conflict.

As the Battle of Rocky Face Ridge was concluding, the Army of Tennessee retired back to Resaca, Georgia on May 13 where it circled the town and trenched in there. Gist's brigade had marched toward Resaca in advance on May 9 and was held in reserve there on May 10.

238 Appendix, Item C.

The Battle of Resaca was waged on May 14-15 followed by skirmishing at Lay's Ferry on May 15 and then the "battle" of Rome's Crossroads on May 16. The 16th regiment was engaged in heavy skirmishing at Lay's Ferry on May 14 but were held in reserve while the battle occurred at Resaca on May 15[239]. The Rome's Crossroads affair was more of a heavy skirmish but Hardee's corps and the 16th South Carolina regiment were involved in the skirmishing at both Lay's Ferry and Rome's Crossroads with the corps on the offensive at the latter. Federal General Corse later described the offensive by Hardee's corps at Rome's Crossing on May 16:

> *"...without any warning, the enemy sprang up from cover in line of battle, and charging the thin skirmish line drove it, in some confusion, back across the Rome Road...it was here that Colonel Burke, commanding the 2nd brigade, was severely wounded in the leg, and Captain Taylor, 66th Illinois infantry, shot through the head, being instantly killed while trying to steady his men. All the time of this charge by the enemy, a rebel battery opened upon some empty caissons and the main road pursued by the troops, now filled with ambulances removing wounded, creating quite a stampede among camp followers, etc., who had by accident ventured too near the front..."*[240]

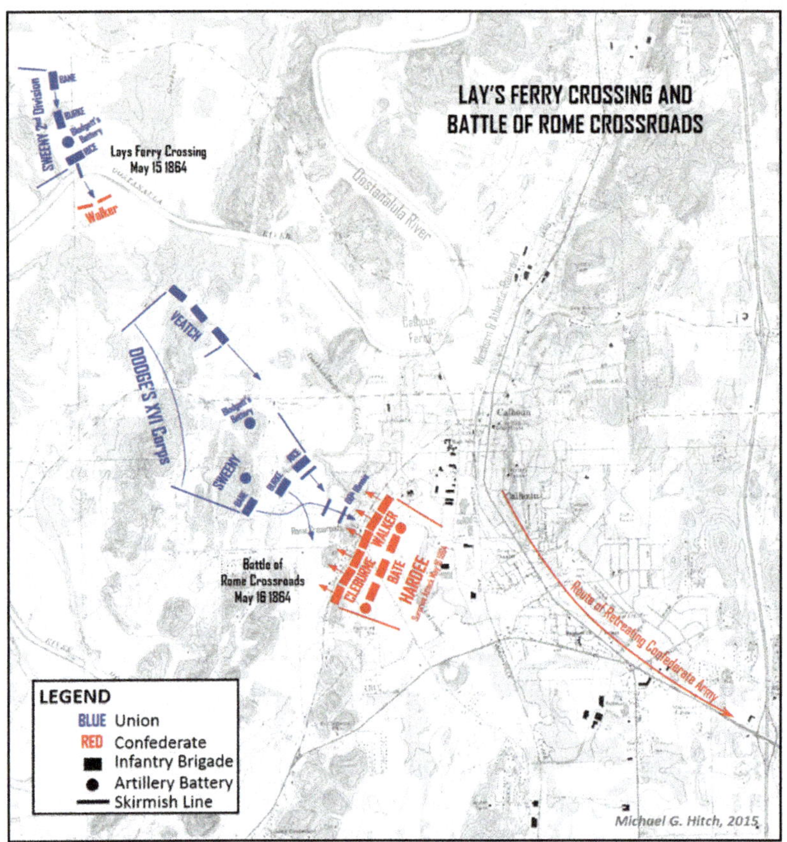

Figure 29 - The action that occurred on the retreat from Resaca. Lay's Ferry provided some minor skirmish action for Walker's Division on May 15 followed by more meaningful heavy skirmishing, especially with the 66th Illinois at Rome Crossroads near Calhoun on May 16 1864. (Michael G. Hitch map, 2015)

We see that Hardee's corps, with Young Hitch participating, mustered up an effective back offensive against the Northern army, especially the 66th Illinois who was in pursuit. After these events, Johnston's army retired to near Adairsville, Georgia on May 17 and then back to near Cartersville, Georgia on May 19. See **Figure 29** for action at Lay's Ferry and then Rome's Crossroads, Georgia. **Figure 30** shows the troop movements after that from Adairsville back towards Cassville.

Sherman had hotly pursued Johnston's army southward after Resaca, where Johnston hoped to find a good defensive position south of Calhoun. Not finding anything he liked, Johnston continued to

---

[239] South Carolina's Military Organizations During the War Between the States; Volume III, The Upstate, Robert S. Seigler, The History Press, Charleston, SC, 2008; page 175.
[240] The Campaign for Atlanta, William R. Scaife, McNaughton & Gunn, 1993, page 40.

Adairsville while the Rebel cavalry skillfully carried out a rearguard defensive action. On May 17, skirmish fire continued throughout the day and evening as the North's Major General O.O. Howard's IV Corps ran into the entrenched infantry of Hardee's corps (and the 16th South Carolina), about two miles north of Adairsville. Three Union divisions prepared for battle, but Major General Thomas halted them due to the approach of darkness and Sherman then concentrated his men in the Adairsville area to attack Johnston the next day.

Johnston had originally hoped to find the valley at Adairsville suitable to deploy his men and anchor his lines with the flanks on hills. The valley proved to be too wide, however, so Johnston disengaged and withdrew.[241] In these general skirmishes, there were approximately 200 Union casualties and an unknown amount on the Rebel side.

Figure 31 shows this movement and the placement of Young Hitch's Hardee's Corps just south of Cassville, Georgia on May 19 1864 and where they stayed until another retirement to near Allatoona Pass on May 19-20 then to near and just to the southeast of Dallas, Georgia by May 25[242]. This fits perfectly with Young's indication of being near Cartersville at the time he wrote the letter of May 22. In fact, they were between Cassville and Cartersville before they then backed up southward to Dallas and then, almost due east towards Marietta, Georgia where, by June 1864, they were stationed near Kennesaw Mountain.

In Young Hitch's letter of May 22 1864, we can see, and practically feel, with his words, the excitement of the activity that has been happening and the anticipation of more to come. He writes:

> *"I am yet alive & tolerably well. I have no strange news to write any more than wee have had heavy skirmishing with the Enemy in the day & hard marching of a night. We are at a halt now & have been ever since Friday Evening but may be on the march again before morning. We have been in some pretty tight places. The yankeys made us ly low behind our breastworks the other day. They threw the shells in amongst us in a hurrah. One of co. (I) got wounded comeing off of the field. A portion of the 16 has had some verry heavy skirmishing with the Enemy. We lost a noble young Liut at Resaca & some wounded."*

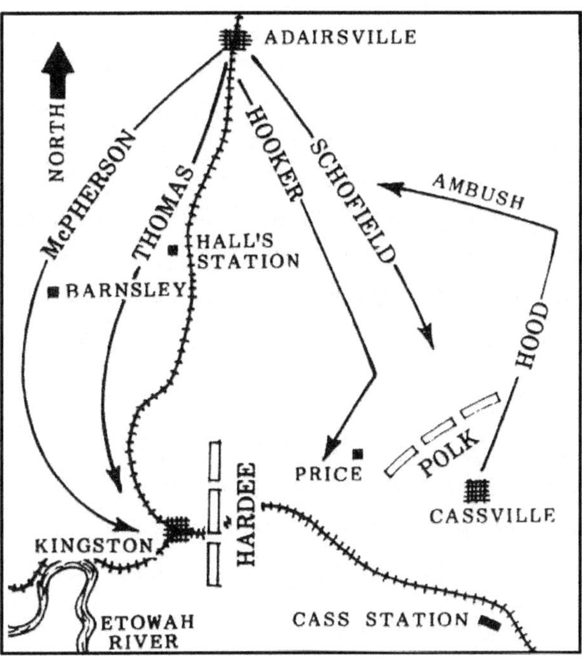

Figure 30 - The route of Johnston's retiring army from Resaca back towards Cassville on May 17-19, 1864. (Public Domain Map, *www.americancivilwar.com*)

241 See *www.americancivilwar.com*.

242 Ibid.

He notes that they had halted their movement Friday evening (which was May 20) but that they may be back marching again "before morning", which would be May 23. He also writes that, during the daylight hours, there has been heavy skirmishing followed by hard marching at night. This accounts for the known activities from the historical record of the fighting during the time and the jostling Johnston did with his army to try and gain a foothold at some location to defend.

When Hitch pens, *"The yankeys made us ly low behind our breastworks the other day. They threw the shells in amongst us in a hurrah. One of co. (I) got wounded comeing off of the field,"* he is probably referring to the action near Cassville, Georgia on May 19 1864. We see that there was plenty of gun fire as well as artillery and one person in Young's Company I, 16th South Carolina regiment was wounded. Then, Hitch goes immediately into a description of what had happened at the Battle of Resaca previously on May 14-15 1864, *"A portion of the 16 has had some verry heavy skirmishing with the Enemy. We lost a noble young Liut at Resaca & some wounded."* The 16th could complain no more about the lack of action, as there was heavy fighting in Resaca in which they lost "some wounded" and a bright, young lieutenant.

Young continues with,

> *"Our regt has been verry fortunate so fare in not getting into a regular Engagement. But in the last two weeks we have been several times as I thought right into a regular Engagement. Wee have had the rear to bring up different times & have been placed in the front line of battle But have been verry agreeably disappointed in not having the Enemy to advance on us."*

This clearly indicates that the 16th had not yet been in a "formal" battle engagement where it can be assumed this meant being formally lined up as a unit and marched directly across the field to an approaching enemy. Rather, the 16th had been engaged in "heavy skirmishing" that would be less formal activity but no less hazardous. They were, however, "several times" in the past two weeks in situations where a formal engagement looked imminent but did not pan out as such. The 16th was "very agreeably disappointed" that the enemy did not advance when they were ready to engage.

He writes no more about the battles in his May 22 letter but states that colleagues (William Berry) Scruggs is well as is (Little) Berry (Edwards). He asks that Mary Hitch tell Caroline (e.g., Caroline Edwards Scruggs, wife of William B. Scruggs) that her husband is "well & hearty." He then remembers Mary's constant worry that he is eating well enough when he states that "Johnson" (e.g., General Joe Johnston) is feeding them pretty well as they have been marching and, his Division has been self-dubbed, "Walker's Cavalier".

The final portion of the letter is a rather moving and poignant passage,

> *"Mary...I do hope that we may have the pleasure of spending a few more days on Earth together. It appears to me that I would be a happy man to be at home to enjoy home & family as I once could do. But I must ask you to forgive the ill treatment that I have given you. Mary I am allmost getting weaned from home in a heap of respects. But still I can call many of our ups & downs to my mind & it is company to me to think of them. Mary you ma wonder if Young aint badly scared*

in time of Battle. Mary it makes me feel verry little indeed but it sorter wears off after awhile. I try to put my whole trust in my Creator believing him to be able to save me."

It shows that Young, faced with the heavy action of recent days, is feeling his mortality and pining for home but, at the same time, thinking he may never get the opportunity to see home again. He then offers to Mary whether she wonders if he gets afraid in times of the battles. His response reflects the fact that he has been away at war for too long as, even the seriousness of a battle, "makes me feel very little indeed" and even that wears off in a short while. Instead, he has resigned to put his fate into the hands of his "Creator" and let come what may.

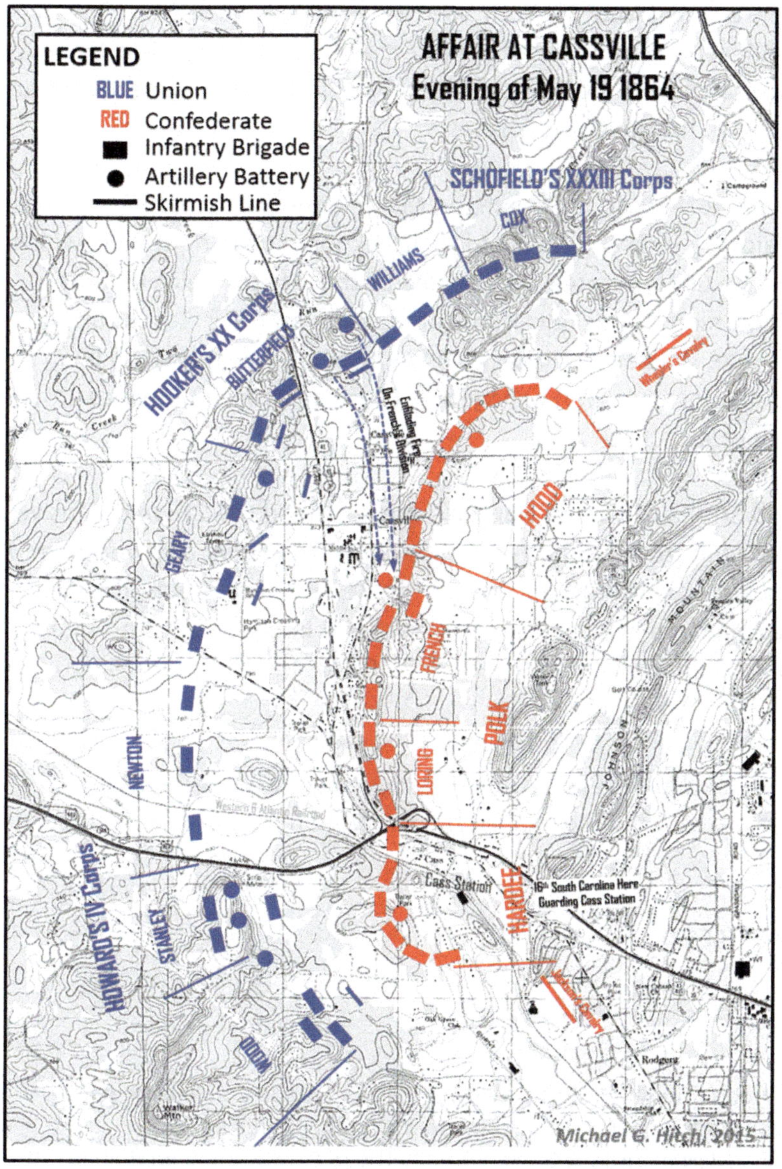

Figure 31 - Cassville area operations on the evening of May 19 1864. Note, Hardee's corps (with the 16th South Carolina) dug in around the Cassville railroad depot. (Michael G. Hitch, 2015)

At last, at the end of the letter, Hitch writes to tell "Ellen" that, "...*while some are lying takeing their ease & Enjoying home others are undergoing hardships. Sutch as marching day or night or lying in some ditch behind breastworks and nothing but Bacon & crackers to Eat & sometimes have it to eat raw.*" He wants to make sure she knows of the hardships the soldiers are bearing to help maintain the freedoms of those at home.

After Young Hitch writes his letter on May 22, in **Figure 32**, we see that, indeed, Hardee's Corps was marching again and reestablishing a position near Dallas, Georgia (New Hope Church and Pickett's Mill) by May 25 before falling back to Kennesaw Mountain in late June 1864. The Battle of New Hope Church was waged on May 25 1864 and significant action was underway near to Young Hitch and the 16th South

Carolina regiment included the following Battles[243]:

NEW HOPE CHURCH: After the Army of Tennessee retreated to Allatoona Pass on May 19-20, Sherman did not want to attack Johnston in such a strong location, so he decided to move around Johnston's left flank and march toward Dallas, Georgia. However, Johnston anticipated the move and met the Union forces at New Hope Church on May 25. Sherman mistakenly thought that Johnston only had a small force there and ordered Major General Joseph Hooker's corps to attack. Hooker's corps took a severe blow from the Confederate forces that consisted of Hood's full division. Walker's division and Young Hitch were marching south of New Hope at the time towards Dallas and therefore saw no action here[244]. On May 26, both sides entrenched and skirmishing continued throughout the day until full action commenced at Pickett's Mill on May 27. The 16th regiment was present but not engaged at New Hope Church[245]. Estimated casualties were 1,600 for the Union and unknown, but much fewer, for the Confederates.

PICKETT'S MILL: After the Union defeat at New Hope Church, on May 27, the Battle of Pickett's Mill occurred when Sherman ordered Major General O.O. Howard to attack Johnston's right flank which he incorrectly thought was exposed. The Confederates were ready for the attack, which did not unfold as planned because supporting Union troops never appeared and the attack was repulsed, causing high casualties on the Union side. Walker's division with Young Hitch was trenching in at Dallas when this battle took place and, hence, was not engaged[246]. Estimated casualties were 1,600 for the Union and 500 for the Confederates.

DALLAS: The Battle of Dallas occurred on May 28 when Hardee's corps probed the Union defensive line, held by Major General John A. Logan's Army of the Tennessee corps, to exploit any weakness or possible withdrawal. Fighting ensued at two different points, but the Rebels were repulsed, suffering high casualties. Walker's division was engaged at Dallas but only as rear reinforcements for Bate's division and saw only limited action[247]. Estimated casualties were 2,400 for the North and 3,000 for the South.

After the flurry of action in late May 1864, the Confederate army was locked down near Dallas and Johnston was still trying to find a suitable place to defend against the overwhelming amount of forces the Union was throwing at him.

JUNE 1864 – MANY SKIRMISHES AND BATTLES

---

[243] Descriptions of the minor battles at New Hope Church, Pickett's Mill and Dallas, Georgia are, in large part, presented from reference at *www.americancivilwar.com*, for the section on the Civil War in Georgia.
[244] The Campaign for Atlanta, William R. Scaife, McNaughton & Gunn, 1993, Battle of New Hope Church map, after page 60.
[245] South Carolina's Military Organizations During the War Between the States; Volume III, The Upstate, Robert S. Seigler, The History Press, Charleston, SC, 2008; page 176.
[246] The Campaign for Atlanta, William R. Scaife, McNaughton & Gunn, 1993, Battles of Pickett's Mill and Dallas map after page 60.
[247] Ibid.

As it entered June 1864, Johnston's Army of Tennessee was located just east of Dallas, Georgia before it would eventually back pedal towards Marietta to the east and what would become the Battle of Kennesaw Mountain on Jun 27 1864 (See **Figure 32**). He was looking for a strong position to defend and, possibly, to get a notable defeat of the Union forces.

In the Mowbray collection, there is one final letter written by Young Hitch and it is dated Jun 2 1864 from near Dallas, Georgia[248]. Since this is the final one from Hitch, it is included in its entirety as follows:

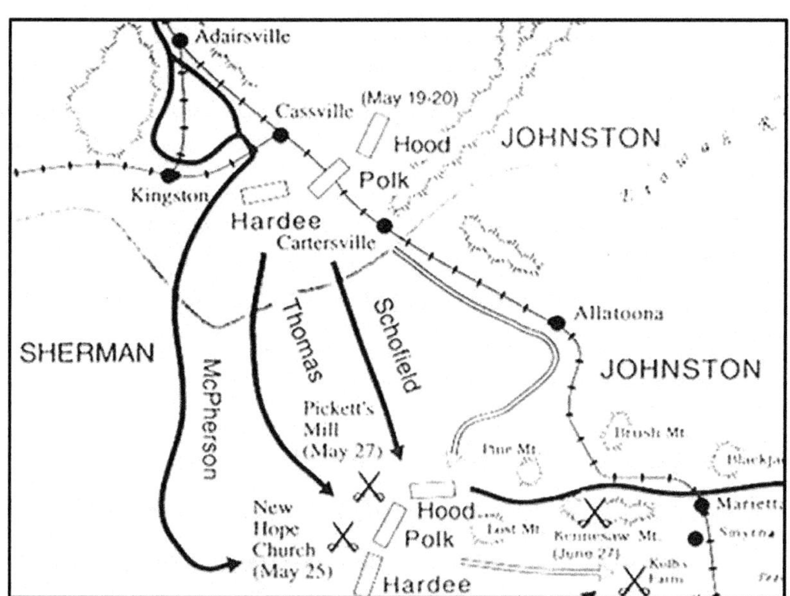

Figure 32 - Detail of the Cassville and Cartersville area in May 19-27, 1864. Note Hardee's Corps position within which Young Hitch was participating. After retiring back from Cassville, Hardee's Corps set up near where the Battles of New Hope Church and Pickett's Mill took place on May 25 and 27, respectively. (Public Domain Map, *www.americancivilwar.com*)

Near Dallas Ga
June 2nd /64

Mrs Mary A Hitch

Dear wife I seat myself to drop you a few lines to let you know that I am still alive & tolerably well.
But I am verry mutch fatigued and tired as we have had but little rest the last month neither day nor night. This is a mountainous country and hard to travel over. Mary I have escaped safe so far. But since Friday last I have been exposed a great deal to the Enemy fire. I was out on skirmish 48 hours. The yankeys fired a many a ball in the tree I stood behind. I done the best that I could for them. I tumbled over one but don't know how bad I hurt him. But one thing I do know I put a stop to his loading & shooting at me. He had been standing behind a tree shooting at me for sometime. But last Sunday night had a hot time. The yankeys thru shot & shell amongst us in a hurra. There is skirmishing on our (right?) this morning. Scruggs is sorter puny worn out I think. Edward is under the weather but I will not say what is the matter. Mary, I hope this may find you and the boys all well. Please write and let me hear from you. The 16 of April was the last. Please excuse this short letter for I may have to break & fall in to the breastworks in a few moments. This may be the last you hear from me. God only knows. But if I fall I hope to fall doing my duty. If I should survive this war let this be my boast that I served as a private in the great struggle for Southern independence.

So I remain your husband
Y.H.E. Hitch

---

248 Appendix, Item CI.

From the letter, we can practically feel Hitch's fatigue from marching and fighting over the past month as he writes, "*...I am verry mutch fatigued and tired as we have had but little rest the last month neither day nor night. This is a mountainous country and hard to travel over.*" Tramping over mountains and always having to be on the alert had to be extremely exhausting. Then Young suggests the fact that he has been in direct fire for almost a week, since "Friday last" which was May 27 and he has been on skirmish duty for 48 hours.

We then get the first glimpse where Young Hitch actually has traded fire with the "yankeys" as they "*fired many a ball in the tree (that he)... stood behind.*" He shows that he returned fire and hit one as he, "tumbled one over" but did not know how bad he was hurt. However, it did "*put a stop to his loading & shooting*" at him after the Yankee had been firing at him from behind a tree for quite some time.

He then mentions his friend (William Berry) Scruggs and Edwards and asks his wife to send another letter and hopes that she and his sons are well. Then he seems interrupted by saying "*...excuse this short letter for I may have to break & fall in to the breastworks in a few moments.*" Then, comes Young Hitch's final pronouncement of all his letters we have had the privilege to read and they are directed to his dear wife, Mary Hitch:

> **This may be the last you hear from me. God only knows. But if I fall I hope to fall doing my duty. If I should survive this war let this be my boast that I served as a private in the great struggle for Southern independence.**
>
> **So I remain your husband,**
> ***Y.H.E. Hitch***

The profoundness of these words would soon profess themselves in a dramatic way in the coming days - quite poignant and quite moving. With little fanfare, LT Jesse James Locke of Company I dies on Jun 4 1864 of disease while on a furlough home[249]. Things are definitely changing, and changing very quickly for Hitch and his unit.

In the Kennesaw Mountain National Battlefield files, there is a letter that provides some additional information of the experiences the 16th South Carolina regiment was having at this time. It comes from Private Samuel McKittrick[250], Young's colleague in Company I[251]:

---

[249] Jesse James Locke (1829-1864) was son of James W. (1800-1863) and Susan (Dacus) Locke (1803-1855) of Greenville County. He married Mary Elizabeth Owens (Owings). Lt. Locke was brother to Company I compatriot, Private George Washington Locke (1827-xx) and, to Margaret Locke who married Private P.E.A. Howard. Jesse J. Locke and his parents are buried in Standing Springs cemetery, Simpsonville, SC.

[250] Samuel McKittrick (1822-1864) was covered earlier herein with the formation of Company I but did not continue due to the reorganization of force in 1862. He did join Company I as a Private in Dalton, GA on Feb 11 1864. Private McKittrick would be elected Lieutenant on Jun 28 1864.

[251] SC-1 file, Kennesaw Mountain National Battlefield Park.

"Sunday June 5 (1864), letter to wife
I will finish my letter today. I never know when I commence a letter that I will have time to finish it without being stopped, as we are frequently stopped in our writing and have to lay all things by to march. We have been ever since the 7th of May marching around and laying in line of battle all the time. We have marched, I suppose, about 150 miles by night and day. We seldom pull off our shoes at night as we have to start so suddenly. We moved a short distance yesterday and struck up camp in the rain, hearing the Yanks were getting to our right we left camp about 12 o'clock last night—and come since 5 or 6 miles in that direction. We are now going to move again this evening. We had a severe time this morning through the mud and rain in the dark. My dear, it is a hard struggle for Independence. I am well today. My bowels are troubling me some. I stood all the hard marching better than I expected to. The troops are very much fatigued. We are now getting more to eat than we did before we left winter quarters. We get enough of meat and bread. My dear wife I hope that your frightful dream will not be realized. Oh, if I could be with you in your confinement, but that you know is impossible. I hope that your neighbors will not let you suffer. I hope that you are getting on with our dear little ones. Be firm in government with them. Tell them all I am always thinking about them and want to see them badly. Tell Turner and Jeffy they must not say bad or ugly words. Tell Rose and Line I have not forgotten them. I want them to be faithful servants, both to you and their God. Tell my dear children I want them to be such good children that if I never see them in this world, we will meet in Heaven. My dear wife, I have had many serious thoughts since I left you about leaving the world. I sometimes fear that I am not prepared, but still I have a Hope that I would not give for any mansion. In the narrow escapes I passed through I felt resigned to the Lord's will. My dear, I have no doubt of your preparation and if we both prove faithful we will soon meet where all the horrors of war will be over. I am sorry I have not got your likeness, but I have it engraved on my heart which nothing but death can erase. Write when you can. Your loving husband
Samuel McKittrick"

Here, we can see the corroboration with Hitch's assertions about the incessant marching that the 16th had seen over recent weeks, although they are eating well. The troops are tired and drained of energy and this is getting worse by the day.

Over the days after the June 2 letter, we do not hear from Young Hitch again. Probably, because he and the rest of the Army of Tennessee were very busy marching, trenching in, marching again and exchanging fire with the enemy. They were gradually being pushed back towards a battle position that would eventually explode into a heavy battle at Kennesaw Mountain on Jun 27 1864.

After the Battle of Dallas on May 28, they stayed trenched in east of there until June 4 when part of the Army of Tennessee marched to set up the Lost Mountain Line while the remainder established a line at Brushy Mountain. Walker's division with Young Hitch in attendance, was among the units digging in on the line at Brushy Mountain. The portion of the army on the Lost Mountain Line, most notably Bate's division who was exposed there out in front on Pine Mountain, retreated to join the others on the Brushy Mountain Line on June 14 and 15 after a Union attack at Gilgal Church. After that, there was another engagement at Mud Creek in June 14-16 and Latimer's Farm on June 18. **Figure 33** illustrates where the units in these areas, and the various engagements, were in the time from June 4-18, 1864.

We also know from the records that Company I gets reinforced with ten (10) transfers in from the Palmetto Battalion Light Artillery on Jun 16 1864.

Most notable for all the events involving the Lost Mountain and Brushy Mountain Lines for Young Hitch happened on Jun 18 1864 near the Latimer House. There was a hinging of the Confederate line there which created an exposed segment that was being defended by Samuel G. French's division, and fronted with his Francis M. Cockrell's Missouri brigade on the left, Mathew D. Ector's brigade in the center and Claudius W. Sears' Mississippi brigade on the right. On that day, three Federal divisions converged on French's position by moving in on the left. To French's left were Walker's division of Hardee's corps that were being driven at by the Federal's Thomas J. Wood's division who was swinging to the left to try and

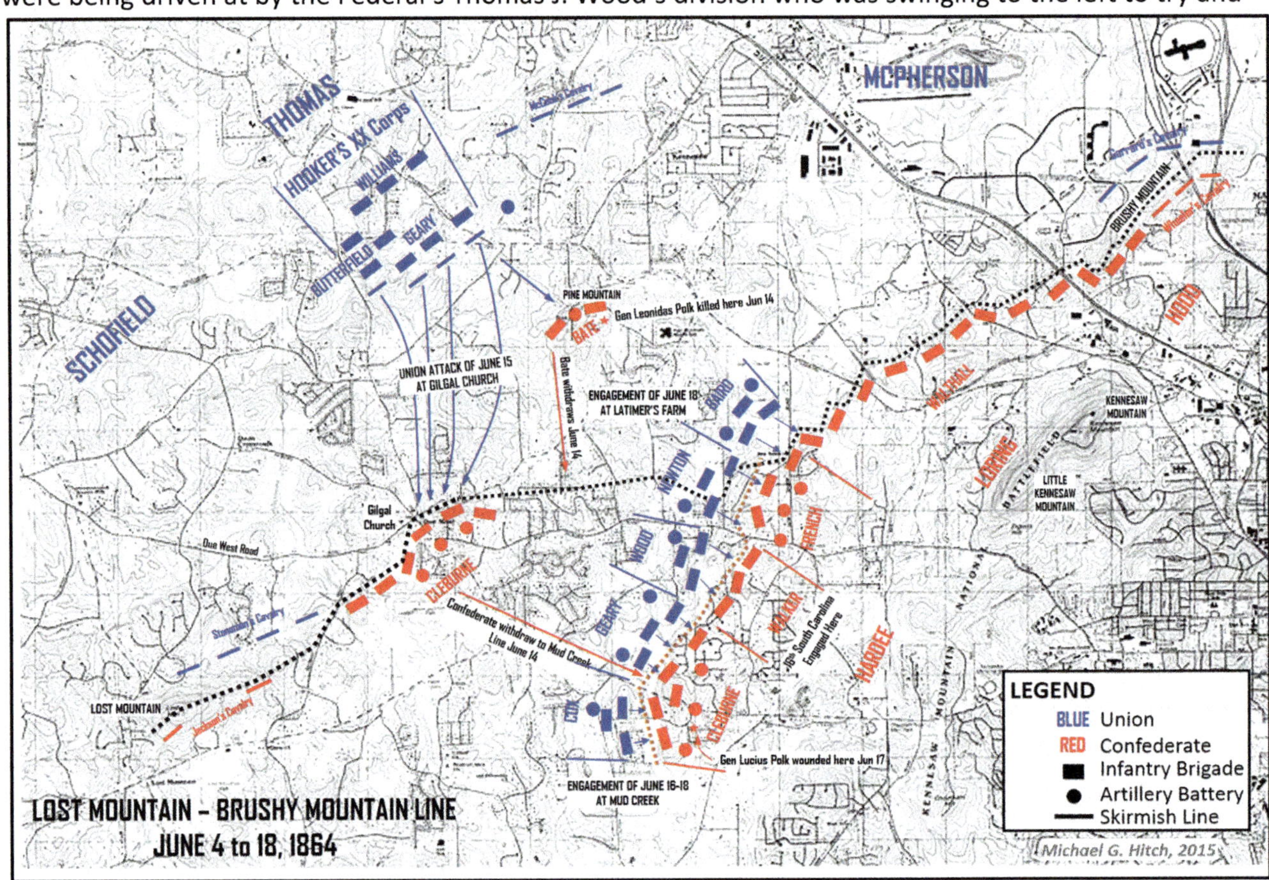

Figure 33 - The Lost Mountain and Brushy Mountain Lines of defense set up by the Army of Tennessee in the time from June 4-18, 1864. Our Young Hitch was entrenched for most of this period with Walker's division on the Brushy Mountain Line between Cleburne and French's divisions where they engaged the enemy on June 18th during the Latimer's Farm affair. (Michael G. Hitch map, 2015))

get behind Cockrell's skirmish lines and gain possession of the Latimer House and force Ector's pickets back into the main Confederate line. General French described the action from the Confederate view:

> *"The way being clear, the enemy soon advanced in line of battle, and with many guns enfladed my line all day. The constant firing never ceased, but I could not induce them to come out and*

make an assault on my front and infantry, and ere night came, my loss was 215 men. Captain Guibor's Battery lost more men today (13) than it did during the entire siege of Vicksburg."[252]

So, more action for the 16th South Carolina who, just two months earlier, had complained of not seeing much excitement of engaging the enemy up until that time. Realizing the vulnerability of the Army of Tennessee's situation due to the hinged line at Brushy Mountain, Johnston withdrew about two miles on Jun 18 1864 to the vicinity of Kennesaw Mountain forming a more formidable line there which would prove fateful for Hitch. **Figure 35** shows the line as it formed in the vicinity of Kennesaw in the days from June 18-22 but, more importantly the spot where Young H.E. Hitch was killed while skirmishing on picket duty on Jun 19 1864 at about 10:00 in the morning.

He was killed by a minie ball that was likely fired by a member of the Union Army's XIV or XV corps who were conducting their own skirmish duty on the enemy's side. The nearest we can get to try and ascertain who killed Hitch comes from the battle maps of the time where we see Col. William Stoughton's 2nd brigade of the Federal XIV Army Corps just opposite of where Gist's brigade was positioned. So, it was likely one of the men in the 11th Michigan or the 15th, 16th, 18th or 19th U.S. regiments of the 2nd brigade who fired the fateful shot that killed Young Hitch.

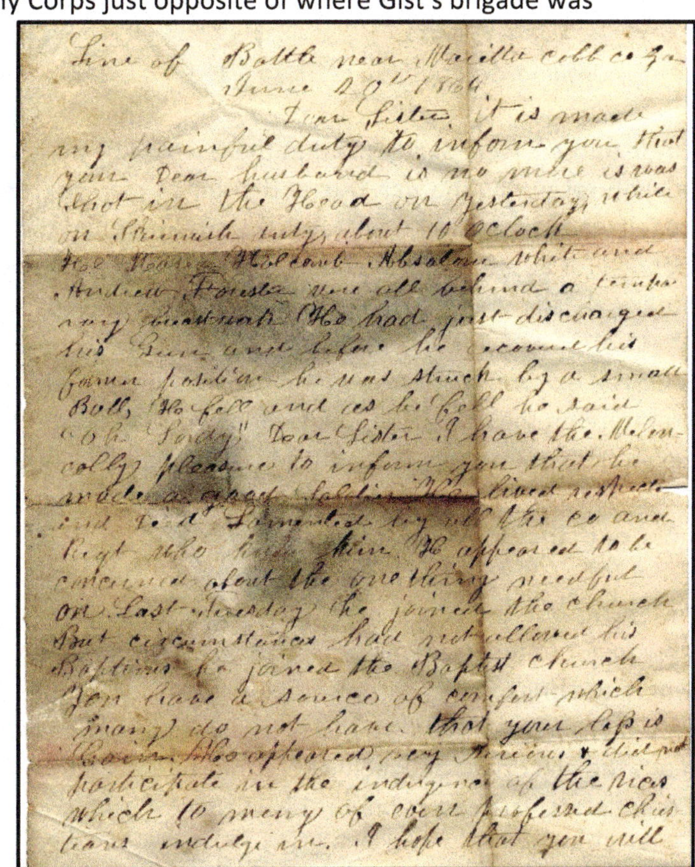
Line of Battle near Marietta Cobb co Ga
June 20th 1864
Dear Sister, it is made
my painful duty to inform you that
your Dear husband is no more is was
shot in the Head on yesterday while
on Skirmish duty, about 10 oclock
He Hosey Holcomb Absalom White and
Andrew Forester were all behind a temporary breastwork He had just discharged
his Gun and before he recovered his
former position he was struck by a small
Ball, He fell and as he fell he said
"Oh Lordy" Dear Sister I have the Melan-
colly pleasure to inform you that he
made a good Soldier He lived respected and died Lamented by all the co and
Regt who knew him He appeared to be
concerned about the one thing needful
on Last Tuesday he joined the church
But circumstances have not allowed his
Baptism he joined the Baptist church
You have a source of comfort which
many do not have. that your loss is
Gain He appeared very Serious & did not
participate in the indulgence of the vices
which so many of our professed Christians indulge in. I hope that you will

Figure 34 - Page 1 of the original letter from William Scruggs to Mary Hitch informing her of the death of her husband, Y.H.E. Hitch (1825-1864). (Mowbray Collection, Edward H. Nabb Center, Salisbury University)

Our beloved Hitch, devoted husband and father, dear friend of many, and memorable family member had breathed his last. His dear friend and brother-in-law, William Berry Scruggs writes news of the occasion on Jun 20 1864 in the following letter to Mary that is included here in its completeness[253]:

Line of Battle near Marietta, Cobb County, Georgia. June 20th 1864

Dear Sister,

It is made my painful duty to inform you that your dear husband is no more is was shot in the head on yesterday while on skirmish duty, about 10 oclock. He, Hosey Holcomb, Absalom White and Andrew Forester were all behind a temporary breastwork. He had just discharged

[252] The Campaign for Atlanta, William R. Scaife, McNaughton & Gunn, 1993, pages 63-64.

[253] Appendix, Item CII.

*his gun and before he recovered his former position, he was struck by a small ball. He fell and, as he fell, he said "**Oh Lordy**." Dear Sister, I have the melancholy pleasure to inform you that he made a good soldier. He lived respected and died lamented by all the co and regt who knew him. He appeared to be conscious about the one thing needful. On last Tuesday, he joined the church but circumstances had not allowed his baptism. He joined the Baptist church. You have a source of comfort which many do not have, that your hope is gain. He appeared very serious and did not participate in the indulgence of the vices which too many of even professed Christians indulge in. I hope that you will feed upon the promises of Him who has said "I will be a father to the fatherless and husband to the widow". Your husband has died in the discharge of duty to his country and I hope to his God. I hope that you will have grace sufficiently given you to bear up under this great affliction. We are now in line of battle but I do not see any more prospect of a battle now than there has been for some time past. Our skirmish duty is very heavy now. Toliver Vaughan was wounded this morning but I hope not mortally. He was struck by a small ball near our camp and line. He was not on the skirmish line. Your brother Edward is well and doing well. I remain yours in brotherly bonds until death.*

William Scruggs

These authors were saddened that there would be no more letters to read from Young Hitch and his adventures during the war. But, at the same time, we were also comforted that Young fought for a cause he felt was just and right. In May 2015, one of us had the serendipitous opportunity to be in Atlanta, Georgia for business and spent an afternoon exploring the Kennesaw Mountain National Battlefield Park.

It was an extremely interesting trip that first led to the Visitors Center which yielded a lot of good literature on the Atlanta Campaign and verified that the 16th South Carolina regiment was part of General Joe Johnston's Army of Tennessee, Hardee's Army Corps, Walker's Division and Gist's Brigade. Once Gist's Brigade was located on a map of the battlefield, help was inquired of a Park Ranger there on how, or if, that spot was accessible.

As it turns out, the spot is part of the National Park and the Park Ranger provided detailed directions on how to get to the location via hiking trails. After some hiking through a pleasant wooded area, the spot where the brigade had entrenched was easily located. It was just to the north of Noses (Noyes) Creek near a place called Hardage Mill and accessible via the Noses Creek and Hardage Mill trail. The latter leads the hiker right between where the Federal and Confederate lines were placed and along the Confederate earthworks on Jun 18-27 1864!

The earthworks of rocks and dirt are still easily seen, even 151 years later, but of course the timber breastworks are long ago lost to time. This was the place, within a few hundred feet, where Young Hitch peeked up out of a trench, fired and lay back to reload and was hit in the head with a minie ball and died as he uttered the words, "Oh Lordy!" that became the inspiration for the title of this book. It was quite surreal finding that spot, now a bucolic and peaceful walk among the trees but, in June 1864, the center of much tension, strife and death.

Anyone can visit the location where Young Hitch spent his last day and is probably still interred within the peaceful earth and among the flora and fauna of that location. **Figure 36** shows the trail map for the central portion of the Kennesaw Mountain National Battlefield Park. On it is added the approximate location of Gist's brigade from Jun 18-27, 1864. The star marks the spot where Young Hitch was killed on the morning of June 19. There is a visitor parking lot denoted on the top, center of the map at the intersection where Old Mountain Road meets Burnt Hickory Road. Noses Creek trail is easily accessible from there and leads directly to Hardage Mill trail.

KENNESAW AFTER THE DEATH OF YOUNG HITCH

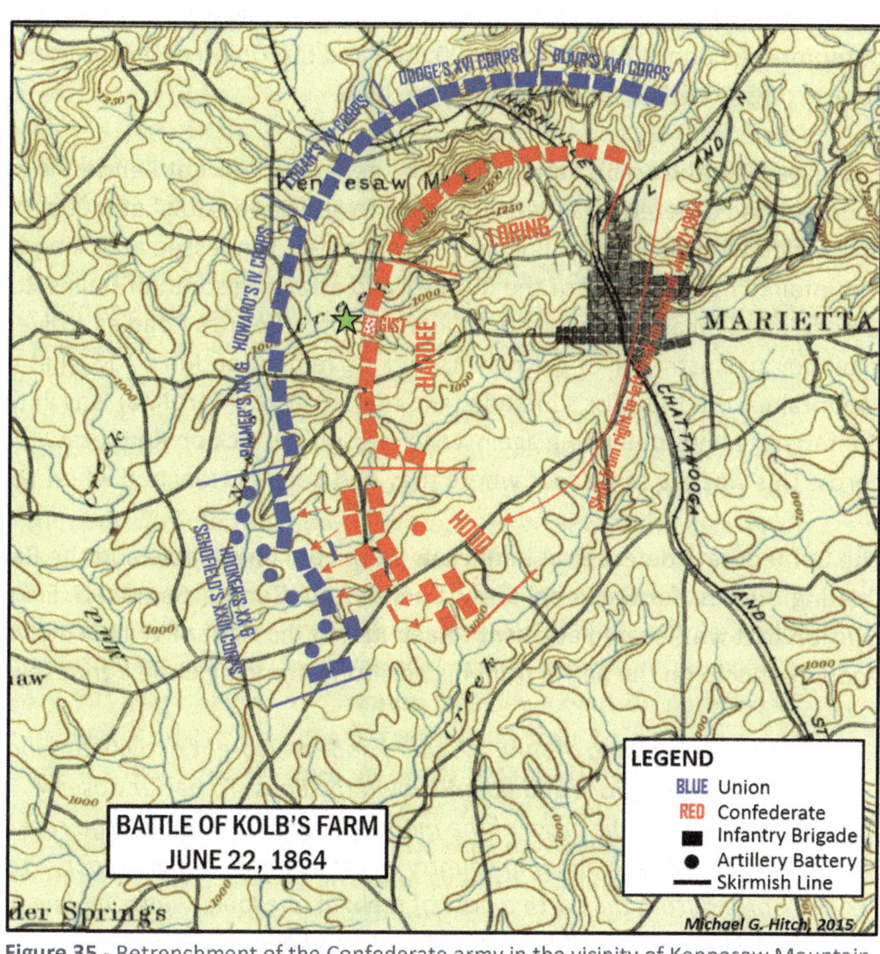

Figure 35 - Retrenchment of the Confederate army in the vicinity of Kennesaw Mountain after June 18th and the action of the Battle of Kolb's Farm on June 22nd. The location of Gist's brigade is shown at a position near Hardage's sawmill. As depicted, this is very near the exact spot where Young Hitch was killed while on picket duty on Jun 19 1864 (denoted by the green star). (Michael G. Hitch, 2015)

In the immediate days following Young Hitch's death, his wife was not even yet aware, given the slow post in those days. It was probably not until about July 1 when she received the letter from Scruggs about Young's fate. By then, a great battle had been fought in the area of Kennesaw Mountain from Jun 22-27 1864 and the Army of Tennessee had retired back to Smyrna, Georgia. Hitch was the first of Company I to die in action during the war. But he was not the last. In fact, the very day after Young was killed, Toliver R. Vaughn of Company I was killed on June 20 as was 16th SCV regimental officer, Major Charles C. O'Neill[254]. Hosea K. Holcomb[255] followed on June 28. For the rest of 1864, the 16th regiment would see much direct action and lose many of its ranks to killed, wounded and disease.

---

[254] South Carolina's Military Organizations During the War Between the States; Volume III, The Upstate, Robert S. Seigler, The History Press, Charleston, SC, 2008; page 169.

[255] Hosea K. Holcombe (1843/44-1864) was son of James and Lucretia (House) Holcombe.

Also near Kennesaw Mountain, Company I member, Private George W.T. Robertson[256], was captured by the enemy on the same day Hitch was killed. Robertson was first sent to Louisville, KY and processed as a POW and then on to Camp Morton, IN on June 27. He was transferred for exchange on Feb 26 1865. Additionally, Private J.S. Thackston was wounded in action on Jun 28 1864[202].

The actual Kennesaw Mountain Battle was really a series of events over several days that opened on June 22 with the Battle of Kolb's Farm (see **Figure 37**). The action at Kolb's farm only involved the left flank of the Army of Tennessee under Hood's corps in which Carter L. Stevenson's division attacked the enemy at 5:30 pm on June 22. History notes that this was an ill-advised attack as Hood was outnumbered about 14,000 to 11,000 men and the Union defenses there under Joseph Hooker were very strong. Confederate casualties were high.

Five days after the Kolb's Farm battle, the general conflict at Kennesaw Mountain broke out, as General Sherman had ordered on June 25 to begin "a general assault" at 8:00 am on June 27. The assault proceeded with General McPherson's Army of the Tennessee attacking the southern slopes of Kennesaw Mountain, Thomas' Army of the Cumberland attacking south of Dallas Road and Schofield's Army of the Ohio feinting an attack to the south along Powder Springs Road as a diversionary move. See **Figure 37** again for an illustration of the players and movement on Jun 27 1864 at the Battle of Kennesaw Mountain. Note that Gist's brigade (and the 16th South Carolina) was in the action at the far left of the Confederate lines defending against McPherson's attack on Kennesaw Mountain opposite Logan's XV corps. This was the same spot where they had been entrenched when Young Hitch was killed on June 19.

The Confederate defenses at Kennesaw were very formidable and the Battle is considered a huge, but fleeting, success for the Rebel army. Confederate General Samuel G. French commanded French's division that was located adjacent to and just to the right of Walker's division in the battle. He writes a good discourse on the battle from his position defending Little Kennesaw and Pigeon Hill:

> *"On the morning of June 27, there appeared great activity among the staff officers of the enemy all along my front and up and down the lines. To better observe, my staff and I stationed ourselves on the brow of the mountain, sheltered by a large rock where we had a commanding view of the surrounding country as far as the eye could reach. Presently as if by magic, there sprung from the earth a host of men. In one long, wavering line of blue the infantry advanced and the Battle of Kennesaw Mountain began.*
>
> *We sat there perhaps an hour, enjoying a birds-eye view of one of the most magnificent sights ever allotted to man, to look down upon a hundred and fifty thousand men arrayed in the strife of battle below. 'Twere worth ten years of peaceful life, one glance at their array! As the infantry closed in, the blue smoke of the musket marked out the line of battle. Through the rifts of smoke,*

---

[256] Little is known of George W.T. Robertson. He is probably the brother to Company I colleague, Private Berry William Robertson (1818-1908), who was son of John and Elizabeth (Holland) Robertson of Greenville County. Berry married Sarah Butler (1823-1898) and they are both buried in the Ebenezer Baptist Church Cemetery, Travelers Rest, SC. Berry W. and Sarah Robertson were the parents of Company I Private John Thomas Robertson (1844-1920). John T. and his wife, Susan (Griffith) Robertson (1842-1906), are buried in the Reedy River Baptist Church Cemetery, Greenville, SC.

we could see the assault on Cheatham (Hill). There the struggle was hard and there it lasted longest. At 9:00 o'clock a courier informed me that General Cockrell's position was being attacked in force and General Ector was directed to send two regiments to Cockrell's aid. The assaulting column struck Cockrell's works near the center, recoiled under the fire, swung around into a steep valley, where exposed to fire from the Missourians in the front and od Sears' Mississippians on their left, it seemed to melt away, or sink to the earth, to rise no more."[257]

The fighting was indeed intense and, even though our beloved Young Hitch had been killed and could not write about it, we can view firsthand what it was like for Company I and the 16th regiment from Samuel McKittrick's letters in the Kennesaw Mountain National Battlefield Files. He had rejoined Company I in February 1864 and was well enmeshed in its ranks by the time the Battle of Kennesaw raged. He writes about the fight in two letters, directly from within the breastworks, one from June 27 and the other June 28. They are included here in their entirety:

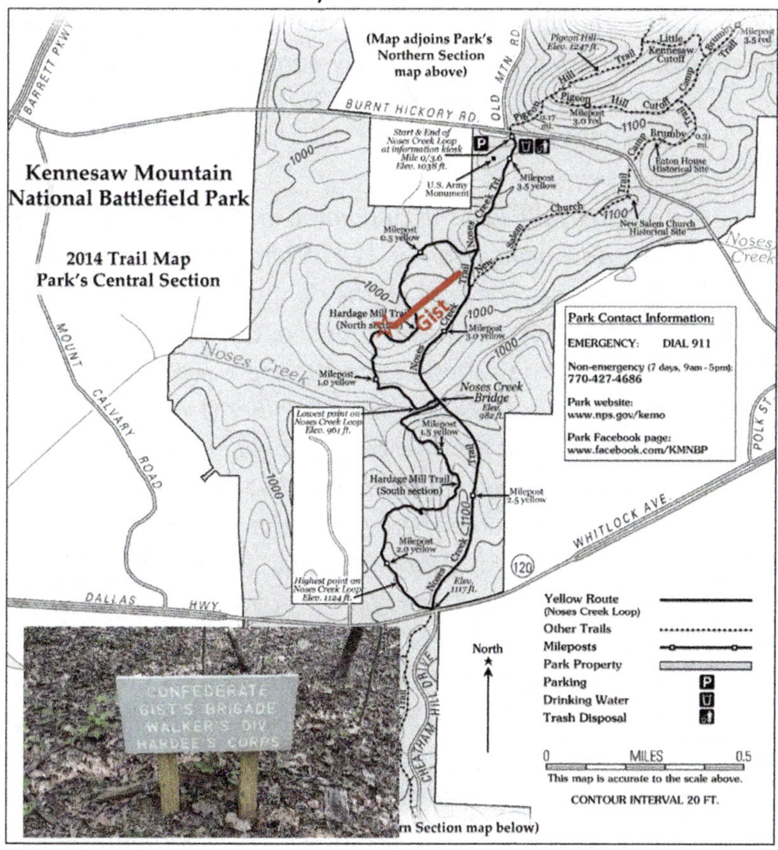

Figure 36 - National Park map showing the trail network and contours of the central portion of Kennesaw Mountain National Battlefield Park (KMNBP). On it is depicted the location of Gist's brigade on the day Young Hitch was killed, June 19, 1864 and the signage on the Hardage Mill trail as it stood in May 2015. (Map of central section of KMNBP used with permission of cartographer Larry Knight)

"Line of Battle near Marietta, GA
June 27, 1864

Dear Wife,
I am by the great Mercy of God well this morning. I write to you under very unpleasant circumstances. We are now and have been lying behind our Breastworks, and the Enemy are about 900 yards in front of us behind their fortifications, their skirmishers occasionally killing one of our men and wounding several others. It is dangerous to step out from our works. Their sharpshooters are ready to pick us out. This is the only fighting we have had here, yet we are hourly expecting an attack. But they do not appear to come on us. Both parties bomb each other but to no great damage. They are both actively engaged this morning in Bombing. My dear, you will scarcely believe how indifferent soldiers become to Danger. This is the 9th day that

[257] The Campaign for Atlanta, William R. Scaife, 1993, page 70.

we have been thus, waiting an attack. We have lost several men in killed and wounded. I suppose had had some 15 killed 65 wounded. Tell Mr. Berditt I have not heard from William. He left the line Greenbury. Austin is severely wounded in the Head. Thomas and John Atkins brothers are both killed."

He clearly states that they (the 16th) had not seen any general fighting in the battles around Kennesaw thus far but were seeing it on June 27 in the form of heavy skirmishing and were expecting a general attack at any time. Casualties were mounting with 15 killed and 65 wounded. He mentions "Austin is severely wounded in the head" – this is John T. Austin[258] of Company I. Official records state that he died of wounds received at Kennesaw Mountain in Caldwell Hospital, Griffin, GA on Jul 16 1864. "Thomas and John Atkins brothers" are Thomas A. and John W. Atkinson of Company A of the 16th SCV, they were both killed in the fighting on June 23. William Burditt of Company I, from whom McKittrick had not heard was actually safe. The next day, June 28, he finishes writing to his wife:

"June 28, 1864
Dear Wife,
I am still well. I was disappointed in finishing my letter yesterday. The news came that the Enemy were advancing upon us. We all had to fly to arms for an attack but they did not come. But they attacked our line both on the right and left of our position. We hear that they were repulsed with a loss of 3500 killed and wounded. Our loss is said to be 150 killed and wounded. A great victory. Gen. Cleburne's division had but one killed and eleven wounded. Gen. Mercer suffered more severely. Our Division namely (Walker's) was not engaged. We may be attacked today. If so I trust God in his Providence will shield our Heads and give us the victory. Our troops are so worn down by Fatigue and Hardships that many of us care but little how soon they come as we have them to fight somewhere and perhaps as well here as any where else. My dear wife, I feel anxious about my dear infant. But I know that an all wise God will do all things right. I also know that your very soul years for its recovery and are doing all you can for its relief. The Lord's will be done. If Providence call her away she will make an additional spirit to our department family formed in Heaven; clear from all the turmoils and troubles of Earth. Oh, if I could be allowed to visit you and spend a few days with my most interesting family. But this Privilege is denied me and I am trying to get along as well as I can by only enjoying sweet Meditation of you. Let us live so that if we never meet on Earth we may make a happy reunion in Heaven. My dear try to train our Dear children for Heaven as there is nothing worth living for on Earth. I truly sympathize with you in all troubles and care and can only bear you to a Throne of Grace. Your loving husband until death, Samuel McKittrick"

Private McKittrick described the scene well at Kennesaw and, later that day of June 28, he would be elected Lieutenant in Company I. Also, on the 28th, Company I lost another member killed - Hosey

[258] There are three Austin men in Company I; Privates John T. and William A. Austin and 2LT Thomas J. Austin. Little is known about the identity of John T. Austin. Private William Anderson Austin II (1821-1885) is son of William Anderson I and Jane (Nelson) Austin of Greenville County, SC. He was discharged on Mar 27 1863 from his one year service hitch at age 42. LT Thomas J. Austin is probably Thomas Jeremiah Austin, son of Captain William Lawrence Manning Austin of Co. F, Hampton Legion. LT Austin was gravely sick with typhoid fever and the records are indeterminate to his fate but, it appears he may have died of it in the summer of 1864.

Holcomb, one of the men who was with Young Hitch behind the breastworks when Hitch was killed, had now met the same fate nine days later. The earlier lamenting that Young Hitch stated in his letters about the troops of his "mess" grousing about not seeing action had come full circle over the previous months, and it had climaxed into very hot activity at Kennesaw. It would not be over by a long shot, either, for the Atlanta campaign itself was crescendoing and coming to a rapid conclusion in the summer of 1864.

At Kennesaw, three and a half hours after the Union attack began, by 11:30 that morning, they knew it had failed. The uncustomary frontal assault cost Sherman 3,000 men in that short period of time. The Federal survivors of the assaulting columns at Cheatham Hill spent the next five days in advanced works only thirty yards from the Confederate position,

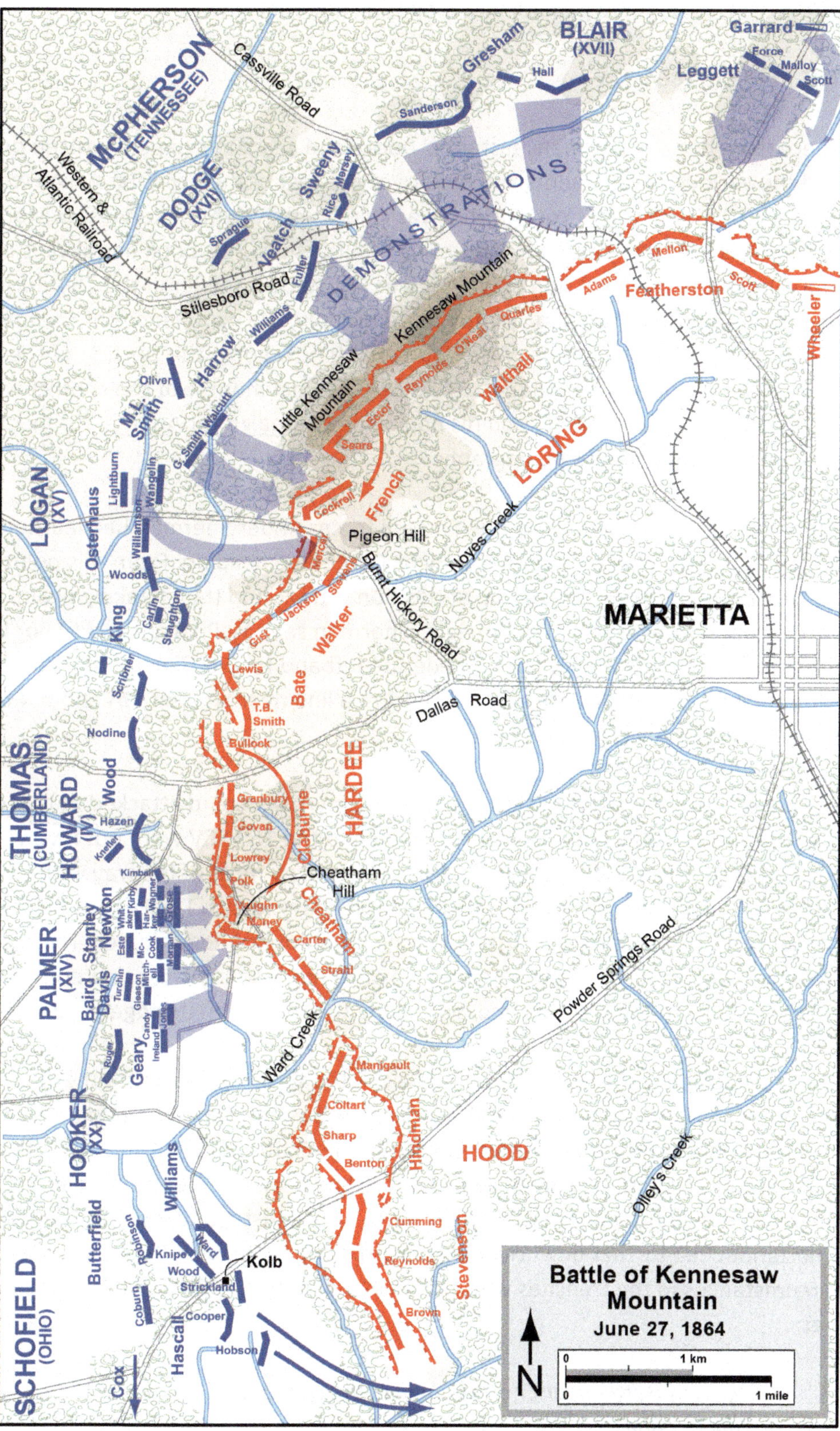

Figure 37 - The Battle of Kennesaw Mountain, June 27, 1864. Note the location of Gist's brigade along the right flank of Hardee's corps to the left side of Walker's division. Young Hitch was probably buried along there among the action that included the remainder of his 16th South Carolina regiment. (Map by Hal Jespersen, *www.cwmaps.com*)

but there was no more general battle fighting at Kennesaw.

THE REST OF 1864

There have been many, many historical books and academic papers written on the Atlanta campaign and the various engagements and politics of the rest of the Civil War which would officially last for another 10 months after Young Hitch was killed within sight of Kennesaw Mountain, GA. The purpose of this book is not to recreate an accounting of all of that. This book has always been to develop a factual storyline of the personal side of what it was like to be a soldier in the CSA during the war through the eyes of Young H.E. Hitch and, slightly more broadly, the experiences of Company I and the 16th South Carolina regiment volunteers. With Young Hitch now gone, this portion of the book briefly covers events later in the war that affected the 16th SCV as the final months of the conflict wore down. We are indebted to William R. Scaife and his book, The Campaign for Atlanta, for much of the background presented in the following paragraphs.

After the fighting at Kennesaw, the Federal forces under Sherman had learned a hard lesson about trying to attack Johnston's Confederate Army of Tennessee head on. From this point forward, he returned to his practice of flanking, letting the opposition retreat and then flanking again, until such time that there was a clear strategic advantage to fight. Sherman sent McPherson and Major General George Stoneman's cavalry around the Confederate left and forced General Johnston to leave the Kennesaw Mountain line and pull his army back to form a line near Smyrna, GA about 4 miles north and west of the Chattahoochee River on Jul 2 1864.

By July 4, the Federal forces closed in on the Smyrna line and attacked at two points, at the town of Smyrna and at Ruff's Mill. Walker's division and the 16th SCV were not involved in these actions directly. Instead Cleburne's and Stevenson's divisions entered most of the fray with the former repulsing the North's William Grose's brigade but sustained heavy losses. The Federal's Fuller's brigade drove Stevenson's troops back but sustained their own dose of heavy losses. The result of the attacks, however, exposed the Army of Tennessee once more so Johnston retired to form the Chattahoochee line on July 5, on the NW side and right along the river from its edge at spots to a half mile in from it.

On approaching the river, Sherman had expected to see a fleeing southern army trying to get across the water before it would encounter the federal troops. Instead, he found a very formidable defense set up by Johnston and his proud Confederates. On the Chattahoochee line, Walker's division with the 16th SCVs occupied almost the dead center of the line between Cleburne's and Brown's divisions. But Sherman would not engage the Rebels here, opting instead to look for fords and passages over the Chattahoochee further downriver to Johnston's right. LT McKittrick writes a brief few words of the circumstances in the trenches with Company I of the 16th SCV and the "Yanks" not willing to engage just yet:

> *"Line of Battle near Chattahoochee River, Georgia*
> *July 8, 1864*

Having a few moments leisure I send you a few lines which by the great Mercy of God leave me in good health. We still here where we were when I last wrote to you. The Yanks have been unusually slow to pursue us the last move we made..."

By July 9, Johnston again retired his army backward towards Atlanta, after burning the rail and wagon bridges and dismantling the pontoon bridge he had built there. His line formed what was called the Outer line, just south of Peachtree Creek and only 1½ miles from the main fortifications of Atlanta itself. No general action occurred for more than ten days as the federals forded the Chattahoochee and set up a plan to continue driving at the Confederate army. The river crossing was completed on July 17 and the federal forces began to move south toward Peachtree Creek. In the official records, we find Colonel Ellison Capers, commander of the 24th SCVs, sister unit to the 16th in Gist's brigade, writing of this time period:

"On the 17th of July the commanding general published an address to the army, and announced that he would attack General Sherman's army as soon as it should cross the Chattahoochee. I had the honor to read the commanding general's prospect of a successful battle. The order of battle was received with enthusiasm, and the most confident spirit prevailed."

However confident the Confederates were, something very profound happened in the CSA Administration in Richmond that altered, if not its final outcome, most assuredly the immediate course, of the war. At 10:00 p.m. on Jul 17 1864, General Johnston received a dispatch from the CSA Secretary of War stating that he had "failed to arrest the advance of the enemy to the vicinity of Atlanta" and that there was "no confidence" that he could further defeat or repel them. Therefore, Johnston was "relieved from the command of the Army and Department of Tennessee" and he was to immediately turn over command to General Hood.

Hood, hearing of this astounding news, suggested to Jefferson Davis that his appointment be rescinded citing that it was a terrible time to be changing leadership. But Davis replied that the order had already been executed and would not be suspended and it was officially enacted on Jul 18 1864. The change of command hit the Army of Tennessee like a proverbial ton of bricks. The confidence that had been slowly building in anticipation of an attack on Sherman's army had had the air let out of it. We wish we had the opportunity to hear what Young Hitch would have said about this event but, lacking that, we can again turn to Colonel Capers of the 24th SCVs of Gist's brigade:

"A courier handed me a circular order from General Hood, announcing General Johnston's removal...It is due to truth to say that the reception of these orders produced the most despondent feelings in my command. The loss of the commanding general was felt to be irreparable...Passing by his headquarters, Walker's Division passed at the shoulder, the officers saluting and most of the latter and hundreds of the men taking off their hats."

The 16th South Carolina regiment, as part of Walkers division, would join in that salute to Johnston. It would also join in the despondency Capers describes amongst his command. But, where the Army of Tennessee was mourning the loss of their supreme commander, Sherman delighted in the change of course saying, "At this critical moment the Confederate Government rendered us most valuable service."

Johnston had planned to attack the federals as they were divided crossing Peachtree Creek. He planned to use a counterclockwise "wheeling" movement in hopes of pinning a large portion of the army into the angle formed between Peachtree Creek and the Chattahoochee River. In doing so, he would strike through relatively open terrain near the mouth of Clear Creek and hoped to inflict serious harm and/or capture a large part of the army. If his attack would fail, Johnston, always prepared, would have his army in a position to safely defend approaches to Atlanta from the enemy and he could retire back to the city's fortifications and fight again from there.

With the change of command, Hood's plan for Peachtree Creek was much different. He looked to force an attack further west from the original plan, in heavily wooded terrain that held deep cut ravines. This topography was wholly unsuited for such a large scale offensive upon which the Army of Tennessee was about to embark. In technical military terms, his move was planned to be a classic "en echelon" in a clockwise direction, completely opposite from Johnston's planned counterclockwise movement. Should this attack fail, Hood's army on the right would not extend far enough to effectively defend the easterly approaches into Atlanta.

Hood orders the attack to begin at 1:00 p.m. on Jul 20 1864. In the final hours before the attack, Hood realized his exposure to the right (Cheatham's corps) which required Hardee and Stewart's corps to lengthen their coverage by thinning and extending their lines so that Cheatham could extend further to the right. This left a very large gap between Hardee and Cheatham and placed the Rebels in unfamiliar terrain and delayed the attack by three hours. By this time, all the Federal troops had crossed Peachtree Creek, thus taking away any advantage of division of their forces that had originally offered. Hood was definitely no Johnston when it came to skill of strategy and cunning on the battlefield.

When the attack began, around 4:00 p.m., Bate's division began but got slowed by the heavy undergrowth in the terrain of the area eliminating any advantage of immediate momentum and surprise. The Federals, in the form of Bradley's 3rd brigade, were able to return heavy fire and stop Bate in his tracks. Then Walker's division, with Gist's (and the 16th SCV), Stevens' and Mercer's brigades, was unable to effectively carry out the "en echelon" movement due to the bulge formed when Bate was repelled. The attack disintegrated from there into a poor frontal assault that was badly fragmented with practically zero success achieved along the entire two mile front of the Confederates. General Clement Stevens, commander of Stevens' brigade, was killed in the assault.

As the Battle of Peachtree Creek was raging, McPherson had advanced his Army of the Tennessee toward Decatur, Georgia six miles to the east with its sights on Atlanta. By 1:00 p.m., the army was within 2½ miles and within range of his 20-pounder guns and they fired the first rounds into Atlanta. The Battle of Atlanta had begun.

Hood decided to try a very bold action and have the Confederate forces conduct a flanking movement against the rear of McPherson's army as it was leaving Decatur for Atlanta. To do so would take near super-human strength from a portion of his army – he would have Hardee's corps do a forced 15-mile march overnight on July 21 and attack. Hoods old corps, then positioned in the area and commanded by Cheatham, would move from its trenches and attack McPherson in its front. This would attempt to pinch McPherson's army on to itself where it would be soundly defeated and many of its men captured.

Hardee's corps with Walker's division, Gist's brigade and the 16th South Carolina began their rapid march at dusk on Jul 21 1864, picked up Cleburne's division when it passed through Atlanta[259], and, as Young Hitch would have stated, "tramped" all night for 12 hours. This was the only way to get them into position for the battle that was to occur on the east side of Atlanta. Scaife proclaims, in his The Campaign For Atlanta, *"Hardee's march continued through he night and his weary troops trudged along the dusty roads, many with empty canteens."* As part of this effort, the 16th South Carolina regiment was being tested to their very core of capability!

General Hood had severely underestimated the time it would take for Hardee to march into position. While he had expected them to attack the flank of the federals by daybreak, it was just after noon before the attack was able to begin with Walker's and Bate's division. The 16th SCV was not involved in a regular and direct engagement as they were part of the force attacking the Union's Thomas W. Sweeney's 2nd division of Dodge's XVI corps.

See **Figure 38** for a layout of the Battle of Atlanta on Jul 22 1864. Walker's division, with the 16th South Carolina, was to the left of Bate's division and attacking the flank of the federal force to try and get in behind their lines and defeat them. Just as the attack began about 12:15 p.m., General Walker, commander of the division that included the 16th South Carolina regiment, was shot and instantly killed by a Federal sharpshooter. General Hugh Mercer assumed his command.

To describe the fighting as fierce is a clear understatement. Major William H. Chamberlain of the 81st Ohio regiment, USA observed the attack coming from the Confederates:

> *"Nor can I restrain a tribute to the bravery of the enemy...they came tearing wildly...with the yells of demons, We had an advantage in artillery; they in numbers. Their assaults were repulsed, only to be fearlessly renewed, until the sight of dead and wounded lying in their way, as they charged again and again to break our lines, must have appalled the stoutest hearts. So persistent were their onslaughts that numbers were made prisoners by rushing directly into our lines."*

By nightfall, the battle was over and the Confederates had retired from the field with the federal line restored to what it was previously. Southern forces had suffered twice the casualties of the Union in almost breaking the Federal stronghold. Dodge's XVI corps had saved the day for the north in repelling Hardee's corps and its incessant and gallant attack. Again, we hear from Major Chamberlain:

> *"Had Dodge's men not been where they were, there would have been absolutely nothing but the hospital tents and wagon trains to stop Hardee's command from falling unheralded directly upon the rear of the XV and XVII Corps in line. Upon what slight chance, then, hung the fate of Sherman's army that day."*

---

[259] Cleburne had pulled back to Atlanta after fighting all day at Bald Hill near Decatur.

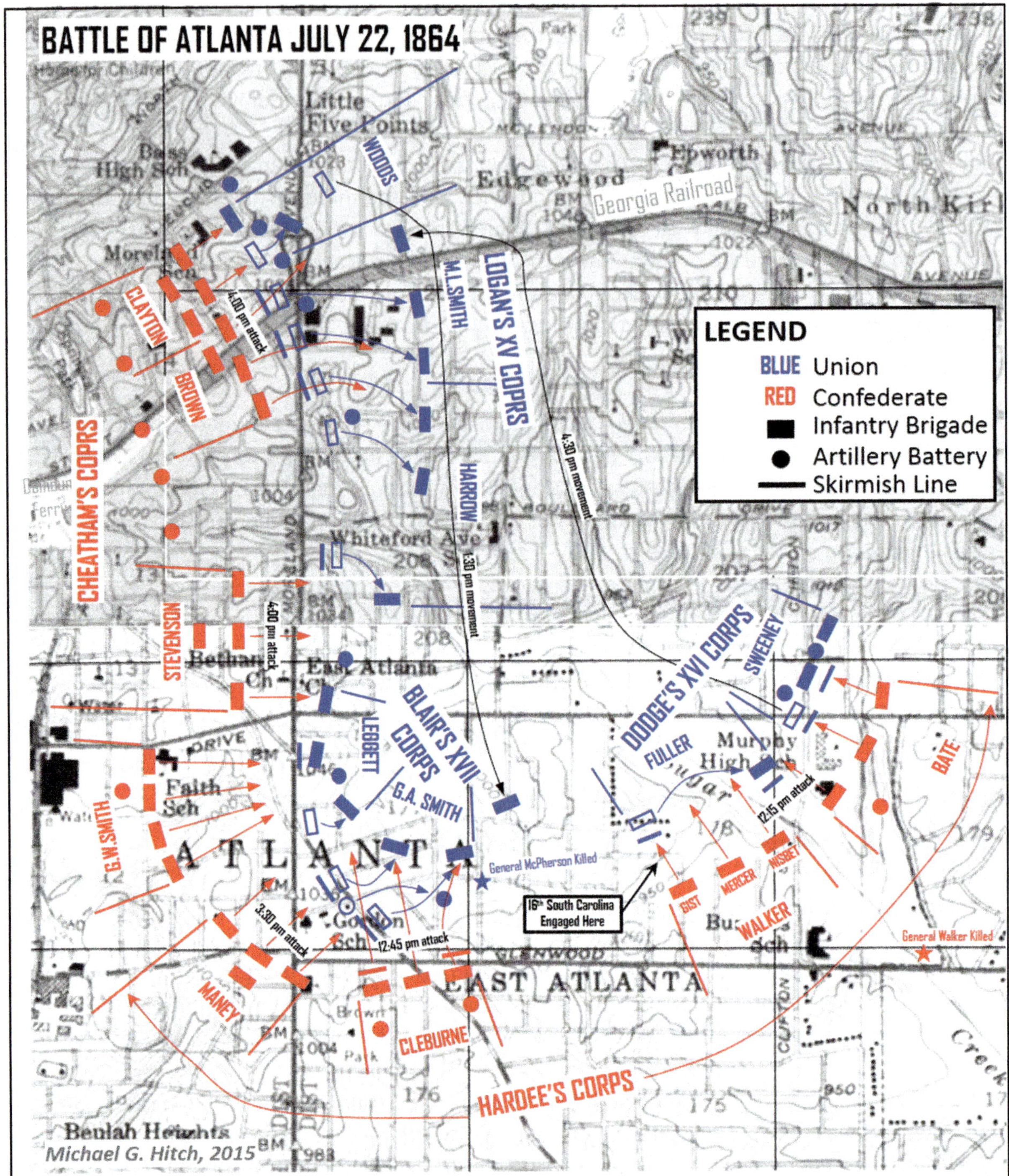

Figure 38 - Battle of Atlanta on Jul 22 1864, the bloodiest day of the war for Company I of the 16th South Carolina. This battle was a last gasp attempt by the Confederates to save Atlanta. While they had some initial success early in the battle, ultimately, the Union army prevailed in capturing the city 6 weeks later. (Michael G. Hitch map, 2015)

The Federals had taken relatively much fewer losses than the Confederates; however, they did not come away unscathed as General McPherson was killed on the field at just after 2:00 p.m. on July 22. The southern army definitely took the highest toll, however, and suffered many killed and wounded. We see evidence of this in the ranks of Young Hitch's own Company I, 16th South Carolina regiment:

Private W.S. Gary[260]	Killed
Private John Graden[122]	Wounded
Private J.W. Jones	Killed
Private S. Linder[261]	Killed
Lieutenant Samuel McKittrick[250]	Died July 23rd of wounds received
Private J.S. Peden[262]	Died July 28th of wounds received
Private John H. Simmons[147]	Wounded
Private W. Henry Stewart[208]	Wounded

Five members killed and three wounded. Company I, with the rest of the 16th South Carolina, had experienced what was, and will be, the bloodiest day of the war for them. In the list, we see LT McKittrick who left us with the letters covered earlier chronicling the original formation of Company I and the 16th South Carolina Regiment Volunteers and, then later, after rejoining Company I in Dalton, GA, letters of the battles fought at Kennesaw. He now lay dead like many of his colleagues in war. Similar to what William Scruggs had done for Young Hitch, Sgt. J.J. McKinney writes to McKittrick's wife to inform her of her husband's passing:

> *July 25, 1864*
> *Dear Friend*
> *I hasten to drop you a few lines which bears the sad intelligence of the death of your husband. He was wounded in the evening of the 22nd in the fight below Atlanta and died next morning in the charge. A brigade on our right gave way and caused our brigade to have to fall back to keep from being captured and in falling back he with Captain Roberts and some others became separated from the Brigade and fell in with General Goven's brigade and went on into the fight and they made a vow to take care of each other if they were shot down and Capt. Roberts being in the front rank did not know when he was hit but a man by the name of Tinsley of our Regiment saw him fall and went to him and took him back a piece but gave out and could not get him any further and got a friend to stay with him until he could come and find our regiment. So about midnight he came and told me where and how he was and as I was in charge of the Company and we were expecting the enemy to advance the Colonel would not let me go myself, but I sent 3 men of the Infirmary Corps to go with Tinsley after him and they brought him by where I was*

[260] Little is known of Private W.S. Gary.

[261] Private S. Linder is Simpson B. Linder (1826-1864) of Spartanburg County, SC. Private Linder had just transferred into Company I, 16th SCVI from Company I, 3rd South Carolina (Palmetto) Battalion Light Artillery (PBLA) on Jun 16 1864. Companies H, I and K of the PBLA were disbanded on Apr 1 1864 since they were declared not to have been legally organized. Simpson Linder married Sarah Allen (1827-1901). Private Willis Lee Linder was their son who had transferred under the same circumstances as Simpson Linder from the PBLA into the 16th regiment.

[262] Two Privates and one Corporal Peden had also just transferred into Company I, 16th SCVI from Company I, 3rd South Carolina (Palmetto) Battalion Light Artillery (PBLA) on Jun 16 1864. Private James Scipio Peden (1821-1864) was wounded in the Battle of Atlanta on July 22 and died six days later, he was the son of Robert and Jane Peden. Private Thomas Carlisle Peden (1837-185) was son of John Simpson and Margaret M. Peden of Fountain Inn, SC and the nephew of Private J.S. Peden. Private John McVey Peden (1821-1891) was promoted to corporal on Aug 4 1864. He was the son of Scipio and Martha (McVey) Peden of Fountain Inn and 1st cousin to James Scipio Peden. All three Peden men are buried in the Fountain Inn Municipal Cemetery.

and I talked with him. Sometime, he said, he was going to die and he wanted me to write to you and let you know that he was perfectly willing to die, but he hated to leave his poor helpless family but he wanted you to reconcile it as best you could and prepare to meet him in Heaven. He was shot through the lungs and was carried to the brigade hospital where he died next morning and was buried by some of our Company who was there. So I must close. Write to me and I will give you any information I can.
Yours respectfully,
J.J. McKinney

Figure 39 - Inscription on Sgt. James J. McKinney's grave stone in the Stonewall Confederate Cemetery in Griffin, Georgia.

McKittrick was mortally wounded but able to say his last goodbye to his wife via his friend and fellow soldier of Company I, Sergeant James J. McKinney. Sergeant McKinney himself would die not too many days later, on Aug 8 1864, in a hospital of wounds received while on picket duty near Atlanta. He is buried in Stonewall Confederate Cemetery in Griffin, Spaulding County, GA.

Probably the largest family impacted by the war from Company I's standpoint was the White family. Private Solomon A. White died of sickness Jul 28 1864 in a hospital in Georgia. His brother by blood and his brother by occupation, LT Anthony White of Company I, was killed while on picket duty in Atlanta eleven days later on Aug 7 1864. He had just been elected lieutenant the day before he was killed. Four other White brothers also served in Company I of the 16th South Carolina; Private John J., Corporal Absalom A., Private William H., and Private Young M. White. Young M. White was killed in Franklin, TN on Nov 30 1864[263] and William H. White died in North Carolina on Apr 2 1865. Absalom White was one of the soldiers behind the breastwork with Young Hitch when he was killed on Jun 19 1864 and therefore one of the last men to see him alive. Of the six White brothers serving together, only two survived the war[264].

There were three other sets of brothers in Company I that did their service without a lot of fanfare. Brothers Green Smith Hamby, John T. Hamby and Stephen Rashar Hamby, all of Greenville County, served together in the unit. All the Hambys were Privates and all survived the war to live long lives[265]. One of the Hamby's sisters, Wealthy Hamby, married Private Paul J. Verdin of Company I as well.

---

[263] Private Young M. White's Confederate Military Service records give no indication of his death but we find him in the Confederate Cemetery in Franklin, TN, having been killed in the battle there on Nov 30 1864.

[264] Privates William H. White (1830-1865), John Jones White (1831-1908), Solomon A. White (1833-1864), Young Moses White (1842-1864), Corporal Absalom Abner White (1836-1905) and Lieutenant Anthony White (1834-1864) were brothers serving in Company I, all sons of Solomon King and Elizabeth (Jones) White of Greenville County. Three died while in the service for the CSA.

[265] John T. Hamby (1824-1897), Stephen R. Hamby (1829-1895) and G. Smith Hamby (1845-1907) were sons of Charles Smith Hamby (1796-1880) and Ermon (Green) Hamby (1807-1857) of Greenville County, SC. Sister Wealthy Hamby (1833-1908) married fellow Company I soldier, Private Paul Joseph Verdin (1837-1896). Paul J. Verdin was the son of Company I Private James Allen Verdin (1820-1900). John T. Hamby and his wife Hannah (Forrester) Hamby (1830-1909) are buried in the Stokes-Hamby family cemetery in Mauldin, SC. Stephen R. Hamby and his

We also have Privates Alfred Jay Hawkins and James Harvey Hawkins, brothers from Greenville County who did their service and returned home after the war[266]. Finally, we have Privates Madison Roland Mahaffey, Hoyt J. Mahaffey and James L. Mahaffey, also of Greenville County, who were all within six years of age of each other[267]. Three sets of brothers eager to serve for their cause among the various other brother combinations in Company I. These three sets of brothers described here are typical of the soldiers who were not killed, captured or seriously wounded but who did their duty gallantly and then quietly returned to their families to disappear into the relative obscurity of history after the Civil War.

One other casualty occurred with the ranks of Company I around this time - Private William Martindale Waldrep was wounded on Aug 15 1864 in the action around Atlanta. Private Waldrep was one of the ten men who transferred into Company I from the 3rd (Palmetto) Battalion Light Artillery (PBLA) on Jun 16 1864. He survived his wounds and lived a long life, passing away just beyond his 89th birthday, in South Carolina, in 1931[268]. There was another Waldrep who transferred in to Company I from the PBLA, Private Little Berry Waldrep. Research does not readily indicate any familial relationship between the two[269].

After the bloody Battle of Atlanta near Decatur, GA on Jul 22 1864, the Confederate Army of Tennessee continued to backpedal from the onslaught of the overwhelming number of forces that were coming from the Union army. There was a battle at Ezra Church, GA on July 28 but the 16th regiment was not engaged there, instead remaining in the trenches outside of Atlanta during late July and August 1864. From there, they marched towards Jonesboro, GA on August 30, arriving there on the 31st. The 16th regiment was held in reserve there while its sister unit, the 24th SCVs were engaged that evening. Both regiments saw action there on September 1. The 16th withdrew to Lovejoy on the night of September 2 and remained in that area until Sep 19 1864 when there was a 10-day truce.

---

wife Rachel (Miller) Hamby (1838-1918) are buried in the Miller Cemetery, also in Mauldin. G. Smith Hamby and his wife Mary (Wilson) Hamby (1867-1930) are buried in the Bethel U.M. Church cemetery in Simpsonville, SC.

[266] Alfred Jay (1831-1899) and James Harvey Hawkins (1837-1916) were sons of James Ichabod (1805-1878) and Mahalia (Hawkins) Hawkins (1813-1850) of Greenville County, SC. Alfred J. and his wife Hannah (Griffith) Hawkins (1853-1902) and James H. and his wife Catherine (Griffith) Hawkins (1847-1896) are buried in Enoree Baptist Church cemetery in Travelers Rest, SC.

[267] Madison Roland (1842-1922), Hoyt Jackson (1845-1934) and James L. Mahaffey (1839-1904) were sons of William Madison Mahaffey (c1810-aft 1880) and Matilda (Wood) Mahaffey (c1810-c1850). Madison R. Mahaffey is buried in Zoar U.M. Church cemetery in Greer, SC and James L. Mahaffey is buried in the Rocky Creek Baptist Church cemetery in Greenville. It is unknown to these authors where Private Hoyt Mahaffey rests.

[268] Private William Martindale Waldrep (1842-1931) was son of James and Catherine (Deshields) Waldrep of Spartanburg County, SC. Private Waldrep is buried with his wife Louesa (Watson) Waldrep (1850-1911) in the Trinity United Methodist Church Cemetery, Cross Anchor, SC. The spelling of the surname comes from his gravestone, his service records show the spelling as "Waldrip."

[269] Private Little Berry Waldrep (1844-1923) was son of Caswell and Rachel (Bagwell) Waldrep, also of Spartanburg County. It is probable that Private L.B. Waldrep was only 16 years old in 1864 as he is listed as age 2 in the 1850 census. Many young men would lie about their age to join the service in the Civil War and this appears to be the case with this Private Waldrep. There is no known relationship between Little Berry and William M. Waldrep but it seems probable that they were at least distantly related.

In the Mowbray collection, there is one remaining letter from Aunt Sarah Hitch, this one dated Sep 15 1864 to Mary A. Hitch[270]. The subject of her letter, after she speaks of her health troubles is the passing of her nephew Young Hitch and the loneliness that Mary must be feeling:

> *"...I have been a wanting to write to you before now but was prevented by sickness and other things. I do hope when these few lines come to hand, they will find you and your little sons all well and a doing well. you said you wanted me to write as often as I could for I was all that you had to write to now. O my dear niece I think I can cympathise for you in your loneliness and would be glad I could hear from you every week for it seems like the oftener I hear from you the nearer you feel to me. There was years passed by when we neither saw each other nor but seldom heard from each other and I felt sometimes like Young was dead and gone. And after he went to the army and commenced writing to me I felt like I wanted to hear from him every week if I could. His letters was interesting to me and I feel very certain that it wont be long that it will be so that you and me will have the privilege that we now have of a writing to each other and a hearing from each other for I feel certain that I shall soon have to go the way of all the earth."*

Sarah Hitch then discusses wanting to correspond with and see Mary and sons Joseph and Lucian and, offers some wise words from a sage, elderly aunt and continues her very religious leanings:

> *"...and I want you to write as often as you can, you and that lovely little J.J. Hitch, which you say is so much the favor of his beloved father. And O that he may be like him in principle and live long on the earth and be useful in his day and generation. May he seek and serve his father and his mother's God in his youth. O my beloved little nephew I want you to remember your Creator in the days of your youth before the evil days come when you shall say I have no pleasure in them. May the Lord have mercy on little Lucian and bless his little soul and teach him as he grows up how to walk the strait and narrow way of holiness. O my beloved niece you don't know how glad I should be to see you and your dear little sons and converse with you and them face to face. But I fear I never shall have that pleasure. I was in hopes when I wrote last perhaps I should have the chance to pay you a visit but I fear new I shall not get the opportunity... J.J. I want you to be certain to write and tell me how you feel about meeting your beloved Father in that happy place where Jesus is. youth is the time to embrace religion."*

Uncharacteristic of the Aunt Sally letters in the collection, this one does not offer much information about the extended family. Perhaps, this is because Sally is writing to Mary and not Young Hitch who would probably know the family members better. Nevertheless, there is a little on the Pitts family, "*E.L. Pitts has gone to the war and its uncertain when he will return whether ever or not. And his people has got so much work to do of one thing and another I fear it will be a bad chance. They have there molasses to make that will take them a considerable time.*" We remember that Edwin Leroy Pitts is the son of Henry and Mary (Hitch) Pitts, Mary Hitch being the twin sister of Young Hitch's deceased father Joseph Hitch. But, by this time in 1864, Edwin Pitts has almost reached the age of 46 and would be quite old to

---

270 Appendix, Item CIII.

Figure 40 - Private David W. Burdette from Company I, 16th South Carolina with his left arm and leg injuries from his wounds of Nov 30 1864 clearly visible (his leg is missing). The photograph probably dates from c1880.

be joining the war even for Civil War standards. This reflects how depleted the southern army had gotten and needed recruits of any age[271].

On Sep 19 1864, the 16th regiment left Jonesboro and marched to and crossed the Chattahoochee River and continued westward to Palmetto Station, GA. They then re-crossed the river on September 29 and began marching toward northern Georgia. The brigade captured a Federal garrison in Dalton on Oct 13 1864 and destroyed 20 miles of railroad track between Dalton and Tunnel Hill, GA.

The 16th regiment marched to Gadsden, AL on October 21 then past Decatur and Florence on their way to cross the Tennessee River into Tennessee on Nov 13 1864. They reached Spring Hill, TN on November 29 and became disastrously engaged at the Battle of Franklin, TN on Nov 30 1864.

Franklin was one of the worst disasters of the war for the Confederate army. General Hood's Army of Tennessee conducted numerous frontal assaults against fortified positions occupied by the Union forces under General Schofield and was unable to break through or to prevent Schofield from a planned, orderly withdrawal to Nashville.

---

[271] Pitts had enlisted with Company D, 4th Battalion South Carolina Reserves on Jul 20 1864 and reported for duty on August 14. He is listed as present on the muster rolls for November and December 1864. The 4th Battalion mustered into state service Apr 16 1864 and then to Confederate service on October 31. Company D was from the Laurens District and commanded by Captain W.J.M. Jones who had been Captain of Company B, 9th Regiment South Carolina Reserves back in 1862/63 when Young Hitch was in Company C of that unit. The 4th Battalion Reserves were in a brigade with the 3rd, 5th and 8th Battalion Reserves under General James Chesnutt from December 1864 to March 1865 when they were ordered to Blanchard's brigade but it is unclear whether that order was ever executed. The primary duty carried out by E.L. Pitts' Company D in late 1864 was to guard the prison camp at Florence, SC. South Carolina's Military Organizations During the War Between the States; Volume IV, Statewide Units, Militia and Reserves; both by Robert S. Seigler, The History Press, Charleston, SC, 2008; pages 200-202.

The Confederates used six infantry divisions containing eighteen brigades with 100 regiments numbering almost 20,000 men, sometimes called the "Pickett's Charge of the West", to assault the federals and it resulted in devastating losses to the men and the leadership of the Army of Tennessee—fourteen Confederate generals (six killed or mortally wounded, seven wounded, and one captured) and 55 regimental commanders were casualties. Included in those killed at Franklin was General States Rights Gist, the illustrious leader of Gist's brigade under which the 16th South Carolina fought for many, many months. One soldier recalled the heroism, and the devastation, of the rebel army at the Battle at Franklin:

> *"The annals of war may long be searched for a parallel to the desperate valor of the charge of the Army of Tennessee at Franklin, a charge which has been called "the greatest drama in American history." Perhaps its only rival for macabre distinction would be Pickett's Charge at Gettysburg. A comparison of the two may be of interest. Pickett's total loss at Gettysburg was 1,354; at Franklin the Army of Tennessee lost over 6,000 dead and wounded. Pickett's charge was made after a volcanic artillery preparation of two hours had battered the defending line. Hood's army charged without any preparation. Pickett's charge was across an open space of perhaps a mile. The advance at Franklin was for two miles in the open, in full view of the enemy's works, and exposed to their fire. The defenders at Gettysburg were protected only by a stone wall. Schofield's men at Franklin had carefully constructed works, with trench and parapet. Pickett's charge was totally repulsed. The charge of Brown and Cleburne penetrated deep into the breastworks, to part of which they clung until the enemy retired. Pickett, once repelled, retired from the field. The Army of Tennessee renewed their charge, time after time. Pickett survived his charge unscathed. Cleburne was killed, and eleven other general officers were killed, wounded or captured. "Pickett's charge at Gettysburg" has come to be a synonym for unflinching courage in the raw. The slaughter-pen at Franklin even more deserves the gory honor."*
>
> - Stanley F. Horn, The Army of Tennessee

From Franklin, what was left of the Army of Tennessee, including the 16th South Carolina, marched toward Nashville on December 2. They were shelled near Nashville on December 4 and skirmished there on December 5, 7, 8 and 15. On Dec 16 1864, the Army of Tennessee was decimated at the Battle of Nashville. By then, the Army of Tennessee retreated with barely half the men with which it had begun the offensive at Franklin and Nashville, and was effectively destroyed as a fighting force for the remainder of the war. The army reorganized the next day at Franklin and withdrew to the south and arrived at Corinth, MS on December 31.

In the action at Franklin and Nashville in late 1864, there were casualties within Company I of the 16th South Carolina. Private David Wilcot Burdette[272] was wounded Nov 30 1864 at the Battle of Franklin via gunshot that fractured the upper 3 inches of his left ulna and his front left thigh. He was then captured while convalescing in a hospital near Franklin, TN Dec 18 1864 and sent for processing as a POW to Louisville, KY. On Jan 17 1865, he was forwarded to Camp Chase in Nashville and then transferred to

---

[272] Private David Wilcot Burdette (1845-1919) was son of Jesse Bramlett and Agnes (Barker) Burdette of Laurens County. He was the brother of Company I compatriot, Private Benjamin William Burdette (1843-1936). D.W. Burdette is buried with his wife, Zeline (McPherson) Burdette (1845-1919), in Simpsonville Municipal cemetery, Simpsonville, SC.

Point Lookout on Mar 26 1865. He took the Oath of Allegiance and was released on Jun 9 1865. What is most interesting about Private Burdette, is the detail given in the records concerning his injury. **Figure 40** is a photograph of Burdette after the war and, even though he is heavily clothed, you can see that he is missing most of his left leg and his left arm appears deformed from the injuries he received in the war.

Additionally, Private Andrew Jackson Allison[273] was also captured, he near Nashville on Dec 16 1864 and forwarded for POW processing in Louisville, KY. He was discharged from Louisville on December 21 and sent to Camp Douglas, IL. No further information is available to where he ends up but he did survive the war so was likely paroled in May or June 1865.

The year 1864 had ended with the Confederate army in tatters and the objective of southern independence hanging by the slimmest of a thread. Many good men had been killed and maimed in the cause but had fought the good fight. Families were suffering the sorrows of death and the extreme challenges of the collapse of the southern economy. The war's end was closing in.

---

[273] Private Andrew Jackson Allison (1828-1873) was living in Greenville County in 1860 with wife Harriett, occupied as a hatter. He and his wife Harriett G. (Howard) Allison (1818-1900) are buried in the Clear Spring Baptist Church Cemetery, Simpsonville, SC. She was sister of Private P.E.A. Howard and 3LT John M. Howard and the mother of Lt. William S. and Private Thomas M. Thackston.

CHAPTER 7
1865 and Beyond

1865 opens with little hope for the Confederate army. The 16th, with its sister regiment, 24th South Carolina, stayed in Corinth, Mississippi from Dec 31 1864 to Jan 10 1865 when it marched to Tupelo, arriving on January 13. Both regiments then went on a long circuitous journey by boat, rail and foot that took them to South Carolina by February 9. They crossed the Saluda River on Feb 17 1865 and made it to Newberry, SC on the 19th. They passed through Unionville on March 2 and moved into North Carolina, arriving at Charlotte on March 11. From there, the men marched to Smithfield on March 20 and bivouacked near there from April 1 to April 8. The 16th and 24th regiments were consolidated on Apr 9 1865 and the Army of Tennessee surrendered to Union forces 17 days later on April 26. All the men remaining in the consolidated regiment were officially paroled on May 1 1865[274]. And, so ends the story of the 16th South Carolina regiment and our focus on Company I.

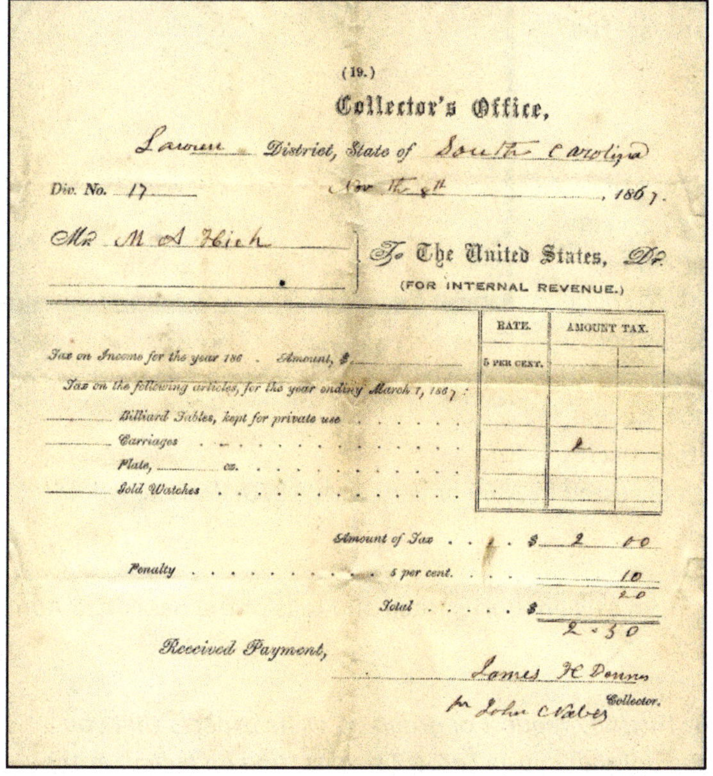
(19.)

Collector's Office,

Laurens District, State of South Carolina

Div. No. 17 Nov the 8th, 1867.

Mrs M A Hich — To The United States, Dr.

(FOR INTERNAL REVENUE.)

	RATE.	AMOUNT TAX.
Tax on Income for the year 186 . Amount, $	5 PER CENT.	
Tax on the following articles, for the year ending March 1, 1867:		
Billiard Tables, kept for private use		
Carriages		2
Plate, oz.		
Gold Watches		

Amount of Tax . . . $ 2 00

Penalty . . . 5 per cent. . . . 10

Total . . . . . $ 20 2.30

Received Payment,

James H Dennis
for John C Nabers Collector.

Figure 41 - Nov 8 1867 Internal Revenue receipt where Mary A. Hitch paid taxes on a carriage she owned. (Mowbray Collection, Edward H. Nabb Center, Salisbury University).

The final wartime letter in the Mowbray collection is a Feb 6 1865 correspondence from John Bradley Edwards to his sister, Mary A. Hitch[275]. John was apparently serving as a Private with Captain R.D. Senn's Company Post Guard of Columbia, SC at the time of this letter, he being age 47[276]. The subject of the letter surrounds the war as he writes, "*Dear sister, I have nothing to right to you at present more than ware newes and I recon you have as much of that as you want to hear. You wanted me to give you my opinion about this cruel ware. I can't tell you when it will wind up but I dont think that it can last much longer. They are a fighting now no they staid above 73 miles ___ hear where I am ___ Ediston? ___ wher I stayed last winter. We are a fortifying this place as fast as wee can but I dont think it will do as much good. Dear sister I am looking every day when I will have to get in*

---

274 South Carolina's Military Organizations During the War Between the States; Volume III, The Upstate, page 177 and, South Carolina's Military Organizations During the War Between the States; Volume IV, Statewide Units, Militia and Reserves; both by Robert S. Seigler, The History Press, Charleston, SC, 2008; pages 88, 89.

275 Appendix, Item CIV.

276 Not much is known about the assignments for Captain R.D. Senn's Company Post Guard. One reference states (in paraphrase), the only record of service for Senn's Company is in Guard Duty at the Richland (SC) Jail. The number of troops indicates they also did service at Camp Sorghum and Camp Asylum, known to be guarded by

to the fight…" He does not think the war can last much longer yet, he is prepared should he have "to get in to the fight." The war would be officially over in 2½ months and John B. Edwards would be paroled with the rest of his unit.

Figure 42 - Young H.E. and Mary Hitch's son, John Joseph Hitch (1847-1915). Photo taken c1889, courtesy of Michael Givens.

There are a few surviving relics in the Mowbray collection from when after the war ends. Additionally, we know from research some of the elements of the family who survived Young Hitch after the tragedy of losing him in the war. There is an interesting U.S. Internal Revenue receipt that Mary Hitch kept from Nov 8 1867 where a tax for $2.00 was applied to a carriage she owned and three penalties of 10c were applied bringing the total amount she paid to $2.30. One legacy of the Civil War that lives on to the modern day is the creation of the Internal Revenue Service, first to collect funds to support the Union effort during the war and then for use during the Reconstruction post-war. This "carriage tax" is one example of the post-war reconstruction effort to collect revenues.

There is also a receipt hand written on a small piece of paper that reads, *"Rec'd of M. Jones Two hundred seventy nine dollars & 34/100 my porportionable part of John Edwards Dec property as my part of my Distribetted shear of all demands. May 27 1871. M.A. Hitch."* This was her portion of her father, John Edwards' estate. We do not know the exact date of his death but, we do know he was living as late as 1864 and had died by the time this receipt was written in 1871. It is probable that his death occurred in 1869 or very early 1870. If so, he would have been 81 or 82 years old at the time.

A letter from Sep 10 1871 to Mary Hitch comes from William Curtis Hitch and tells of the passing of Aunt Sally Hitch[277]:

> *"I will give you a little sketch about Sally Hitch by request of grand pa as he expects that you have not heard it She was struck with the palsy at cousin Leroy Pitts a setting on a chair in the piazza. She fell from the chair and they run and helped her up but she could not talk for a while She was struck in the throat but she could not talk plain when she got so she could speak. she was struck on the last day of August and died on Sunday the 3rd of September. she bid adieu to earth and the earthly things. she told them before she died that she was a going to die and that*

Local Defense troops. The number of men in the unit was large since the men had war-related factory jobs. In addition to POW guard duty, there is some evidence that they assisted in maintaining civil order and guarded the various bridges and military resources of the area. (Post of Columbia, Richland Jail Post Guards, Senn's Company, *www.sciway3.net*)

[277] Appendix, Item CVI.

she wanted to be buried at old poplar Springs Church. her funeral was preached before she was buried. she lost her speech before she died and she made motions to all that was standing around. they went up to the bed and she taken hold of their hands and rub their hands and would look up that is good as to say that she was a going to die and go happy that she was willing and ready."

Aunt Sarah Hitch had spent her final days at Edwin Leroy Pitts' home and had died there on Sep 3 1871 at the age of 75. William C. Hitch notes that "grand pa" wanted Mary Hitch to know, he being Louther Douglas Hitch (1798-1886), Aunt Sally's brother. She died of the "palsy" which would be a stroke in modern-day terms. She had made her peace with dying and was able to go out on her own terms, something that Sally did throughout her life – always conducting things on her terms!

Mary Hitch died on May 11 1880, a little over a month shy of her 53rd birthday. She was laid to rest in the Cedar Grove Baptist Church Cemetery, Fountain Inn, Laurens County, SC. She lies by herself as Young Hitch's body was never recovered from the place he was shot near Kennesaw Mountain, GA. But the love shared by the two lives on forever in the letters she and her husband exchanged while he was away serving for his cause from 1862 till his death in June 1864. From November 1862 to his death, Young Hitch only saw his home, farm and family a total of six weeks in that 19-month period. He missed home terribly so, and she missed him being home even more terribly. But she would not see him in person again after Mar 27 1863 so she relied upon his letters in order to glimpse him in her mind's eye. Then, after he died, she kept every letter and, one can imagine, would turn to them to read as she mourned her husband from the time she had learned from William Scruggs that he had been killed in June 1864 till she passed away herself sixteen years later, on May 11 1880.

After Young Hitch died, the farm and homestead was passed to Mary A. Hitch via his will to be held "during her life or widowhood." Afterwards, the provision was that it would be equally divided between his sons John J. and A. Lucian Hitch. After Mary dies in 1880, we find land record transactions where 115 acres of the land was laid out to Joseph Hitch for $164.00, land bordering John Mock, A.L. Hitch, Ray Thackston, Berry Edwards "and others." The other half of the land was laid out as 108 acres to A.L. Hitch for $1.00, land bordering W.T. Parks, Edward Hughes, Ray Thackston and J.J. Hitch[278].

The letters in the Mowbray collection continued to survive through the years, probably primarily descending down through the family lineage of Young Hitch's youngest son, Augustus Lucian Hitch, although a few came through Joseph Hitch's lineage. There is one final item in the collection that dates from Aug 11 1893 where A.L. Hitch purchases a house and lot in the town of Fountain Inn, SC. The purchase price was $800 which he promises to pay to Julia A. Snow by Nov 1 1893 for the deed to the property that was "on the corner of Weston and Hellams streets." He completed payment for the property on November 10.

At the time of the 1880 census, Lucian Hitch was still living on the Hitch farm with his brother, Joseph's family as a farmhand. He probably stayed there until he married Sarah Elizabeth Bryson on Nov 29 1883,

[278] Both land transactions are recorded in the Laurens County, SC Land Records, Book A, Page 219, Mar 25 1882 and registered, Oct 27 1882. There is also a survey of A.L. Hitch's plat dated Jul 27 1880.

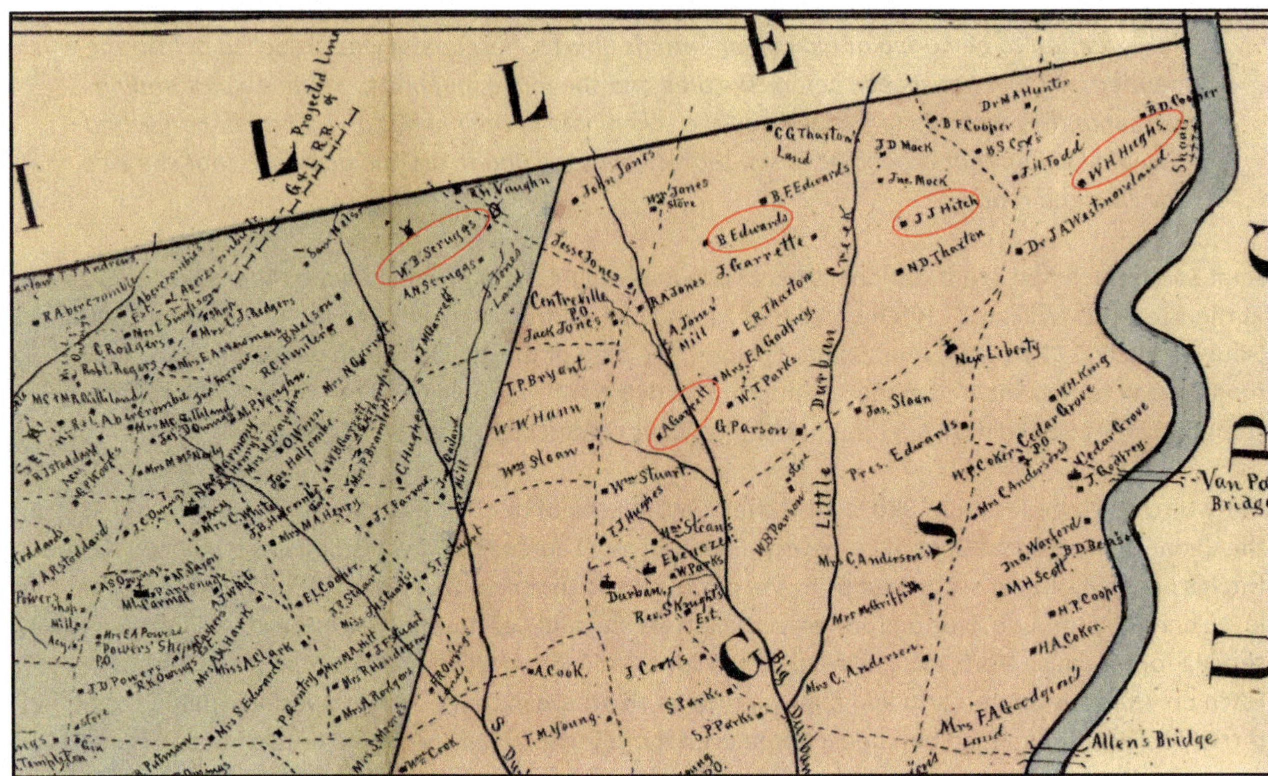

Figure 43 - Portion of an 1883 Hellam's map of Laurens County, SC. This is the northwest portion of the county with north oriented about 30 degrees up from right relative to the image. Note the location of J.J. Hitch and others around the forks of Durbin Creek in the pink area which is Youngs Township. This is where Young Hitch's farm was located that he was so fond of and wrote so much about while away serving with Company I, 16th South Carolina Volunteers. (Michael G. Hitch files)

she the daughter of Robert M. and Nancy Rebecca (Stoddard) Bryson of Greenville County. They likely continued to live on the farm from 1883 to 1893, when they decided to purchase the house in Fountain Inn.

Lucian and Sarah Hitch had only one child, Nancy Mary Elizabeth Hitch, born Dec 18 1887. She went by the name of Bessie Hitch and she married Fred Bascomb Holland on Nov 24 1910. Lucian Hitch died just eight months after the Hollands were married, on Jul 3 1911 and is buried in Fountain Inn. The Hollands had two children, Azilee Hitch Holland and Eleanore Mae Holland and the former married Thomas Mowbray in 1942. They in turn had four children one of which, the co-author of this book, still possessed the cache of original letters from Young Hitch and other documents that have become the Mowbray collection. We are deeply indebted for the line of this family from Mary (Edwards) Hitch down to the Mowbrays for taking good care of these priceless documents through the years!

Young and Mary Hitch's oldest son, John Joseph Hitch, went on to marry Margaret Jane Garrett, daughter of Young Hitch's good friend and 16th regiment compatriot, Miles Rainwater Garrett and his wife Nancy (Stoddard) Garrett. Miles R. Garrett had died of sickness 3½ months after Young Hitch, on Sep 30 1864 in Forsyth, GA. J.J. and Margaret Hitch had four children; Dr. Young M. Hitch, Nannie Mae, Eula and Zula Hitch. Young M. Hitch, named after his grandfather Private Young Hitch, married Daisy Williams in 1898, Nannie Mae married John Wesley Givens Sr. in 1898, Eula, or Mamie as she was known, married Samuel C. Fulmer in 1906 and Zula married Dexter Edgar West in about 1909.

Less than two months after Mary Hitch passes away, on Jul 16 1880, Margaret J. Hitch transferred one-half of her personal estate to John J. Hitch "in consideration of the natural love and affection which I have to my husband." This estate included "my one-half interest in a cotton gin on the waters of Little Durbin Creek, one mule name Patsy, seven head of cattle, six hogs, five sheep, my buggy, my household and kitchen furniture, my one-half interest in a wagon now at my Mothers, all rents and profits now due

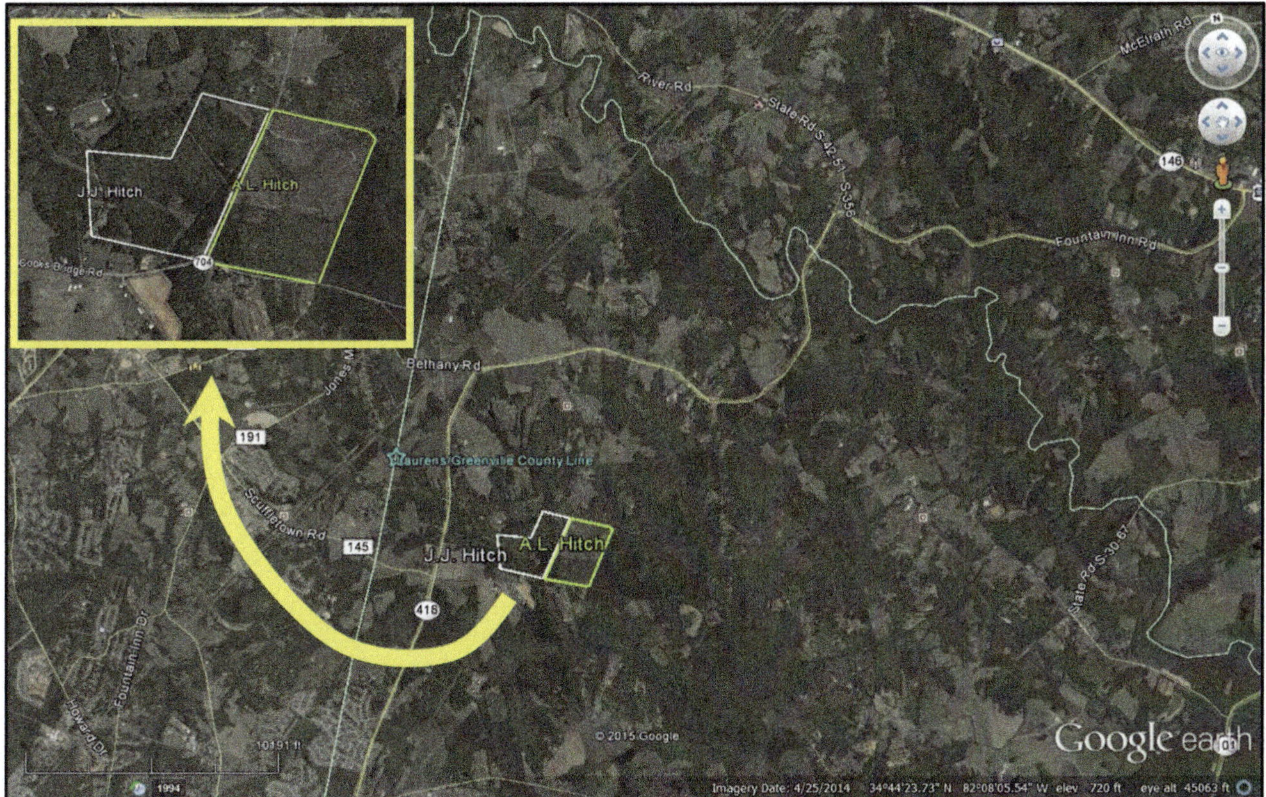

Figure 44 - Map showing approximate boundaries and location of the original Young Hitch property as descended to sons J.J. and A.L. Hitch on a modern satellite image. Note the Laurens County line depicted as this is the far north point of the county. Young Hitch's farm was approximately 225 acres and sits straddling modern-day Pennington Road at its intersection with Cooks Bridge Road. (Michael G. Hitch map adapted from Google Earth).

me or hereafter to become due, all notes now in my possession and belonging to me, my interest in three bales of cotton..." Further, she gives all her rights in her real estate "in a certain tract of land lying and situated in the County..." that included 227 acres bordering Edward B. Hughes, Mrs. A.E. Brown, William Parks and others. This transfer was witnessed by A.L. Hitch and E. Lafayette Edwards on Aug 13 1880[279]. The transfer of property was probably in support of the preparation of dividing the property between the brothers J.J. and A.L. Hitch per the provisions set forth in Young Hitch's will. This division formally took place as previously shown in the deeds of March 1882.

Figure 43 shows the area of Laurens County where J.J. Hitch was living in 1883, near Little Durbin Creek in Youngs Township. A.L. Hitch was probably still living with J.J. there at the time. On this map, Fountain Inn is not shown but would be in the area of the "projected line of G&L R.R." shown there, though the

---

[279] Laurens County, SC Land Records, Book A, Page 178, recorded Aug 13 1880. Note that this was the full extent of the original Young Hitch homestead – 227 acres. Margaret seems to be relinquishing her right to it so that it can be split between J.J. and A.L. Hitch per the original provisions of Young Hitch's will.

town was not incorporated until 1886. Note the presence of Young Hitch's old friends Archibald Garrett, William H. Hughes, Billy Edwards and William Berry Scruggs as nearby neighbors. One can imagine those men telling J.J. and A.L. Hitch stories of their father in the War through the years. **Figure 44** shows the same land in a modern-day (2014) satellite image. The two tracts shown are the segments that went to Joseph Hitch and Lucian Hitch per their division of the Young Hitch farm in 1882. The Lucian Hitch tract was still in the family and owned by one of the descending Mowbrays in 2015.

John Joseph Hitch died on May 31 1915 as his obituary from a newspaper in the Fountain Inn, SC area reads, "J.J. Hitch died at 4 o'clock Monday afternoon, after a long illness. He was 68 years of age. Mr. Hitch was born 5 miles northeast of Fountain Inn, and had lived his life in this neighborhood. He was one of those few men of whom it may truthfully be said: 'Everybody loved or respected him.' He had long been referred to as one of the best men in the country. The funeral service was held at the residence at 2 o'clock, conducted by Dr. J.D. Pitts. The deacons of the Baptist church were pall bearers. Mr. Hitch is survived by his widow, who was formerly a Miss Garrett, and by four children: Dr. Y.M. Hitch of Hodges, Mrs. J.W. Givens, Mrs. S.C. Fulmer and Mrs. D.E. West, the latter of widow. During the war between the sections, Mr. Hitch offered his services but was refused. He weighed only 65 pounds."

CHAPTER 8
Final Thoughts

The writing of this book has literally been a labor of love for the authors Hitch and Mowbray. From the very moment Mr. Hitch discovered that Ms. Mowbray had found the cache of old documents belonging to Young Hitch in her attic, he knew the story must be expressed in print. Serendipitously, Ms. Mowbray had already had the same thought before the two met and the partnership that culminated in the writing of this book was formed.

Ms. Mowbray took on the monumental task to transcribe all the old records and Mr. Hitch worked to weave them into a documentary of the life and times of Young Hitch. As the work was refined, both worked together to bring the work into state of final presentation that hopes to please the reader. However, no true justice can be provided in mere words on paper that would adequately describe the trials of the time leading up to and during the war. Most families in the local area of Laurens and Greenville counties, where Young Hitch grew up, experienced incredible upheaval and hardships during that time. But none could be worse than losing a husband, father and good community man as the Hitch family experienced.

Both Hitch and Mowbray felt the emotions of the time 150 years ago relived in conducting the transcriptions of Young and Mary Hitch's letters and those of their sons and friends and other family and while weaving the story into a book. They knew that, on Jun 19 1864, Young Hitch would fall victim to being shot and killed by a minie ball near Kennesaw Mountain, GA just a few days before the massive battle there as the Union army advanced towards Atlanta. This image would remain in the back of their thoughts as they wrote, building to a tragic climax that they knew was to occur, and wishing that it would not happen and yet were powerless to change it. A good man, a good father and a good husband was going to be killed on the battlefield and there was absolutely nothing they could do about it. How sadly tragic this was and it came through as a crescendo of emotion as the book came together.

Perhaps, if there is any good that may have come from the tragic end of Young Hitch, is that he and his fellow soldiers now live on for posterity in this interpretation of his words and his time with Company I, 16th South Carolina regiment volunteer infantry. Had he not died in the conduct of his cause, then the letters and documents from the time may not have survived. They were no doubt carefully saved in the years after the war by the family – especially his wife and sons – to try and maintain some small token of remembrance of their precious husband and father around the Hitch farm as they lived out the remainder of their lives. Hitch's body was never returned home from the battlefield, but his spirit and story live on through his writings and his legacy through this book and the memories of his family. It has been our pleasure to have been a part of it.

Michael G. Hitch
Elinor H. Mowbray

APPENDIX
The Mowbray Collection[280]

In this Appendix, we present transcriptions of the elements within the Mowbray collection including the correspondences, scribblings, and other items like receipts. The various items as transcribed are presented here in chronological order and date from 1846 to 1871. Ms. Elinor Mowbray, great-great granddaughter to Young Hitch, discovered the collection at her residence and completed all of the transcriptions herself. She also has graciously donated all of these original items to the Edward H. Nabb Center at Salisbury University in Salisbury, Maryland for preservation and use by researchers in the future.

The letters from the time of Young Hitch's service in the Civil War are primarily from him as the author with only a few that his wife Mary Hitch penned and sons Joseph J. and A. Lucian Hitch. This is because the letters saved were mainly those written to Young's address in Laurens County and stashed away in the attic. Most of the ones written to Young while in the field do not survive unless he sent them back with his own correspondence later. Unfortunately, most of those letters are lost. However, from Young Hitch's responding letters, we can often glean the majority of the content that had originally been part of Mary Hitch's or his son's letters.

LETTERS (UNTIL AUGUST 1862) DATING FROM BEFORE THE WAR TO YOUNG HITCH'S TIME IN COMPANY C, 9TH SOUTH CAROLINA RESERVES

I. "Scribbling" Notes of Young Henry Elkanah Hitch dating from 1846 and from several pages that were folded inside an 1806 school notebook of his father, Joseph N. Hitch.

An interesting set of three pages where it looks as if Young was practicing his penmanship as a young man. There a couple of interesting additions as well relative to family.

State of South Carolina Laurens District July 5th 1846 young

At Dover dine Geary Brown Esq. Good Christopher Finch and David Friar?
Young H.E. Hitch is my name and single is my station and Laurens District is my dwelling place and happy will be the girl that marrys me I hope. H

A man today in rich array to morrow may be laid in clay.
Jane. Young H.E. Hitch is my name single is my station Laurens District is my dwelling place and happy will be the girl that marrys me I hope.
This is my hand and pen Young H.E. Hitch
State of South Carolina Laurens District A.D. 1846. 1846.

280 All items are part of the Mowbray Collection except two exceptions where noted.

Never lament and weep for things which you cannot keep.
When this you see remember Young H.E. Hitch A.D. 1846 July 5th ill
The reverend T. Robeson & H. Hit are to preach at North 1846
Many persons marry in haste and repent at leisure July 6th 1846
Many persons marry in haste and repent at leisure. Young H.E.H.
Quick matches in matrimony may some times prove beneficial July 6th
State of South Carolina Laurens District July the 19th 1846
God made man and man made money God made bees and bees made honey
Quick matches in matrimony may sometimes prove beneficial
This is the first Sabath in July A.D. 1846 Young H.E. Hitch
Command you may your mind from play every hour in the day

I bought a beaurau of Rubin bramblet the 11th day of July A.D. 184 price $12- Young Henry Elkanah Hitch
A man today in rich array tomorrow may be laid in clay.
When this you see remember Young H.E. Hitch July 12th A.D. 1846

(Page 2)

Though I am young yet I may die
And hasten to eternity.
There is a dreadful fiery hell
Where wicked ones must always dwell.
There is a heaven of joy and rest
Where godly ones with Christ are blest.
To one of these my soul must ply
As in a moment when I die. ---

A man of wit any understanding may kiss a maid with out asking.
State of South Caralina ina Laurens District.
Death is the doctor that cures all maladies. July 19th
Miss M.A. Martin.
This is the Sabbath day which God appointed for rest July 19th
Young H.E. Hitch is my name and single is my station and Laurens District is my dwelling place and happy will be the girl that gets me I hope. July 17th A.D. 1846. 1846.
Young H.E. Hitch his hand and pen February 12 1850
Many persons marry in haste and repent at leisure July 18th 1846
Of all earthly enjoyments money beares the sway July 19th 1846
Commenced ciphering in the single rule of three the 10th of July A.D. 1846.
My true loves name is in this letter and you made read it over and be none the better
Read it over and over and be none the better yet my true loves name is in this letter.
By diligence and care you may learn to write fair.
South
Many persons marry in haste and repent at leisure

Young H.E. Hitch is my name & single is my station & Laurens District is my dwelling place and happy will be the girl that gets me I hope.

(Page 3)

July the 20th A.D. 1846. Monday the 20th of July 1846. 1846.
A man today
A man today in rich array tomorrow may be laid in
Death is the doctor that cures all diseases. Young H.E. Hitch
Death is the doctor that cures all maladies. July 19th 1846. 1846
Life time is swiftly. Life is sweet and death is certain. July 20th
Command you swift from your mind from play every hour.
A man of wit and understanding may kiss a maid without

Young H.E. Hitch August 16th A.D. 1846. Y.H.E.H..

Society friendship and larie? divinely best avned? on from man.
A man wishing to gain popularity should act studiously
Remember well and bear in mind that a trusty friend
A of wit and understanding may kiss a maid without asking.
What is everybodys business is nobodys business I say 1846.
What is everybodys business is nobodys business I say 1846.

William Brown Esq. a hog thief and a liar you better believe it.

Health and competence are a thousand recompenses A.D.
Health A man to day in rich array to morrow may
Kings may command but subjects must obey. Young H.E. Hitch
This is the sabath day the third sabath and the 16th day of August.
This is my hand and pen August 16th A.D. 1846.
Many persons marry in haste and repent at leisure
Many damsels marry in haste and repent at leisure
When this you se remember Young H.E. Hitch
Command you may your mind from play every hour

The following are excerpts from the pages folded in the 1806 Joseph N. Hitch notebook that were written by Young Hitch from 1846-1854:

Young H.E. Hitch Oct 1st 1846 State of South Carolina Laurens District
Young H.E. Hitch is very sleepy this evening.
Alfred Holcombe his hand and pen Oct the 1st 1846
Miss E. Halbert Young Henry Elkanah Hitch Tama whacker
By diligence and care you may learn to write fair
Young H.E. Hitch was born August the 30th 1825

Joseph Allen Hitch, P.P. Hitch, L.D. Hitch
Capt. William Brown Esq a hog thief and a liar 1846
Rozannah Martyn. Emila M.L. Brown 1846
Mary Elizabeth Martyn. Martha Jane Martyn
Two days after date I promise to pay James B.F. Bruce Ten cents for value received of him. Sept 23rd 1846
My true loves name is in this letter And you may read it over and over be none the better
Read it over & over & still be none the better
Yet my true loves name is in this letter.
Twelve months after date I promise to pay James B.F. Bruce or order Ten dollars for value rec'd of him
Young H.E. Hitch Esq a hog thief and a liar

June the 30th 1850 By Y.H.E. Hitch
Joseph John was born Dec 2nd 1847

Young H.E. Hitch May the 25th 1850
M.A. Hitch
May the 27th 1850 John Joseph K.M. Hitch
Mary Ann Hitch
This is a verry warm day May today May 28 1850
Today wee had a severe rain and hail storm Sunday June the 2nd 1850

Y.H.E. Hitch Dec 15 1854 (sic)
J.J.K.M. Hitch
Dec the 24th 1853 wrote Young H.E. Hitch Christmas came this year on Sunday
Young Hitch January 5 1854
Augustus Lucian Hitch A pretty little babe A lying in the cradle A playing

II. The "Grand Rascal" Letter, James B.F. Bruce to Y.H.E. Hitch dated September 30, 1851, Laurens District, South Carolina

September 30 1851
South Carolina Laurens District

Dear Sir I take the pleasure in writing you a few lines to inform you that through the mercy of God we are as well as could be expected. The child is on the mend and I think will get well if no backset and I wish to answer your letter. You say that your reason that you talked about me the way you did you didn't want her and me to marry. Well sir if you can help your self do it. I ask you no favors and I think that you had a very poor excuse and you say that you never talked to nobody but to Emily and it is a lie sir. Did you not come to the mill, sir, and talk to her father? You did, sir, or his family tells wrong tales and you say that when I get blood out of a turnip that you will acknoledge and not before and when you get so that you can stand on your head and shit and jump from under it, then you get my friendship but not before and to give you my opinion about you. I believe you to be a grand rascal. That's my sentiment about you and the man that you said wanted my note or the pay is no better than you and you are no better than a certain miller in my knowen has been. You rote that it hadn't been long since I had broke up a match with Pyrence and Nathan Woods. Sir, it is a lie and I can prove it since I went and asked Pyrence whether I did or not and she said not. She asked me why I told her and then I asked mother and she said it was a lie and she told me to tell you that you had better be at something else than using Pyrence's name for fear you get in worse business than ever. You said that you never talked to nobody about me but Emily. Did you not talk to her aunt, sir? You certainly did or she has told a sorry tale. Did you not talk to Mr. Edwards, sir? If you didn't, sir, I have heard wrong tales. You say that you can help to kill a (__) killing of hogs without speaking, sir. I can help three times without speaking, sir. You rote that you didn't try to scandalize me. You are a liar, sir. If you ain't tried to scandalize me, I don't know what hipocrating is. What I have to say I am very plain about it. You are a grand hypocrite and a liar in the bargain, sir. I would like very much if I could have the time to meet you on the halfway ground and knock it out. It would be a great deal of comfort. I had rather be ketched with a stolen sheep on my back than to be gilty of stealing from a poor widdow woman. I hant time to write as much as I would do as I am in a hurry to get off so I hope that you won't think hard of me for not writing no more and sooner to. I bid you a farewell to this knight and luck to your children. So if you choose it and can make it come upright I would be glad to meet you in the field so no more at the present. Dear sir, I wrote you a friendly letter at the start and you wrote me an insulting one at the start and I wish to give you the same kind of a dost so no more.

Jas B. F. Bruce to Y. H. E. Hitch

Envelope addressed to Mr. Y.H.E. Hitch Favored by a friend

III. Young Hitch's List of Members of Number 1, 2nd Battalion 41st Regiment of the Beat Company, January 14, 1854

The List of Beat Camp No. 1, 2nd Battalion 41st Regt.
Commanded by John D. Pattan
South Carolina

Augustus Lucian Hitch

(There is a date written here as)January the 14th 1854 By Y.H.E. Hitch.

List of officers commissioned and non commisi

John D. Pattan	*Capt.*
W.E. Garrett	*1st Lieut*
J. Landrum Riddle	*2nd Lieut*
Bird Phillips	*3rd Lieut*
Y.H.E. Hitch	*1st Sergent*
S.F. Riddle	*2nd Sergt*
S.K. Henry	*3rd Sergt*
Tatiller Garrett	*4th Sergt*
Richard Jones	*1st Corp.*
John Jones	*2nd Corp.*
Wm Massey	*3rd Corp*
Thos Canady	*4th Corp*

T.J. Wallace *Clerk*
Alfred Sloan
K___ Jones
A___ Eweings?
A___ Holcombe
J.___ Meadar
John Jones
R.H. Vauah?
J___ Jones
J.S. Cox
Dr. Lucas
John Grumbler
Jeremiah Gilbert
J.T. Simmons
T. P. Massey
Wm Stephens
E.A. Smith
U.W. Pain
James Spele?
Joseph Lang
Reuben Lang
Newton J. Lyons
Sterling Smith
Stephen Griffith
Richard Compton
Thos Parks
O.P. Jones
Charley Sloan
Hosey Holcombe
James Holcombe
B.W. Holcombe
Derias Garrett
Wm M. Patton
John Edwards
Jesse Godfry Senr
Jesse Godfrey Junr
Elijah Scrugs
Jno F. Burdit
Wm Stephens
U.W. Pain
Thos Edwards
Samuel Nelson
John Massey
C.P. Jones

Joseph T. Bardit
Carter Holcombe
E.J. Fairbairn
Elis Riddle
Simeon Riddle
Wm Waddle
Mansil Garrett
J.F. Leopard
J.H. Templeton
J.F. Stewart

IV. Letter from "Nan" to Y.E. and Mary Ann Hitch dated June 20, 1854 from Marshall County, Mississippi

June the 20 1854
Mississippi Marshel county

Dear brother an sister
I once more take the opertunity to write you a few lines to let you all no that we air yet alive an tolarb health at this time but we hav ben sick this summer with the bowel complaint an a tuch of the flu. I was sick for three or for days that I dident set up any at tall only what time I was helping Robert to cook but he dun the most of it. Maryan, Robert can make up doe an put down a very nice pone of bread an bake it too an he can milk very well to tho he hasnt milk any for a few days. He has a large bile on his backbone an cant stoop about much tho he is peart as ever an dont complain of it much. John was sick at the same time I was tho he only lost one or too days with his sickness. Ther is a great deal of sickness about hear with the flu an bowel complaint an the cholery have ben very bad in Memphis about thirty miles from whear we live an I have hird of som few cases only a few miles of from us. Maryan I want you to rite to ous when you git this leter and rite all you think I want to know. Maryan, I rote some to you when I rote to father an you an I rote some to Caroline to an neth of you haint rote never a line yet. If you have I havent got them yet an I you to rite the reason why you don't rite. I receivd a leter from father but I haint roat him no answer but I saw Mr. Harry Gilbert an sent word by him that we got his leter an how we was. Maryan, I reckon you will want to know whether I am satisfide or not. I can tell you I aint and the reason for it is because ther aint no water hear in the summer only water is in the wells. People hav to draw water ou of ther well for all of ther stock an the women dont make no cloth an that dont soot mee. Tha by all tha war but when I git in a (__) I intend git mee a wheel and cards an loom an make our close an then we can save money to pay our dets back. Ther meany. We aim to pay you what we owe you an all the wrest of our dets if we live ever git money anuf to come back ther an pay them of. John sais if hee can ever make money anof to pay of his dets he intends to com back ther an bring mee an the children an I set a great deal by makin moey an coming back ther independent so more at present.
Only remain your sister until death.

V. Letter from William P. Edwards to Y.H.E. and Mary E. Hitch dated February 2, 1855 from Lauderdale County, Alabama

Alabama Lauderdil County
February the 2 1855

Dear brother and sister After hearing from you I seat myself to drop you a few lines to let you know I am well hoping these lines will find you all in good helth. I hant eney good news to rite to you more than we have plenty to eat. Tha corne is $35⁰ cts pur bari four $10 dollars pur baril. Coton is worth 5 cts pur pound. Hard times to get money tho I am owing rite smart and cant get eny money to pay off what I owe. you sed you wanted me to rite to you how mutch I was owing. 800 dollars is as near as I can come to hit with thout counting up. I cant rite hardly eney. You sed you did not want me to think hard of you for not scending eney money to me. You mout know that I wod not think hard of you and I dont want you to think hard of me for scending word for you to make hit out of John if you coud. I must close as I have to rite another or two by saing I want you to rite to me as soon as you can after you get these lines so fare you well for this time.
Wm P. Edwards

Y.H.E. Hitch
Mary E. Hitch

VI. Letter from William Scruggs to Y.H.E. and Mary Hitch dated August 16, 1855.

Georgia Forsyth County
August 16th 1855

Dear brother and sister

After hearing from you again I will seat myself to drop you a few lines to let you know that I hant forgot you but I hant got mutch to rite more than we air all well at this time and hope these few lines will find you all well. And (__) got home on Sadduraday after he left there and he told us that you all was well when he left there. I recon hit is no use to tell you about my crop. I recon that and (__) talk about it. I has had a bad chance this year for we all has been sick some but I think that I can live next year.

You name in your letter about my (__) I will tell you about hit. I did take hit a fact for I think hit the best way for I was as fast as I was when I hast uncle Jac and never seed him. You sed that you recon that I ware out a (__) of my trouse but I didnt for I was in my shirt tale but I has got too sons & a daughter that I will show with eny body. I will be glad to spend a few hours with you once more but I recon that hit will be a long time before I will. I want you to rite to me every chance that you have for I am glad to hear from you. I must come to a close so no more at present. A little for Caroline to Mary. I hant got mutch to rite at this time. I must tel you about my little gal that I has had since I left you. She is mity little but she grose fast but she is the crass as the dayes is long. You sed in your letter that you recon that I wood look for a coat for youse name sake but I dint (__) for the sake of the cats. I name hear for her ants an graney.

Tell Samantha that I got that coat that she sent to her name sake and I though hit was purty but if she cood see her she wood think that she is purty according. Mary I want you to rite to us every chance that you has for I am glad to hear from you. If you did know how often I thought of you when I was sick. I think that you wood rite to me for I wood of been glad to a got to read a letter from you when I was on my bed for hit wood of been some pleasure to me if I coont see you. tell father & mother that (__) not (__) coming out to see us for (Next line illegible) to come an see us. Once more I cant rite all I want to for my chance is bad an I make a bad out aritin but I recon that you can read some of hit. I was glad of then pees that you sent me but I will try next time to save seed an not (__)

Mary I must tel you a little more about my sickness. I was sic so long that I got so week that I cood hardly (__) git in the house when I went out of dorse. You don't now wha I wood of give to of seed eny of you out ther but I hadd nether father nor mother, brother nor sister or cusin to see me (__) I can tel you that William was father & mother, brother & sister & husban to if hit is possible that one body cood be all of them to me for he waited on me day an knight till I got well. I want you to rite to me. Tel the rest of our kin that we will rite to them as soon as we can for we hant forgot them. I must come to a close. I recd your letters to me to (__)

William Scruggs
(__) Scruggs

Y.H.E. Hitch
Mary Hitch

Envelope addressed:
South Carolina
Larance District S.C
Senterville Post of
To Mr Young Hytch

VII. Letter from "Aunt Sally" (Sarah) Hitch to Y.H.E. and Mary Hitch dated April 25, 1856.

Sarah Hitch (1796-1871) was daughter of Louther Hitch and, hence, the paternal aunt of Young Hitch. She never married or had children.

April the 25 1856

Dear nephew and niece
Its with pleasure that I take my pen to send you a few lines to let you know I am in moderate health at present. Hoping that these lines will find you and all yours in good health. I am often a thinking about you all and the pleasure I enjoyed amongst you when I was with you. I should be happy to see you all again. But as I know not whether I ever shall see any of you in this world again or not, I take the opportunity of sending you a few lines to tell you a little about how the times has been amongst us since I saw you. Your Uncle Pitts family has been greatly afflicted since I came home. His son John first took down and had a severe attack of the winter disease that's so prevalent in the country. And before he was able to see to the business out, the negroes all took down. That is the men, four of them. Pretty much the same disease. His old negro Jo had a spell before Christmas sometime. He has never got so he can labour yet and his oldest boy he raised, Jack died of a lingering disease, something like a consumption. There

has been a sight of affliction in our neighborhood. Sarah Ann Milam has had a very severe spell and three of her children but all better at present. Isaac Boyd and some of his family has been sick. John Coopers family. Leroy Pitts family has all shared more or less the afflictions of providence. Eunice Duvall and family. Young Pitts and family is I believe in moderate health at present as far as I know. There has been several deaths close in the neighborhood and the sickness is still a going on. Almost every day I can hear of one and another taken down. Your uncle Louthers family is last account just in tolerable health. we are told in Holy writ that when the Judgments of the Lord are in the world, the inhabitants of world will learn righteousness. There surely is a loud call at this time to us all. Saying aloud watch. and be ye also ready for in such an hour as ye think not the Son of man cometh. O my beloved niece and nephew I want if I never should see you any more this side of an awfull Eternity to meet you at the right hand of God on high. I feel like trying by the Grace and help of God to get to that happy place where parting will be no more. O my beloved nephew, I want you if you never have come out on the Lords side, if you have a small hope that God for Christs sake has pardoned your sins. You know not how long you have got to live. Come out from amongst the world and join in with the people of God and say by your actions to the people of God as one of old, thy people shall be my people and thy God my God. If you have got the Religion of Jesus you never will enjoy it as you would do in making an open profession of his name. our blessed Lord was never promised to bless the disobedient while living in it. While all the promises and blessings are promised to the faithful and obedient. Give not sleep to your eyes, nor slumber to your eyelids till you discharge your duty to God in what he requires at your hand. If you are one of his redeemed ones, may the Lord enable you to do your while duty is the humble prayer of your very unworthy but affectionate aunt. I long to hear from you all very much. I want you to write to me as soon as you can and tell me all about your situation, both spiritual and temporal as nigh as you can. It is with much difficulty I have made these few scrawls with a trembling hand and weakness of body and mind. I shall begin to come to a close as I know not whither you can read what I have already scribbled. Your aunt Mary says she would be very glad to see you and would be glad to come to see you if she was able and had the opportunity. As your father and her were it seems nearer to each other or felt as being twins than the rest of us, you therefore feel particular near to her. Your most sincere and affectionate aunt and well wisher. Farewell.
Sarah Hitch

Envelope addressed to Y.H.E. Hitch
Beneath that in a different handwriting: A letter from Aunt Sally

VIII. Letter from Elijah and Emily Scruggs to Y.H. and Mary Hitch dated May 16, 1856 from Marshall County, Alabama

Elijah Scruggs (1823-1902) married Amelia (Emily) Gilbert (1825-aft 1900), they apparently had no known surviving children. Elijah was son of John Edwards Scruggs and Mary Edwards, Mary being the sister of Mary Ann (Edwards) Hitch's father (Elijah and Mary Ann are first cousins). Elijah Scruggs ended up serving for Company I of the 43rd Georgia Volunteers (Reynold's Brigade).

Alabama Marshal County
May the 16 1856

Dear cousins, I embrace the present opportunity of informing you that we are yet living and enjoying tolerble health. Hoping when these lines come to hand that they will find you all enjoying the same blessing we are well satisfied with the country and neighbors. We come by Wm Scrugs and tuck dinner with them. They are all well. Caroline is the fattest I ever saw her and her children is as fat as little pigs. Caroline was as proud to see me as she could be. She talked a great deal. She said that she had herd that your father had a notion of joining the church. She told me that she had a hope but she had not joined then. She said that she intended to move out here and be a neighbor to us. She told me that if she could not get to meeting that she wanted me to go but I hav no chance to go here for the meeting house is so fer off I cant go often. I think if Y.H. Hytch was here that he never would go back to old Carolina. I would be glad to see you come to this country for I can tell you a thousand things I cant rite. I want you to tell cousin anna hughs that I am well and well satisfied and that I have not been as smart as Silvy Gilbert was. I want you to rite to me all the news you can think of and not put it of for I want to here from you all. Tell Lafayett Brown that we want him to come out here and preach for us for there aint many preachers here. Tell him there is lots of pretty girls here. Rite to me and then I will rite more. I will come to a close so no more but remain your loving cousin untill death.
Eligah and Emily Scrugs to Y.H. and Mary Hytch

Direct your letters to Big Spring PO
On back of letter:
To Mr. Young H. Hytch

IX. Letter from Sarah Hitch to Y.H.E. and Mary Hitch dated September 26, 1856

So. Ca. L. District
Sep 26th 1856

Dear and much esteemed nephew and niece
Its with pleasure tho in weakness I sit down to write a few lines. I am in a puny state of health at present. But o what reasons for thankfulness thats as well with me as it is. Through the mercy and goodness of an allwise Creator I have had as good health the past summer as I've had for several years past. I hope when these lines reach you, they will find you and your little family enjoying good health. Your uncle Henrys family at this time is tolerable well except himself. He is at this time while I am writing lying a resting after throwing up. The rest of the relatives I believe as far as I know are all able to be up. I often think about you all and think again how glad I should be to see you although if I could believe that you did esteem and love me as I how I do you, we surely could get to see each other oftener. You surely could throw down your work a day or too and come and see us old people one time before we die. My will is good to come and see you if my opportunity was. You may say your opportunitys are not good neither. But I mean in the way of conveyance as for my work or any thing of that kind is no bar in my way tho I think I love to labor when able as well as any one believing it my duty. O my beloved nephew I still want to be a knowing about your spiritual welfare. I love your soul and desire its welfare above every thing else for the word of eternal truth tells us if we should gain the whole world and lose our own souls what would it profit us. It is said again set your affections on things above not on things on the earth. O my beloved nepew an niece try to love the Lord and serve him with your whole heart, soul mind and strength. O that your unworthy aunt could do the same. I do think if my own heart deceives me not I do

desire to love him and serve him. May the Lord enable us all to love and serve him is the prayer of your unworthy aunt. I want you to write as soon as you can. I love to hear from you often if I could. O if you knew what pleasure it gives me to get a letter from you, you surely would grant me that favor as often as possible. I want you when you write to let me know how James Templetons family is. Tell Katharine Stewart to tell Ann Templeton. I want her to write to me and let me know how they are all a getting along. I shall have to a close as I feel very weak and feeble at this time and I've already scribbled as much as perhaps you will like to take time to read unless it was move interesting. May the God of peace dwell richly in you both is the prayer of your unworthy aunt. So fare you well.
Your afectinate aunt until death.
Sarah Hitch

X. Letter from Sarah Hitch to Y.H.E. Hitch dated March 20, 1857

South Carolina
Laurens District
March 20th 1857

Dear nephew. I once more take the opportunity of writing you a few lines to inform you that at the present I am enjoying as good health as I ever expect to. through the mercy and goodness of my kind Creator I have had as good health the past winter as I have had in several winters past. Your Uncle Henry Pitts family is tolerable well at present. Your Uncle Louthers family was well last account a day or two a go. I suppose you have heard of his heavy affliction in the death of Pinkney. He was sick a very short time. He was a complaining on the Sunday previous to his death of a small pimple on the side of his face but himself nor none of the family thought it any thing serious. On Monday it grew worse and still worse and at lenth it became very painful and his face on one side became so swelled that he scarcely looked like himself. On Tuesday evening he took a long severe chill and suffered on severely till Friday afternoon when he ceased to breathe. I feel to hope that hes gone to a better world than this. You said in your last letter that some of your family had been sick but at the time you wrote they were all better. I hope when this reaches you it will find you all in good health. You say times is hard. You say you have reapt a sorry crop last year. and now my dear nephew we must learn to be cheerful in adversity as well as prosperity. It appears from your letter your in very low spirits conserning your worldly prospects. and now pray tell me how and what your prospects are for a better and heavenly country. My beloved nepew I long to hear of you a coming out on the Lords side. If it is your duty marvel not if you meet with chastisements by your disobedience. I don't want you to think hard of me for speaking so to you on the subject of religion. I do it because I love you and wish you well. You said you did not want to hurt my feelings in telling me that it would not suit me to spend the winter with you for the several reasons which you have given. I reckon it was all right. I have spent the winter or the most of it with Pinkneys widow and two little children whose names are William Leander and Luther David, two lovely promising little boys. Your uncle Henry and aunt Mary desires very much that you should visit them with all your little family one time at least. It might be possible you might not lose any thing by it. The old people and myself cannot be here many more days according to the course of nature. Its an old saying. The young may die but the old must die. Your uncle and aunt pitts wishes to see Mary-ann and the children one time as neither of them has ever seen them and in all brobability if you do not visit them soon they never will see them. I myself would be so glad to see you all one time here on Reedy River. I want to hear from James Templeton and and family. I think I

wrote to you one time before to tell Catharine Stewart to tell Ann Templeton I want her to write if she can to me. I have heard of Templetons distresst situation and feel to sympathise with the family and himself knowing the fewest number is ever cured of that disease. I shall begin shortly to draw to a close lest I should weary you with my disinteresting letter. I want you to write to me often as you can. I am always glad to see a letter come from you if it was as often as once every month. I want you next time you write send the name of your post office. I may at some time send by mail. So I remain your loving and affectionate aunt untill death. Farewell.
S. Hitch to Y.H.E. Hitch.

XI. Y.H.E. Hitch Diary from Jan to Aug 1858

Y.H.E. Hitch was born Aug 30 1825 Jan 1858

Jan. 5th 1858 brought from Mill the flower of 2½ bus. of wheat.----
At the same time the meal of 1½ bus. of corn. ----
------next page
Saturday the 9th had Liberty shod with old shoes & ribbit put in pot hook. ----
Y.H.E. Hitch
Monday 11th commenced hovling for John Edwards at 4 P.M. & continued until the 14th day 3 oclock P.M.. -----
------next page
Saturday 16th burnt sedge.
Saturday 9th 1858 made settlement with S. Templeton for sawing bill $13.70 cts paid $6.50-cts in cash & gave a note for seven dollars & 70 cts. Paid up the above account.
15 of Jan bought of M.M. Garrett 3½ lbs of sole leather 40 cts per lb. Paid the above $1.40
16 Jan of the same one pair of Showes 1.60 whitch he proffers to take peas and rawhide in exchange for. --- Paid the above
Mr. Edwards Vicy died Thursday 14th 1858
------next page
February

Took to M.M. Garrett today one rawhide Jan 26 1858 weighing ten & a half pounds. ---
Rec. payment for the above April 17.

Feb 11 1858 Brought home today the meal & flower of two and a half bus. Of grain each.
Feb 12 1858. Got up this morning & found the ground covered in sleet & continued falling untill night half after eight oclock.
Feb 12.. My crib half full of corn now. Wind very high.
------next page
W.W. Hitch left here this morning Feb 12 1858

Feb 12. We have four little lambs here.
Feb 17th M.M. Garrett Dr. to two and a half bushels of peas. 75 cts per bus.
Rec. payment for the above April 17.

Feb 15th commenced on the Jones flower.
------next page
Feb 22nd 1858 today bartered at Greenville C.H. 22½ doz Eggs and 3 lbs of butter for

$1.00 worth of Sugar	*$1.00*
One dollars worth Nails	*$1.00*
Half dollars worth Rice	*$0.50*
Half pound Salt 5 cts	*$0.05*
One pound Copperas 5 cts	*$0.05*
One bunch tacks 5 cts	*$0.05*
Four boxes matches 5 cts	*$0.05*

	$2.70

John Joseph Camiller Hitch was born Dec 2
------next page
Feb 23rd 1858 A cold windy day
Wroth by Y.H.E. Hitch

April the 14th 1858 Sold at Laurens Court House Thirty seven and a half dozen Eggs at ten cts per dozen.
Bought of Joshua Gilbert one thousand & forty four feet of plank at seventry five cts per hundred foot whicth amounts to seven dollars & eight three cts. April 16.
Gave my note for the above account.
April 13 sold to Mary Scruggs half bushel corn 75 cts per bus. and rec. of her 10 cts.
April 17th Planted Cucumbers today.
------next page
Paid J.M. Edwards $41.15 for a bale of cotton April 16th 1858
Paid John Edwards $30.30 for his bale of cotton April 15 1858.
Mr. Zeddock Cooper was buryed today April 17th 1858
April 19th and not a grain of corn planted yet at Hitch's. Call him late beginner wont you yessir
The third Sabbath in April is a cloudy dark day. Y.H.E. Hitch

Different writng at bottom of page:
Jan the 6 1864 to day was brought Home the flower of two bushels Jan 6 1864
John J. Hitch
------next page
April 19th Commenced planting corn
April 23rd Finished planting corn
April 24th Finished beding cotton land
April 23rd Beans kild by frost
Sunday 25 A cold cloudy day

Brought home to day from mill the flour of two and a half bushels of wheat. April 24 Y.H.E. Hitch
Wednesday morning April 28th A killing frost the fruit all or the biggest part of it killd I suppos
April 24th Bruce's Children came here today & left the 1st of May. John himself staid all night 1st May.

------next page
May 1st Planted cotton seed and goober peas. ---
May 2nd A Sunday the skie hazy & muddy looking very warm to.---

June 16th Laid by the bottom on the other side the branch.
Saturday 19th Laid by the other side of the creek or begun it.
June 20th A warm dry day & not mutch appearance of rain to be seen.

Mr. Y.H.E. Hitch June the 18 18 John J. Hitch Dec 1st
Young Hitch Mary an
------next page
June 24 Bartered at Greenville C.H. with Mr. Ray

Twenty two & half dozen Eggs	*$2.25*
Five & three fourths lbs Butter	*$0.85*

	$3.10
Thirty six lbs Bacon	*$3.60*

	$6.70
Bleaching 6 yds 10 cts per yd	*$0.60*
Linen 2½ yds 60 cts per yd	*$1.30*
Pants 1½ yds 37½ per yd	*$0.50*
Alpaca 1 yd 37½ per yd	*$0.37½*
Bottle Oil 25 cts	*$0.25*
Needles 5 cts	*$0.05*
¼ lbs pepper 20 cts per lb	*$0.05*
Soda 10 cts 1 lb	*$0.10*
½ lb Ginger 12½ cts per lb	*$0.06¼*
Pair of Scissors 37½	*$0.37½*
Four deep plates 30 cts	*$0.30*
½ lb Starch 10 cts per lb	*$0.05*
One set Knives & forks	*$0.75*

	$4.75¾

------next page

1 ball of Shoe thread	*$0.05*
1 Gimblet 5 cts	*$0.05*
1 Box of blacking 5 ct	*$0.05*
4 yds Braid 4 cts per yd	*$0.04*
2 yd Ribbon 7½ cts per yd	*$0.15*
Shirt Buttons 10 cts	*$0.10*
Bolt of Sheeting 37 yd 7 ct per yd	*$2.59*

	$3.03

	$4.75
One dollars worth of coffee	*$1.00*
7 lbs	
Fish hooks 5 cts	*$0.05*
Candys 15 cts	*$0.15*

	$8.98
	$6.70

	$2.28

(Bottom of page written by different hand)
The third Sundy in June there was a grate flush in the Turtle Creek
The year of our Lord 1867.
------next page
June 25th There fell a heavy shower of rain about 12 oclock at this place.
June 26th at five oclock P.M. a good rain fell nice to doo good.

Sowed some stubble land today in peas for the first this season.

July 7th Finished laying by corn
on the same day ploughed out the potatoes
The cow cald Beaut brought a young calf up Tuesday 29 of June.
The cow called Sarah brought a young calf up Wednesday 7th of July 1858.
Young H.E. Hitch
------next page
July 10.. dressed out the garden and taken up unions
A very warm day this but a fine growing time for all growths
July 14th Finished sowing peas to day P.M.

(Bottom of page, different ink)
This is a cloudy day Sunday dec the 13th 1863
When this you see remember Me Though ded and burred I may be
John Joseph Camiller Hitch Young Hitchs Sun
Dec the 13 1863
------next page
Wednesday 18th 19 days and a half
Thursday 19th
Friday 20th
Saturday 21st
Monday 14th Sept 58 made sash untill Friday 12 oclock then made a door shutter that evening
Monday 22nd Shutter & chim
Tuesday 23rd ney borad
Wednesday 24

Thursday 25   Thursday 25
Friday 26
Saturday 27   Days 27.50

Bought on borrowed of John Edwards 26½ lbs beef
Young Hitch Nov 13 1858
------next page
Wednesday morning 21st of July went after J.B. Edwards chest of tools. He worked that day out for me & Thursday at Mr. Edwards.
A friday untill twelve for me after twelve I took a load of corn & bacon up to his house for him.
Monday 26th of July
Tuesday 27
Wednesday 28 for Mr. Edwards
Thursday 29th
Friday 30th
Saturday until twelve after twelve went to mill
------next page
Friday 23 of July sold to J.B. Edwards four bushels of corn at 75 cts per bushel $3.00
J.B. Edwards worked for me
Mo 2nd Aug 58
Tu 3rd Aug 58
We 4th Aug 58
The balence of the week for Mr. Edwards $2.50
Aug 9th on Monday
Tuesday 10th
Wednesday 11th
Thursday 12th the rest of the week for Mr. Edwards
Monday Aug 16th
Tuesday 17th from 12 untill night.

XII. Letter from Caroline L. Brown and Emily (Brown) to Y.H.E. Hitch dated May 30, 1858 from Marshall County, Alabama

Caroline L. Brown and Emily (Brown) Bruce were half-sisters to Young Hitch as was Frances Brown mentioned in the following letter.

Ala. Marshall
May 30 1858

Mr. Y.H.E. Hich
Dear brother
I now take my seat to fulfill the long neglected promise of writing to you. I beg you to excuse me for not doing it before. We are all well except Frances and aunt Margrett. They have been sick but are recovering. I hope we will have good health after we are naturalized to the climate. This seems to be a

great place to make grain but money is allways scarce. every one about will (__) can live (__) but they need not think of finding refinement when they come here for the people are everything else but refined either in manners or morals. Young as you are a farmer I must tell you something about the crops. Corn looks well indeed and wheat did fair to (__) well. I want you to write soon. So no more but remain your affectionate sister.
C. L. Brown
P.S. my beau says to ____ he is well. Caroline

(On same letter)
South Carolina
Laurens District

Dear brother
It has been a long time since I have written to you but I have at (__) found time and opportunity which gladly I embrace. I have passed years without the hope of seeing father or any of my brothers and sisters. But have been blessed beyond expectation in seeing them all again and am now living here with them all and I could be very glad indeed to see you too. I feel like I could talk a week if I could see you. I have never seen the day that I could not have got some one to have written to you but thought it best to let it lie a while. I was verry well satisfied in Mississippi in everything only the lands being so high father wrote to us to come hear and he would give us land. So we have come and he expects to close the trade for a place in a short time and if we get it I am s(et) for life. I have three (girls) and two boys that look like (torn manuscript) *prospect for raising corn. the worst of it is the(re is) no market for it hear. I want you to write to (me). So no more but remain (your affection)-ate sister.*
Emily L.M. B(ruce)

A few lines to Mary... I am doing very we(ll with) chickens and gardening (for a?) new comer. I have wor( ) the few lines you wr(ote) when I was in Mississ(ippi) and I hope you will w(rite) again. So no more.
Emily L.M. B(ruce)

Note: above underlined text in parentheses are conjecture as the letter was torn and words missing.

XIII. Letter from J.C. Brown to Y.H. Hitch dated August 7, 1859 from Marshall County, Alabama

John C. Brown was half-brother to Young Hitch and Caroline (Brown) Lyons mentioned in the letter his half-sister.

Marshall Co Ala
August 7, 1859
Mr. Y.H. Hitch

Dear Sir
I write to inform you where I am which I ought to have done sooner, as I have been here nearly two months, but I have been too busy to write letters. I left Florida on the 8th of June and arrived here on the 14th. I was teaching a school in Maddison Co., Fla., but having a small school I concluded to abandon it,

and took a notion to come back here. I traveled on foot and by a stage conveyance up to Albany, the terminal of the Southwestern railroad, took the car at 3 o'clock p.m. and at 10 o'clock found myself in the city of Macon. This is a large city and I should have liked to have spent a day here, but for the expense. At 12 o'clock I took the Macon & Western train, an against daylight I could look out at the car window and see the hills and oak woods which was a great pleasure to me after being so long in that low, level, pine woods country. Arrived at Atlanta at 9 o'clock in the morning. I thought it a very cold day, having made so sudden a change of climate, and while I was in Atlanta everybody was complaining of the hot weather, but I could not sit in the shade. After a few days, however, it seemed as hot as in Florida. If I had traveled slowly I should scarsely have perceived the difference of climate. I left Atlanta at 12 o'clock and at 4 in the evening was at Rome. I then took it on foot the rest of the way here, which took me three days. I have been that particular to give the details of my journey, only to fill my space in this letter. I have been at work for father since I have been here. I found his farm in a sad condition, he having had a good for nothing set of hands hired. I am not decided yet whether I shall continue at work or take charge of another school. I would rather have a home of my own and be a farmer, if I could get married; but that is what I can not do. I have traveled a good deal, but have never found the girl yet that would suit me. I am really afraid that I shall be a bachelor for the end of my days. I want you to write to me. Direct to Guntersville, Ala. Caroline wants you to answer her letter. Not Miss Caroline Brown, but Mrs. Caroline Lyons.

Yours truly,
J.C. Brown

XIV. Letter from ____ Hughes to John J. Hitch dated April and May 1860

Interesting two letters addressed to John Joseph Hitch when he was but 12 years old. They seem to be from a 'secret' admirer to whom he paid mutual admiration.

S.C. Laurens Dist
May (__) 1860

Mr Hitch, Dear Sir
It is with the (__) pleasure that I embrace the following opportunity of droping you a few lines to let you know that I am well. hoping that these few lines may find you well. I received a letter from you but it has been so long and I did not write that I was ashamed to write. I want to know why you asked me if I had got in a good humor a Sunday. If I have made you mad I beg pardon for I did not wish to do so and I hope that you will not think I did. You will pleas forgive me for haveing offended you. I do not like to write letter wile I am going to school. I mite have plenty to studdy about without my book. It is a pitty that we are so (__). I can not write anything that would interest you at preasent for times are so very dull now. You wrote that you feared I cared nothing for you. Fear not for I carrie a very warm heart. You must not feel at all slighted. I am so very bashful I feare that you will take a slight when it is not given. I will quit as I expect that I have wrote this so very bad that you cant read it. If you can you will get tired of my noncence and foolishness.
Yours truly (name blacked out) Hughes

Envelope addressed to:

Mr. J.J. Hitch
By the politeness of M Thackston

On a scrap of paper enclosed:
Mr. J.J. Hitch I will send a letter to you to cary to M Edwards. I want you to take it to him in the morning before you go to the Sunday school if you please and don't let nobody see it but him. He will not be there to knight.
your friend
M. Thackston

On another scrap of paper:
Enna___ April 11th 1860
Dear friend
I will write you a few lines to let you know that I have received your letter and that I was glad to hear from you as it had been so long since I have seen you. I felt very much ashamed to wright to you for it the first time that every I attemped to wright to a yong gentenmen but I thought that you would feel slighted if I did not try to wright. I ame to go to the Sunday school if ther doesn't anything happen. (next line illegible) I felt very much ashamed to wright because I am so young to be writing to the young man. I was ashamed to wright you when you wrote me. So I expect I have wrote more than you can read. I expect I will quit. Please excuse bad writing and spelling.
Your true friend. (name cut out)

To Mr. J.J. Hitch

XV. Letter from John C. Brown to Y.H.E. Hitch dated July 3, 1860 from Marshall County, Alabama

Dear Brother
What on earth is the reason you do not write to me? I wrote to you some time ago, I do not recollect exactly when, though it must have been early in the spring; at any rate it was since I received the last letter from you. I suppose, however, that letter never reached you. Caroline has received your letter of May 13, in which you had something to say to every one of the family and kindred, except me and Fayette, and wanted to know where we were. From your not knowing where I was and what I was doing I conclude that you had not received my last letter. I am living this year at Father's, working in the farm, and think I shall be a working man for the rest of my life. I have abandoned the business of school teaching. I intend to work, and devote only a portion of my time to scientific and literary pursuits. Fayette is traveling over the country, sermonizing and selling books, etc. You can write to him either at Guntersville or Houston, Ala. When you write to me, always direct to Guntersville, Ala. We have some very fine looking corn; but if it does not rain within a few days there will be a light crop. We have had abundance of rain this year, but none for the last ten days, and the earth is as dry as it ever gets in a month without rain in your county. We are all well We have a relative with whom you are perhaps unacquainted – a little girl by the name of Ella May Lyons. I should like very much to see you all, but as I cannot have that pleasure the next thing to it is to have a long letter from you – write often. You invited Fayette over to dine with you on slice potatoe pye. Now I think myself greatly insulted in not being invited

also; for I am very fond of that sort of pye, especially if they are of Mary Ann's cooking. I am going to a fourth of July celebration to-morrow.
Yours truly,
J.C. Brown
Marshall Co, Ala
July 3, 1860

Y.H.E. Hitch

XVI. Letter from Sarah Hitch to Y.H.E. and Mary Hitch dated July 25, 1860

South Ca. La. Dis.
July 25th 1860

Dear nephew and niece. I have seated my self this evening tho weak and feeble to try to write a few lines to you to tell you I am tolerable well only at present. I have not enjoyed but very little good health since I saw you last. A part of the time I have been confined to my bed. This morning I had a disagreeable head ache it went of and left a weakness which I still feel at this time I am a trying to write. I hope if these few lines should reach you that they will find you and your little family all well. Uncle Henrys family is well at present uncle Louthers is well as far as I know. There is not very much sickness at this time in the neighborhood. Tho there has been some very sudden deaths around us. The crops about in this section looks solem. To look at corn fields it looks awfully discouraging. Uncle Hs corn in the spring looked beautiful but in consequence of the draught it has dried up and withered so that it looks cribs will almost remain empty. Not only his but I hear it from different parts and places. But now let us pause and think from whence comes all the blessings that we do or ever have enjoyed it looks like a scourge sent on us as a nation and for what. Not for our righteousness. But for our sins. And now my beloved nepew I want to hear from you very much if you have never yet taken up the Cross and come out on the Lords side. I wanted to have a conversation with you on that subject while I was at you house but I put it of till Sunday when going to church. I thought I would have an opportunity of talking it all over. True it is a cold and lifeless time of religion amongst Christians at this time. but my beloved nephew if God for Christ's sake hath pardoned your sins its your duty to confess him before men. For he hath said in his holy and blessed word. He that is ashamed to confess me before men him will I be ashamed to confess before my Father and his holy Angels. O Young you don't know how it would rejoice my heart to hear that you had found Him of whom moses in the law and the prophets did write Jesus of Nazareth. And had come out from the world and joined Gods Holy army to help to fight against the enemy of Gods people. For he is said in scripture to be going about as a roaring lion seeking whom he may devour. I received a letter a few days since from Katharine Stewart. She said in her letter that your old father in law had become convinced and believed it to be his duty to follow his Savior into the watry grave. O Young when I heard of it I though surely surely if Young had religion that such a sight as that would stir him up to a true sence of his duty. And now my beloved nephew can you say with a clear conscience before your God that you never have at no time felt it your duty to join the Church and be baptized. If you have now I beseech you in the name of my Master to put it not of by saying I am too mean and I am not fit you may say too. I see so many of the professed followers of Christ that act do and say things that I dare not. But my beloved nephew does that make it any less your duty to do what your Savior has commanded you to do. I think not. I have tried in

my weak way to pray to my Heavenly Father for you, that he would direct and show you your duty if he never has and grant you grace and strength to perform the same. I want you to remember that the time is short when we shall all have to bid this world adieu prepared or not. So my dear nephew if you think you are not a fit subject for baptism, I pray you be up and a doing. Give not sleep to your eyes nor slumber to your eyelids till you have found Christ presious to your soul. the chiefest amongst ten thousand and altogether lovely. I fear that I will make my letter too long so that you will become tired of reading it. If you can read it atall. But I can not leave of until I talk a little to Mary Ann. My dear niece I doubt not but you pray to God dayly in behalf of your beloved companion. Pray on sister and continue to pray. It may be God will hear and answer your prayers in his own good way and time. I must now begin to draw to a close. I want you to be sertain to write when you receive this and I don't want it to be long for I feel that my sojourn here cant be long and O if I could feel a full assurance that I should be received at God's right hand. I care not how soon for there is no real pleasure in this poor world. Young I do want you and Mary Ann come and see us old people one time. I say one time. I want you to write to me Mary and tell about your fathers affliction experience and baptism. So Fare you well at present
Sarah Hitch

XVII. Letter from William P. Edwards to Y.H.E. and Mary Ann Hitch dated March 11 1861 from Marshall County, Alabama

Alabama Lauderdal County
March the 11 1861

Dear brother and sister
I have seated my self this beautiful morning to rite a few lines to you all to let you hear from me one more time I am not very well but able to work hoping thes lines will find you all in good helth I hant mutch time to rite and not mutch to rite more than the times is hard money is scarse as hen teeth. YHE this is one thing that I want to knowe if you will let me knowe hit that is why is the reason that I (__) yet no anser from father is hit the reason that he don't get my letters or is hit that he don't rite to me I have rote 2 or 3 letters and no anser yet and I want to hear from him and hear howe he is I wod of come and seed him tho I did not have the money to come on and that is my excuse and all of my excuses and cood not get hit for the best of men hant got nor cant get. I want you to rite as soon as you get thes lines for I want to hear from you all and hear howe you all is I must close in a short time for (__) are waiting. I want you to rite whither South Carolina has with severed from the union or not and what tha are doing ther. tha have caried thing big hear tho tha are sorter settling down like a warme of bees since Cing li wham (apparently a reference to Representative Sydenham Moore) has taken his seet. I don't hear mutch noyes nowe all camm as a lamb tha was a grait noyes that he shod not take his seet tho I heard that he had taken hit. Thes big men cood not get thos little men to goe and keep him from his seet. I must close in short I want you to rite as soon as you get thes lines (__) more at this time only. I remain yor brother until death so fare well for this time.
Wm P. Edwards
Y.H.E. Hitch
Mary Hitch

Mary Ann I wod bee glad to rite to you tho I hant time tho I was with some pretty galls yesterday. You out to see them tho I aind mared yet and I don't expect to marry in a good while yet if I ever do. I want you to rite how large Joseph is and tell him I hant forgot him yet rite whether ther is eney pretty galls ther or not. So no more at this time
Wm. P. Edwards
Maryan Hitch

XVIII. Letter from G. Lafayette Brown to Young Hitch dated June 25, 1861 from Moulton, Alabama

Gilbert Lafayette Brown (1834-??) was Young Hitch's half-brother and is listed as a "Christian Clergyman" in the 1860 Census for Winston County, Alabama.

Moulton Ala June 25th 1861

To Yong Hitch
Dear brother
I have writen to you several times and hav received now answer what is the matter are you yet in the land of the living or not. Hav you forgot G.L. Brown or are you determined never to write to me again. I wrote to you last fall. Shortly after I was married. And I forgit where I said for you to address me at. If you hav written to me at Guntersville I supos that some of fathers family would hav forwarded the letter to me. I now write to let you know whare I am my address etc and if you do not write me you never expect to git another line from me.
Yours till death with out an answer
G.L. Brown

Well young I hav not an angel for a wif but as near so as any human being on earth but She is a good little wife I am devoting the energies of my life to the building up of a kingdom that can not be moved If you think worth while to write to me mark your letters to G.L. Brown Moulton Ala. Dear Brother do you ever expect to be a Christian or will you live and enjoy the blessings of God and never obey the easy Gospel of Christ. What think you but you say how can I turn a Christian or how can I obey the commands of Christ: I answer
1st believe in Christ with all thy heart (that you do and hav done for years)
2nd Repent of all you Sins that is Sins to do bad and born to do well (that you hav partly don for you have so far as you could Seased to do eavil for years. now if you will learn to do well by or in obeying the gospel all will be right So far as repentance is concerned)
3th Confess the nam of Jesus Christ as the Son of God with the mouth before men.
4th then arise and be Baptised and wash away your Sins calling on the Nam of the lord: Acts 22 ch and 19 verse Allso Acts 2 ch and 38 verse
Then if you will do what I hav said do (__) ward for it you will be pardoned by the lord.
But you say must I not not hav evidence of pardon before I be Baptised. I say emphatically now you ask again if I must not hav assurance of grace before I be Baptised. I say now you are required to relate an experience to get into a Baptist Church But not to get into Christs Church. what then should be required of me before I am Baptised. See Acts 8th ch and 37 verse with the conviction. You say then I don't believe

in experience then I say I do for I believe in all the Bible sais any thing about but I don't believe in a person having all the Experience he ever has before he is Baptised. in Romans 5th ch 4 verse with the conviction is all that the Bible sais about Experience. (__) you see that after a person has been a Christian for years he has experienced som things (__) he has some things to tell. Now you may learn from Example how persons became Christians in the days of the apostles. You will find an account of all of the conversions recorded in the bible in the acts of apostles. In the 2nd chapter we have an account of 3 thousand being converted in one day. In the 3 or 4 chapters of 5 thousands. In the 8th Chapter of all Samary and so on (__) three. And you will see also that persons coud believe repent confess and be Baptised the same day the saime hour of the knight. Now will you have the patience to Examine all the cases of conversions or turnings to the lord recorded in that book. It is all contained in the following short sentences. Do good and you will feel good. Com to the point whare God has promised to pardon you. Then you can believe that you are pardoned. Then you can feel good and happy because you believe you are pardoned. But I have spun this out longer than I thought I would at the start. So God bless you a your family. Let me know how your boys are growing off.

XIX. Two Letters from W.P. Edwards to Y.H.E. and Mary Hitch dated September 11, 1861 from Lauderdale County, Alabama with codicil from J.P. Garrett

Ala Lauderdal County
Sept 11th 1861

Dear brother and sister
I again take the blezure of droping you a few lines to let you know that I am in tolable helth kindly hoping these lines will find you in the same state of helth I hant mutch to rite to you more than I receive a letter from you whitch gave me plezure to hear from you and to hear that you was well and I receive one from father whitch gave me great Sadisfaction to hear of him and to hear that he was no worse off than he had bin for some time An I will be glad to see him and all of the rest tho I don't expect to see eney of you soon if ever for money is very scarce in deed and ther is two parties in this country not so mutch tho as there is in this Lyneing stat of tennisee whitch I am on the line I ben hear of devilment being done rite close by hit tis thought that hit is the younion men that dos hit Throweing down fence and puling up corne and I wod not bee badly so soprized if ther aint a little battle fought here after a while tho the most of the union men says that if tha has to fight tha will fight for the sothern confederate stats I have bin tending to a grocery for the last month tho I expect to quit tomorrow and hier to pull fodder and after fodder gathered I don't know what I shall doo. Mr Reynolds sed the other day that he expected he wod want me to help him till this winter and if he dont I expect I shal volunteer to protect our little confederate stats. You tell Father that I wod rit more to him but I thought I wood writ a week or tenn days and a maby I wood have something knew to rite to him About and I am yet Single and expect to remain so for some time yet wheat crops was very good and corne crops in tolable good. Mary I might drop you a few lines to let you knowe that I hant forgot you yet and I wod bee glad to see you tho I aint able to come to see you and I will ackolege that I hant don as I ought of don or I wood of bin able to of come bee fore nowe tho if this ware wod sop(?) I wod make my self able to come and I wod come tho I don't know when I ever will come or whither ever or not tho if life last long enouf I ame to come one more time if I don't goe to the ware and if I doo and live to see hit ended I will come then and I want you

to rite to me as son as you get thes lines. So this morning I will bid you a dew for a while so I remain you brother until death
W.P. Edwards
Y. H.E. Hitch
Mary Hitch

Ala Lauderdal County
Sept 11th 1861
===
Alabama Lauderdal County
September 11th/61

Dear brother and sister
I take the plezure of droping you a fewe lines to let you knowe that I have heard that my father seems like that he is dissadusfide and I have heard howe things is Young on thear and I think that he is dissadusfide on the o count of the weiy that tha are a many doing and I want you to find out and send me word an if that is hit I will come if I have to walk. I shoad that letter that I got from that friend to J.P. Garrett and eney of you find out hoo sent hit to me no he want tell hoo sent hit to me. I heard hit from a friend and I recon you all wonder hoo hit tis tho you all may wonder tho you wont find out from me. I wod of thought that you or Mary or some of you wod of rote to me how things was going on ther nowe. I have heard of howe things is going on I recon you will rite as I ask you to doo hit and I want you to find out what he is dissadusfide him and send me word and it hit tis eney thing that I can do I will try to sadusfie him so I want you to rite as soon as you get these lines no more at this time
W P Edwards

Y.H.E. Hitch
Mary Hitch

On the next page in a different handwriting:
At Capt A.P. Reynolds
(__) YHE Hitch tell the boys that I and family are all well at this time.
Sept the 11th 1861
J.P Garrett
Cosen mary one thing I wish to know if you pleas as a friend that is about them goslings thoes they are yours (__) (__).
J.P. Garrett
South Carolina Laurens District

XX. Letter from S.R. Thackston to Young Hitch dated October 7, 1861 from "Army of the Potomac", Fairfax County, Virginia

An interesting letter that discusses….

Flint Hill

Advance forces Army of the Potomac
Fairfax County Va
Monda Oct 7th

Mr Young Hitch Dear Sear

I have thaugh evry since I have bin in oald Virginia I would try to write a few lines in a way to let you know how I am gitting a long I had tolerable health until I had the measles. Since then my health hant bin so very good I think that I am improving we have bin exposed so much no wonder our health has bin bad. I don't recon I art to grumble my life has been spared while many others has bin taken a way from them. I have nothing new to write to you.

War the cry we air looking for a fight constant and the most of the men think hit will be in a few days. Let hit come and I think wele whip the fight at least I hope so. We have bin here in sight of our enemy for some time and I have had a peasable time only the last few days they have got roused up a little. I think if we get engaged agin that we will sette the fuse. if not I think it will be a longe war.

They had a fight a few days ago in the western part of this state whitch our side ganed a grait victory. I cant tell you how many was kild in the fight but our men kild and taken prisen. General Rozencrantz they did not hit General Rozencrantz but wound him and taken all his forces that was good. I wish we could git some more of their generals. He was won of their (___) men. So I learn this news was got from this one paper. I have bin hearin a pur heavy firen all the morning down near Washington. I expect they are fighten. If so you wil hear from hit be fore many days.

Tell Cosin Mary I would be glad to see her and tell her all about the Virginia girls. Also tell Bery and Phratus to write to me. So I will close by requesting you to write to me

S.R Thackston
Looke over al bad speling and writin and write soon and give me the news E.R. and maning and Lacy is well. So hope these few bad spelt and written lines may come to hand in dew time and find you all well give my love and respects to all enquiren frends if they be any such
your truly S.R Thackston

XXI. Receipt from E. Watson to Y.H.E. Hitch for Confederate States War Tax dated July 12, 1862

July 12, 1862

Received of Y.H.E. Hitch Five Dollars and 25 cents for War Tax of the Confederate States under Act of Assembly of SC passed Dec, 1861.
War Tax $5.25
Less 5 percent on .26
Amount paid before 31st July 1862 $4.99

E. Watson T.C.

XXII. Note from Capt. S.D. Thackston to Y.H.E. Hitch to be Captain of a patrol dated August 16, 1862 at a Camp near Charleston, South Carolina

Mr. Y.H.E. Hitch

You are hereby appointed Capt of the patrol in beat company (___) with the men whose names are hereunto anexed. You will ride at least once a fortnight and make return on oath the 2 Saturday in Oct. next.

This August 16, 1862
S.D. Thackston, Capt

On the back:
L.B Edwards
J.J. Brown
Goodin Parsons
(_) Thackston

On back of order is written:

Times we rode patrol
Monday, Sept 8
Sunday Sept 14
Thursday, Sept 25
Sunday Sept 28
Wednesday, Oct 8
Camp near Charleston S.C.

LETTERS (UNTIL MARCH 1863) DATING FROM YOUNG HITCH'S TIME IN COMPANY C, 9TH SOUTH CAROLINA RESERVES

XXIII. Letter from Y.H.E. Hitch to Mary A. Hitch dated December 8, 1862

Dec 8. 1862

Dear wife I seat myself to drop you a few lines to inform you of my health and wherabouts. I am at this time enjoying tolerable health, better than I expected to after being broke of my rest as I have been. I arived at this place Charleston yesterday morning at three oclock. The night after I left home I slept none. The next night I left Columbia at dusk & got to this place at three. I then with others gathered up my good with the exception of my box, that I had to leave until morning. I went back to the Depo in the morning & got my box. When we left the car we started for the Camp a mile from the depo & just after we started we met some of our men coming to meet us. When we got to the camp we warmed by there good fires in Camp. Myself and A.Y. crawled in to W.H. Hughes & J.M. Edwards tent to sleep I got good warm & slept good. Yesterday Sunday myself & Capt. Stewart. & others went to see the brest works. We got back in time to hear Uncle Tol Robertson preach & I hope to be able to hear him again as he is going to preach here on the coast. Mary we had some good singing in camp last night the preacher gave out some hym books & some of the soldiers was using them. Mary I haven't any news to write. I think they are looking for the Legislator to do some thing before there is any alteration made in this Regiment. The regiment in good health so far as I know. J.J. & A.L I have seen a great deal but cannot tell you now.
Y.H.E. Hitch

Envelope addressed to
Mrs. Mary A. Hitch
L st So C
Dec 8

XXIV. Letter from Young H.E. Hitch to Mary Hitch dated December 10, 1862 from Charleston, South Carolina

Charleston South Carolina
Dec 10. 1862

Dear Mary
My health is not verry good to day. I did not drill this morning not being unable. I have take a fresh cold since I left home. This evening I feel a great deal better. Last night I sufferd severly with head achk. My back & hips is verry sore just now but hope to be better Soon. I do hope this may find you & our two sons enjoying a reasonable share of health. J.M. left here last night. I sent some word to you about a bed tick & knapsack & haversack. You can make them & have them ready so if John Garrett brings a box you can send them to his house & if he cant, mabe some one els will be coming that you will have a chance to send them. Mary don't put yourself to to mutch trouble for so long as we remain here I can do verry well without those things but if we should move I then will need them. If it is so that you can you may send me some butter and onions. I have not tasted my butter yet I have 25 or 26 cakes yet. Jonas can tell you

more than I can write to you about our fare & what we are a doing here. Joseph and Lucian two large guns was drawn up here today eight horses each large enough for a man to put his head in the mussel. Dear Sons be good to your Ma. Mary I cant write that that you wish to hear yet. But try & do the best you can. I hope that I will be able to give you the newes. So I bid you farewell.
Young H.E. Hitch

Mrs. Mary Hitch

XXV. Letter from Mary A. Hitch to Y.H.E. Hitch, undated (but possibly December 1862)

Letter from Mary

(Undated)

I could not get much sence from A.Y. You must gess what was the matter. I want you to write to me what you wish me to send to you. I will send you enny thing that you want that I can send you. I want you to rite to me wether you have the measles. I dred to hear from you for fear you have them. I dred them for you. I want you to rite to me wether you got your bed tick and napsack. I want you to rite to me as soon as you git this letter so I can send by A.Y. Garrett. he ses I can git an (__) from you befor he start back. I must close nin short.
Mrs Mary A. Hitch

Y.H.E. Hitch
Young I must send you that 20 dollars bill to you.

Back of letter:
Git off if you can do so how happy I wood be
I hant ben to preaching since you left me.
Addressed to: Y.H.E. Hitch, Confidential

XXVI. Letter from Young Hitch to Mary Hitch, undated (possibly December 1862).

Mary I have not tried to get of yet perhaps I will soon. I may be mistaken but I think my chance is better than it has been but if I do get off it may be after Christmas before I can leave camp. You may think that I could come as well as A.Y. Garrett but Mary, I could not of got through with that barrel of salt. And in the next place I am not lucky as some & to act as some do I wont. I am above quirking like some. W.H. Hughes for one a good Baptist. As to my mess I can get along with them. I must close in short. Let me hear ever chance. Here is a form to back your letter.

On the back:
Mary Hitch
Confidential

XXVII. Letter from Young H.E. Hitch to Mary Hitch and his sons, dated December 20, 1862 from Camp Means, Charleston, South Carolina

Young H.E. Hitch
Camp Means Charleston S.C.
Dec. 20, 1862

Dear wife I am yet through the blessing of God in the land of the living. Although I am somewhat pestered with pains. This morning I verry unexpectedly met up with J.B. Edwards & from him I got some news from home whitch I was truly glad to receive. Mary you don't know what a pleasure it was to me to hear from you. John stayed but a short time, but took dinner with us & then I went a piece of the way home with him. He insisted on me a going home with him but I did not go. But promise to go the first opportunity. He is stationed some seven miles from here on the other side of the branch as some call it. I am looking for John Garrett back hopeing to get late newes by him. We all like to hear from home. The sun has set & no John Garrett yet I was verry mutch in hopes he would arrive to night. Mary if you wish to know our fare I can give it. We get corn meal & beef a plenty. Then we get potatoes, rice and sugar vinnegar soap and candles. Our allowance of salt is rather small. We our mess had to by a quart the other day. Mary so long as we get as mutch as we have been getting we will not perish. I can boil beef & bake bread pretty well. Mary I have no newes of importance to write only we have verry cold weather & our soldiers have severe colds & caughs. We also have some measles in camp. Yesterday or the day before their was a man taken from camp to the hospital said to be a case of the measles. This morning their was another taken of one that was sitting by our fire yesterday a few moments. So if I do not get them it will be Providence providing better for me. I dread them & worst of all there is several others with myself to have them. Joseph I made every word of your letter out. I got a little stalled at the part where you wrote about G.T. Hughes wedding not thinking of sutch a thing.
Dear sons myself & Capt Stewart last night went down to the Depot to see if any of our folks had come down. And while standing looking on at the passengers get aboard the Augusta train I saw an old man come along with several bundles to put them on board the car & as he was handing them in he dropt one bundle on the ground near a young man that was sitting close by. Boys what do you think this youth did why sirs instead of his pict it up & giving it to the old man as an honest yout should he slipt it up to his feet the old man got a board the car & the youth put the bundle in his own knapsack. Dear sons you cant guess what I then thought of my thoughts was these. Is it possible that Each Either of my sons whoo I have tried to teach better should be guilty of sutch a crime. But I sincerely hope better of them. O that they may be better boys. Mary I don't have any pertickular use for Money just now an if you can't make the change after paying for you salt just let it aloan. I have bin thinking if salt still keeps falling I would get some more. The payrool has bin made out but when we will get pay I don't know it may be in a few days or it may be several. So I thought A.Y. probably would be the best chance to bring me any thing from home. please hunt up one of them old knives and a fork. I don't care if the prongs of the fork isn't but one in long its just good enough to loose or get stolen here. A.Y. is going to bring a box & you can drop them in. Joseph Every thing ma sends you rap & tie it up then put my name on them so when they are put in with others they will be known. Some are forgetfull whitch is whitch.

Boys Pa has not got the measles yet. I must close.
Here is the form of address for you to put on your letters

Y.H.E. Hitch Charleston
9# Regt 1st corp of Reserves
In care of Capt William Stewart

Letter includes envelope.
On the front is:
To Mrs Mary A. Hitch
Laurens S.C.
J.J. Hitch

On the side of the envelope is:
Favored
By .W. H. Hughs

On the back of the envelope is:
Mr. Y.H.E. Hitch
Adams run 16 regt S.C.
In care of Capt N. Babb

XXVIII. Letter from Young H.E. Hitch to Mary Hitch and his sons, dated December 22, 1862 from Camp Means, Charleston, South Carolina

Dec. 22. 1862
Camp Means Charleston

Dear wife again I take my pen in hand to drop you a short letter. Mary I have nothing of great importance to write. But as A.Y. Garrett is going to start home I will drop you a few lines. I can say to you that I am well with the exception of bad cold & pains. I haven't drilled any to day we are not compeled to drill if we are not well. John Garrett landed last night with the Articles you sent to me also your letter whitch I was glad to receive. And thankfull to hear that you was all upon foot whitch we should all be. A.L. you ast me to come & eat squirrels with you. Dear son I would gladly come & dine with you if it was so that I could But as I cant come to help you you must eat my part & yours both. A.L. I will send you some rice for your Ma & some salt to salt your part with.
Mary you wish me to come home Christmas. Willingly would I comply with your request. But mary those whoo come here first all want furloughs & it would cost me at least ten dollars to visit home. But I think if I live I will come before the time is out to see you. Ten days & cost ten dollars is pretty tough.
Joseph glad to hear that you have your grain all sowed and that your taters is sound. Eat of them all you can for our tatar here are roting fast. J.J. A.L. & your Ma must go to se gran Pa at Christmas times.
Joseph you said you was verry loansom & wished to see me. Dear Son I hope you don' feel more so than I do myself. And you may think that I might return home again, but is you was situated as I am you might do diferenly
Young H.E. Hitch to
Mary Ann Hitch
J.J. Hitch

A.L. Hitch

Written on front of envelope: Mary A Hitch at Home
Dec 22 1862
Written on side on envelope: In the Politenss of A.Y. Garrett
Written on back of envelope: Young. H.E. Hitch J.J.

XXIX. Letter from Mary A. Hitch and John J. Hitch to Young H.E. Hitch dated December 25, 1862 from Laurens District, South Carolina

South Carolina Laurens District
Dec 25th 1862

Dear Young I seat mi self to drop you a few lines to let you know I am gitting along not so well. I just con eat a nuff to keap onn foot When I set down I think of Young fair I am full I go all day & don't eat as much as I aught to eat at one meal I hope the time will soon cum that mi Joy will be as grate as mi Sorrows is Now Young Pa has ben verry kind so fair sent & had me som wood hold. he told me when I buirnt that up he wood send then & hold me more.Young ever time I git a letter from you PA want me to bring them & read them to him Young I want you to thank him for his kindness towards me in your next letter So I bid you farewell.
Mary A. Hitch } Y.H.E. Hitch

Back of letter
South Carolina Laurens District Dec the 25th 1862

Dear PA I receive your letter the 25 I was sorry to hear you back was sour yet I hant got much to rite we ar all on fat to day & I thank God ar it. PA. AY took dinner with us to day. PA I must tell you how much our spoted hog waid. He was fat you ma depend. PA gran pa had our wood hold for us. PA I want you to write as soon as you git this letter for I want to know wether you want enny thing if you do wee will send it by AY. Pleas rite what you ruther have. I want to knoo this is a dull Christmass with us. PA I must close for it is time to feed. rite soon forgive mi bad riting & spelling.
JJ Hitch

Y.H.E Hitch

Envelope addressed to Y.H.E. Hitch, 9th Reg, 1st Corp of Reserves
in care of Capt Stewart Charleston

XXX. Letter from John and Rebekah Edwards to Y.H.E. Hitch dated January 5, 1863

Confederate States of America Jan 5 1863

Dear (__)
I seat my self this Evening for the perpos of Droping you a few line for the first time. We are all well as common & Mary & the children is two & hoping when thes Few lines comes to your hand they will find you enjoying the same good Blessing & the rest of your old friends. Wm Scruggs & Family & C.P & Samantha is well but little John is very bad sick with throwing up & running off at the Bowels Dear Yon I have no news of importance to write no more Edward Hughes got himself married the other night to Miss Caroline Parson & at the infaire Mr. William Jone got his white horse leg broke, the left fore leg right above his nee I believe the latest news I have no I forgoton Mr. Henry Linsey decease Dec 31st & was buried Jan. 1, 1863 at Cedar Grove. Dear Mary has kill one of her hogs & it waid very well it waid 220 lbs neat so I will turn over.

Back of letter:
Dear Brother I wish you to excuse my bad writing & spelling so I must this time in short so write soon if you have the chance. So remember all of your friends
John Edwards E.L.E.
Rebekah Edwards L.B.E.
To Mr Y.H.E. Hitch

XXXI. Letter from Young H.E. Hitch to sons Joseph and Lucian Hitch, undated (but possibly 1863)

Undated (possibly 1863)
Joseph and Lucian Hitch
Boys, we have just drawn our guns. We have drawn Enfield rifles this evening. Boys, I feel just like I could take a few pops at a Yankey with my gun. It is not near so heavy as I supposed it would be. Lucian, I have seen the largest river that I ever saw. Joseph, I visited the slaughter house Sunday evening. Saw them butcher eleven beeves in a few minutes. You see I wanted to see what sort of beef I have to eat. Joseph, feed the hogs good and get them fat. Perhaps I will get some salt for you to salt them with. Lucian, you feed the sheep good and keep them alive if you can.

Young H.E. Hitch

XXXII. Letter from Young H.E. Hitch to Mary A. Hitch, undated (but probably Jan 1863)

Dear wife

I have read the letter from you. Your letter found me enjoying pretty good health. You stated you was not verry well and that you could not eat for thinking about my fare. Mary I do cincerely hope that you not study so mutch about that. One thing I want you to do, that is not to believe half you hear. If you do you may allways expect to be in troble. Mary if you could be here & here the lies that is told it would make you shudder just to think what tales men tell. Mary instead of studying about my fare so mutch. Ask him

that is able to prepare some way for us better than we can see. I think that I have had help from above. Since it has bin so ordered that we should be separated I am verry certain that I have been blessed beyond my expectations. Probably you think this reg is all down with the measles. To the best of my knowledge there has been three cases of the measles only & they have been taken to the hospital. I have not had them yet. I take good care of myself for fear that I may take them. Capt Stewart, Hand E. Holcombe & two or three others in this camp has never had them. Mary sorry to hear that you have not heard any preaching since I left you. I have been at church ever Sunday since I left home. I dont know when the opportunity may cease. I prefer going to church to sitting in camp. Mary I hope my prospects for eternity is brightening. I have nothing mutch to tell but little as it is I prize it verry high. I hope to see home once more then we can talk. Mary you stated that your father has been verry kind to you. I am verry glad to hear & to think that someone is kind enough to assist you in my absence. I have tried to ask help for you as well as for myself. Tell Mr. Edwards I thank him kindly for his kindness to you. Allso tell him to please excuse me for not writeing to him for I have not wrote to no one but my own folks yet but I knew that he would hear from them. I thought when I was at home, that one a week would be as often as I would want to write but it is not. Mary I wrote the 25 what I wanted. First to pay A.Y. Garrett for the salt he takes you & the freight on it. 2nd you may bake me some corn dodgers in the oven or a light pone of either corn or wheat. If you have any hog head and feet soused send some of it. Coffee, send me a little bunch more & one of them old knives and forks. Instead of Twenty dollars send me Ten. I hope I will not need that mutch. I have spent $7.12 cts since I left home. Write soon & let me know if you got the salt & my likeness. I am afraid it never reach you. I received the articulars you sent me. Please wrap up all you start to me & put my name on it so it will be known. Joseph your hog weighed well, if you can make the other as good you can do pretty well Mary it is gitting late & I must close by saying that I hope to be at home before long but if it is God's will otherwise let us submit without a murmur. Let us trust in him so long as we live and pray that if we never meet on earth we may meet in Heaven. So fare you well.
To Mary A Hitch From Young H.E. Hitch
We are not equipt yet & until we are we will remain here.

XXXIII. Letter from Y.H.E. Hitch to Mary A. Hitch dated January 10, 1863 from Camp Means, Charleston, South Carolina

Camp Means Charleston S.C. Jan. 10th 1863

Dear wife I embrace the present opportunity of writing you a short letter to inform you that I am Enjoying a reasonable share of health at present. And hoping this may find you & our sons Enjoying the same like blessing. I have but little news to write. But as Capt Stewart is going home I will send you a few lines. We had some neighbors to come in Thursday evening last three regs of Georgians but the same night at one or two oclock they got orders to leave for N.C. so they left before daylight. Mary, I was vacinated yesterday evening. A great many were vacinated in the regt yesterday. The measles have not caught me yet but I don't know how soon they may. Mary I have been thinking about coming home & I hardly know what to do. If I can't get off next week the time will be so short that I hate hate to be at the expense & run the risk on the road home the old cars run of so often. I would like verry mutch to see home again & hope that I may some of these days. Some say our time will be out the 5th of Feb. & some say the 17th of Feb. but I don't know when the time will be out. But let it be long or short, I am in for the war. Those over 40 may be out when the 90 days are out. But if I should not get to come home before the

90 days is out, I hope then I can come and stay awhile with you. Mary, tell your father that I am stationed at Camp Means one mile from Charleston & am able to eat cornbread & beef & it seems to agree with me. Tell him that I weigh 154 lbs. Saturday 10. So I must close, farewell Mary A. Hitch }
Y.H.E. HItch

On back of letter:
Mrs. Mary A Hitch
Jan. 10. 63 the 15
Mr. YHE Hitch

On the side of the back:
In the Politeness of Capt William Stewart

XXXIV. Letter from Y.H.E. Hitch to Mary A. Hitch and his sons dated January 13-15, 1863 from Camp Means, Charleston, South Carolina

Camp Means, Charleston S.C. Tuesday 13th 1863
Dear wife I seat myself this Evening to write you a few lines to inform you of my whereabouts & health. I am tolerable well at this time, a little sore from guard duty. Myself and eleven others were detailed Sunday to guard the Charleston jail. We went on guard half after one oclock & remained on guard until one a Monday. I stood ten hours out of 24. but the night was pleasant & I stood it pretty well. There is several points to be guarded. The regiment that have been guarding those points have left for north carolina. And we have to take there place. We are yet campt at the same place. The jail is about three miles from our camp. We have no drilling all guard duty now. Our regiment is small so it takes us all or near it to guard this town. Boys I spent last Sunday Evening in & around jail, locked up at that. We lay in the jailors office by a stove of fire & slept a little. Oh boys the stinkingest place you every saw, a perfect shit hole, 130 white and 40 black prisoners all our own men, no Yankees in there.
Jan. 14th boys I stood guard again last night at the camp. I guarded the commissary store. I had my choice to stay here or go of to some other station & this was mutch the lightest. Dear Sons I find that the man who trys to do his duty in camp fares the best in some respects. My name come in again to go on guard a Tuesday but my Capt said Hitch should not go again so soon whitch I thank him verry kindly for. Boys, please write & let me hear from you often. So I must close my letter Eat dinner & sleep a little. Hitch to Mary & Sons

Written upside down on the letter;
Jan 15th I am well. We drawed cartridge & cap boxes yesterday.
Hitch

Mary, please write & let me hear from you often for I have not forgotten home & home friends. Let me know whoo shaves your father now, what Scrugs is driving at & W.E. Garrett & what has become of the Grubbs. Let me know whether your Potatos both Irish & Sweet is keeping or not. Tell me how the barley is a growing. Tell how mutch more salt you want. Please excuse this bad spelt & written letter for I am so sleepy & lazy that I cant do mutch better. Tell L.B. I rec. his letter on Sunday evening tell him I was in jail

when it came to hand & will answer it soon as convenient. So I shall quit my scribbling & not weary your patience any longer.
Y.H.E. Hitch.
Jan 14, 1863

On the back of the letter:
Mary perhaps you are looking for me to come home soon. I would like verry mutch to come home but the chance to get of now is not verry good now. I thought of coming this week but I know not whether I can or not. Capt. Stewart has tried to get of a time or tow and faild. So don't look for me until you se me. I am Enjoying Camp better than you may suppose. If I can just have good health & you can Enjoying the same blessing I can do pretty well whitch I do hope may be granted to us, if Capt Stewart should get to come home he will bear this to you. If you can Mary cheer up and be a man. I wanted to be at home next Monday, the 19th of this ist. But fear that I cant. But the 90 days will roll off by-n-by & mabe I can come then & stay a little while at old home again.
Y.H.E. Hitch

XXXV. Letter from Y.H.E. Hitch to Mary A. Hitch and his sons dated January 18, 1863 from Camp Means, Charleston, South Carolina

Camp Means Charleston So. Ca.
Jan 18th 1863

Dear Mary I am only tolerable well today. I have just returned from picket & feel verry mutch werried from losing sleep & being in the cold. We have had verry cold weather for a few days past the coldest winds I ever felt. There is not much ice here but the wind off the rivers is verry cold. Mary, I have been on guard three nights out of eight. The posts we have to guard are in town. The distance from one & a half to four miles from camp. This morning from 6 to 8 I had to guard in a house where the wind could not strike me whitch was a great favor on me. Mary I think you & the boys had better be vacinated get the doctor to vacinate you. My arm is pretty sore but not bad as some yet. Mary you may wish to know whether I intend volunteering or not. Well I cant say what I will do yet. The drum has beat for preaching. Uncle Tol Robertson is to preach to us. Just now rec. your letters & one from E.R. Thackston verry glad to hear from you all. Sorry that I cant give you an answer fully not having the time just now.

(continued letter after preaching) I have been to hear Uncle Tol. text was St. John 14.15. If you love me, keep my commandments. My Capt is to bear this to you if he can get off. If not, I will mail it. J.B. Edwards was well yesterday Saturday 17. I thought I would be at home tomorrow the 19th but it is out of my powers to do so. But hope to see home soon. Dear sons. be good boys and try to get along the best you can and look to him that is able to help. So I must close. But still remain your devoted husband.

Mary A. Hitch } Young H.E. Hitch

To Mrs. Mary A. Hitch
In the politeness of Capt Stewart

XXXVI. Letter from John W. Pitts to Young Hitch dated January 19, 1863 from Simpsonville Post Office, Laurens District, South Carolina

From J.W. Pitts to Young Hitch
South Carolina, Laurens District
Simpsonville PO

Jan the 19 1863

Dear Coson

I will take the pleasure of droping you a few lines to inform you that my health is not much better than it was the last time that I saw you or I would of bin up to of sean you befor now. The wether has bin so coald that I was afraid to turn out. There is som young laides that I promis to come up to sea to and I never has went yet and therefore if you will come down when the wether gets better I will go home with you and stay a week with you and the gals up ther and I want you to rite to me when you will come and let me know whither Miss Cox is married yet or not. If not tell her to hold on till I come up. I never saw her but the one time and that was at the factory. I thought very well on her at that time and maby when I sea her again I will lover still more. I want you to give her my love and respect. She had on a red dress when I saw her.

Dear Coson, I can say to you that my mother still keeps up and about but she is very puny at times. And aint Sally, she is as stout as ever most that is as she has bin for the last year.
Dear coson it is got to be a solem time. the men all that is able to join is gone from this naborhood and a grate many gon that will be of no service in the army & would be here at home. I am as willing to go if I was able as aney body but a camp life is no place for a sick man without he is tired of living, thar he will soon die.
Dear coson I will close for this time by saying to you that I want you to rite to me as soon as you get this and direct your letter to Simpsonville PO Laurens Dist SC.
I will sine my name as your affectionate coson till death. JW Pitts

John W. Pitts, Simpsonville PO, Laurens District
To Young Hitch, Centerville PO. Laurens District, SC

XXXVII. Letter from Mary A. Hitch to Y.H.E. Hitch dated January 20, 1863

Look hear young, if you hant volunteer, dont no wa hit can benefit. don't think hard of me for writing to you to not volumeteer for I think it best from what little I can find out ther is no chance for a man that volumteer to git off.
We are all well this morning the Jan 20th 1863

Y.H.E. Hitch
Mary A. Hitch

XXXVIII. Letter from Mary A. Hitch to Y.H.E. Hitch dated January 24, 1863

South Carolina Laurens District
Jan the 24 1863

Young you say you have ben to preaching ever Sunday since you left home that is more than I can say for I have not heard enny preaching since you left home I cant say when I will Young When you go to Preaching think of Mary and Pray for hear & our two souns. Young I may be Decive but I fell like if it is godds Will to call me I am prepared to go. Young I Want to know wether you aire ready ar not. Young When you rite to me aboute this matter rite hit on a pease to hit self Young pit (Pitts?) Stewart & Crugs has Never ben to See me Sence you left home. they air god brothers laws (sic, brother-in-laws?) they never have ben. they men that sed one time mary if you wont enny thin Dun I will asist you in it. Young I want you to cum home & tell me what I had better do as I Don't now whether Ginney will Git Well ar not. Young if I ever is to See enny More Trubble than I am seeing now it will be a pitty but I try to bair it the best I can Young god is able to help me & I trust he will I will Stop riting for I feair you Cant read what I have rote. Fair Well Dear Young S:C rite son. rite ofting and let me hear from you. The Doctor Sed this morning That he wood Vacinateed us the next week I dredd it for it is pirty hurting Sum Verry bad. the Doctor tet(?) for one he says that it don't go in his arm enny more.
Mary A. Hitch
To Mr. Y H E Hitch

XXXIX. Letter from John J. Hitch to his father Y.H.E. Hitch dated January 28, 1863

1863 J.J. Hitch Jan the 28
South Carolina Laurens District

Dear PA I am enjoying pirty good helth and hoping these few lines Ma find you in good helth I got your letter Standing dated the 21 & I got hit the 28 and I Was glad to hear from you & glad to hear that you was well PA Wee have go Sum New nabors Close bye but I hant ben to See them. Mr. Edward Hughes & Mrs. Caroline Parson is living down at Cusen Mansel place. PA hurry home for I am invited to Candi pullings ever Week but I hant bin to enny uv them I hant forgot my promis yet Shorly you Will Never you Cum home you Will turn Me loose for a few days PA Miss Mary Brown had a candi pulling last week and invited me to it but I did not go to it
PA I never have left MA nairry Night Senc you left home and if I can bea at home with Ma I Will bea hair. PA uncle J.M. Edwards and Aunt Clairry Cum & Staid With us last Night & ther 2 least sons PA the Wa hit snowd last night. PA you mapend Wee had ruf time PA uncl J.M.E hope me cut up Some Wood this morning in the snow Whitch was A grate favor on me. PA if you plea I want you to forgive mi bad riting & spelling but I Do the best I Can PA you Sed A.Y. Garrett give 30 cts for a paper and needles but you think that is a big price a paper and needles hear is A Dollar a paper. I must Close by saing rite soon. Fair Well

J.J. Hitch } YHE Hitch

Envelope addressed to Mr Y.H.E. Hitch 9th Regt 1st corps of Reserves, Charleston, SC
In care of Capt William Stewart

XL. Letter from Mary A. Hitch to Y.H.E. Hitch dated January 29 (probably 1863)

Mary A. Hitch Jan 29th (likely 1863)
South Carolina Laurens District

Dear Husban I Seat Mi Self To in form you of mi helth I am on ly tolerable Well to night but a grate deal better than I have ben Young I have ben Verry unwell for Some time The doctor ses it is Cold that aild me. A.L. is not well. I have Just give him Some pills. J.J. is well as common I hope When those few lines Come to hand they ma find you in good helth Young I have nothing Verry Strang to rite to you. Young ginney has got So She Will eat Young I am sorry truly sorry I did not send you Sum thing to eat. Pray don't think hard for not Sen ding nothing to eat far I was looking for you home but you have not return yet but I hope you will soon Young Please bye me Some needles for I hav not got but one that I can soe with. I cant git then. A thought paying one dollar for a paper a paper of pins is three dollars Ol So git me Some camfer for I need some Verry bad Young don' think hard of me for riting to you So Much to Come home for it is mi hold desire for you to cum home. I receive your letter the 28 Young Me & J.J. has a ruf time feeding. Our lot is shew mutch deep in mud & snow. PA dont shoot all your powder away at a pine(?). Cum home & kill me a Mes of squirrels for they air verry plenty. I must Cum to a Close as it is giing late rite Soon & offting & let me hear from you as I Cant see you fair well Young.
Mary A Hitch
all on foot the 30 not Verry well.
Mary A. Hitch
YHE Hitch

XLI. Letter from J.J. Hitch to Y.H.E. Hitch , undated (possibly January 1863)

Undated
South Carolina Laurens Dist.

Dear father.
I take my pen in hand to inform you of my helth and A.L. and Mother wee air all onn foot but not verry well at this time. But hoping that when these few lines comes to hand that they may find you a live and in good helth. And I hope that it may be god's will to give you good helth and spair your life and you may return back to your home and injoy home a gain and you (__) whether wee all will meet onn earthe enny more ar not but I hope that if wee don't all meet onn earth that wee will meet in that world whare wee wont part no more whare thir will bee no war nor toiling and grief and pain But wee must think a Chrit this solom war for it is god's work and it is rite ar it was and not be a so but still wee can put our trust in him to bless uss and keep us from all harm I think a meny of a time how you air in the army struggling while others is at hom doughing nothing Me and Mother al in the field working and toiling for to make sum thing to eat and live on but I hope that when wee leave this world that wee may be at rest Dear father I hope that you may cum home yet hav it to say that you stade in the army till it was over and Now you was going to stay at home as long as god seed cause to let you live so no more.
J.J. Hitch To Mr Y.H.E. Hitch

XLII. Letter from Y.H.E. Hitch to Mary A. Hitch dated February 9, 1863 (with note from February 28, 1864 on back) from Camp Means near Charleston, South Carolina

Camp Means near Charleston, So.Ca.
Feb. 9. 63

Dear Wife

I seat myself to drop you a few lines to inform you that I am not well today. I have a very severe cold. And maybe takeing the measles but I think it is just cold. I got verry cold the other night & suffered that night severely with the headache. Last night the latter part of it suffered badly with the back and limbs aching. Today I have lain the most of the day. Since dinner today I have washed myself & put on clean cloths. I have bin to that old jail until I have got some of them nasty lice on my clothing. I want to have the cloths that I pulled of washed & maybe it will kill the nasty things. I heard last night that J.B. Edwards was in the hospital today. A.Y saw him at the hospital. He is better up on foot. It is thought that we will be disbanded on the 15 inst if so we will be at home the first of next week if we are spared to be alive & able to make the trip. I think I am better this evening & hope to improve. I hope this letter may find you all in good health. I write this in haste to get it ready for B.W. Knight to bear to you. I did not know that he was a going home until a few moments ago. I haven't any news of importance to write to you. it is said this place will be attacked shortly but I think it uncertain allthough there has been some heavy cannonading on the islands today. Mary you need not write again untill you see or hear from me again. I hope to see you soon. I have ben home three times since I came to camp but when I awoke it was all a dream A.Y. is not well. So I bid you farewell. Look not until you see me at the gate.
To Mrs Mary A. Hitch at home
Y.H.E. Hitch

Back of letter addressed:
To Mrs. Mary A. Hitch
At home
Favord by B.W. Knight
15

(It appears Joseph practiced his writing on the back of this letter☺

On back of letter:
Mary A. Hitch
Y.H.E. Hitch Feb 28
Mar AH mar ann

Well this is the losomes iss day that I ever Past I think Sholey feb 28 1864

Mary A Hitch
Laurens Dist feb 28
A L Hitch J J Hitch

A man is bornd a few days & (__) off truble
This a world of truble
J.J TEM Hitch
Feb 19
When this you see remember me though Ded and a burred I May Bea.
John J Hitch

Well Young this is a losom day with Me indeed you Know these times is Losom indeed
J.J. Hitch

Mrs. Mary A. Hitch
Mary Y.H.E
Wife   Wife
John Joseph
Hitch Y.H.E
Sun John Joseph Hitch

LETTERS (UNTIL JUNE 1864) DATING FROM YOUNG HITCH'S TIME IN COMPANY I, 16TH SOUTH CAROLINA VOLUNTEER INFANTRY

XLIII. Letter from Y.H.E. Hitch to Mary A. Hitch dated March 31, 1863 from Camp Croft, South Carolina

Camp Croft SC
March 31st /63

Dear wife

I arived at this place yesterday. I stood the trip pretty well and found the boys generally well. I have nothing very strange to write. I am going to the run to see Mr. Hughes as I did not think to hunt him up as I came by the run yesterday. I will get him to bear this to you. The boys drawed their guns last night. I have not the time to write today. I will write soon & give you the news. Please write to me.
Y.H.E. Hitch

Envelope addressed to:
Mrs. Mary A Hitch

Favored by G.T. ? Hughes

XLIV. Letter from Y.H.E. Hitch to Mary A. Hitch dated April 5, 1863 from Camp Roberts, South Carolina

Mary the mess we have are some I can tell you if Jerrey can be beat I don't want to see the boy. Mat will sorter do. Berry is a very good boy. Billy is our main dependence for cooking & getting things done. The boys will do anything if you can catch them at the right time & place, but that is very seldom I can tell you, And some can eat like dogs. That is any thing that is good to eat. Billy tells me that sugar they can not keep for they eat it as pigs do corn all at once and then do without until they draw again. Mary my little bottle of brandy has done me but little good some rogue got half of it but they was neighborly; they left me a little, probably a half tumbler full. I had treated two or three before the rogue came along. So when the measles git hold of me I will not have any of my own. Miles Garrett has brought in a box with a lock & key to it so we can lock our sugar up hereafter. I have half of my pone of bread We have all our flower yet & the most of my meat. I have all my fruit and some of the potatoes.

Back of letter addressed to:
Mrs Mary A Hitch
At home alone with two little sons.
Confidential
Camp Robberts S.C.

Also on the back of the letter:
From Y.H.E. Hitch

To his wife at home.
This Aprill the 5th/63
Late Sundy night
God grant that this may find my friends all well.

XLV. Letter from L.B. Edwards to J.J. and A.L. Hitch dated April 6, 1863 from Camp Roberts, South Carolina

Camp Robbards
April 6 1863

Dear frind
I take mi pen in hand to write you a few lines to let you now that I am well at this time and hoping when this comes to hand that hit may find you all enjoying the same good blessing. I have nothing to write more than we have move again and we have drand new guns and I hav shot mine three times and I think that hit will dought to depend on. J.J. I have seen a rattle snake five feet long hit had eleven rattles and a button. I tell you what hit was one. A.L your father and uncl Bill is gon up to the run today but they is as well as common. I want you to tell father and mother that I am well. So I must come to a close for this time. I hope you will excuse for not writen no sooner. So write soon.
L.B. Edwards
To J.J. Hitch and A.L. Hitch

Envelope addressed to:
Mr. J.J. Hitch
Fountain Inn, SC

Written on the side:
April the 11th
Recive

XLVI. Letter from Y.H.E. Hitch to sons J.J. and Lucian Hitch dated April 13, 1863 from Camp Roberts, South Carolina

J.J. Hitch
April 13th /63
Camp Robberts Slands Island, So. Ca.

J.J. Hitch,
Dear son I take the present opportunity of droping you a short letter. I wrote a letter to your ma & mailed it this morning. But as Berry is a going to start a letter home I thought I would write a letter & send in his letter. The paper that I talked of ordering for you I have never attended to. I stopt but a short time at Columbia. If I knew exactly how to write to the Editor I would try to get it sent to you. You ask Mr. McNeely to write to the Editor to send you the paper. You ask ma to give you the money for it. You must send the money before you can get the paper. And if the Cola. does not grant you the favor let me know

& I will then see what I can do. I hope you will try to read all you can in them. Hannah Moors Tracts they are verry good to read. Above all use no bad words, Joseph, and ask your brother to do the same if he loves his Pa.
Well Lucian I wonder if you would like to see pa by this time. If you don't pa would be glad to see Lucian. Lucian I was detailed this morning to chop firewood with two other men from company I & by being so detailed it clears me from drill untill dress parade this Evening. We was gone about two hours only but the gnats allmost eat us up. I had to work to keep them from Eating me entirely up. Lucian I have drawed a pair of shoes today the moste of the men drawed shoes today. Hurah Boys & be little men if you are left to shift & no one to assist you. I hope if you both do your duty as you should that you will be blessed with help from on high. So be industrious & good as fare you know how & are able, if you are not able immediately you will be some day. We have a warm day today. Joseph I fear your corn will never come up its being so cold. Let me know how you are getting along.

So farewell Sons.
Y.H.E. Hitch

XLVII. Letter from Y.H.E. Hitch to Mary Hitch (and Joseph Hitch) dated April 18-19, 1863 from Camp Roberts "near Adams Run", South Carolina

April 18th /63
Camp Robberts near Adams run, So.ca.

Dear wife today finds me rather unwell but up. The pains pester me a great deal last night & today. Scruggs & Mat are both well. Berry is grunting with his leg. M.R. Garrett is not well but better than he has been. J.J. Brown was taken sudenly sick the other day & was taken to the hospital. I have not heard from him today.
The 19th of April 63
I heard from Jerry Brown yesterday. He was verry bad but the doctor thinks there is some little hopes of him recovering. I thought yesterday awhile that I was about to have a severe attack of the bowel complaint. But fortunately for me it has stopt for the present. My mess are all on foot but Brown. I dont know how long it will remain. so for we have made arrangements to have chicken and dumpling. Vaughn and mess find the chicken and me and mess the flour to make the dumpling. So I must get out and assist in making the dumpling.
On a separate piece of paper:
Joseph, I rec your letter yesterday 2nd inst. Glad to hear from you. Glad to hear your wheat & rye is looking well. I hope it may please God to spare you & your ma & brother so as to get it saved, if it should not meet with no accident before the time to save it. If your wheat comes good it will be a great help out to you in the bread line. Your barley to will make you coffee. That I have tried done fine I tell you. That will save your bread for you can not eat that in bread & anything to save bread. Joseph the eggs you spoke of come pretty safe. There was about a dozen broke but not lost. There was a few broke so ar to be of no use. But I had a good look to what Mr Vaughn had. He got to camp a Tuesday evening & his boxes landed today in a verry bad condition. Mr Vaughn toted out about as mutch pies and chickens as he could in his arms & threw it a way. His eggs was broken up shockingly. Well Joseph I have wrote a heap but it does not amount to mutch. So I shall come to a close. So I bid you farewell.

Y.H.E. Hitch

XLVIII. Letter from Y.H.E. Hitch to Mary A. Hitch dated April 19, 1863 from Adams Run, South Carolina

Mary Hitch
After eating a verry hearty dinner of chicken & dumplings & then standing two hours immediately afterwards, you may guess that I am very warm at the present time. Yes, me and Tol Vaughn got a splendid dinner & have all but M.R. Garrett eat verry hearty of it. What will be the result of our feast I don't know. But I hope nothing serious. The weather is getting pretty warm and dry. No rain hardly since I come to camp. The sands is getting quiet dry & dusty. It is said the Yankeys are leaving for some other point. Some think that we will leave after a while for some other point. And some think differently, that we will remain on the coast whitch looks reasonable. Enough. it is said furloughing will begin soon, probably by the 1st of May next. We have drawed nothing but guns and (_rings) & some shoes. We have new harness out & yet(?) so fare we have no knapsacks or canteens yet. if we had them we would be harnesst in full.

Adams Run, So. Ca. April 19 /63
Please write & give the newes I like to hear from home. I want to know how your garden is getting on. Let me know if that corn that hope plant is come up so as not to plant over. Tell grandpa Berry is getting on plenty well & has his own fun with the boys. Mary I shall come to a close. The tent is verry hot & I want to get out in the shade & cool before I have to go on post again. I hope this will reach you in due time & find you all well.
Y.H.E. Hitch

Mary A Hitch

Envelope addressed to
Mrs. Mary A. Hitch
Fountain Inn, P.O
Greenville District So.Ca

XLIX. Letter from Y.H.E. Hitch to Mary A. Hitch dated April 25, 1863 from Camp Roberts, South Carolina

Mary Hitch. April 25th /63
Camp Robberts Slands Island So.Ca

Dear wife
My health is just tolerable today. I have been sorter puny for the past few days with my bowels, not serious though & hope I will not get verry bad. Lieut. Thackston is a going to start for home tomorrow or the day after. If so he will carry some things for me to you & some money. I will pack up my things tonight & then write to you what I put in for you. Mary I rec yours of the 20th and 21st on the 23rd verry glad to hear from you but sorry to hear of your health being no better. I hope when this reaches you it

may find your health improving. Allso our sons enjoying good health. Mary I shall stop until I see what I can get in the box. Well Mary I have put in the box one pair of shoes & leggins & a little bunch of sugar for you. Scruggs & Edwards Nelson & M.R. Garrett have an interest in the box, allso Lieut. Thackston. Mary, I send these shoes to you for you to swap or make the most of them you can. They are badly made, my old ones will do me more service than those. If you could se see Taylor he can by putting a piece to the toe of those leggins, make you a nice pair of guaters lace them up on the inside of the ankle. If you can get enough soles to bottom them you can have a nice pair for yourself & the shoes besides. If you can go to see Lieut. Thackston, he can show you some that has been made in camp but they are not made right. They should be sowed up at the side & open in front. Mary, I think I will give Lieut. Thackston some $65.00 for you to do the best you can with it. Please write to me when you get this how mutch you have on hand. I must come to a close by saying to you that I wish you to remember me in your prayers as you say you have been doing. And I will try to return the favor. I sincerely hope God will hear our feeble petition and smile upon us.
To Mary A. Hitch } Y.H.E. Hitch

Envelope addressed to:
Mary A. Hitch
At Home
By the politeness of Lieut. Thackston
April 26

L. Letter from Y.H.E. Hitch to Mary A. Hitch dated May 1, 1863 from Camp Roberts, South Carolina

Camp Robberts Slands Island, So. Ca. May 1st 1863

Dear Wife,
I seat myself to inform you of my health. Mary I have been verry unwell a few days last Sunday morning I eat pretty hearty breakfast & that was the last to call any thing until Wednesday evening & but little then. I past off more blood than I ever did in all my life before. Mary I was about in sutch a fix as I was some few years ago. The pains at the same time, I had in the time of it a spell of colick or cramp in my stomach as I did last summer whitch was severe indeed. This morning finds me better how long it will last I can't tell. My mouth is verry sore the Doctor give me me medicine that salivated me severly. But I think my mouth is a little better this morning. Mr. & Miss Vaughn got here Tuesday evening. There box has not come yet. Mr. Vaughn left them in Charleston. I dout there gitting them at all. Mary I have no newes to write to interest you yesterday was general inspection but I mist it by being sick or the officer did as he past inspecting haversacks & tents ast me what seemed to ail me & he spoke kindly to me. Mary, there was one well man got a furlough today. I supose his father is lying low and he has not been home in nine or ten months. I think Richard Farrow will get a furlough if not a discharge. His health is verry bad & no likelihood of its being much better. Mary, the provisions you sent got to us yesterday Friday in time for dinner all right or near it. We took dinner of the hen and corn pone. Supper of eggs boiled with butter and corn pone and coffee. Today breakfast fried corn pone and coffee. Dinner fried shellots & light wheat pone, a most excellent mess.

Lucian, try to save seed of your shellots for they are most the best dish that I have had lately. Lucian, you and Joseph, work your unions good. And don't get out of heart hurra & be little men & make your own bread.
Joseph, don't get out of heart if your old land corn don't gro off fast for it don't grow of fast like fresh land would. Hurrah work and get your bread honestly. Perhaps it may please God for us all to get together some time. So I must close. Farewell } Young H.E. Hitch

Envelope addressed to
Mrs. Mary A. Hitch
At Home
So.Ca. Coleton Dist.
On side of envelope:
Favord by R.H. Vaughn

LI. Letter from Y.H.E. Hitch to Mary A. Hitch dated May 1, 1863

Young H.E. Hitch
May 1st /63
Confidential
Mary I rec. a letter the 28th of this Inst. from Mr. A.Y. Garrett. I see from that letter he is aiming to still this summer. He proposes to by your fruit & do all the gathering, or still on the share, and wishes to know of me whitch way I had rather do. he says that he wants to still all that he can for it's about all the chance to make money now. Mary, I want you to do what you think to be the best. I can't tell you now what would be best. Only this fare if there is money to be made you and the children should have the best right to it. If the fruit should be good and you could, you ought to try for it will be valuable and your pigs can eat a heap of them. My notion is that the fruit has been so injured with frost that it will drop off. But I shall not tell Garrett what I will do until I get an answer from you & you need not be in a hurry untill you can see whether there is any fruit to dispose of. He proffers to pay ten dollars per stand. And if I had that big jug here, I could get more than ten for one quart. I haven't the least dout of it getting $50.00 per gallon to retail it out. Mary, don't treat everything that passes for it is too costly. If you can sell any & wish to do so at a good price, do so, but keep some for yourself untill you see if there is any new made. Mary, Billy is doing tolerable well. His health is very good. You may tell his wife that I found Billy more of a moral man than I expected to. Also tell her that I don't recollect of hearing him swear any since I come to camp. But there is a sight of profane language used here. Mary, I do not know for certain who took my brandy but have a verry good idea whoo it was. Mary, I don't think that I ever told you of paying my fare from Greenville to Columbia. The reason was Capt. Stradly had given orders to the conductors not to rec. transportation unless printed and the fare was $4.25 and that the quartermaster would refund it over to me. But unfortunately, being green on the road, I did not have him to endorse on the back of my paper. Then I neglected to cut the part at the top off from the other. So when the second conductor came around and waked me up I handed the paper to him and he took both the first and second part. The third past me from the Citty to the run. The error was all in the first part and if I had been smart that should not happened. The boxes cost me just one dollar drayage from the Charleston to the Savannah depot. I brought a box for another man that was put in my care on the road. He has not paid me yet and one of the mess has not paid his part. Both together is the big sum of 45 cents. Counting my fare which I may

get, it all amounts to $6.30 since I left home for myself. I tell a story for I give fifty cents the other night for John Graden who has had the luck to get everything burnt night before last. Jessy Knight made him a little smoke to keep the gnats off & went to sleep & dropt his pocket book or rather it shift out of his pocket into this little fire whitch burnt pocket book and sixty dollars he said burnt. Knight will not get any mad up for they say he won't send hardly any to his wife. Graden was his house and home that got burnt leaving wife & children out of doors. I shall stop writing and go to bed.
Confidential
Mary, I have never dreamed of seeing you or of being at home since I come in to service this time. Mary, you say you pray for me dayly. I hope you will continue to still pray on for me. I try to pray for my self & my family. The past week has been a trying one with me for I have suffered severely. But, Mary, I have the New Testament to read and the more I read it the more I delight in reading of it. I find in it sutch rich promises. It appears more plain the more I read it. I see in that little volume that it is best that we should have trials and difficulties to undergo, whitch I believe. Mary, I believe that the war and my afflictions will be an advantage to me in a coming day. Difficulties and trials cause us to feel more sensibly our dependence in the Almighty.
Joseph, gladly would I comply with your request if I could see any chance. You surely do not want to see Pa worse than he wants to see you. It is said distress furloughs have started. If so I hope well furloughs will start soon but the whole company will get off before me, but perhaps I, if no accident, will get to come the last of the summer or first of the fall.

LII. Letter from Y.H.E. Hitch to Mary Hitch dated May 3-4, 1863 from Colleton District, South Carolina

May 3rd / 63
Mary, today is Sunday. I thought this morning that I would like to be at home and go to Cedar Grove but I can't so I must put up with things as they are. Mary, my health has been pretty bad the week past. I have done no duty since last Sunday morning untill this morning I went out on company inspection. I don't feel quite so well as I did yesterday. I think that probably I eat too mutch yesterday although I was as careful as possible. My head aches. My bowels are running off again some today, not passing blood, yet that is today. Mr. Vaughn starts home in the morning and I sent in our trunk Williams flask with four other bottles, tickets on them. Also one pair of drawers to work up as you think proper. If you have no other use for them, you can hang them up and put seed beans this fall in them. Be sure you save them. Mary, if you have the chance, send me a patch or two to patch with after awhile. I don't need them now but will by & by. So no more at present.
To Mrs. Mary A. Hitch } Y.H.E. Hitch

On the back of the letter: May 4th. I am alive this morn and upon foot. Truly hoping this may find Mary, Joseph and Lucian all well and doing well both for time and eternity.
Y.H.E. Hitch, So. Ca., Coleton Dist.
Mrs. Mary Hitch at Home
Confidential

LIII. Letter from Y.H.E. Hitch to Mary Hitch dated May 6, 1863 from Camp Roberts, South Carolina

Camp Robberts. So. Ca. May 6, 1863
Dear Wife. I sate myself to drop you a short note. I am Enjoying tolerable health at this time. Truly wishing this may find you all well. Mary, we are now packed up and packing up ready to start to the railroad for the purpose of taking the car for Vicksburg, Miss. You will see W.E. Garrett, tell him that we send a box of flour and other things sutch as we can not carry with us. We send them to Greenville marked to him, he will please go after it. The little polk of rice and sugar is M.R. Garrett's. You will know the rest. W. Scruggs sends his best love to Caroline and his children. L.B. sends the same. Mary, I bid you and the boys farewell, if we never more meet on earth God grant that we may meet in heaven.
Y.H.E. Hitch

LIV. Letter from Y.H.E. Hitch to Mary Hitch dated May 9, 1863 from West Point, Alabama

West Point Ala.
May 9th / 63
Dear Wife,
Through the mercys of providence I am once more permited to drop you a short note to let you know my whereabouts & health. I am at or on the Ala. side of the Chattahoocha River. My health is better than it has been but am pretty well or nearly worn out for sleep & rest. Last Wednesday 3 p.m. we we left Camp Robberts for Vicksburg, Miss. We got aboard the car at the run after a warm march of seven miles about dusk. Arived at the Savannah Depot, Charleston about 11 or 12 o'clock the next day. We marched over to the So. Car. Depot & at 4 p.m. we left for Augusta Ga, arived there 11 a.m. and left there at 2 p.m. for Atlanta, Ga, arived there at day break this morning Saturday. Left in an hour or two for West Point 2 p.m. at whitch point we are at. We have put up our tents. How long to stay I can't tell. If we go on to Vicksburg there is two other regiments to go before ours. The 24th South Carolina Regt of Volunteers and 46th Ga Volunteers are here at this place. I heard it said since we got here that there was as good a chance to get to go back to Augusta as to go on to Vicksburg or Jackson, Miss. Where we will go and when we will go, I can't say. Our regt. all are opposed to going to the west. Mary you need not write untill you hear from me again. I will rite soon and give you the newes. I hope this may find you all well. Please excuse me for not writing more. So I bid you farewell Dear wife & Sons. Tell Mrs. Brown to excuse me for not calling to see her and Jerry for I did not have the opportunity to do so.

Envelope addressed to
Mrs. Mary Hitch
Fountain Inn, P.O.
Greenville Dist, So. Ca.

LV. Letter from Y.H.E. Hitch to Mary A. Hitch dated May 14, 1863 from McDowell's Landing, Alabama

Ala. Mcdowels Landing, May 14th 1863
Mrs. Mary A. Hitch
Dear Wife. I take my pen in hand to write you a few lines.
My health is just tolerable. The limestone water does me for salts. It only quenches my thirst so long as I am drinking of it. When I wrote to you last I was at West Point. On Monday last we left there for Montgomery at 10 a.m., arived at Montgomery at dark there at 12 p.m. Took the steamboat down the Coosy River to Selma, arived there 8 or 9 a.m. There took the car for Demapolis at 3 p.m., arrived at sundown there. at 8 a.m. took the steamboat down the Tombigbee River 4 miles to McDowel's Landing at whitch place we are yet at. A part of our regt. is gone on & the rest of us should of been gone if it had not of been for a little accident. We just had got on the train about dark last night and the car started and one box run off the track whitch caused us to stay all night here. Fortunately for us it happened to be right by the side of a (__) house & we took lodging in it whitch is very pleasant for it is pouring down the rain. How long before we leave I don't know. The old train is preparing to leave. My mess are enjoying tolerable health at present. We had to leave our Capt at West Point on account of sickness. We are in one hundred and fifty miles of Jackson, Miss. From what I can learn we are going where there will be something to do. Great fighting expected to come off soon in the State of Miss.
Joseph and Lucian, I will give you the places where we stopt and shifted cars and boats.
Charleston to Augusta 136.
Augusta to Atlanta 171
Atlanta to West Point 86
West Point to Montgomery 87
Montgomery to Selma 110
Selma to Demapolis 50
Selma to McDowels Landing 4
We are now 644 miles from Charleston, not so fare from home quiet. If I could see you I could tell you a heap more than I can write to you. Whether I ever shall have the pleasure of conversing with you God only knows. There is nine chances to one for me never to get home, yet I still hope to be spared to see you all again on earth. Boys, I have seen some verry rich land in the Ala and south corn fields I never did see. I have seen hundred of acres of corn that the corn was as high as your shoulders, A.L., and green as poisen. & wheat that will do to cut next week. If it is a good crop year there will be an abundance of bread stuffs made this year, no cotton being planted hardly. Boys, I have seen lots of the Yankey but they was all prisoners. We meet them every day, bring them to Atlanta & Augusta, Ga. I have heard them talk. Some of them say we will whip them while others say we never will.
Lucian, yesterday I saw a little Yankey boy hardly as large as you sitting by the side of his pa eating of a cracker and a piece of raw meat that one of our men give to him. Him and his pa was pasengers on a boat when they was taken prisoners. Boys, I hope you will be good boys in every respect. Always keep it in your mind that you have to die & leave this world & there is a hell for you to shun & heaven to seek for. So if you wish to go to heaven, you must be good boys. Work & do the best you can for your ma as your pa is deprived of helping of her. Be good to her. It is your duty to do so & I hope that you both love your ma so as to honor & respect her as long as you all live. I hope you will write as soon as you get this and let me hear from you all. I expect to be, if no accident, about Jackson, Miss by the time that your letter

can get to me. Please tell the friends of my mess that we are all tolerable well. Let me know if Doc. Mock has got home yet. I suppose if we get started directly that we will get to Jackson some time to knight. I will close in short as we have to start. So fare you well.
Young H.E. Hitch

LVI. Letter from Y.H.E. Hitch to Mary A. Hitch dated May 15, 1863 from Lauderdale County, Mississippi

Mrs. Mary A. Hitch. May 15th / 63
Dear Wife I am not well today. My bowels are yet running off, that & traveling on the car together has worn me very mutch. I am very weak. Our traveling on the train yester & last night was the roughest I ever had. The road was rough & they stald frequently. A portion of our regt. is gone on to Jackson or in that direction. Whether they reached there or not I don't know. We are waiting for further orders. What they will be I can't tell you now. It is a pretty noisy time, a heap of lies afloat. I wrote a letter yester before we left McDowel's landing to you. Since then we have traveled 60 miles to this place, Meridian. I hope this may find you all well.
Y.H.E. Hitch
Berry says tell his friends that he is well, hopeing they may be well & doing well.
This May 15th /63 11 oclock. A.M.
Below that in a different color of ink:
Lockeby County Mississippi

LVII. Letter from Y.H.E. Hitch to sons Joseph and Lucian Hitch dated May 15, 1863 from "Hospital Ward 5", Meridian, Mississippi

Dear Sons

I hope when this reaches you it may find you both well and a doing well. I have no news verry interesting to write. Only just now I hear that Johnson and Loreing are at Jackson, their Headquarters at the citty of Jackson. Boys, I bought a dozen hen eggs yesterday. I paid one dollar for the dozen. I have eat two of them. Eatables are verry high in this state. Sutch sweet breads as your ma bakes in the little baker would be worth one dollar & upwards here. Some grumble at their fare. As for my self, I can do pretty well.
Young H.E. Hitch.

Written upside down on the same page:
May 25, 1863 my health is as it has been for some days, well except pains whitch troubles me to get about.

Written on the back of the same page:
Boys, our nurse's little son whoo is not as big as you, Lucian, road eight miles to stay all night with his pa & I thought it would please me to see one of you coming to see me. I want you on Sundays if you can, to go to church. If you cant go to church, get your books and learn all you can. Whatever you do keep off the creek with rude boys who might cause you to do more than you would if you was alone at home. I hope to hear from you soon. If not let us try to be prepared to meet in Heaven.

Young H.E. Hitch

On a second piece of paper enclosed with the above:
Lucian I hope you are well & a doing well & hope that you are a good little boy to your mother. Allso I do hope that you will use no bad words in your conversation whatever. Lucian men hear whoo are looking more like they would die than live swear the hardest you ever heard. Don't get mad, son, at good advice from one who wishes you well both for time and eternity. I hope to be able to see you again on earth, if not let us try to be prepared to meet in Heaven where we will never be separated again.
So farewell, A.L. Hitch.
Lucian, take good care of Brutus and Toby Pig. Y.H.E. Hitch

Written on back of second letter:
Joseph, I hope you are well and doing well. Allso I hope you will not get out of heart at trifles and little accidents. You may expect many crosses in your life. Tell me in your next how your steers are getting on. Tell me if your barley is doing anything. Tell how Jinney is getting on. Tell me how our Dr. D.D. Westmoreland is getting on. Joseph, you will back your letters after the form here below.
Mr. Y.H.E. Hitch,
Meridian P.O. Mississippi
Hospital ward five

LVIII. Letter from Y.H.E. Hitch to Mary A. Hitch dated May 16, 1863 from Meridian, Lauderdale County, Mississippi

May 16th 1863
Mississippi Loterdil County Meridian P.O.
Mrs. Mary A. Hitch,
Dear Wife I embrace the present opportunity of writing you a few lines to inform you of my where abouts health etc.
Mary, I am at a hospital in two miles of a little town called Meridian. My health is rather bad today. I come here yesterday. I did not feel able to do duty yesterday & was advised to come here. Myself & five others of my company come here together & one come in today & I fear us is not all by a heap. Out trip has been verry fatiguing indeed on us. Mary, I suppose you have heard a great many tales. Probably you have heard that our regt. has been cut off. I think that to be a false rumor. True our regt is divided but I was told just now that the rest of our regt started this morning to join the rest of our regt some fifty miles from hear. That portion of the regt that went on first must be in 30 or 35 miles of Jackson. It is said that Jackson has been retaken by our men, as to the certainty of it I can't say. Mary, you can't think how I hated to leave my company and come here but the soldiers have to do as they can, not as they wish. There is something over 100 men in this hospital, not all in one house, but they are in three or four houses all situated in the woods. The water drinks pretty well but a great ways off well water the most of it. One good spring between hear & the town. All of us that are well enough to walk to the table, go. It is as fare as I want to go. It's about 300 yards from where I stay to the eating house. There is seven men & myself in the room that I stay in, about the same number in the adjoining room & in another little house close by there is some twelve or fourteen. Four of our company are in the little house & me in the big house with strangers but so long as I can get up and walk about, I can go in the other house to see my

friends. I have just been to the well to get some coal water the best that I have drank lately by a good deal, but it made me swet to get it. If I understand it right the men whoo are able to wait on themselves are sent to this house.
Mary, I learn this morning, Sunday the 17 of May that the Yankeys who have Jackson in possession have burnt the principal buildings & preparing to leave the town. But it is said that our army is closing in on them on three sides of them. From what I can learn there is either something verry bad or verry good just a going to hapen for us. Notwithstanding the enemy have Jackson in their possession & may get Vicksburg, it may all be for the best for us at last. This is said to be the boldest attack that the Yankeys have ever made here. They are getting further out from their gunboats. Some are expecting the enemy to be here soon at this town. It is said that we fellows at the hospital when discharged from here will be assigned to the nearest regt, let it be what regt it may be. I don't know that that rule will work for the men. All will want to join their own companys again soon as able so to do. There is one thing I don't like, that is our troops can't get transportation as I think they should. We were 9 days traveling 644 or 50 miles. Something wrong in the conductors, I think. We should of been to Jackson by the time that we got to this place. It may all be for the best for us. Mary, I have just been after a bucket of water & took a look at a very pretty garden. I thought while looking at that garden of one in South Carolina & the loved ones that I had had the pleasure of walking in it with & how I would like to have the pleasure of so doing again. But I hope to be able to see you sometime if so spared.
Well Boys, you may want to here from your Pa by this time my opportunity to write has not been as good as you may suppose, and I can't write all that you probably would like me to write to you. I have seen a great deal, some things that was not very pleasant but expect if I last long, to see a heap of things that is not pleasant. Boys, you make think that Pa is starving but that is not so. I get as mutch as I want at present. I have been for some time that I care nothing for anything strong. I get as much bread & coffee as I want & we get beef & some bacon with a little rice. I hear a heap of grumbling about our fare. This morning at breakfast I heard one remark that if a man could just live through this war that there would not be any danger of his diing afterwards. I must close in short. So Fare you well.
Sunday, May 17th 1863
Mrs. Mary A. Hitch } Young H.E. Hitch

LIX. Letter from Y.H.E. Hitch to Mary A. Hitch dated May 21, 1863 from Lauderdale County, Mississippi

May 21st /63
Lauderdale County Mississippi May 21st /63
Mrs. Mary A. Hitch

Well Mary probbably you may wish to hear from Young again. I can say to you that through the mercys of God I am yet alive, although not well. so far today I feel better than I did yesterday. My bowels is sorter checked just now. How long this will remain so I cant say. I am verry weak in the back & legs. I have Exercised more today than any day since I come to this hospital. Mary how long I will stay at this place I do not know. I am not able to do duty if I was with my regt. And if I was its uncertain about me getting to my regt. I cant hear anything at all from the regt since I left it at Meridian last Friday. In fact I can get but little news to rely upon from the seat of war. We get news but a great deal is false so that when the truth does happen to come I don't know that it is truth. We have beautiful weather for our

troops to march in & I expect they have to do some of it a long now. I heard that two of our men & the Capt went on yesterday that had been left behind. They are going on after the regt. Mary write to me. Direct your letters to Meridian P.O. Mississippi Hospital ward five. If I should be so fortunate as to get to go to my regt the letters that are sent to this hospital can be sent on to the regt. I should of told you in my other letter to you. I want to hear from you bad. Allso the neigbors generally. Pleas let me know if any other of our men have had to hul out since I left home. Tell A.Y. Garrett that I have not forgoten him and tell him to drop me a few lines. Tell your Pa that I would be glad to see him & his folks all of them. Tell E.L. Edwards to drop me a letter & give me the news in general. Mary I truly hope this note may reach you in due time & find you & the children Blessed with a reasonable share of health.
Joseph and Lucian, I hope you are getting on as well as you are able to with the farm. Hurrah do all that you are able to do. Be honest in all your dealings. And I hope you will be blest in so doing. Tell me if J.J. Brown is at home & how he is getting on. I want to know how many of your cows & sheep have died since I left home. I must close in short.
So farewell Mary A. Hitch, J.J. Hitch, A.L. Hitch
Young H.E. Hitch

LX. Letter from Y.H.E. Hitch to Mary A. Hitch dated May 24-25, 1863 from Meridian, Lauderdale County, Mississippi

May 24th 1863
Lauderdale County, Meridian P. Office Miss.

Mrs. Mary A. Hitch
Dear wife
Through the mercys of God I am able & so permitted to write you a few lines. I am yet at the same place that I was at when I last wrote to you. My health in some respects is better. But I am troubled yet verry mutch with rheumatism. How long I shall have to stay here I don't know. I can get no strait account of my regt. I hear a heap of news; sometimes hear the enemy have whipt, then hear that our men have whipt the enemy. It is said that Johnson is at or near Vicksburg but has not yet formed a junction with Pemberton. The other men whoo come with me here are with me yet. They say as soon as they can get the chance to get to there regt they are going on. Mary the steward told us at breakfast that he wanted us all that was able to be present after dinner to hear preaching. Whitch orders pleased me verry mutch. I hope to be able to attend for I want to hear some preaching once more. Mary this is a lonesum place to stay although it is quiet a pleasant place. The wether is beautifull dry & not very hot. Well Mary I have been to preaching & have heard a good sermon & prays & the preacher gave us some tracts to read the first that I have seen since I left home. I think text Hebrews 4 chapt & 9th verse. There remaineth therefore a rest to the people of God. Mary, I hope these troublesum hard times have not had the same effect upon you that it has on the soldiers. It seems to me that the most of our men have forgotten that they ever have to die & appear before their Maker to render an account for the deeds in life. Mary look forward. Don't give over. But pray that you may get strength from God to ennable you to bear with your trials and troubles. And please remember Young in your petitions.
May 25th
Mary I don't believe I ever told you that I drawed twenty dollars the day we left Charleston. I did not have the opportunity of sending any of it to you. So I have kept it. It may be that I may want it myself before I

draw any more as I am away from my command. The boys are speaking of trying to go to the regt if the doctor will let them go. I don't know but what I shall try to go with them although I am not able for service. I will tell you in the if I go or not.
Young H.E. Hitch

LXI. Letter from Y.H.E. Hitch to Mary A. Hitch dated June 2-3, 1863 from Meridian, Lauderdale County, Mississippi

June 2nd 1863
Lauderdale County Miss. Meridian P. Office

Mrs. Mary A. Hitch
Dear wife
As I dont know whether you have ever rec ary letter from me since I left Charleston. I will write one more letter to you. I have wrote three letters to you since the few lines I wrote about the time that we left So.Ca. Also one to your father. Yesterday I heard that there had no letters been rec from the 16 regt & that you had learned that our regt. had been cut to pieces. I have got no sutch news yet though I get but little newes here. I wrote to your father the other day & thought I would not write to you this week but after hearing you could get not newes from us I have concluded to drop you one more letter, thinking maybe you might sorter begin to want to hear from me by this time. The best newes I have to give you is my health is better than it has been. Nothing the matter with me now but rheumatism & hip pain as you know I am subject to and was before I left home. I have been here at this Hospital two weeks last Friday. When I will leave her I cant tell. It may be soon or it may be some days. just when the doctor says go. Mary pleas write to me I want to hear from you bad. I will again tell you where to direct your letters to. Direct them to Meridian P.O. Lauderdale County Miss. Hospital ward no. five. 16th regt, So. Ca.v. so if I should be here when a letter comes I can get it. If with my regt the letters will be sent on after us to our regt please write & give me all the newes that you have. The last few days has been verry warm indeed. Wee have had some pretty showers of rain lately. This is a very poor part of God's creation around here, sure it is. The land looks a good deal like the land about Cola Mcneelys only it is verry mutch broken & the pine is verry heavy & of the long leaf kind.

June 3rd a.m.
I hear this morning that General Johnson is moving on toward Vicksburg. The certainty of it I don't know. We can get but little news here from the seat of war that is reliable. It is thought by some that the struggle now on hand at Vicksburg will be the deciding struggle. Someone has prophesied that it would be decided in the great valley of the Miss & we all hope it may be settled soon and hope it may be decided in our favor. Mary my clothing holds out verry well. I expect when I have to leave this place to have to dispose of some of them perhaps through them away. The weather is warm & my clothing to heavy to toat on a march. I have been offered eight dollars for the coat that I brought from home. I believe if I can get that for it I will sell it. My plain pants are getting a little slick & thin. I shant mind throwing of them away so bad. My uniform is as good as new. It has not been worn but a few days. I may try to make it convenient to loss my roundabout coat & keep my other coat although the roundabout will suit the summer the best. My jeans pants is verry good yet. I will hold on to them as long as possible. I have a verry pretty fitting uniform. The first things I aim to dispose of will be my bedtick & the plain pair

of pants & one haversack. The next one of my coats, my jacket I don't know what I may do with it. But two shirts, two pair of drawers, three pair of pants, two coats, one vest, one bed tick & two blankets & other trappings is more than I can carry through the heat of this summer, I fear.
Wel boys, I hardly know what to write to you as I fear that you have not received the letters that I have wrote to you. I have wrote in the letters before this one to you & given you an account of our trip to this place & the length of time that it took us to make the trip. Dear Sons I have the pleasure of saying to you that my health is better than when I last wrote to you. And I truly hope when this reaches you that it may find your & your Ma enjoying a reasonable share of health. I have no news of any importance to give you at the present. I hope that you have got the letters that I have started to you. I would be verry glad to be at home to assist you in takeing care of your wheat next week. I hope your wheat is doing well & that you may get it saved some how. The weather is fine here for the small grain, dry & cool. Hurrah my little sons be good boys to your ma. And make your own bread if it is in your power. Take as good care of what little stuff you have as you can. And if I should be so fortunate as to get home again I want you paid. If I never return it is your mas & yours what little there is. So I must close. Please write soon.
Young H.E. Hitch

Envelope addressed to:
Mrs Mary A. Hitch
Fountain Inn P. Office
Greenville Dist. So.ca.

LXII. Letter from Y.H.E. Hitch to son Joseph Hitch dated June 4, 1863 from Hospital Ward 5, Meridian, Lauderdale County, Mississippi

Mr. Y.H.E. Hitch
Meridian P. Office
Lauderdale County Miss
Hospital ward no five
16th regt S.c.v.Com (I)

Joseph, let me know how your stock is getting along, your steers in particular and your milk cows, whether old Sarah is alive or not. Tell me how J.J. Brown is getting on and I wish to hear from your granpa. Also tell how J.D. Mock is or whether he has ever got home. Tell old Mr. Mock Howdy for me.
This June 4th 1863
Young H.E. Hitch

This letter was written on the back of an old envelope that had been addressed to:
Mr. Y.H.E. Hitch, Adams Run,
16 regt SC v.
in care of Capt Newton Babb.
Date on side of envelope: April 23rd /63

LXIII. Letter from Y.H.E. Hitch to son Lucian Hitch dated June 5, 1863 from Hospital Ward 5, Meridian, Lauderdale County, Mississippi

June 5th, 1863

Lucian, I dreamed last night of seeing your dog Brutes and I called him by his name as I thought. And he did not know me and you do not know how it hurt me to think that he did not know me. I have dreamed of seeing your ma and Joseph. But have never dreamed of seeing A.L. Hitch. Mary, I have been at this hospital three weeks today. Mary I am able to be up & nock around & has never faild to be able to go down to the dinner house to get my meals. True I have not been able for duty since I came here. Mary, there is but little honor in lieing in a hospital, but there is a heap of dishonesty going on in this war. And if I don't try to take care of myself, no one else will. I have not reported able for duty yet neither is it worth while for I would just be sent to meridian as others have been that reported able for duty.
Mr. Y.H.E. Hitch
Meridian P.o.
Lauderdale County Miss
Hospital ward no five
16th regt So. Ca. V. Com (I)

Young H.E. Hitch

Back of letter:
From Young H.E. Hitch
Mrs. Mary A. Hitch
Confidential
June 5th 1863
Meridian P.O. Miss

LXIV. Letter from Y.H.E. Hitch to Mary A. Hitch and sons J.J. and A.L. Hitch dated June 8, 1863 from Jackson, Mississippi

Jackson Miss June 8th 1863

Dear Wife, I left the hospital Saturday after dinner for Meridian & yesterday, Sunday, took the car for this place Jackson. I got here a little before night. Myself and Mr. Forester is the only two that belong to my company. There is one more man going on with us who was at the hospital with me & Forrester. Wee will take the Car this Evening at four P.M. for Cantton our Command is there if they have not left lately. We may not get up with them yet. Pretty stiring times here. Something to be done I think from what I can see. It will be some two days or more before I can reach my company. This leaves me tolerably well at the present I want you to write to me, the 30 of April was the last letter I got from you. Direct your letters to Jackson, Miss. So I wish you & children well Both for time & eternity. Mary, as this may be the last letter that you may ever get wrote by me to you, if it should be my lot to get killed or die, I want you not to grieve after me at all for I hope when I am no more here on Earth that I will be at rest in heaven. Mary I

may be deceased but I hope you will still pursue your course as you have been doing. Let us try to be prepared to meet God in peace. So I bid you farewell.
Mary A. Hitch }
J.J. Hitch }
A.L. Hitch } Young H.E. Hitch

***This letter included a drawing of a woman (probably Mary) enclosed with letter.*

LXV. Letter from Y.H.E. Hitch to Mary A. Hitch dated June 12, 1863 from Yazoo City, Mississippi

Yazoo City Miss
June 12th 1863

Mrs. Mary A. Hitch
Mary through the mercy of providence I am permited to drop you a few lines. I am Enjoying moderate health But verry mutch fatigued from my march. I footed it forty miles in about two days. I left Meridian the 6th and arived at Camp the 11th P.M. I found the boys my mess all but M.R. Garrett in moderate health. Garrett is sorter puny. Our men generally look bad. They seem to be verry mutch worn down. We are campt in 3 miles of Yazoo Citty on the creek cald Short Creek. With the exception of a pretty shade, it is surely the roughest country that you ever saw, although verry rich. Yazoo Citty undoubtedly must be the Stern End of Miss. Mr. I. Forrester was the only one of Com (I) that went on with me from the hospital. I got with Capt. Babb yesterday morning. I was verry glad to meet up with him but would have been more so if he had brought me a letter. Mary I rec a letter from you bearing date May 22nd I got the letter from the boys when I got to camp. It is the only letter that I have got since the one that Mr. Brown brought to me. I have wrote to you regular as mutch as once a week & expect to as near as I can. The Capt said when I first come up with him that he thought he had a letter for me but if he did he has lost it on the way. Mary you speak of your trobbles when you heard of my comeing to Miss You may suppose that it troubled me verry mutch. I dont know what I would of give to of seen you & the boys before I started. I was truly sorry to hear that Joseph was so puny as he is. I hope this may reach you in due time & find you all well. Mary, we have as you say great room to be thankful that Providence has been so merciful to us. And can we not trust in him for the future. Let us try so to do. So Fare well.
Mary A. Hitch Young H.E. Hitch
J.J. Hitch
A.L. Hitch

Includes envelope with stamp. Postmarked Yazoo, June 13.

LXVI. Letter from Y.H.E. Hitch to Mary A. Hitch dated June 15, 1863 from Camp Woods, Mississippi

Camp Woods, Miss
June 15th 1863

Mrs. Mary A. Hitch
Dear Wife today find me in tolerable health & hopeing this may find you all well & doing well. We have just been stript of our knapsacks and all the baggage that we can spare. The weather is warm & hard marching to be done. Where I don't know. I have brought my turn down to one blanket, one oilcloth, shirt, pants, drawers, socks and gloves besides the suit on my back. Probably I yet have more than I can carry. You need not think strange if you do not get letters from us soon as the communication will be stopt. Miles Garrett is gone to the hospital. The rest of my mess are tolerably well at present. Berry & Mat hold up fine. I hope to survive this war & be spared to reach home & see you all on earth once more. If not I hope to meet you in heaven.
Y.H.E. Hitch

Written on the back:
My last letter should have been 12th not 22nd.
Includes envelope with stamp. Postmarked Canton, June 18.

LXVII. Letter from Y.H.E. Hitch to Mary A. Hitch dated June 16, 1863 from Madison County, Mississippi

Madison County Miss
June 16 1863

Mrs. Mary A Hitch
Dear Mary I will write a few lines to you this morning perhaps I may not have the opportunity of writeing again soon. We may start to march tomorrow. Where I can't tell but maybe to Vicksburg. If so, we will have several days marching to do. And probably some fighting to be done before we can get thare. The 16 has not yet come up with any Yankeys yet but I fear that they will in the course of ten, fifteen or twenty days. We come here last Sunday Evening we may leave here tomorrow it will not be many days before we leave at most. This country is alive with our soldiers. The face of the hole earth all most covered with men waggons horses mules and beefs. Mary, no doubt but you think that we are liveing verry hard. Yes we are living hard, indeed we are. Our fare at Charleston was a feast to our fare here. We get a plenty of corn meal and beef. The meal is so coarse it is allmost impossible to turn a hocake. I have found several whole grains of corn in the bread. The only chance to get any of the brand & silks out is to get the meal in a pan & shake it until the brand & silks rise to the top & then blow them off. Probably when we get on the march we will get some bacon. I hope those times will not continue as they now are. I think there will be a change soon, either for the better or the worse. I hope it may be for the better for us. Although there may a many a noble fellow fall before it is decided. I have wrote to you concerning our fare not to trouble you but just to let you know. Our water is standing pon water, the creek at home

would be mutch better. The water is the worst thing we have to contend with. This leaves our mess all well as common. I hope to be able to see you sometime if it be Gods will.
Mary A Hitch Y.H.E. Hitch

LXVIII. Letter from Y.H.E. Hitch to Mary A. Hitch and sons J.J. and A.L. Hitch dated June 22, 1863 from Madison County, Mississippi

Young H.E. Hitch
Madison County Miss. June 22nd /63

Mrs. Mary A. Hitch
Dear wife I embrace this opportunity of writeing you a few lines I have nothing strange to write. My health is not as good as it has been. I have taken some medicine this morning & hope to be better soon. I have a severe cold & may be taking the measles. But it is not time for me to take them from L.B. yet. But if I don't take them from him, I don't know how I will take them for I lay by his side last Thursday night & he had a high fever & severe cough. L.B.'s case is the only case of measles that I know of in camp. I (__) talked in camp today that there is some probbability of us being sent back to So.Ca. soon but I fear it will not be our lot to be so fortunate to get back so near home. Our regt would shout at the order to start back to Adams Run. As me it would please me verry mutch, then I could hear from home oftener & see people from home. Mary I rec. your kind letter on Saturday 20th of this inst. glad to hear from you & to hear you was all alive. Tell J.J. that I was verry glad to hear of his getting home tell him that he need to be thankful that he is at home with his ma instead of (__) I was sorry to hear of E.K.s misfortune. Hurrah with your bees & be sure to save the honey & eat it & not do as we did last year let the worms eat them out instead of yourselves. As you wish to know who went with me to the hospital I will give their names. Augustus Howard, Isaac Forrester, John Simmons, James Bramlet, John Gault, Joseph Fowler & a ga. man, myself, Forrester & Simmons (__) of the seven that has got to the regt yet. Mary truly would I comply with your request & hope it may yet be our lot to take the walk you speak of. I often think of our home the yard & the garden that I set so mutch by. Take care of my Bervene. I trust I may see it again.
J.J. Dear son you can't think how it pleased me to get a letter from you. I expected to hear that you was not well but glad to hear that you was not confined to a sick bed. Glad to hear that your stock are all alive or so near it. Glad to hear that (__) well & hope you may get (__) seasons so as to make your breads. Glad to hear that you can plough so well. Hurrah Joseph Support yourselves if you can. I hope if you will act your part that God will bless you.
A.L. Dear son glad to hear from you but sorry to learn that your health is like mine not good I would be glad to come home & se you & would be glad to have an opportunity to help you to Eat your union. You say you think of your pa when you Eat unions & wonder if you shall see him any more. Lucian I hope to be able to see you again but God only knows whether I shall or not. Dear Son be a good boy do your duty towards your Ma.
*Mary, you & the children notwithstanding that you are left in a sad condition and in a verry lonsom one to, you need to be verry thankful that there is not an army near you. You have no idea what a misfortune it would be to have (___) (*paper torn and words are missing*). Some better this morning than I did yesterday morning. The rest of my mess are doing pretty well. Berry is doing tolerable well this morning. I hope he will soon be up again. Mary, we have all sorts of amusements in camp. Just right close to me are three bunches of men playing cards, some reading the scriptures, some cooking, some eating, some*

sleeping, some shoe mending and the rest doing nothing. Tell (__) that I will try to answer his kind letter in a few days. Allso tell E.K. Thackston to be sure to write that letter & give the news. Mary I hope you will write often as you can & let me hear from you. glad to hear that you are all as near all shod with shoes for the winter as you are. My old shoes hol out well yet. So I will add no more at the present only I wish Mary to remember one that loves her above all others.
Mary A. Hitch } Y.H.E. Hitch

Envelope addressed to:
Mrs. Mary A. Hitch
Fountain Inn P. Office
Greenville Dist
So. Ca.
June 22

Postmark: Canton

LXIX. Letter from Y.H.E. Hitch to Mary A. Hitch dated August 11, 1863 from Scott County, Mississippi

Scott County, Miss.
Aug. 11th 1863

Mrs. Mary A. Hitch,
Dear Wife.

I seat myself to write a few lines to you to inform you that I am yet alive. I am not well but am well to what I have been. I was very unwell with pains when I took the measles & we were on the march to Vicksburg & the weather was awful hot. The first day on the march I got to ride in an ambulance. The next, the first of July, I had to get on a loaded waggon with nothing to shelter me from the broiling hot sun shine. It was a day to be remembered by me for it seemed to me that it was all that I could do to sit up without being exposed to the hot sun & being jolted as I was on the second of July. I got to ride in an ambulance two or three miles when we came to the house where I was left. Mary, you have no idea how thankful I felt when I was told that I could get to stop & get some kind of a shelter. The doctor gave me blue pills before we left Vernon and after I got to Mr Odoms the doctor came back & cald in to see us. He gave me another blue pill & my Bowels then runing off severely. The water where I stayed was the verry strongest of limestone spring water whitch did not agree with me at at all. It kept my Bowels runing off all the time. And they never got any better until after I left Mr Odoms. Mary you can form no idea my feelings for the first two weeks after I was left. It was but a few days after our army passed on to Vicksburg until I heard that they was retreating back. They passed by Brownsville within six miles of where I was & the Enemy pushing them closely. I could heare them fighting at Jackson. There was one week that I expected every moment that the Yankeys would step in & get me but if they had they would not of got mutch for I felt more like diing than living just at that time. But the Enemy retreated back the same road that they come & never give the neighborhood where I was a call. The negros in the section have a great many of them left and gone to the Yankeys & the Yankeys have taken a great many horses *from the Miss. & pretty well all there meat & chickens. Me & J.M. Garrett started for our regt 1st of this inst & reached our regt 7th five days traveling 60 miles & got to ride 23 miles of the 60. we only was out two dollars on the road. I paid two for our breakfast one morning. J.M. is not verry well. he has had a bad spell & ot not to started so soon. L.B & W.B are tolerably well. M.R. Garrett is in camp well as common. Tell E.L. Edwards that I got his letter when I got to camp & was verry glad to see it. It was dated July 8th I think. Mary I have no news to give. It is said that we will be sent to some other place soon, some say back to Charleston, some say to Savannah & some say to Mobile or Tennisee. So I think it uncertain where we go to. But hope that we may rec orders to go back to Charleston soon. Mary, I had just 38 dollars and 50 cents when I was left at Mr. Odoms & a pack of envelopes, some of them had stamps on them. I don't remember how many now but several. When the Yankeys come in so close I slipt $20 into one of my suspenders. So when I went to leave I just had $18.50 in my pocket book. I told the gentleman it was not worth while to ask him his charge, that I would pay according to my pile so he took $13, whitch left me $5 in my pocketbook. I now only have 22 dollars. I did not get here in time for the last draw & the capt would not draw for me & Mat not knowing when we would come up. Mary, I haven't got any letter from you in a long time. There has come several from you to me in my absence from the regt and in the fight at Jackson they destroyed them just as I would of done myself had I had anybodys letter in my hands. I must come to a close by saying that I wish that this may find you all well & doing well. give my best love to all enquireing friends if enny. So I bid you farewell,*

To Mary A. Hitch from Young H.E. Hitch
Aug 12 /63

LXX. Letter from Y.H.E. Hitch to A. Lucian Hitch dated August 20, 1863 from near Morton Station, Scott County, Mississippi

Scott Co, Miss near Morton Station
Aug 20th 1863

Mr. A.L. Hitch
Dear son,
I take this opportunity of droping you a short letter to inform you where I am and how I am a getting along. I am in the hospital at the regiment. This is the third day I have been in this hospital. Dear Son, I have suffered a great deal since I saw you last. I suppose that you heard of me having the measles and me being left behind allmost right amongst the Yankeys. Lucian, Pa fared rough with the measles. I thought one week that I could not live. But for sum cause God has spared my life a little longer. Lucian, I calculated on being captured by the Enemy while I was sick. The Yankey passed in six miles of me on their way to Jackson & they returned by the same road. I was about halfway between Jackson and Vicksburg. The people where I staid treated me as good as I deserved probably but not as good as they could of done. I paid him $13.00 & would of give him as mutch more if they had acted more gentlemanly with me. My health a little better today

August 21 – Lucian, you ought to be here to see how fruit & watermelons, cakes, pyes and sutch like are selling. Peaches & apples $1.50 to $2.00 per dozen. Mellons from three to twelve dollars a piece, ginger cakes from $1.00 to $2.00 a piece. Small fruit pyes, sutch size as your ma frys $1.00 to $1.50 a piece

without shortening, spice or anything but flour & fruit & sometimes a little salt in them. Biscuits six to the dollar. Bacon $1.50 to $2.00 per lb. Flour $1.00 per lb. Lucian, I would like to be at home to help you to eat Irish taters & unions & some stewed chicken & dumplings of your Ma's cooking & some of our eggs. I got some verry good bacon and beans, squashes and collards at Mr. Odoms. Lucian, I have eat peach pye made out of rye meal & fritters too. And have eat wheat meal not batted, just sifted. Both does fine. Save all your rye for it does fine to make fritters. It's worth $10.00 per bushel Lucian, let me hear from you. Let me know how your dog, Brutus, and Tompy are getting on. Write soon. So I have to close. Farewell A.L. Hitch.
Y.H.E. Hitch

Envelope addressed to
Mr. A.L. Hitch
Fountain Inn P.O.
Greenville Dist, So. Ca.

On side of envelope:
Private Y.H.E. Hitch
Co I, 16th regt, So.Ca. v

LXXI. Letter from Y.H.E. Hitch to Mary A. Hitch dated August 21, 1863 from Morton Station, Mississippi

Morton Station, Miss
Aug. 21st 1863

Mrs Mary A. Hitch
Dear wife
I seat myself to drop you a few lines to inform you of my health. Mary, I am not well. I have been here in the regimental hospital some days. How long I will remain here I don't know. I am not able to drill. I just can poke about. My legs is stiff & I cant use them sufficient to drill. They may send me off to the hospital unless I improve soon. If I am sent to the hospital I may get better soon. I can't improve lying here on the hard ground with the disease that I have. Garrett may come home soon. I don't know whether you need to try to send any thing more than a letter to me for its uncertain about me being with the others but I hope to be. Mary the last few days nothing sets well on my stomach. I took calamel & oil the other day & then lay upon the hard ground which is against my disease. Mary I hope to see you again but God only knows whether I shall or not. I wish you well.
To Mrs Mary A. Hitch } From H.Y.E. Hitch

Written across the back of the letter between a list of names:
Mary, please excuse me for writing on old paper. I pict this up after losing my stamps. I have not had the chance to get any more is the reason why your letters are not paid. I supose you can pay for them. Mary if I am spared today I will write you a confidential letter soon.
List of names on back of letter. Appears to be names of men who were sick:
John H. Rice 929 C

S.F. Clary 930	*G*
F.T. Trammel 931	*H*
John Kelly 932	*"*
W. Bryant 933	*"*
Th. Morris 934	*A*
W.B. Lock 935	*"*
W.M. Burton 936	*D*
Augustus Howard 937	*I*
W.W. Goodwin 938	*"*
E.R. Yeargin 939	*B*
James Holcomb 940	*H*
W.P. Smith 941	*F*
Jessie James 942	*"*
R.I. Vaughn 943	*"*
T. Vaughn 944	*"*
P.B. Watson 945	*"*
James Wiganham 946	*G*
T.W. Johnson 947	*"*
H.D. Coleman 948	*"*
J.A. McCreary 949	*I*

Envelope addressed to:
Mrs. Mary A. Hitch
Fountain Inn P.O.
Greenville Dist, So. Ca.
"Due 10"

Written on side of envelope:
From Private Y.H.E. Hitch
Co. "I", 16th Regt, S.C v.

LXXII. Letter from Y.H.E. Hitch to Mary A. Hitch dated September 7, 1863 from "Three miles west of Rome," Floyd County, Georgia

Floyd County, GA
Three miles West of Rome
Sept 7th 1863

Dear Wife,
through the mercys of a kind Creator I am yet alive allthough not well. But as well as I have been for some time. I hope this may find you all in the best of health. I have nothing verry strange to write any more than we have been traveling a great deal of late. I have seen a good deal of the country but could of seen a heap more had I of been well and sound. We left Miss for Ten. & went there and stayed five or six days only when we got orders to leave there for Rome, Ga. So we landed here yesterday. This is a

verry good farming country, this & Ten both. Mary, we had to leave Scruggs at West Point sick have not heard from him since. Mat Garrett is dead as you know. M.R. Garrett is not verry well. L.B. Edwards is tolerable well. We are sorter expecting to meet some of our Enemy soon & it would not surprise me mutch if we don't see them this time. Mary, I have been looking for that letter that Lucian spoke of in your last. Mary, I would write to you about some clothing but things are in such an uproar at present that I will wait awhile before I write. It may be that I have Enough or more than I can carry. Mary, write when you can. Maybe I will get one sometime. Give me all the news you have for I love to hear from you. Mary, I hope you will remember Young in your prayers. Pray that when death comes all may be well with him. So I still remain your most affectionate husband until death.
Young H.E. Hitch } Mary A. Hitch

Letter was written on the back of a list of soldiers who had been sick. The list included name, rank, regiment, company and type of illness.

N.A. McKinney	*Private*	*16th*	*(page torn)*	
W.A. McHugh	"	"	*(page torn)*	
G.W. Lyons	"	"	*(page torn)*	
E.H. Boles	*Lieut.*	"	*G*	
A.J. Howard	*Private*	"	"	
W. Brown	"	"	*F*	
S.E. Smith	"	"	"	
S.P. Mims	*Sargt*	"	*A*	
H.T. Fisher	"	"	*D*	
H.M. Bishop	"	"	"	
Jerry Fowler	"	"	"	
M.C. Cantrell	"	"	*H*	
J.H. Stansil	"	"	*E*	
James Hunt	"	"	*C*	
John Crafford	"	"	*E*	*otitis*
C.R. Twitty	*Sergt*	"	*A*	
John Wallace	*Private*	"	*A*	*Diarrhea*
T.M. Cox	"	"	*A*	
I.L. Henning	*Corp*	"	*A*	
I.G. Barton	*Private*	"	*A*	*Diarrhea*
L.C. Collins	"	"	*D*	*Dysentery*
F.M. Lenderman	"	"	*B*	*Catarrh*
C.W. Bridges	"	"	*B*	*Constipation*
James Hester 971	"	"	*K*	*Enteris Fever*
H. Springfield 972	"	"	*G*	*Dysentery*
H.W. Clayton 973	"	"	*C*	*Surditas*
George Shannon Green 974	"	"	*F*	*General debility*

In this month are recorded four names which count in 974, then discharged as being on sick report.

Between the names on the list Y.H.E. Hitch wrote:
Tell me who thrashed our wheat for you, whether Hughes or Stone.

Mary, direct your letters to Rome, Georgia. If I am spared, I will write again soon.
Lucian, I have seen a heap of big towns in my travels but wish that I could see your little home in Laurens.
Joseph, let me hear how you come out in pulling of your fodder.

LXXIII. Letter from Y.H.E. Hitch to Mary A. Hitch dated September 18, 1863 from Kingston, Georgia

Friday Sept 18 /63
Kingston Georgia

Dear Wife, I seat myself to drop you a short note. My health is as has been for some time. We are here at Kingston this morning on our way back to Ten. We came here yesterday and I suppose we will leave at 12 today for Ten. A great many soldiers passing this place. Troops from Virginia are rolling in. The 3rd regt of South Carolina passed last night. I saw Simeon Thackston & talked awhile with him. He was well and in high life. Sim said O.H.P. More was on bord but I did not see him. This morning is quite cool. Last night it clouded up and sprinkled rain a little and is yet cloudy & wet. I haven't heard from Scruggs since we left him at West Point. Berry is tolerable well. He has cold & pretty bad cough but is better of that. We got us some sweet potatoes last night & have eaten hearty of them and some gingerbread whitch was very good. We have spent 3 dollars at this place for tater cakes. Mary, I wish I could get some letters from you. I don't know where to say for you to direct your letters now as we are on a march but it don't matter mutch for letters come sometimes directed to no certain point. We can't go as far on railway as we did before on account of the bridges being burned. Probably we may have a heap of marching to do. Mary, you may want to know if I have any money. I only have 12 dollars. I have not made arry draw since May. I have a half dollar in silver whitch is as good as five dollars of Confederate money. I am a most oblige to spend some and can get but little ever thing is so high. Please excuse this short & badly composed letter for the mail leaves in a few minutes. I hope this may find you all well and doing well. So I remain your loving husband untill death. Write soon and give me the news.

To Mrs Mary A. Hitch } Young H.E. Hitch

LXXIV. Letter from Y.H.E. Hitch to Mary A. Hitch dated November 6, 1863 from "near Chattanooga, Tennessee

This letter is so badly faded only about one-third of it is readable. The portion that is, is transcribed below:

Near Chattanooga Tenn   Nov 6th 1863
Mrs Mary A Hitch

Dear wife I seat myself to drop you a short letter. I left a very fine Ga the 4th at 1 oclock P.M. for Atlanta left Atlanta at 9 oclock same evening for Chattanooga Station then left thare for the command on the 5th at 12 oclock same day on fast _____ a _____ trip are it. I found the regt today before revelrie? Found L.B. & Garrett in tolerable good health. The ____s some of ther _____ rather ____ I hear since I come to the camp of the Death of two (this line is unreadable)

Post Mark is Dec 2

LXXV. Letter from Y.H.E. Hitch to Mary Hitch dated November 15, 1863 from near Chattanooga, Tennessee

Badly faded letter that is almost unreadable.

Confidential Mary Confidential
__________ near Chattanooga Tenn Nov 15th 1863

Well Mary I am once more permited to write you a few Lines. I am as well as common today. I have no newes to get? of interest. Berry is well & is of? from? the mountain to ___ I again to ____ William Scruggs says tell his folk he is well. Pretty ____ ____ Mary I have b____ that young Howard with (Much more unreadable)

A Soldiers Letter
Co / I / 16th Regt. S. C. V.
Mr. J.J. Hitch
Fountain Inn P. Office
Greenville Dist. SC

LXXVI. Letter from Y.H.E Hitch to Mary A. Hitch dated December 19, 1863

This is another letter that is badly faded so only partially transcribed.

Mary we have not put (__)
I told (__) that if he (__)
Will now have
Mary you once asked me how Billy was a doing. (__) just Billy (__) & he will (__) byes (__) bring them in (__) (__) to sell. From what he told me he made about $30 the other day. Mary you think (__) I
Mary I shall have enough to answer for some day without (__) to (__).
Mary, Berry is fat as a hog & lazy to kill. He is a full brother to Billy Edwards. He is verry (__) & sullen with the boys in talking. He is not as well liked now as he was when he first came to the regt. Me & him gets on fine. Please read & burn this. I don't wish to start up a fuss.
I hope you are all well. So I remain your moste loveing husband

M.A. Hitch
Young H.E. Hitch
Dec 19 /63

Written on the back:
Jan 2 1864
Confidential
Mary A. Hitch

At home in Laurens Dist, SC

LXXVII. "Anniversary Letter" from Y.H.E. Hitch to Mary Hitch dated January 19, 1864 from camp near Dalton, Georgia

Camp near Dalton, Ga
Jan 19 /64

Wel Mary seventeen years ago today if I remember right me and you were married. What a great difference there is in our hopes and expectations now and then. True we are hopeing for this war to close so that we may have the pleasure of being at home together and enjoying life together again. But our hopes I fear will never be granted. Yesterday is our anual wedding day and it comes on the same day of the week that we were married. It brings to my mind a heap of things. Our hopes then was bright for peace & pleasures. Dear Mary we have enjoyed our lives while together as well as any I rekon. And I now am proud to be able to say it. I now am glad that I stayed at home with you and the children while I had the opportunity. And it grieves me to think that I can't be at home with you now. I want to be there to instruct our boys. I studdy a great deal about them. I fear that they will forget there promises. But I hope they are trying to right and act right. I hope that they will recollect to act mannerly both at home and abroad. And when at church behave like men not like some do. I want them to not call men and women by name but Mr. and Mrs. them as they should do. Mary this is a sun shiny morning with a light snow upon the ground whitch fell last night. The weather is a little colder than it was this day seventeen years ago. Oh how happy I would feel if I could have the privilege of starting this evening to see you. I would feel proud indeed. I should not know how to contain myself until I could get home. The cars would not run fast enough for me. Mary it has been a long time since I have had a hug and kiss. I would not say go away to you now I don't think as I have often done. But I hope that you will forgive all sutch offences. Let them pass by. But separated as we are have we not growd to be thankful to our maker for many blessings. Have we not enjoyed many blessings while living together. Yes we have room to be verry thankful. Mary let us look far away to him that is able to help. If we are not blest in this life I do hope that we will be in the other world. So let us not murmurs at sutch as we can't avoid hoping that it is all for the best, This leaves me in tolerable health only rheumatism. Write soon as you can. I rec. a letter from E.L. Edwards the other day. I remain your loving husband
Y.H.E.Hitch. Jan 19th 1864 10 am in the morning.

LXXVIII. Letter from Y.H.E. Hitch to Mary A. Hitch dated January 25, 1864 from camp near Dalton, Georgia

Jan. 25, 1864
Camp near Dalton Ga.

Mrs. Mary A. Hitch
Dear wife

Garrett landed here yesterday evening Sunday. He brought me some letters only nothing else. Mary if their has been any falling out in our mess I know nothing of it. What hapened while I was absent I cant tell. Scruggs quit our mess while he was on patrol guard because he had to be there all the time or nearly so. But they have broken up that guard and he comes back to camp. He has not been more than three hundred (__) us all the while. He thought I suppose that he could have some chance (__) over there. Mary I was glad to get a letter. I was not hardly disappointed in getting anything by him. I suppose the trunks (___ ___ ___ __) are left at Greenville. C.H. he says he could not bring but two trunks through. He could of brought Vaughns through if he had of tried for (Adai__?) would of alarmed them and brought them through. We look for the trunks some time. Mary I am sorry that you did not get any letter before Garrett left. And more so to think that he would tell you such a tale. True my clothes are good sutch as they are and do verry well so long a (__ing) at this place ever get socks, gloves and a cap. I have pants some three weeks before Christmas but if I had not taken care of them they would of last. They would have had the seat worn out by now. But enough on t__ (__). Mary if you think you can stand the trip out and wish to come to see me I want you to use your own choice in the matter provided you can get Mrs Vaughn and Mr. Vaughn to come with you or some person that you can depend upon. If I understand you hant put in the little things in the trunk for me. If you do come be sure to wrap yourself up in clothing. Bring me a coat and pair of pants. If it is cold you can put my coat on and wear it. You need not put buttons on. I will furnish them. If you don't leave and Vaughn comes let him bring the coat and pants. Mary I (___)

[there is another half page here but it is difficult to read.]

Mary I think hard of some but not you in the least you start with money enough if your___ ___ ___ ___. (__) along with you & if you have a small trunk you could bring a jug___ by packing it____ with clothing & other things. Tell A.L. to take care of his wound and get it well & try the timber again. This leaves me in tolerable health. Tell me whitch trunk you started? & get your____?

Young H.E. Hitch

LXXIX. Letter from Sarah Hitch to Y.H.E. Hitch dated January 31, 1864 from Laurens District, South Carolina

This letter from Aunt Sally to Young reports on many family members and serves a great genealogical purpose.

So.C. L. Dist.
Jan 31st 1864

Dear Nephew, I received your kind unexpected letter on the 30th inst. It found me enjoying as good health as I ever expect to have. Through a kind and merciful God I have been enjoying as good health for a year or two except a spell I had last summer as I have for a number of years. I feel sorry truly sorry to hear of your afflicted situation but the good word says all things shall work together for good to them that love God. I hope and trust that God will spare your life to return to your beloved family again and that you may have the opportunity of offering yourself to the Church and be baptized and go on your way rejoicing. O my beloved nephew you don't know how glad I was to hear from you and to hear that you had a hope that when you was done with this troublesome world you would have a resting place in heaven. O glorious thought that there is a resting place for the weary traveler where there will be no more parting with friends and relatives. You said you asked me to remember you in my prayers. O my dear nephew I don't think I shall forget you. I thought for a long time you had entirely forgotten me. The last letter I wrote to you you gave me no answer. I waited and looked for a long time for one but it never

came. I wrote to Ann Templeton to know of her if she knew what was the matter that you did not write to me. She said Adellar saw Mary Ann at meeting at Clear spring Meeting House and she said she said she could give no reason but through neglect. I then gave up on a writing to you any more till you wrote to me. I have wrote to them that is Katharene Stewart and An Te when they heard from you when I would write to them. I had just lately heard you was in the Camps. It is a hard task for me to write. It takes me so long to write a letter. I will begin now and tell you a little of my troubles since I saw you last for it would take me a long time to tell you all. Your Uncle Henry you know is no more. And John W. Pitts also is no more. And worst of all your Aunt Mary is no more. She died the last day of Oct last. And o the trouble I have seen and felt in consequence of the conduct of that spoiled child emeline. She got so after the death of her father that she wanted to make me leave there. And would abuse me in the shamefulest manner you ever heard and would threaten to hit me if I did not keep out of her way. She would urge her mother to make me leave. I saw no satisfaction when I was there. I staid at Eunice Duvalls the most of my time but when I would go back there again I would have to bear the same abuse again or worse. It would trouble her mother very much. She would tell her frequently to hush and then she would abuse her mother. Her mother said to me one day maybe you had better go to uncle Louthers or somewhere awhile and stay a while and so I did. I went down to Duncans Creek to Susan Duvalls last Jan. and staid six months and came back and it was no better but still worse and worse. She wanted no one to stay with her mother but herself so she could have the whole rule and control of every thing in and out. Her brother John had to leave his mothers and go to eunices and die on the account of the abuse that she gave him while at his mothers. Em was always a teasing of her mother to make a will and will all or the most of her property to her but she never could get her to do it till within a few days of her death and there is but few that believes it to be her mothers will but her own making. The rest of the children except Isaac Boyd is a trying to break it and the reason he is not is because em has promised to give something to him. O my beloved nephew this is a world of trouble and distress. I am at this time at eunices but rather expect I shall live at D.M. Milams the man that married Sarah Ann Pitts. Em is a living at the same old place where her father and mother died a keeping house her and the negroes such a keeping of house as it is. She has but little company only of men and negroes. Leroy P and family and John Cooper and family, Eunice D. and family and uncle Louther and family are all well at present as far as I know. Marian Duvall went to Virginia and staid I think something over a year and became diseased and came home and died some few weeks ago of the brain fever. And now my dear nephew I do hope that God permits you to return home again. You will not fail to do your duty lest a worse thing come upon you. You say you have suffered affliction. It may be because you did not your duty that God had required at your hand before you left home and he has followed you as he did Jonah of old and has been a chastising you with his rod of affliction. I hardly know how to leave of but I must come to a close by saying to you I want you to writ as often as you can. Now I heard from you I shall want to hear from you worse than ever. If you get home be sure to write. So no more at present but remain your loving aunt till death. So fare you well to Y.H.E. Hitch.
Sarah Hitch

LXXX. Letter from Y.H.E. Hitch to Mary Hitch dated February 2, 1864 from camp near Dalton, Georgia

Feb. 2nd 1864
Camp near Dalton Ga

Dear wife I take this opportunity of writing a few lines to let you hear from me again. I have no strange news to give particular. My health is tolerable. I have been verry bad off with cold but I hope that I am getting over it. I have had a powerfull caugh but it seems to be getting better. I hope when this comes to your hand that it may find you all doing well. We have beautiful weather now. If this weather should hold as it is I fear the enemy will cause us to have to head out from our little town. The roads are improving verry fast so that the enemy can begin to travel again. And it will go pretty hard with us to have to leave our shantys and turn out all at once. Mary, I have just bought half a square of this sort of paper. I give two dollars for it. And I just bought me a new pair of socks. I paid a five dollar bill for them. And I have just six dollars fifty cents of money in hand at present. Mary, I dismissed my old shoes yesterday morning Feb. 1st. they have been faithful old friends to me and have carried me over many a rough mile of rocks. The shoes that I have on are not worth mutch but they did not cost me a thing. They were a pair of the donation shoes. Mary, today has been wash day with me. I washed two pieces, a shirt and pair of drawers. Got them clean & white too. I recon that you have got the letter by John Jones by this time & mabe you have all the news. Our men are getting off to come home occasionally. John White left the other day and Lieut. Austin today. Mary I have wrote to you in answer to the letter that Lieut. Garrett brought. I hope you have got my letters to you may know better what to do about coming to see me. I have wrote to you to come if you wished to & could get the right company. If you do come you should try to get here pretty soon as wee may have to leave soon. True wee may have to leave in a few days or weeks. And we may be allowed to remain here until April next. But I dont think it. Mary pleas tell me in your answer what you do your hauling with. I want to know whitch you haul with, the mare or the steers. You speak of hauling this, that & the other. But don't say what with. Mary when you write let me know whether you did start Mr. Mocks trunk to me or not. Berry says that the keg that was sent to him is frate's keg. Mary tell Joseph I thank him verry mutch for his present that I have read it different times. Mary, pleas tell me who your preacher is this year at Cedar Grove. Let me know if any body has joined since S.R. Thackston. Scruggs has a severe fresh cold at present. But up and baken bread & boilen beef for our supper. You can hear a heap of new about the 16 regt. I would repeat but you must not believe it. (next line is impossible to read) wicked set of men you may believe it all. Mary there is but little difference between a professor & the worldling here in camp. I shall have to come to a close as my paper is short. Mary don't forget your husband when you try to pray. Write soon as you can. So I remain your
Young H.E. Hitch.

LXXXI. Letter from Y.H.E. Hitch to son A.L. Hitch, undated but probably early February 1864

Undated – pale yellow notepaper same as other letters in 1864

Mr. A.L. Hitch
Dear Son, yours of Jan 26 and Feb 1 is now before me. Sorry to hear of you being so puny & being so crippled up but you must (next line illegible) good care of your foot & (__) perhaps it will soon be well

again. Lucian glad to hear of your ma getting plenty of milk & butter to use. I wish I was there to help you eat some of it. Nurse your pigs as good as you can & make your own meat if you can. Please tell me if you can manage tolerably you and Joseph. You must nurse (__) good and save him if you can. I would like to be at home to help your ma eat biscuits & honey. Mabe I can come in about twelve months if I live that long. You want to know how fat I am and how my hair & beard is. I think I am about as fat as I was I had my likeness taken & my beard is about as it was that time. The hair is not near so thick on my head. last July when I was sick my hair pestered me so I got Mr Odom to shear my hair. Then (__) has (__)at the Has (___) in Oct. my hair shed out almost as bad as when I had the fever. I had it cropt the long leathering? hairs before Christmas and it is thin enough now for me to comb with a fine comb without a course comb. So if you want to see me just get my likeness you will see me. Only my hair is (__) my beard is about the same. (next line illegible) a time or two. As to my teeth I have not lost any but I would like to lose one or two of them for they hurt & sometimes are verry sore. Lucian, you want to know if I think the war is near at a end. I have been afraid that we were whipt. But we are not quite defeated? yet.

LXXXII. Letter from Y.H.E. Hitch to J.J. Hitch dated February 8, 1864 from camp near Dalton, Georgia

Feb. 8th 1864
Camp near Dalton Ga

Mr.J.J. Hitch: Dear Son I have just come off of Battalion drill this morning and now I will you a short letter. My health is tolerable good at this time and truly hoping this may find you well. The weather is prety cold at this time but not freezing like we have had. Joseph we have to drill twice a day and attend a big review one day out of every week. The two last Fridays we had to go to Dalton to the review. Last Friday I saw the most men that I ever saw at one sight I am verry sure. It was supposed that their was 35 or 40 thousand men their. It was said that there was 32 brigades there. I saw as many men on the days of the missionary ridge fight. But never saw so many at one look. They was situated in an open field so that they could be seen to an advantage. There was three strings I think about a mile & a half long. It was so long that it took General Jo Johnson a good while to lope his pretty bay mare around. It is three miles to Dalton & we went to the other side & then back to camp something near ten miles. M.R. Garrett allowed that the city(?) would not last mutch longer. There was so many men to eat. I think if the weather remains dry the rest of the winter that we will not get to stay here long. Joseph you ought to be here see sutch a nasty mess of provisions as is in the trunks & boxes verry near all of the cooked is spoildt. The trunks have all come but Berrys & I don't expect it will come at all. I saw Mr. Bozeman & asked him about it he thinks that he never started with it from Greenville C.H. so when John Jones comes I shall look for the coat and pants. But after that I don't intend to look for anything to come to my mess at all. Looks strange that everybody also can get things from home but us. M.R. Garrett got his box and trunk both today. I hate it on the account of the socks and gloves etc. But however we will try to make out. I would not mind it so bad if it was that a most everybody else in the company are feasting on their daintys from home. Joseph I have just rec. your letter by Thos. Mchugh glad to hear from you but sorry to hear of you all being so unwell. Also I got J.C. Browns letter & one from Uncle Jonas Edwards. I will send you a letter that I got from Aunt Sally Hitch if I can think of it when I go to mail this letter. Joseph you wish me to be at home to advise you about your farm. I have been thinking of giveing you a letter on the subject but have not time at present. But the best thing for you to do is to hurrah and get your land

broke as you can. Your mare you must not push to hard but keep steady a looking. I fear your land that you have to tend this year will be hard for you to manage. But the main thing is to get it in a good fix before you plant it. Break your land as good as you can (__) stiff part of the bottom don't break it too deep the first time to make it cloddy. Take as good care of your mare as possible & mabe she will pay you for your trouble. Hurrah work & do the best you can let others do as they please. I hope to be able to see you sometime. This leaves me tolerable well. Fare well.
Young H.E. Hitch

LXXXIII. Letter from Y.H.E. Hitch to Mary A. Hitch dated February 28, 1864 from camp near Dalton, Georgia

Camp near Dalton GA. Feb 28 1864
Mrs. Mary A Hitch
Dear wife I seat myself to drop you a few lines to let you hear from me again. Through the blessings of God I am enjoying tolerable health. true I am troubled some with pains as usual but that is common with me of late you know. But so long as I can keep on foot & a going I think that I am a doing well & should feel verry thankful to my Creator for sutch blessings. Well Mary we have just got back to our cabbins again this morning. Wee left on Tuesday last & went out to Dalton and fortunately for us we got to ly there untill this Sunday morning when we returned back to our old camp. You probably will get a truer account of the fight than I can give. We were near enough to hear the small arms verry distinctly. Thursday last they put their shots in like hail all day long. What has been done I can't say now report say that we lost 110 men killed dead, the loss on the enemys side I don't know. Fortunately for our brigade we did not get hitcht in. If they had of come on wee would of got in as we had one road to guard that the enemy were a coming. But as it was we had a verry pleasant time the weather was dry and not so verry cold. We have found all of our huts a standing as wee left them. How long we will get to stay in them I don't know for we may have to leave before tomorrow morning again. All around here looks sorter like home. I had rather stay here untill the winter is over. Mary nary letter have I got since by Mchugh. It seems strange that I can't get letters. Edwards & Scruggs are like myself only get a letter now and then. M.R. Garrett scarcely ever miss a week without getting a letter from home. If Henry Stewart comes surely I will get a letter from you. I want to hear from you all badly. I have wrote once a week or about so to you I don't know whether you get my letters reggular or not. Yesterday eleven months ago since I saw you I hardly I can think how you look & the same by the boys. I can come nearer seeing how Joseph looked than any of you. I wrote in my last for the boys to send me there weight and hight. You don't know how bad I want to see my boys. I see a heap of boys but not Joseph and Lucian. Mary from what I can learn there has been a heap of slurs throughd at the 16th regt. I should like to know what we have done that they should talk about us so. We have not done any fighting I know. But whoos fault has it been tell me will they. There is one thing I do know & that is that the 16th has done as mutch hard marching as any of them. She has generally reported when ordered so far as I know. This western living is rough in the summer season. The water is so bad (__)some of them are so bad off I do hope that peace may be made without the 16th fireing a single gun but enough on that subject. I hope this may find you all well. Please write soon as you can. So I remain your Husband
Hitch

LXXXIV. Letter from Y.H.E. Hitch to Mary A. Hitch dated March 6, 1864 from camp near Dalton, Georgia

Camp near Dalton Georgia
March 6, 1864
Mrs. Mary A. Hitch,
Dear wife I seat myself to drop you a short note. I have but little to write. Henry Stewart arived in camp yesterday he brought me a letter from you. Glad to hear from you & more so to hear of you all biding well Enough to be up & able to go. Your letter found me not verry well. I was on guard the night before & it was verry cold & I was not verry well before. But I feel tolerable well today. Wee have the suddenest changes in the weather hear that you most Ever saw. The weather has been quiet mild except some cold spells that wee have had that was cold to kill. But however the winter I hope is a most over although March & the first of April may be pretty rough & cold. Mary I am sorry to learn of you fathers being so kind to you, but it is just like I expected it would be. But you must bear it as well as you can. It hurts my feelings to think of your situation but the best that I can sa will not help you mutch. I can only wish you well. But you can't look for mutch help from your father for he has Enough with him to consume all he has in a year or two. So do as I have done in some things just give it up And say that you hope to be as well off when you come to leave this world as any of them. I have known or believed that it would be just as you say it is. But you have gained some honor since I left you that is that you are trying to live with in your self. It is just the same case here Everyone is taking Every advantage that he can if it mant that I hate to write it. I could tell you something that you would not believe. But Enough of this. We must get along the best that we can it appears to be a hard old world to get along through verry mutch so if we do our duty. Our people appears to be growing more wicked Every day. I sometimes think that times will never be any better for us not in our time no how. If wicked has brought this war on us I fear it will not End soon. It seems that all is aiming to make a speck some way. And some is not particular how they make it. Mary I have been in the army long enough to be getting verry lazy & you know that I was lazy Enough before I left home. But I think if I was at home I could get your firewood. But hearty as I am I cant chop nor toat a great deal my back never has been as well since I had the measles as it was before. It may be if I could work steady & not be out in the night or bad weather that I could do more. There is a heap of the time that wee are doing nothing. Then again run like all the world. So no more.
I remain your Young H.E. Hitch

LXXXV. Letter from Y.H.E. Hitch to J.J. Hitch dated March 7, 1864 from camp near Dalton, Georgia

Camp near Dalton Georgia
March 7th 1864
Mr. J.J. Hitch,
Dear Son I embrace this opportunity of writing you a few lines to let you hear from me again. I am not well this Evening verry mutch painafied. The weather is unsettled whitch makes me worse than if the weather was good. You are getting on pretty well with your ploughing. Your land is sutch that I fear you will not be able to manage it. But if you can get it well broke before you plant perhaps you can tend it & if you have good luck & seasons you will make corn. I wish I could be at home to help you to plant it to lay off the rows anyhow. You say you have a fine colt at your house. Take as good care of it as you can maybe you can make something of it. I cant think of any name for it without you call it Prap Pats or

Picture or something easy & short to call. I would be glad to see your colt to see if it is well formed. If you want to & can you may raise you a mule colt this Season. I think David Studdard has a good jack. It is a good ways down there but it might save your mare from being taken from you next winter. They will not want a mare that is in fold. But you & ma must do as you think best about the matter. Mr Jones has a jack but unless he has growed since I saw him he is verry small. If he is large Enough to age you can put your mare to him if you wish to. Joseph you wrote to me to pray for you to pray that your sins might be forgiven you & that you might be prepared to be baptized. Joseph I have often tried to pray for you that you might see that you was a sinner and that you must repent of your sins. Dear Son I hope that you have been thinking of the matter. And if you have don't give it up but keep trying. And even if you don't feel that you are fit to join the Church you can try to do that that you know to be right. Don't just because you are a worldling give up to sin. For do the best you can you then will have Enough to answer for. Dear Son if the Spirit has been striving with you I hope you will yield to it. And I hope that you may get through & join the Church & be baptized. Be sure to steady the matter over well before you do your do. Joseph I hope you may receive a pardon of your sins & join the Church. You know that you have to dy & after death appear before your Creator. You may soon have to leave home for camp. And if so you will find camp a poor place to try to get religion. So I hope that you will have yours before you leave home & then try to hold on to it. If I had a good opportunity I could write a good deal more on the subject. But I hope you may get through. And be able to write it to me. So I bid you fare well for this time.
Young H.E. Hitch

Envelope addressed to:
Mr. J.J. Hitch
Fountain Inn P. Office
Greenville Dist. S.C.
Postmarked Mar 12, Dalton, Ga. No stamp. "Due 10"

On the side of the envelope;
Private Young H.E. Hitch
Co (I) 16th regt. S.C.

LXXXVI. Letter from Y.H.E. Hitch to Mary A. Hitch dated March 13, 1864 from camp near Dalton, Georgia

The following letter is from the Michael Givens collection.

To Mrs. Mary a. Hitch at home. Y.H.E. Hitch
Camp near Dalton, Georgia, March 13, 1864

Mrs. Mary A. Hitch,
Dear wife, as I sent you no letter by H.G. Vaughn I will drop you a few lines. I don't feel very well to day I have cold or may be takeing mumps, though I may not taken them, but wee have one case of them here in camp. Mary you may rest easy about my clothing, the way everything has turned out I have done pretty well, as we have had cabbins to stay in most of the winter and the winter has not been as hard as some winters. True I would rather have the coat you made than these short jackets when it rains. But as

it is I have as much or more than I can pack and toat on a march. So I want you to put that suit in the drawer & keep them until next fall maybe you may yet see me put them on. Mary I have three cotton shirts two are getting smartly worn, and two flannel shirts. If it had been clean I would of sent Joseph my red shirt for it would come nearer of fitting him. I have three pairs of drawers one is old. I have a pretty bad pair of pants on & drew a good pair the other day. They are just plain homespun but they are lined & well made. I also drew a pair of shoes my old ones are thin & rather tight. My new ones are rather large, But I can wrap my feet up with rags & keep them warm. I have one pair of socks that I hant wore any yet. If you have any socks you may send me a pair by Vaughn. I would as soon have cotton ones. You may send me a pair of suspenders and some sewing thread. If H.G.V. can fetch it you may send me a little honey & brandy for I could sell the brandy & get something to eat. I had of thought yesterday I might of sent you some buttons for pants for you may need some. Mary I told Vaughn to go to see you & the boys & to tell you to treat him to some honey & brandy for me that I could not get there to get any of it myself & that I wanted a friend that could drink some of it. Mary I can't write all that I want to so I must stop. I rec. yours of the 7th to day glad to hear from you, I hope this may find you well. Hitch

LXXXVII. Letter from Y.H.E. Hitch to J.J. Hitch dated March 20, 1864 from camp near Dalton, Georgia

Camp near Dalton Ga
March 20 /64
Mr. J.J. Hitch

Dear Son I seat myself to write you a few lines. I am tolerable well today & hope this may find you well. I have just come in from preaching. I saw the M.E. take the sacrament today. There appears to be a revival of religion in this army. This Evening half after three oclock there will be preaching in our regt. But I may have to be on guard, if not I will try to attend. This morning wee had inspection as wee always do on Sunday morning. Wee have a heap of big kickups of late. Wee get to go to Dalton Every two or three days to have a division drill or sham battle or some review. Wee have verry pretty weather now. It is windy like March generally is. Joseph I weighed the other day I weighed 158 ½ the most I think that I Ever weighed before. So you see that I am fat or well stuffed. The stuffing is mostely cornbread & water. This morning I had a good breakfast good hoecakes, cornbread & boild fat beef & some rice. And for dinner I had some pancake of the flower & meat that your ma sent me but it is nearly out. We lived fat while Stewart Garrett & our little Provisions lasted. Today Scruggs & Garrett is both sick so I fried some pancake for them & myself for dinner. Joseph let me know in your next if the upper string of fence has ever washed away since I left home. You say your wheat look verry bad. Mayby it will come out. You must recollect the moste of your land is poor & it will not grow off so fast as if was bottom land.
Now a few lines for A.L.
Dear Son it maybe that you may have the pleasure that you speak of sometime this summer. It may be if we don't have to go the Kentucky Tenn or some where else that I can get to come sometime this summer. if furloughing is kep up as it has been for a few weeks my turn will come after awhile. I hope to live to se it. I may get to see you all. I would of wrote to your ma to tried to get me a recruit if I had known of ary one to get. But I cant pay sutch prices like some are for a ten days furlough. Me & Garrett like to of quarreled on the subject last night. He is wanting to see home Enough worse than I do. So do all that

have been home lately. Dear Sons I hope this may find you all well. So fare you well. If wee never meet on Earth let us try to be prepared to meet in heaven.
Y.H.E.H.

LXXXVIII. Letter from Young H.E. Hitch to Mary A. Hitch dated March 24, 1864 from camp near Dalton, Georgia

Camp near Dalton Georgia
March 24 /64
Mrs Mary A. Hitch.

Dear wife
Yours of the 13th come to hand on Tuesday night of the 22nd. It found me tolerably well & on guard. I expected to about freeze that night but come out better than I commonly did. The night of the 21st there was a good big snow fell. Tuesday evening the wind blew verry cold but after dark the wind lay. The orders is for all to stay at the guard house when not on post. But they could not stay & have fire & shelter there. So the most of them slipt to their quarters to their fires & I slipt into the Officers fire at the guard house & stayed the first two hours by a good fire, then went on post two hours. I did not get mutch cold. I was pretty well wrapt up. I had my feet well fixed two pairs of socks & a large pair of heavy shoes so when my two hours was out I slipt to my quarters to & stayed till near time to go on post again. So yesterday the sun shined all day & has melted the moste of the snow. So I got through with another day & night of the war safe & sound. Mary you have often heard of snow balling. If you had been here yesterday & the evening before you could of seen the biggest one you ever did sure. Tuesday evening Jacksons Brigade made an attackt on ours & I am sure I never saw snow fly before. And yesterday I never saw & heard the like it was not just a few men it was hundreds against hundreds. One Brigade would charge another & fight until the ones they had charged would get to hard for them when they would break for home & the others after as hard as their heels could carry them. And then sutch whooping you never heard. Each side would take prisoners all they could. I was on post a part of the time & then on my line and on each side they did not aim their missiles at me at all but I was in the hot place, one army on the one side & the other on the other. Their balls flew around me thick & heavy. I did not take any part with them for I was on guard & would not no how. Mary as to thinking hard of you concerning the provisions & the clothing I dont in the least. I dont see why I should it is not your fault. The worst I hate is your having the trouble & expense & then loosing all. I know that you hate it bad enough. Keep the suit of cloths as I wrote to you to do. When you have the chance you can send me a little but dont send but little at a time for it is hard to get every thing that is started to us. So if you send and I get anything I will be verry thankfull if not I will not think the least hard of you atall. So no more but remain your most unworthy Husband
Young H.E. Hitch

LXXXIX. Letter from Young H.E. Hitch to Mary A. Hitch dated March 27, 1864 from camp near Dalton, Georgia.

Note – this letter comes from the Michael Givens collection. He descends from Young Hitch through his son John J. Hitch.

Camp near Dalton Ga.
March 27th 1864

Mrs. Mary A. Hitch.
Well Mary to day one year ago I left home. My health at present is something better than it was at that time. I have seen & felt aheap since I left home more than I ever thought of liveing to see. Wee rec. our trunk yesterday But not mutch in it. I will tell you what I got. I got the cap gloves socks & scarf all good. I got a sack of flour & a piece of meat & some coffee I suppose it to be I hant opend it yet. The fruit was loose that I took to be mine in the trunk. The fruit smartly hurt but will do to use by suning a while. The cake you sent was not hardly fit to eat. There was some of a big cake that was burnt a little that had not soured mutch. I am glad that the trunk did come although there was not near what was started in it. Wee start the trunk back to Greenville C.H. by Mr. Bozeman to day. Please tell E.L. (Euphrates Lafayette) Edwards for Berry that he starts the trunk to Greenville C.H. by Bozeman And that the trunk is marked in his name. Mary I sent you my old shoes you can have then worked on a little & you or joseph can wear or trade them they are rather small & light for mee. The leather straps are for Joseph to use as he see proper. The big strap will make a haim string by triming. The buttons & little buckle is for Lucian they are in the toe of the shoe. That just reminds me of the sewing thread & the suspenders you sent I got them they come in time of need as you may see by the old ones that are around the shoes. I just lacked from last night till to day of wearing them twelve months without washing. I wish now that I had not of told you to send socks & suspenders by Vaughn. I must close my letter as there is going to be preaching in our street now soon. I send this letter by Bozeman. This leaves the mess all on foot. I hope this may find you & the boys well. Let me hear from you when convienint. So here comes the preacher for preaching. Good by Mary. Some talk of us going to Verginy
Young H.E. Hitch
Upside on the top of the second page:
A beautifull day this is March 27th 1864. H.

XC. Letter from Y.H.E. Hitch to Mary A. Hitch dated April 21, 1864 from camp near Dalton, Georgia

Camp near Dalton, Ga
April 21st 1864

Mrs Mary A. Hitch
Dear wife
I this morning will try to write you a short letter to let you know that I am yet liveing & have not forgotten you yet. I am just tolerable well at present but better than I have been. A Sunday night I was on guard & it was a rough time to be out. Tuesday wee had to go to Dalton on a big review a heap of doublequicking to do whitch give me out I tell you. Yesterday our regt were ordered out near Dalton on the Cleaveland Road to work. The work was throwing up a battery to place cannon & rifle pitts and sutch like. The 16th done the biggest days work that she has ever done since I have been with it. Every three men has so mutch to do there was no slideing out. But this morning I feel better than I expected to after sutch tramps. Mary on Tuesday at one time I was so mad when they was runing us so that I felt like I

could of throughed hot shot at them. Mary the Enemy & our Headquarters are only 14 miles apart. The Enemy is at Ringgold. Ours at Dalton. There may be fighting done hear about Dalton. Mary I rec a letter from aunt Salley on the 16th last. Her health is not so good as it has been. From what she writes she has no regular home yet. She speaks of Milams haveing but little house room not enough to take all her plunder & she wants to all together. She is at Leroys at present. It may be that she would like to live with you. You can do as you please about it. Mary wee have good preaching here & pretty good attention. Some are joining the Church. There is a little warmth of religion of late in our camp & I am glad to see it. There is service a moste every night when the weather is suitable near our cabin. Prayer is offered for mouners they have from three to six I believe generally when I have been out. Mary I have rec no letter since Vaughn come. I am anxious to hear from you. I must come to a close for my ink is so bad that you cant read it I fear. And I want to write to aunt Salley. Write soon & give me the newes. Let me hear from your Pa. I have not wrote to Ellen yet. I have not mutch chance but think I will soon as I can.
So fare you well
Young H.E. Hitch
April 21st /64

Envelope addressed to Mrs Mary A. Hitch
Fountain Inn P. Office
Greenville Dist. So. Ca.
Postmarked Dalton April 22

Written on side of envelope:
Soldiers Letter Co (I) 16th regt. So. Ca. vol.

XCI. Letter from Y.H.E. Hitch to sons J.J. and A.L. Hitch dated April 21, 1864 from camp near Dalton, Georgia

Camp near Dalton GA April 21st 1864

To J.J. A.L. Hitch,
Dear Sons this leaves me just tolerable. I am stuffed up with cold and have been the most of the winter. I have a caugh that hurts me pretty bad at times. I have had it the hole winter through & was it not for me having the measles last summer I would be uneasy about it. But I hope this may find you both well. Lieut. Garrett will bear this to you he is going to start for home tomorrow. He leaves us for good. He will join some other command I suppose. But will get a good furlough before he joins another. Boys we have plenty of drilling to do we had a big review Tuesday last it come the nearest wearing me out of arry one that we have had yet, but I was in a poor plight for it for I was old guard & had a bad cold & pains to kill allmost seemed to me. But I made the trip although in a great deal of pain yesterdays work did not hurt me near so bad although I had to use a pick & shovel. Today a short company drill this morning probably a Battalion or Brigade drill this evening. Boys I must tell you of there takeing our Enfield rifles from us and giveing us the Austin rifles whitch are a rough looking gun at best. And you may know that I was not pleased with the swap. My Enfield had kept me off of the guard lines six weeks hard going and one week besides & had I been allowed to keep it I could of got the premium the next Sunday morning. But the second Sunday after getting our new guns me & another man tied so we had to draw for it & I lost it but

it was said that my gun was the cleanest. If nothing happens I will make some of them rub for the premium next Sunday morning. Col. Toor said to me the first Sunday after we drew the Austin rifles that he believed I always would have a clean gun. Some say to me that they won't work on a gun like I do. But they bought sandpaper & wore it out on there guns & I beat them without any sandpaper then I laugh in my belly good. It pays mighty well to keep a clean gun sutch weather as we have for there is no fun in standing twenty four hours in bad weather. I hope you will write soon as you can & let me hear from you. We may leave hear soon but write the letters will or at to be forrowed on to us. Please give me your highth both of you. Joseph your present came in a verry good time to me. And will answer my use verry well. Hurrah knock on the best you can and may by you can get a long so fare you well.
Y.H. E. Hitch

XCII. Letter from Y.H.E. Hitch to Ellen (?) dated April 21, 1864 from camp near Dalton, Georgia

Camp near Dalton Ga
April 21st 1864

Well Ellen you probbaly think that I have forgotten you but I hant. I hope that this letter may find you & your children all well. Ellen I often think of you, your children & the old folks on your plantation. Ellen it makes me mad Enough to bite the nails off of my fingers allmost when I think of some things I have propesied for some things that are a coming to pass as fast as possible. But the worst is yet ahead yet to come. I would be glad to see you to hear from you all but so it is I cant. But Ellen if I was at home I do not know whether I could go to see them or not. I am afraid I could not. I am sorry to hear of the loss of kin. I do not see how you are to get along But I suppose you have another in her place. Ellen these are hard trying times. It is trying the souls as well as the boddy. If we was only sure of our happiness after death it would be a happy change for us. I have seen some sorry times since I left my home and Expect to see worse if I live. But I hope there will be some way provided better than I can see. As to perishing you don't I hope know anything yet. Wee don't get Enough here wee say, yet we are fat Enough. Ellen I hant perished yet but I have eat a many a meal off of corn bread and water. Time of the Lookout Mountain fight I picked a chunk of corn dodgers up in an old camp that had been throughed out eat it & thought good. And I saw some men on the retreat bring some bacon skins out of a meat house and broil them to eat. The other day I seen a man with about 15 inches of a cows tail skind to eat. But I hope you will have plenty if you hant (__) (__) on one little farm ought to do a heap of work. But you have to do so mutch for the (_____) get (__) done at home but do the best you can. Times will change some day for the better or worse one. Ellen let me hear from you again soon as you can. Let me know how you are getting on with the (__). Ellen you know I yous to love to stay at home But if I ever am so fortunate as to get back I will be worse to stay at home than ever. I could help Mary to (__) up wash or any hard drudgery with pleasure. Wee are lazy to kill in camp. So I must come to close as there is wood to get to cook our rations with & it is a raining now. The old man is on guard. Scruggs is standing guard two hours for another man but will be in soon. So good by Ellen
Young H.E. Hitch

At the top of the second page:
Joseph read this to Ellen if you please

XCIII. Letter from Y.H.E. Hitch to sons J.J. and Lucian Hitch, undated (probably Spring 1864 sent with a letter to Mary Hitch)

Undated – probably spring 1864 based on contents

To JJ – got a letter from A.Y. Garrett speaking of the late spring and the neighbors being behind with their work. He said you were ahead of the neighbors with your work. We have to be thankful that we are as well off as we are. Suppose your ma had no meat at all and your whole dependence for something to eat was in the milk and butter from your cow. And think soldiers was to come and drive her off and kill her for beef. Leave you nothing to eat but a little dry bread. Just sutch a case took place near this camp. No, don't you think you see hard times but wait until the army comes along, they will steal the last thing that you have to eat.
To Lucian – I have just come from preaching and eat my dinner. I saw several baptized or sprinkled. And they are now gone to the river to baptize them that joined the Baptist. I felt to lazy to walk to the river. Berry is gone I think. Scruggs is on guard. I lost the premium today again. Had I of worked on my gun as the man did on his this morning who beat me, I would of beat him. I generally clean mine on Saturday so it rained last night and I done as good as nothing to mine this morning but I make them work. I don't spend a great deal of labor on my gun. I hope you and Joseph will never let it be said that you let your mother suffer for something to live upon.

XCIV. Letter from Y.H.E. Hitch to Mary A. Hitch dated April 25, 1864 from camp near Dalton, Georgia

Camp near Dalton Georgia
April 25 /64

Mrs Mary A. Hitch
Well Mary today finds me only tolerable. My back is very weak and hurts me pretty bad. Just come off of guard yesterday morning. I have had nothing to do today not until dress parade this evening. I have been troubled verry mutch of late with pains. I fear that I will get on the lift again. My health otherwise is good as to an appetite. I have a good one. And if it was not for the pains and weakness in my back & legs I could do fine. The moste of our regt are gone to Dalton for Provoste guards two companys and a piece left in the camp. It begins to look a little like spring the last two or three days. It appears to be a verry backward spring here and I suppose it to be the same with you or verry near the same. I suppose you get the Army news as soon as me & it is not worthwhile for me to say anything on the subject to you. Also of the stoping of furloughs. If the furloughing had kept on I would of got to of come home this summer. But as it is God only knows when or whether or ever or not. But I trust there is a better day a coming soon. We appear to be getting the best of the war this year. Mary I feel like that if we could just humble ourselves all of us both soldier and citizen and ask the Lord to assist us and aid in the Battling with the Enemy, I do think we could have peace in our land again. Mary I want to come to see you bad but not bad enough to run away to get to see you yet. Mary I am tiard of soldiering but I cant say what some say. That is peace any way just give them peace. They dont care whitch side gains just so they get out of the war. I know that I have never been in a battle but I have been near Enough to see a good deal. But I am not willing to stop just on any terms as some speak of. Mary I hope that I can come to see you sometime

& when I do come have it to say the war is over & that I have come to spend the remainder of my days with you. Mary was it not for being so troubled with rhumatism I could enjoy myself in the army fine. Wee soldiers should recollect what we are fighting for & try to be content even if wee do have a heap to undergo. Mary I hope this may find you well and in good spirits. When you pray for me, pray that I may be ennabled to do my duty as a soldier & that I may be ready & prepared when death comes let it be soon or late. So fare you well Dear wife
Young H.E. Hitch

XCV. Letter from Young H.E. Hitch to Mary A. Hitch dated May 1, 1864 from camp near Dalton, Georgia

Camp near Dalton Ga.
May 1st 1864

Dear companion
I seat myself this Sabbath morning to drop you a few lines. I am as well as common today. I am troubled smartly with pains as you know I am subject to. I recd your most kind and loveing letter yesterday by A. White bearing date of April 26. I was truly proud to get a letter from you. I had not recd ary letter since the one by Vaughn. Glad to learn that you was all well. I was afraid that you were all sick by me not getting no letters. Mary, I have but little news that will interest you. A Friday last there was some appearance of a fight. I was at Division Headquarters on the road & the Couriers flew a round in a hurry. The cannonading was pretty heavy. I don't know the result yet But hear that the enemy have retiered back to Ringold. We are in our old holes yet it will soon be five months since we came to this camp. We have got to stay a heap longer than I expected when we come here. The weather is warm this morning is cloudy a raining a little. The woods have got green verry fast for the last week. Some of our men that have just come in from Greenville say that the trees are greener here than at Greenville. But I suppose it about the same. Mary you say for me to come home & you will give me something to eat. I will try to comply with your request as soon as possible. It may be some time before I can get off though. Mary I often think of home & the past & gone by days of pleasure that I have spent with you. I hope that I may live to get home again & that we may Enjoy a few more days on Earth together. I want to see my old home again verry bad. I would be glad to see the old chicken coop or the sheep house. And I would love to see them pretty shade trees & the rose bushes in the month. Tell me if the wooly vine and the big monthly is yet alive & standing. To come home would be a treat to me sure at this time. Mary there is a great revival of religion going on now in this Brigade mostely of the 24 SC v and some of the 46 Ga & eighth Ga Battalion. There has some few joined of the 16 SC reg. There will be Baptising done some time today. I don't know that I will get to go yet as the inspections is not over. Mary let me know how Cedargrove Church is getting on of late & if any have joined of late. Also the same from old Durbin. M.A. I hopt this may find you well & in good spirits. And if I never more meet you on Earth I hope to meet you where there will be no more troubles.
Your Husband
Young H.E. Hitch

Envelope addressed to Mrs. Mary A. Hitch
Fountain Inn P. Office

Greenville Dist. S.C.

On the side is written:
A Soldiers Letter
Co. (I) 16 regt S.C.

XCVI. Letter from J.J. Hitch to father Young H.E. Hitch dated May 1, 1864 from Laurens District, South Carolina

May 1st 1864
South Carolina Laurens Dist

Mr. Young H.E. Hitch
Dear Father
I take my pen in hand to rite you a few lines to let you know that I am yet a live and in tolible Helth. I have got the head ack a little this even but I hope that when this letter cums to hand that it may find you well and doughing well. Dear father. I hant go mutch to rite at this time only wee air dun planting corn. Wee finished the 30 of April. Wee got all the bottom planted. Father that old bottom is a going to bee cloddy the loar end of the rows. I Bedded the ends of the rows in the old Bottom and onn the other side of the branch the ends of the rows. Well now the Wheat, the Wheat looks sorter small. I think that wheat will bee late to save and I am afrade that the rust will ketch it and ruin it all together. Oh daddy cum home and help us set out cabedge plants. We have got sum Just as purty as you ever saw. Wee want to set out sum as soon as it rains and I think that in a week I will have sum tobacco plants big Enuff to set out. The rye and barley looks very bad indeed it has ben Sutch a bad winter on it until it like to of killed all the barley. Father as ruff a winter as it has been your birveany is yet alive and a blooming out verry pretty and Mother has got the best Stand of Beens that you ever saw in the garden for they air as thick as you ever saw beens and Sum peas they have got Sum blooms onn them now and Sum cucumbeirs up and Shallots wee have plenty of them too and Sum ounions and a Sallet bed and the irish potatos I don't now what they will do but they air cuming up verry pretty and our potato patch it will be Just where you told us to have it last year below the garden. wee had our potato patch thair last year and this year again in the same place. Pa cum home and I will give you a big mess of Eggs rite brand new ones. I have got four ar five duzen rite at this minit in the cubard and that wont be all that wee will give you to Eat for I think Ma wood kill a hin and stuff hir besides the eggs friers grows as fast you ever saw a colt in your life. Well father now my hight and wait. Five feet one inch and a quarter I way ninety lbs. Now A.L.'s wait and hight four feet five inches and a quarter and ways sixty 2 lbs. I am just about as high as Ma. I recken you know how high Ma is. father you told me that you wanted me to find your squair but I hant never found it yet. I dremp of it but did not (__) (__) you told me too you told me when I drem of it not forgit whair it was but I forgot whare it was. I will cum to a close in short. Rite soon fair you well.
J.J. Hitch

XCVII. Letter from Young H.E. Hitch to sons J.J. and Lucian Hitch dated May 7, 1864 from camp near Dalton, Georgia

Camp Near Dalton Ga
May 7th 1864

Mr. J.J. Hitch,
Dear Son
Through the goodness and kindness of our Creator I am enjoying tolerable health & am once more permitted to drop you a few lines to let you hear from me. I have no strange news to give more than the Enemy is said to be advancing on us slowly. They are coming on the Cleveland Road. We are still preparing for them. The Ladys have been ordered to leave hear. Wee had a fly round Tuesday & Wednesday last out to the Spring Place some ten or twelve miles. My company was sent out on pickette that night. But we saw yankeys. In a few minutes after wee got back to camp there come orders to be ready to leave at a moments notice. And we keep our crust ready baked for a tramp. I hear today that wee have gained a great victory in Virginia. I hope it may be so. There will no doubt be a great battle fought near Dalton soon. How it will turn out time will only tell. I cant help but dread it for I know that some will be sure to fall & I may be one of them. Joseph please write to me. I rec. a letter from you & your ma on Wednesday last of the 15 April.
So fare you well J.J.
Young H.E. Hitch.

Well Lucian a few lines for you. I am tolerable well my legs are a little sore from the tramp to the Spring Place the other day. The calves of my legs have been verry sore indeed. The weather the two last days quiet warm but the night verry cool. The first of the week was verry cold frosty today this morning cool but will be warm when the sun gets up. Today is Saturday so I must rub up my rifle for inspection tomorrow morning so as not to have so mutch work to do on Sunday. Also sweep around our cabbin. I sometimes can curtail my work on Sunday by doing a part on Saturday. Then what I cant do on Saturday & am compelled to do on Sunday I don't think I will have to account for. Boys I wish I could be at home to help you plant your corn for I know you need some help. But hurrah (__) along the best you know & can. And when you need advice you must go to some old person for it. I know you feel at a great loss often times. I am away from you so as to be no help to you atal. But while you are struggling to make something to live upon your father is struggling hard to gain our independence & freedom. And I do hope that we may yet gain our independence though I may fall in the struggle. I hope you two sons may reap some of the benefit of our independence. So fare you well A.L.
Young H.E. Hitch

Boys the best of meetings going on in the Camp.

XCVIII. Letter from Y.H.E. Hitch to Mary A. Hitch, undated but probably early May 1864

Undated – notepaper same as May 1864

Mary you speak of your visitors. My advice is for you to shun company all you can. I think it right for its not for your benefit that they visit you. Its for their own interest and after you are eat out they will stop coming to see you & tell Joseph to feed light & if they don't like it, it will take the less to do them. You know nothing yet about folks. You had better shell your corn as fast as you can & if no better pile it up in the little room and box up your bacon & put it upstairs. Mary take good care of everything that is to eat. You will have to be verry stingy. Let the people say what they may. Be sure you & the children eat a plenty your selves. Mary as to me getting off I cant tell you any more than you know. I can not double quick when they go at that I step out of rank. But I suppose when the war is over I will be discharged, probably before by death. If so God grant that I may be prepared for Eternity, Death and Judgement oh that I may be ready.

Envelope addressed to:
Mary A. Hitch
Fountain Inn P. Office
Greenville Dist, S.C.

On inside of envelope:
Favored by Mr. Young Howard

XCIX. Letter from Sarah Hitch to Y.H.E. Hitch dated May 9, 1864 from Laurens District South Carolina

Another beautiful Aunt Sally Hitch letter full of family information.

S.C.L. Dist
May 9th 1864

Dear nephew
I seat myself this morning to write you a few lines to let you know how I am and where I am. Through a kind providence I am tolerable well again at present. I have moved to E.L. Pitts and I expect perhaps to live with him the rest of my days. I hope when this comes to hand it will find you well. I received your kind and welcome letter on the 8th of this inst and was glad to hear from you one more and to know that you was still in the land of the living and on pleading ground with your God. Every letter I get from you I fear it may be the last I shall ever hear from you. You say you are having a good time there amongst you in religious meetings. You say they are a joining the Church out here and now my beloved nepew try to do your duty as others are a doing. You said in your first letter you sent me you was not satisfied in not offering yourself to the Church while at home and now you have the same priviledge as others have to join the Church and I would advise you as a friend you would embrace the opportunity. you don't know that you will ever have a better opportunity and then get a letter and send it home to the Church where your companion is. No doubt it would rejoice her heart to have your name enrolled on the Church book

with her own although it would be more desirable for to be present with you when you joined. But you should not neglect doing your duty on that account. If you are a Christian and I hope you are you will enjoy your self in the comforts of religion amongst your Christian brethren a great deal more than you do out of the Church. You can make free in talking of the subject of religion what you can out of the Church amongst your friends. You said you had two of J. Cooks boys to see you. I would like to hear from them all and to know where they all are and how they are a doing. I want you to tell them if you should see them again to tell them to write to me and tell them where to direct their letters to direct them where you do yours. James Duvall, Eunices son has been in the armmy a considerable time. He has been in three or four battles and got wounded at chattanooga if I recolect right and came home and has never got so he could walk without his crutches for he was wounded in the ancle or in the leg near the ancle. He has been at home seven months. Young Pitts, Leroys brother is somewhere in the armmy. the last account he was in the illenois in the hands of the yankeys. Leroys oldest son is in the armmy also Joseph A. Hitches oldest son is in the armmy. Joseph A.H. has been in it himself but is now at home sick. He got sick at the camp and I fear he never will get well any more. I received a letter from Ann E. Templeton the 1th of March. They had all been sick but was then better. Her two little boys is agoing to school and she says a learning very fast. They both wrote to me when there mother wrote. I have been a wanting to write to Mary Ann but did not know for certain where to direct my letters whether at the same post office or not where I used to direct them at Centerville. I reckon you have perhaps heard of the death of Marian Duvall, Susan Hitches husband. He was in the armmy over twelve months and came home on a furlough and took the brain fever and died in a few days. He was a living at his fathers old place. He had put up a small house up on the road near where the old machine stood and susan is a living there this year but I don't know whether she will continue there any longer than this year or not. Pinkney Hitches widow is a living over in Abbeville on a little place she has rented and her two little sons with her. J.A.H. lives on his fathers land near him. I shall begin to draw to a close lest you get tired a reading my blotched writing. I do here enclose a little thread to mend your cloths when you tare them. I sent some thread to Marian Duvall when he was in camp and he was very glad of it and I thought perhaps you might need it. I want you to write every chance you can get for it does me good to hear often from you. I do hope that this unholy war will shortly come to a close so that all of you will get to come home to your fammilyes one time more. May God spare your life to return to the embrace of your fammily is the wish of your affectinate aunt: So fare you well at this time.
Sarah Hitch to Young H.E. Hitch

C. Letter from Young H.E. Hitch to Mary A. Hitch dated May 22, 1864 from near Cartersville, Cass County, Georgia

May 22nd / 64
Cass County Ga near Cartersville

Dear Wife
I am yet alive & tolerably well. I have no strange news to write any more than wee have had heavy skirmishing with the Enemy in the day & hard marching of a night. We are at a halt now & have been ever since Friday Evening but may be on the march again before morning. We have been in some pretty tight places. The yankeys made us ly low behind our breastworks the other day. They threw the shells in amongst us in a hurrah.One of co. (I) got wounded comeing off of the field. A portion of the 16 has had

some verry heavy skirmishing with the Enemy. We lost a noble young Liut at Resaca & some wounded. Our regt has been verry fortunate so fare in not getting into a regular Engagement. But in the last two weeks we have been several times as I thought right into a regular Engagement. Wee have had the rear to bring up different times & have been placed in the front line of battle But have been verry agreeably disappointed in not having the Enemy to advance on us. Mary I got a letter from aunt Salley yesterday. She is living at Leroys. She says she is well. But I will send you her letter. Scruggs says to tell Caroline that he is well & hearty. Berry says tell his folks that he is well. I hope this may find you & the boys all in good health & in good spirits. Mary Johnson is feeding us pretty well since we have been on the march. We call ourselves Walkers caviller. So I must close so fare you well Mary
Young H.E. Hitch

Mary you in your last asked my pardon in regard to some particular matters. And I honestly do grant it. So I want you to rest easy on the subject. But I do hope that we may have the pleasure of spending a few more days on Earth together. It appears to me that I would be a happy man to be at home to enjoy home & family as I once could do. But I must ask you to forgive the ill treatment that I have given you. Mary I am allmost getting weaned from home in a heap of respects. But still I can call many of our ups & downs to my mind & it is company to me to think of them. Mary you ma wonder if Young aint badly scared in time of Battle. Mary it makes me feel verry little indeed but it sorter wears off after awhile. I try to put my whole trust in my Creator believing him to be able to save me. Mary let me hear from you as soon as you can. Tell Ellen howdy for me tell her that I am as well as common. Tell her that I have got up several times at one or two oclock at night & start on a march after being up late throwing up breastworks that wee expected to fight behind the next morning. Tell her while some are lying takeing their ease & Enjoying home others are undergoing hardships. Sutch as marching day or night or lying in some ditch behind breastworks and nothing but Bacon & crackers to Eat & sometimes have it to eat raw. But when me & Scruggs are well our lives are about as mutch Satisfaction as some whoo are at home I Expect. So no more
Young H.E. Hitch

CI. Letter from Y.H.E. Hitch to Mary A. Hitch dated June 2, 1864 from near Dallas, Georgia

Young Hitch's last known letter before being killed.

Near Dallas Ga
June 2nd /64

Mrs Mary A Hitch
Dear wife I seat myself to drop you a few lines to let you know that I am still alive & tolerably well. But I am verry mutch fatigued and tired as we have had but little rest the last month neither day nor night. This is a mountainous country and hard to travel over. Mary I have escaped safe so far. But since Friday last I have been exposed a great deal to the Enemy fire. I was out on skirmish 48 hours. The yankeys fired a many a ball in the tree I stood behind. I done the best that I could for them. I tumbled over one but don't know how bad I hurt him. But one thing I do know I put a stop to his loading & shooting at me. He had been standing behind a tree shooting at me for sometime. But last Sunday night had a hot time. The yankeys thru shot & shell amongst us in a hurra. There is skirmishing on our (right?) this morning.

Scruggs is sorter puny worn out I think. Edward is under the weather but I will not say what is the matter. Mary, I hope this may find you and the boys all well. Please write and let me hear from you. The 16 of April was the last. Please excuse this short letter for I may have to break & fall in to the breastworks in a few moments. This may be the last you hear from me. God only knows. But if I fall I hope to fall doing my duty. If I should survive this war let this be my boast that I served as a private in the great struggle for Southern independence.
So I remain your husband
Y.H.E. Hitch

LETTERS (AFTER JUNE 19 1864) DATING FROM THE TIME AFTER YOUNG HITCH WAS KILLED IN ACTION

CII. Letter of Young Hitch's being killed from William Scruggs to Mary Hitch dated June 20, 1864 from "Line of Battle, near Marietta, Cobb County, Georgia"

Line of Battle near Marietta, Cobb County, Georgia. June 20, 1864

Dear Sister,
It is made my painful duty to inform you that your dear husband is no more is was shot in the head on yesterday while on skirmish duty about 10 o'clock. He, Hosey Holcomb, Absalom White and Andrew Forester were all behind a temporary breastwork. He had just discharged his gun and before he recovered his former position, he was struck by a small ball. He fell and, as he fell, he said "Oh Lordy." Dear Sister, I have the melancholy pleasure to inform you that he made a good soldier. He lived respected and died lamented by all the co and regt who knew him. He appeared to be conscious about the one thing needful. On last Tuesday, he joined the church but circumstances had not allowed his baptism. He joined the Baptist church. You have a source of comfort which many do not have, that your hope is gain. He appeared very serious and did not participate in the indulgence of the vices which too many of even professed Christians indulge in. I hope that you will feed upon the promises of Him who has said "I will be a father to the fatherless and husband to the widow". Your husband has died in the discharge of duty to his country and I hope to his God. I hope that you will have grace sufficiently given you to bear up under this great affliction. We are now in line of battle but I do not see any more prospect of a battle now than there has been for some time past. Our skirmish duty is very heavy now. Toliver Vaughan was wounded this morning but I hope not mortally. He was struck by a small ball near our camp and line. He was not on the skirmish line. Your brother Edward is well and doing well. I remain yours in brotherly bonds until death.
William Scruggs

CIII. Letter from Sarah Hitch to Mary A. Hitch dated September 15, 1864 from Laurens District, South Carolina

So. C.L. Dist
Sept. 15th 1864

Dear and much beloved niece
It is with pleasure I seat myself today to drop you a few lines to let you know how I am a getting along. I have had a tolerable bad of something like neuralgia or neumonia. it was three weeks last Sunday since I took sick. I was not confined to my bed all of the time quite. I have never sat up a whole day in the time. My head has been my greatest distress but through a kind merciful Creator I am at present so I can get about again a little. I have been a wanting to write to you before now but was prevented by sickness and other things. I do hope when these few lines come to hand, they will find you and your little sons all well and a doing well. you said you wanted me to write as often as I could for I was all that you had to write to now. O my dear niece I think I can cympathise for you in your loneliness and would be glad I could hear

from you every week for it seems like the oftener I hear from you the nearer you feel to me. There was years passed by when we neither saw each other nor but seldom heard from each other and I felt sometimes like Young was dead and gone. And after he went to the army and commenced writing to me I felt like I wanted to hear from him every week if I could. His letters was interesting to me and I feel very certain that it wont be long that it will be so that you and me will have the privilege that we now have of a writing to each other and a hearing from each other for I feel certain that I shall soon have to go the way of all the earth. and I want you to write as often as you can, you and that lovely little J.J. Hitch, which you say is so much the favor of his beloved father. And O that he may be like him in principle and live long on the earth and be useful in his day and generation. May he seek and serve his father and his mother's God in his youth. O my beloved little nephew I want you to remember your Creator in the days of your youth before the evil days come when you shall say I have no pleasure in them. May the Lord have mercy on little Lucian and bless his little soul and teach him as he grows up how to walk the strait and narrow way of holiness. O my beloved niece you don't know how glad I should be to see you and your dear little sons and converse with you and them face to face. But I fear I never shall have that pleasure. I was in hopes when I wrote last perhaps I should have the chance to pay you a visit but I fear new I shall not get the opportunity. E.L. Pitts has gone to the war and its uncertain when he will return whether ever or not. And his people has got so much work to do of one thing and another I fear it will be a bad chance. They have there molasses to make that will take them a considerable time. But O my dear niece if we never should be so fortunate as to meet here may we be so happy as to be prepared to meet in heaven where sorrow is known no more and where trouble never come. O my dear niece let us try to bear our troubles and our trials here with patience knowing that it is but a ten days tribulation when it will all be done. O my dear it is delightful thought to think when we leave this sinful world of a going to one where sin never enters. I shall have to come to a close as it is nearly night and I want to send it to the post office tonight and I feel fatigued being weak. I want you to be sure to write when you get this and tell me all about how you are a getting along. J.J. I want you to be certain to write and tell me how you feel about meeting your beloved Father in that happy place where Jesus is. youth is the time to embrace religion. And I must bid you all farewell at present. May God and his Holy Spirit be with you to guide, direct, and comfort you in all your troubles I hope is the prayer of your affectionate aunt.
I remain your affectionate aunt until death.
Sarah Hitch to Mrs. Mary A. Hitch

CIV. Letter from J.B. Edwards to sister, Mary A. Hitch dated February 6, 1865 from Camp Reston, South Carolina

Camp Reston,
Columbia SC
February 6th 1865

My Dear Sister
I this evening through the mercy of God I am blest with the privilege of taking my pen in my hand to drop you a few lines to let you no that I am yet alive and as well as common. Kindly hoping that these few lines may reach you in dew time & find you & your little boyes both well. Dear sister, I received your very kind leter last Saturday 4th baring Sat 21st of January 1864 which I was proud to see & glad to hear that you all was well. Dear sister, I have nothing to right to you at present more than ware newes and I recon you

have as much of that as you want to hear. You wanted me to give you my opinion about this cruel ware. I can't tell you when it will wind up but I dont think that it can last much longer. They are a fighting now no they staid above 73 miles___ hear where I am___ Ediston?___ wher I stayed last winter. We are a fortifying this place as fast as wee can but I dont think it will do as much good. Dear sister I am looking every day when I will have to get in to the fight. Dear sister you said that if could see me that you could tell me more than you could right. I wish I could sad all but God only knows whether I ever will be fortunate to see you eny more in this world or not but I hope that I will live to see this unholy ware come to a close. Dear sister I cant get no leters from home since the Mail Man has march? away and you don't know how__ I am. I am hear with about half anuff to eat and none of my connection don't think anuff of me to right to me. your leter is the second leter that I have got from eny of my brothers or sisters. I have right to Jonas but he dont right to me. I want you to tell him & Caroline Scruggs that I haven't forgot them & that I would be glad to hear from them & I want you to right to me again. Dear sister I must come to a close soon by saying that If I never see you no more in this world I hope that we will meet in heaven where my 4 little boys is gone. May the God above have heaven? around? you & your 2 little boys and save us all is the sincere pray of your loving brother. So fare well. Right soon.
J.B. Edwards

Mrs Mary A. Hitch
Please tell your mother to right to me.

CV. Letter from W.C. Hitch to Joseph Hitch dated March 16, 1869 from Laurens District, South Carolina

Laurens Dist, SC
March the 16 1869

Dear Cousin
I seat my self this cool and cloudy Tuesday evening in order to let you know that I am well at this time and the rest of them is as well as common. Hopeing when these few lines comes to your hand that they may find you well and a doing well and all of the rest. we got home safe and sound that comeing Sabbath in the evening about two o clock but I have been back nearly up there again. I got as far as the Dials Church and stop there to here preaching. I thought when I got there that I would see you there but I did not. I seen a good many good looking girls there but they was all strangers to me. You may laugh at my strait writing but the paper is not ruled all of the way but I recon you can make out to read it. I am in a hurry so that I can not take pain enough to write. I have to quit writing now and go to work. I now seat my self this morning again to drop you a few more lines to fill out as much as this side. I am a bad hand to compose a letter. I never can think of any thing worth writing to any body. You must excuse bad writing and spelling for I never take pains enough to write any better. I want you to write as soon as you get this and let me know how you and all of the rest are a getting along.
Your friend W.C.
Turn over
And I want you to write when you are a coming down. I would be very glad to see you come if you would come so that you could stay till Sunday. We would go to meeting and I would show you some of the prettiest looking girls that you ever saw. Come as soon as you can and write as soon as you can and let

me know how you are a getting along. So I will come to a close by saying to you I still remain yours until death. When this you see remember me tho many miles apart we be.
W.C. Hitch
To Joseph Hitch

Direct your letter to W.C. Hitch
Brewerton P.O. Laurens Dist S.C.
In care of Jack F. Smith

W C H i t c h
23.3. 8 9 20 3 8
Write soon.

CVI. Letter informing of Aunt Sally Hitch's Death from W.C. Hitch to Mary A. Hitch dated September 10, 1871 from Laurens County, South Carolina

Laurens County S.C.
Sept the 10th 1871

Dear cousin I seat my self this evening in order to let you know how we are all a getting a long we are as well as common at this time. my little babe has been very sick but has got well he is enjoying verry good health at this time and I hope when these few lines come to your hand that they may find you all well and a doing well. grandpa and grandma is not so verry well but they keep up and about. I will give you a little sketch about Sally Hitch by request of grand pa as he expects that you have not heard it She was struck with the palsy at cousin Leroy Pitts a setting on a chair in the piazza. She fell from the chair and they run and helped her up but she could not talk for a while She was struck in the throat but she could not talk plain when she got so she could speak. she was struck on the last day of August and died on Sunday the 3rd of September. she bid adieu to earth and the earthly things. she told them before she died that she was a going to die and that she wanted to be buried at old poplar Springs Church. her funeral was preached before she was buried. she lost her speech before she died and she made motions to all that was standing around. they went up to the bed and she taken hold of their hands and rub their hands and would look up that is good as to say that she was a going to die and go happy that she was willing and ready. I must begin to come to a close by saying to you to come down and see us all so that the circumstances that I have just related can be related more perfect and with greater understanding. So farewell for this time.
W.C. Hitch to Mary A Hitch

If you can not come down write as soon as you get this. Direct your letter to Brewerton PO Laurens County SC

Envelope addressed to:
Mary A. Hitch, Huntersvill P.O., Greenville S.C
Handwritten on the side of the envelope:
Brewerton SC Sep. 14

INDEX

CPSIA information can be obtained
at www.ICGtesting.com
Printed in the USA
LVOW02s0250010416
481666LV00001B/1/P

9 781478 762478